S0-BIX-777

Bradford
College
Library

Measuring Environment Across the Life Span

Measuring Environment Across the Life Span

EMERGING METHODS AND CONCEPTS

EDITED BY

Sarah L. Friedman and Theodore D. Wachs

AMERICAN PSYCHOLOGICAL ASSOCIATION • WASHINGTON, DC

Published by
American Psychological Association
750 First Street, NE
Washington, DC 20002

Copies may be ordered from
APA Order Department
P.O. Box 92984
Washington, DC 20090-2984

In the U.K., Europe, Africa, and the Middle East, copies may be ordered from
American Psychological Association
3 Henrietta Street
Covent Garden, London
WC2E 8LU England

Typeset in Goudy by EPS Group Inc., Easton, MD

Printer: United Book Press, Inc., Baltimore, MD
Cover designer: Berg Design, Albany, NY
Technical/production editors: Tanya Y. Alexander and Jennifer Powers

Library of Congress Cataloging-in-Publication Data
Measuring environment across the life span : emerging methods and concepts / Sarah L. Friedman, Theodore D. Wachs, editors.
p. cm.
Includes bibliographical references and index.
ISBN 1-55798-561-8 (case : alk. paper).—ISBN 1-55798-567-7 (pbk. : alk. paper)
1. Environmental psychology. I. Friedman, Sarah L. II. Wachs, Theodore D., 1941– .
BF353.M395 1999
155.9—dc21

98-49321
CIP

British Library Cataloguing-in-Publication Data
A CIP record is available from the British Library.

Printed in the United States of America
First Edition

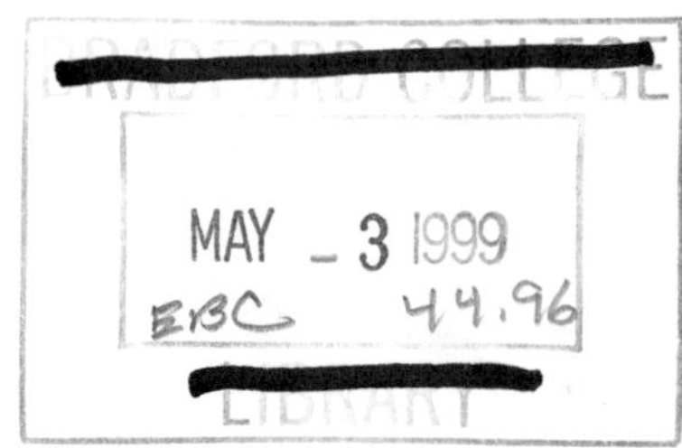

For Moshe, Daphne, and Yossi,
whose profound influence cannot be fully assessed.
S.L.F.

For Helen, John, and Emily
Close in heart, distant in miles.
T.D.W.

CONTENTS

CONTRIBUTORS

Jo-Ann Amadeo, Department of Human Development, University of Maryland

Robert H. Bradley, Center for Research on Teaching and Training, University of Arkansas at Little Rock

Urie Bronfenbrenner, Department of Human Development and Family Studies, Cornell University

B. Bradford Brown, Department of Educational Psychology, University of Wisconsin

Gary W. Evans, Department of Design and Environmental Analysis, Cornell University

Sarah L. Friedman, Center for Research for Mothers and Children, National Institute of Child Health and Human Development, National Institute of Health

Sarah Harkness, School of Family Studies, University of Connecticut

M. Powell Lawton, Behavioral Research, The Philadelphia Geriatric Center

Milbrey W. McLaughlin, School of Education, Stanford University

Jill K. Posner, Wisconsin Center for Education Research, University of Wisconsin

Carmi Schooler, Laboratory of Socioenvironmental Studies, National Institute of Mental Health, National Institutes of Health

Daniel Stokols, Program of Social Ecology, University of California, Irvine

Charles M. Super, School of Family Studies, University of Connecticut

Joan E. Talbert, School of Education, Stanford University

Deborah Lowe Vandell, Department of Educational Psychology, University of Wisconsin

Theodore D. Wachs, Department of Psychological Science, Purdue University

INTRODUCTION

This volume[1] has been conceptualized with multiple goals in mind. These were (a) to delineate state-of-the art concepts and methods for assessing the environment across different contexts and for different age groups, (b) to explore the fit between environmental models and the methods utilized for describing and assessing the environment, and (c) to integrate approaches and methods for environmental assessment that have been developed by investigators studying different age groups, different settings, or both.

Although interest in the environment as an influence on behavior and development can be traced back to biblical times, scientific studies of environmental influences are a fairly recent phenomenon (Wachs, 1992). Bronfenbrenner and Crouter (1983) delineated three phases of scientific research on the question of environmental influences. From the late 1880s to 1930, research emphasized the question of whether the environment influences development. From the 1930s to the late 1950s, research emphasized the question of what aspects of the environment were relevant for behavior and development. From the 1960s on, researchers have increasingly focused on questions involving understanding the structure of the environment, as well as the processes, whereby environmental variability relates to behavioral or developmental variability. For the most part, research on environmental influences has been the province of the social and behavioral sciences, including disciplines such as developmental psychology, environmental psychology, education, sociology, and anthropology (which are all represented in this volume). However, it is important to note that the importance of environmental influences has been increasingly stressed by researchers from other, more biologically oriented domains,

[1]The conceptualization of the volume, its editing, and the writing of this introduction, all taken together, represent an equal partnership of Sarah L. Friedman and Theodore D. Wachs.

including behavioral genetics (e.g., Plomin, 1990), developmental neuroscience (e.g., Greenough & Black, 1992), and nutrition (e.g., Pollitt, 1988).

In the study of environmental influences over the past quarter century, two factors stand out. First, there is an increased understanding of the interrelated, multilevel–multidimensional structure of the environment. Rather than a series of unrelated contexts, the environment is conceptualized as a hierarchical structure consisting of multiple levels (e.g., culture, neighborhood, schools, and home). Being interrelated, the various levels and subunits of the environment act together as a system (as exemplified in the chapters by Bronfenbrenner and by Bradley). However, the different levels and subunits of the environment are rarely studied as an interrelated system (for an exception, see the National Institute of Child Health and Human Development Early Child Care Research Network, 1996, 1997a, 1997b). Furthermore, there are multiple environmental units that make up a given context (e.g., the chapter by Talbert & McLaughlin shows how the school environment can be characterized on the basis of teacher practices, teacher values, administrative policies, and pupil characteristics).

Second, it is now generally accepted that researchers cannot hope to understand the nature of human behavior and development without reference to the context within which the individual functions. Consequently, studies on the role of environmental influences have broadened well beyond the original emphasis on early experience to encompass a wide variety of age groups—a fact that is emphasized in this volume with chapters describing the environment of preschool-age children, school-age children, adolescents, and adults.

Unfortunately, the increased understanding of the multilevel—multidimensional nature of the environment and the expansion of the study of environmental influences to diverse populations have not been associated with increased communication among investigators. Environmental researchers from different disciplines, even though all are studying the same general topic (environment), may be focusing on very different populations or very different dimensions or domains of the environment. Environmental researchers from various disciplines and domains of study rarely interact with one another or know each other's work. This lack of interaction is particularly disappointing, given that environmental researchers who work with different populations across the life span, or who are from different disciplines, may be wrestling with similar methodological and conceptual problems. As a result of fragmentation, environmental researchers studying one domain or population may be unaware of contributions from environmental researchers working in other domains or disciplines that could illuminate their own work. The lack of interaction among environmental researchers from different disciplines and domains means that the isolated research practices do not reflect the nature of the phenomena under study: namely, an integrated multilevel–multidimensional environment.

A similar disjunction is seen in relation to the assessment of the environment. Optimally, the decision to assess specific aspects of the environment should be guided by the hypothesized relationship between specific dimensions of the environment and specific behavioral or psychological outcomes. This is rarely done. More frequently than not, the selection of assessments is determined by the availability of instruments and the ease of measurement. This volume was planned so as to counteract this situation and to establish conceptual and methodological links across different fields and across researchers studying different aspects of the environment. Although the volume is expected to move researchers closer to this goal, it is not as comprehensive as we would have liked it to be. Obviously, no single edited volume can represent all aspects of the environment. As a result, we were forced to choose which environmental domains would be represented in this volume. Our choice of which environmental domains to omit was based, in part, on detailed coverage of these domains in recent books or review articles. For example, we chose to omit focused coverage of the conceptualization and assessment of social and historical changes and life-course events, given the focus placed on these aspects of the environment in a recent volume by Moen, Elder, and Luscher (1995). A similar decision was made in terms of the mass media as environment, given a special issue of the *Journal of Youth and Adolescence* (e.g., Arnett, 1995), as well as a number of books and book chapters devoted to this area (Danish & Donohoe, 1996; Strasburger, 1995). We similarly chose to omit coverage on discrimination as an environmental experience, given the availability of reviews on both historical (Liddell, Kvalsvig, Shabalala, & Masilela, 1991) and concurrent aspects of this problem (Garcia-Coll et al., 1996; Garcia-Coll & Magnuson, 1997).

Coverage was also limited by the unfortunate fact that some chapters describing specific environments, which were planned and contracted for, were not delivered (e.g., neighborhood, marital relations, and poverty). Getting these chapters replaced would have delayed the volume beyond reasonable time limits. Readers wishing information on neighborhood environments can find relevant information in a recent article by Wandersman and Nation (1998) and in a new edited volume by Gorlitz, Harloff, Mey, and Valsiner (1998). Excellent sources on marital relations as a form of environment can be seen in a recent review article by Hetherington, Bridges, and Isabella (1998), as well as more comprehensive review chapters by Sanders, Nicholson, and Floyd (1997) and Wilson and Gottman (1995). Finally, current evidence on the conceptualization, assessment, and impact of poverty as an aspect of the environment can be found in a review article by McLoyd (1998), a chapter by Brody, Flor, and Neubaum (1998), a monograph from the National Research Council (Bridgman & Phillips, 1998), and an edited volume by Duncan and Brooks-Gunn (1997).

Finally, we deliberately chose not to include a chapter reviewing recent approaches to analyzing the environment from a behavior genetic perspective, with particular reference to concepts arising from this research, such as the distinction between shared and nonshared environments and covariation between genetics and environmental characteristics. A most readable and balanced summary of this evidence is found in Plomin (1994). This omission does not mean that we feel that this perspective is unimportant when attempting to understand or assess the environment. For example, the distinction between shared and nonshared environmental sources raised by behavior genetic researchers is discussed in this volume (Wachs, chapter 12) within the framework of the concept of environmental specificity. To the extent that siblings living under the same roof encounter different microenvironments, the action of specificity will produce results similar to what behavioral genetic researchers call "nonshared environmental influences." The degree to which siblings living in the same household encounter different microenvironments is an important question, because such differences imply the operation of reactive and active organism–environment covariance. These forms of covariance form a natural bridge for conceptual overlap and collaborative research between behavioral genetic and environmental researchers (Wachs, 1993). Some behavior genetic researchers use evidence that children with different characteristics elicit different reactions from others in their environment (reactive covariance) and search out different "niches" in their environment (active covariance) to conclude wrongly that genes "drive" environments (Scarr, 1992) and that all but nonextreme environments are thus irrelevant for development (Rowe, 1994). Unfortunately, this line of reasoning perpetuates the scientifically unproductive focus on the nature versus nurture dichotomy. Such conclusions ignore the all too obvious fact that genes essentially drive amino acid sequences. Beyond this stage, there is a long complex chain between genes and environment, with multiple potential mediators acting at every stage of this chain. Such conclusions also ignore the fact that any contributions of genes to environment are truly due to probabilistic covariances. As Plomin (1994) has noted: "Research on the genetics of experience, as in any genetic research on complex dimensions and disorders, does not imply genetic determinism. It refers to probabilistic propensities rather then predetermined programming" (p. 160).

Aspects of the environment discussed in this volume that are correlated with individual genotype will reflect the specific environmental contributions to gene–environment correlation processes. It will be the job of behavior genetic researchers to identify the specific genetic contributions to such processes. Once the relevant contributions from the genetic and environmental domains have been identified, researchers can begin to profitably study how the covariance between genes and environments relates to individual developmental variability, as was most elegantly demonstrated in a recent article by Ge et al. (1996). It is our hope that those behavioral genetic researchers interested in integrating genetic and environmental contributions will find this volume a resource when trying to understand what the environmental portion of the equation encompasses, without necessarily feeling neglected by not having a chapter of their own.

In terms of what is contained in this volume, the chapters are organized into five sections. The first section consists of one theoretical chapter by Bronfenbrenner, who has done more than anyone to provide a strong conceptual basis for understanding environments, their interrelatedness, and their relation to human behavior. Much of what follows in the remaining sections derives from the theoretical principles that Bronfenbrenner discusses.

The second section of the volume focuses on environmental settings that are commonly encountered by most individuals at a specific age. The nature and assessment of the family environment or the home setting as experienced by children from infancy onward are discussed in a chapter by Bradley. As the world of children expands beyond the environment provided by their immediate family, children encounter peers. In the next chapter, Brown focuses on the variety of peer environments that adolescents encounter and discusses how to best assess them. In late adulthood, the world of individuals contracts and typically includes the family home, retirement community, or nursing home. The chapter by Lawton presents a conceptualization of these environments and their assessment.

The third section of this volume focuses on settings that act to organize the activities of individuals, usually through the existence of rules and regulations pertaining to the operations of these settings. Here we refer to child-care settings, school settings, after-school settings, and workplace. Friedman and Amadeo describe a wide range of child-care characteristics, methods for assessing child-care settings, and issues of validity and choice associated with selecting among methods of assessment. The assessment of the after-school environment is described by a team of the pioneers in that area of investigation, Vandell and Posner. Talbert and McLaughlin describe innovative methods for the assessment of different aspects of the school environment in the context of other aspects of the environment. Schooler provides a review of his long-term programmatic research about the workplace environment and its assessment.

The fourth section of the volume sheds light on the larger context within which are nested the specific contexts described and discussed in the previous sections. Evans describes the nature and assessment of the larger physical context as a source of stress. Working within the framework of psychological anthropology, Super and Harkness describe the nature of culture and the tools by which cultural contexts can be assessed.

The fifth and final section of the volume integrates ideas presented and discussed in previous chapters from two different, yet interrelated, viewpoints. Writing from the perspective of an environmental psychologist, Stokols integrates and expands these viewpoints, with particular emphasis on the role of new communication technologies as environment. Writing from the perspective of a developmental psychologist, Wachs also integrates and expands on previous chapters, placing his emphasis on the question of whether researchers can or should assess the environment independently of the individual.

REFERENCES

Arnett, J. (1995). Adolescents use of the media for socialization. *Journal of Youth and Adolescence*, *24*, 519–533.

Bridgman, A., & Phillips, D. (1998). *New findings on poverty and child health and nutrition*. Washington, DC: National Academy Press.

Brody, G., Flor, D., & Neubaum, E. (1998). Coparenting processes and child competence among rural African–American families. In M. Lewis & C. Fiering (Eds.), *Families, risk and competence* (pp. 227–244). Hillsdale, NJ: Erlbaum.

Bronfenbrenner, U., & Crouter, A. (1983). The evolution of environmental models in developmental research. In W. Kessen (Ed.), *Handbook of child psychology* (Vol. 1, 4th ed., pp. 357–414). New York: Wiley.

Danish, S., & Donohoe, T. (1996). Understanding the media's influence on the development of antisocial and prosocial behavior. In R. Hampton, P. Jenkins, & T. Gullotta (Eds.), *Preventing violence in America* (Vol 4., pp. 133–155). Thousand Oaks, CA: Sage.

Duncan, G. J., & Brooks-Gunn, J. (Eds.). (1997). *Consequences of growing up poor*. New York: Russell Sage Foundation.

Garcia-Coll, C., Lamberty, G., Jenkins, R., McAdoo, H., Crnic, K., Wasik, B., & Garcia, H. (1996). An integrative model for the study of developmental competencies in minority children. *Child Development*, *67*, 1891–1915.

Garcia-Coll, C., & Magnuson, K. (1997). The psychological experience of immigration. In A. Booth, A. Croatia, & N. Lansdale (Eds.), *Immigration and the family* (pp. 91–131). Hillsdale, NJ: Erlbaum.

Ge, X., Conger, R., Cadoret, R., Neiderhiser, J., Yates, W., Troughton, E., & Stewart, M. (1996). The developmental interface between nature and nurture. *Developmental Psychology*, *32*, 574–589.

Gorlitz, D., Harloff, H., Mey, G., & Valsiner, J. (Eds.). (1998). *Children, cities and psychological theories*. Berlin: de Gruyter.

Greenough, W., & Black, J. (1992). Induction of brain structure by experience. In M. Gunnar & C. Nelson (Eds.), *Developmental behavioral neuroscience* (pp. 153–232). Hillsdale, NJ: Erlbaum.

Hetherington, M., Bridges, M., & Isabella, G. (1998). What matters? What does not? Five perspectives on the association between marital adjustment and children's adjustment. *American Psychologist*, *53*, 167–184.

Liddell, C., Kvalsvig, J., Shabalala, A., & Masilela, P. (1991). Historical perspectives on South African Childhood. *International Journal of Behavioral Development, 14*, 1–19.

McLoyd, V. (1998). Socioeconomic disadvantage and child development. *American Psychologist, 53*, 185–204.

Moen, P., Elder, G., & Luscher, K. (1995). *Examining lives in context*. Washington, DC: American Psychological Association.

National Institute of Child Health and Human Development Early Child Care Research Network. (1996). Characteristics of infant child care: Factors contributing to positive caregiving. *Early Childhood Research Quarterly, 11*, 269–306.

National Institute of Child Health and Human Development Early Child Care Research Network. (1997a). The effects of infant child care on infant–mother attachment security: Results of the NICHD Study of Early Child Care. *Child Development, 68*, 860–879.

National Institute of Child Health and Human Development Early Child Care Research Network. (1997b, April). *Mother–child interaction and cognitive outcomes associated with early child care: Results from the NICHD Study*. Poster symposium presented at the biennial meeting of the Society for Research in Child Development, Washington, DC.

Plomin, R. (1990). The role of inheritance in behavior. *Science, 284*, 183–188.

Plomin, R. (1994). *Genetics and experience*. Thousand Oaks, CA: Sage.

Pollitt, E. (1988). A critical view of three decades of research on the effects of chronic malnutrition on behavioral development. In B. Schurch & N. Scrimshaw (Eds.), *Chronic energy deficiency* (pp. 77–94). Lausanne, Switzerland: International Dietary Energy Consultative Group.

Rowe, D. (1994). *The limits of family influence*. New York: Guilford Press.

Sanders, M., Nicholson, J., & Floyd, F. (1997). Couples relationships and children. In W. Halford & H. Markman (Eds.), *Clinical handbook of marriage and couples interventions* (pp. 225–253). New York: Wiley.

Scarr, S. (1992). Developmental theories of the 1990's. *Child Development, 63*, 1–19.

Strasburger, V. (1995). *Adolescents and the media*. Thousand Oaks, CA: Sage.

Wachs, T. D. (1992). *The nature of nurture*. Thousand Oaks, CA: Sage.

Wachs, T. D. (1993). The nature–nurture gap. In R. Plomin & G. McClearn (Eds.), *Nature, nurture, and psychology* (pp. 375–394). Washington, DC: American Psychological Association.

Wandersman, A., & Nation, M. (1998). Urban neighborhoods and mental health. *American Psychologist, 53*, 647–656.

Wilson, B., & Gottman, J. (1995). Marital interaction and parenting. In M. Bornstein (Ed.), *Handbook of parenting* (Vol. 4, pp. 33–55). Hillsdale, NJ: Erlbaum.

I

THEORETICAL OVERVIEW OF THE STRUCTURE OF THE ENVIRONMENT

1

ENVIRONMENTS IN DEVELOPMENTAL PERSPECTIVE: THEORETICAL AND OPERATIONAL MODELS

URIE BRONFENBRENNER

In selecting the theme and title of this volume, the editors have set a demanding, dual criterion—one seldom imposed, and even more seldom met, in either social or developmental science. The first topic the authors were asked to address was the structure of the environment—clearly a theoretical challenge—and then, the second topic, no less exacting, was implications for measurement. The dual expectation is clear. Not only are both conceptual and operational models to be clearly specified, but the second must be derived from the first. In addition, the authors were urged to incorporate, presumably within both domains, any "issues of continuity versus change through the life course."

Taken as a whole, that is quite a tall order. In accepting the assignment, all I can assure the reader is that the wisdom reflected in formulating the issues to be addressed will not be matched by the answers presented in this chapter. However, if the English poet Robert Browning's injunction that "a man's reach should exceed his grasp" be as valid for science as for art, then I qualify at least to make the attempt. For many years, I have been engaged in a concerted effort to develop a theoretical and operational model for investigating the role of the environment in shaping human development through the life course. For anyone engaged in such an endeavor, the phrase "in developmental perspective" has a second, albeit secondary significance, for it applies not only to the phenomenon under investigation but also to the *evolution* of the scientific models used for that purpose. In my own case, that evolution has a long history, going back to an article published almost four decades ago (Bronfenbrenner, 1958)[1] and undergoing successively more complex reformulations[2] to attain its present, still-evolving form. At a broader level, however, it is useful to distinguish two periods: the first ending with the publication of the *Ecology of Human Development* (Bronfenbrenner, 1979), and the second characterized by a series of papers that call the original model into question, and then proceed to incorporate its former components, along with new elements, into a more complex and more dynamic structure eventually referred to as the *bioecological model*. The present chapter constitutes the most recent product of that evolving effort, but with a special focus on the role of the environment in processes of human development (Bronfenbrenner, 1995; Bronfenbrenner & Morris, 1998).

DEFINING PROPERTIES OF THE BIOECOLOGICAL MODEL

To turn, then, to the "new beginning" since 1979: The first important theoretical development after the publication of the original ecological model was the introduction of a critical distinction between *environment* and *process*. Traditionally in developmental research, such phenomena as mother–infant interaction—and, more generally, the behavior of others toward the developing person—have been treated under the more inclusive category of the environment. In the *bioecological model*, a critical distinction is made between the concepts of environment and process, with the latter not only occupying a central position, but also being defined in terms of its functional relationship both to the environment and to the characteristics of the developing person. This formulation appears in the first of two propositions stipulating the defining properties of the model. To place Proposition 1's meaning in context, I cite Proposition 2 as well.

[1]Indeed, Cairns and Cairns (1995), in a recent article entitled "Social Ecology Over Time and Space," traced the origin of the ecological model back to a passage in my doctoral dissertation, published in 1943. When Robert Cairns quoted the passage at a symposium, identifying it only by date of publication, I failed to recognize it and panicked at the thought of having missed citing work of someone else so relevant to, and far ahead of, my own PhD thesis.
[2]For relevant references, see Lüscher and Jones, 1995.

Proposition 1

Especially in its early phases, and to a great extent throughout the life course, human development takes place through processes of progressively more complex reciprocal interaction between an active, evolving biopsychological human organism and the persons, objects, and symbols in its immediate external environment. To be effective, the interaction must occur on a fairly regular basis over extended periods of *time*. Such enduring forms of interaction in the immediate environment are referred to as *proximal processes*. Examples of enduring patterns of proximal process are found in parent–child and child–child activities, group or solitary play, reading, learning new skills, studying, athletic activities, and performing complex tasks.

A second defining property identifies the threefold source of these dynamic forces.

Proposition 2

The form, power, content, and direction of the proximal processes affecting development vary systematically as a joint function of the characteristics of the *developing person*, the *environment*—both immediate and more remote—in which the processes are taking place, the nature of the *developmental outcomes* under consideration, and the social continuities and changes occurring over time during the historical period through which the person has lived.

Propositions 1 and 2 are theoretically interdependent and are subject to empirical test. An operational research design that permits their simultaneous investigation is referred to as a *process–person–context–time model* (PPCT).

Note that, in point of fact, the characteristics of the person appear twice in the PPCT model: first as one of the four elements influencing the "form, power, content, and direction of the proximal process" and second as developmental outcomes; that is, the characteristics of the developing person at a later point in time as the result of the joint, interactive cumulative effects of the four principal components of the model. In short, in the bioecological model, the characteristics of the person are both a producer and a product of development.

Because within the bioecological model the concept of proximal process has a highly specific meaning, it is important that its distinctive properties be made explicit, particularly as they relate to the environment. The following features of the construct are especially noteworthy in that regard.

1. For development to occur, the person must engage in an activity.

2. To be effective, the activity must take place "on a fairly regular basis, over an extended period of time." An occasional weekend of doing things with one's mom or dad does not count, nor do activities that are often interrupted.
3. One reason why this is so, is that to be developmentally effective, activities must take place long enough to become "increasingly more complex." Mere repetition does not work.
4. Developmentally effective proximal processes are not unidirectional; there must be initiation and response in both directions.
5. Proximal processes are not limited to interpersonal interaction; they can also involve interaction with objects and symbols. Under these circumstances, for reciprocal interaction to occur, the objects and symbols in the immediate environment must be of a kind that invites attention, exploration, manipulation, elaboration, and imagination.

OPERATIONALIZING THE BIOECOLOGICAL MODEL

The foregoing constitute the principal elements of the theoretical model. For its scientific validity to be assessed, the model must be translatable into operational form. Is that a practical possibility, given its complexity? As yet, no systematic effort has been undertaken to address this question, but nevertheless, some relevant examples do exist. They appear in the form of what I have referred to elsewhere as "latent paradigms" (Bronfenbrenner & Crouter, 1983, pp. 373–376)[3]; that is, theoretical models that are not explicitly stated, but that are implicit in the research designs used in analyzing the data.

A first example illustrating the model is shown in Figure 1. The data are drawn from a classic longitudinal study by Drillien (1964) of factors affecting the development of children of low birth weight compared with those of normal weight. The figure depicts the impact of the quality of the mother–infant interaction[4] when the infant is at age 2 on the number of observed problem behaviors when the infant is at age 4 as a joint function of birth weight and social class.[5] As can be seen, a proximal process (in this instance, mother–infant interaction across time) emerges as the most

[3]Indeed, a partial precursor of the bioecological model appears in the 1983 handbook chapter under the rubric of a "person–process–context model." However, what is meant by process is never specified, and the overwhelming majority of the examples cited do not include a process component as defined in Proposition 1, nor does the formulation contain any reference to time as a key component in the model.

[4]Assessed in terms of the extent to which the mother was responsive to changes in the state and behavior of the infant.

[5]Figure 1 does not appear in Drillien's (1964) monograph, but it was constructed from data presented in tables included in the volume.

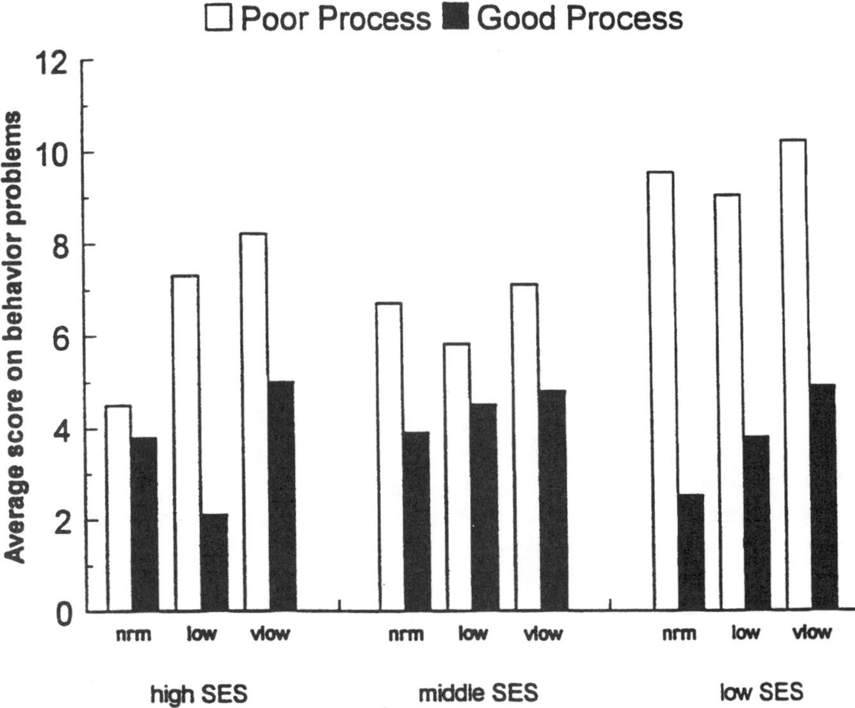

Figure 1. Effect of mother's responsiveness on problem behavior of the infant at age 4 by birth weight and social class. nrm = normal birth weight; low = between normal and 5.5 pounds; vlow = 5.5 pounds or less; SES = socioeconomic status.

powerful predictor of developmental outcome. In all instances, good maternal treatment appears to reduce substantially the degree of behavioral disturbance exhibited by the child.

Herein lies the main justification for distinguishing between proximal processes, on the one hand, and, the environments in which they occur, on the other; namely, the former turn out to be the more potent force in furthering developmental growth. Furthermore, as stipulated in Proposition 2, the power of the **process** varies systematically as a function of the environmental **context** (in this instance, social class) and of the characteristics of the **person** (in this case, birth weight). Note also that the proximal process has the general effect of reducing, or buffering against, environmental differences in developmental outcome; specifically, under high levels of mother–child interaction, social class differences in problem behavior become much smaller.

At this point it is instructive to ask to what extent the defining properties of the bioecological model are to be found in the "latent structure" implicit in Drillien's (1964) research design. To be sure, the four key elements of process, person, context, and time are all represented, but not in sufficient detail to permit fulfilling the requirements of the theoretical model in full. In particular, even though the data on mother–infant interaction when the infant is at age 2 were gathered in home visits over an extended period of time, no information is provided to permit assessment of the model's regularity, freedom from interruption, or extent to which it became "progressively more complex." Also, for infants at age 4, only one type of developmental outcome was examined: the frequency of problem behaviors (e.g., hyperactivity, unresponsiveness, and temper tantrums).

The absence of data on other kinds of outcomes precludes investigating a key component of the bioecological model; namely, the stipulation that the effect of proximal processes will vary systematically as a function of the nature of the developmental outcome under consideration. For example, in the present instance, it was anticipated that the greater developmental impact of proximal processes on children growing up in poorer **environments** is to be expected only for indexes of developmental **dysfunction.** For outcomes reflecting developmental **competence** (e.g., mental ability, academic achievement, and social skills), proximal processes are posited as having greater impact in more advantaged and stable environments. In this context, the term *dysfunction* refers to the manifestation of difficulties in maintaining control and integration of behavior across a variety of situations. By contrast, *competence* refers to the demonstrated acquisition and further development of knowledge and skills.

The theoretical expectation that proximal processes will differ in their developmental effects on children depending on the quality of the environment rests on the following basis. In deprived and disorganized environments, manifestations of dysfunction in children are likely to be both more frequent and more severe, with the result that children attract more attention and involvement from parents, whereas in advantaged and more stable environments, such manifestations are less intense, and parents are more likely to be attracted by, and respond to, gratifying signs of their children's developmental progress.

In addition, most human beings at all socioeconomic levels, and especially parents, have the capacity and the motivation to respond to the immediate physical and psychological needs of their children. The situation is rather different, however, with respect to enabling their children to acquire new knowledge and skills. In this domain, either the parents must themselves possess the desired knowledge and skill or they must have access to resources outside the family that can provide the needed experiences for their children.

Taken together, the foregoing considerations lead to the hypothesis of the differential impact of proximal processes as a joint function of the quality of the environment in terms of the available resources, on the one hand, and the nature of the outcome in terms of competence versus dysfunction, on the other.

Some indication of the validity of this hypothesis is provided by the

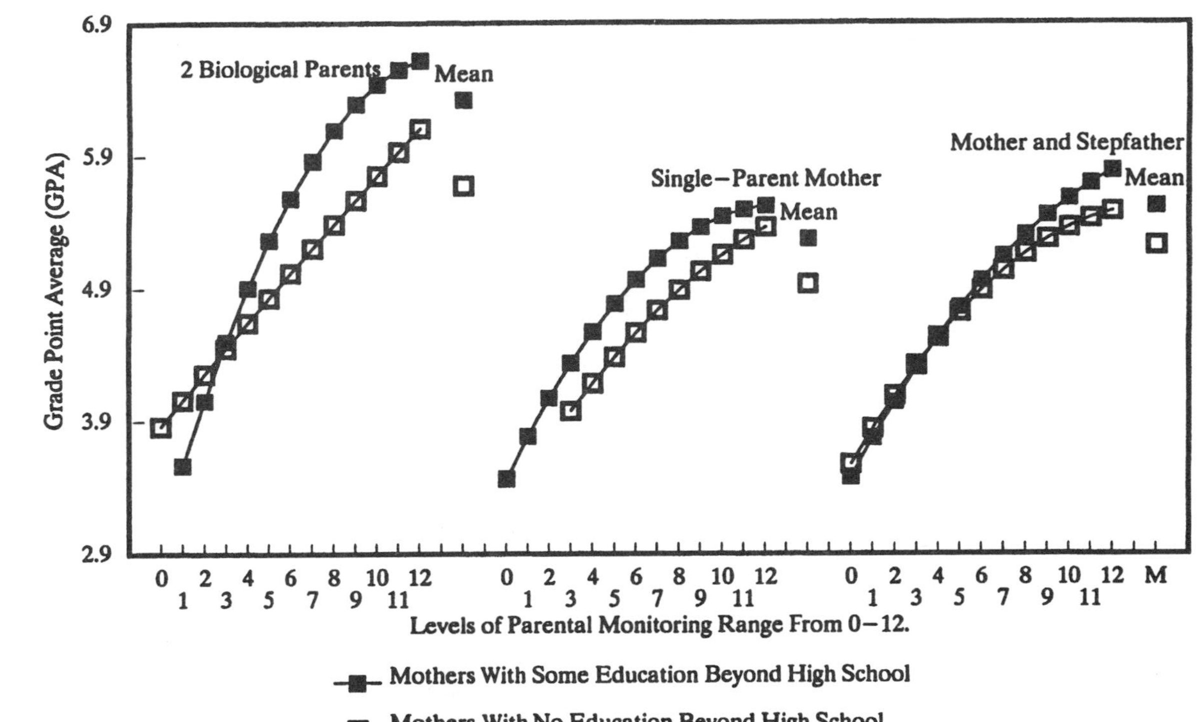

Figure 2. Effect of parental monitoring on grades in high school by family structure and mother's level of education. GPA Scale responses ranged from 2 (*mostly Ds or less*), 3 (*½Cs and ½Ds*), 4 (*mostly Cs*), 5 (*½Bs and ½Cs*), 6 (*mostly Bs*), 7 (*½As and ½Bs*), to 8 (*mostly As*).

results, shown in Figure 2, of an analysis depicting the differential effects of parental monitoring on school achievement for high school students living in the three most common family structures found in the total sample of over 4,000 cases.[6] The sample was further stratified by two levels of the mother's education, with completion of high school as the dividing point. *Parental monitoring* refers to the effort by parents to keep informed about and set limits on their children's activities outside the home. In the present study, it was assessed by a series of items in a questionnaire administered to adolescents in their school classes. Levels of parental monitoring, ranging from 0 to 12, are shown on the horizontal axis, grade point average (GPA) is shown on the vertical. The markers to the right of each curve record the mean GPA for each of the six groups.

Once again, the results reveal that the effects of proximal processes are more powerful than those of the environmental contexts in which they occur. In this instance, however, the impact of the proximal process is greatest in what emerges as the most advantaged ecological niche—families with two biological parents in which the mother has had some education beyond high school. The typically declining slope of the curve reflects the fact that higher levels of outcome are more difficult to achieve so that at each successive step, the same degree of active effort yields a somewhat smaller result. Thus, in this case, for pupils who are not doing so well in school, parental monitoring can apparently accomplish a great deal by ensuring stability of time and place so that some learning can occur. However, superior school achievement would in addition clearly require high levels of motivation, focused attention, prior knowledge, and—especially—actually working with the material to be learned, all qualities that stability of time and place by themselves cannot provide. This fact focuses attention on the key importance of the dynamic interrelations between the four components of the bioecological model and their implications for research design.

THE BIOECOLOGICAL MODEL AS AN INTERACTIVE SYSTEM

I begin with the two principal structural features of the theoretical paradigm. The importance of both their separation and their dynamic interrelationship is already illustrated in Figure 1. Here the environmental context appears in the form of social class, and characteristic of the developing person is the child's birth weight. The distinction between these two domains is typically not made in other research paradigms. For example, Garmezy and Rutter (1983), in their important work on stress and

[6]The data on which the analysis shown in Figure 2 was based were generously provided by Small and Luster (1990) from their state-wide studies of youth at risk in Wisconsin.

coping in children's development, did not differentiate between those protective or disruptive forces emanating from the environment and those that inhere in the biopsychological characteristics of the person. Yet, as illustrated in Figure 1, these vectors do not always operate in the same direction (i.e., proximal processes exert their greatest positive effect in the most disadvantaged environment, but with the most advantaged organism).

A second feature of the bioecological model, retained from its earlier prototype (Bronfenbrenner, 1979, 1993), involves the conceptualization of the ecological environment as a set of nested systems ranging from the "micro" to the "macro." Although the particular design shown in Figure 2 includes only these two extremes, it already illustrates a general ecological principle; namely, the power of developmental forces operating at any one systems level of the environment depends on the nature of the environmental structures existing at the same and all higher systems levels.

Let us now consider a critical difference between the bioecological model and other analytic designs typically used for measuring the contribution of environmental (and other) factors in producing developmental effects. By far the most common of these is the linear multiple regression model. This model provides estimates of the "independent" effect of each factor included in the research design. I put the term *independent* in *italics* for a reason. As I have spelled out elsewhere (Bronfenbrenner, 1993, Bronfenbrenner & Morris, 1998), the multiple regression model, as typically applied in psychological research, requires the assumption that the various factors affecting the outcome operate *independently* of each other and that, therefore, their combined effects can be only *additive*. In mathematical statistics, this is known as the assumption of *homogeneity of regression*. However, in most psychological research—and in developmental research in particular—this assumption is rarely met, not just statistically, but—what is more important—theoretically and substantively as well.

For example, in Figure 2, the assumption would require that the same increase in parental monitoring, what one might call "the bang for the buck," have equal effect in each type of family structure at both levels of the mother's education; in statistical terms, this means that the slopes of the regression lines would have to be the same in each context. Clearly, this is not the case. Had a regression model been applied to control for both social class and family structure, the results would, on the one hand, have appreciably overestimated the power of parental monitoring in single-parent families (particularly those in which the mother had had no education beyond high school) while considerably underestimating the effect of the same degree of monitoring in well-educated two-parent families.

Had the same kind of regression analysis been applied to Drillien's (1964) data, one would never have seen that the beneficial effects of responsive maternal care in reducing infants' problem behaviors had their greatest impact on families living in the most disadvantaged environments (a finding that has since been replicated in a number of studies).[7]

Distortions of reality arising from unwarranted assumptions of homogeneity of regression are even more likely to occur through the use of what an increasing number of researchers regard as the most sophisticated scientific strategy for analyzing data in the behavioral and social sciences—the statistical technique of causal modeling or structural equations. The higher risk of distortion arises from the fact that the model, as generally applied and incorporated in computer programs, does not allow for the inclusions of interaction terms. Under these circumstances, the only way for taking such theoretically based possibilities into account is to apply the procedure separately in each of those domains of major scientific interest in which homogeneity of regression cannot be assumed. Because the analysis of structural equations is a very time-consuming and expensive process, this is not a very practical undertaking. Moreover, even after it is done, there is no systematic method for assessing whether the results of the separate analyses are reliably different from one another.

DYNAMIC ELEMENTS IN THE IMMEDIATE ENVIRONMENT

In the two examples considered thus far, the effects of proximal processes have considerably exceeded those of environmental contexts per se. (See Figure 2.) This same pattern reappears in each of the comparatively few reports of sets of data I have been able to find in which measures of proximal processes are available for individuals studied in different environmental contexts. However, the developmental importance of the environments in which processes take place should not be underestimated, for there are some contextual features that, once introduced, can have substantial effects on subsequent psychological development. To be sure, in accord with what has already been seen, these features exert these effects indirectly—either by setting proximal processes in motion and sustaining their operation at a high level or by reducing opportunities for their initiation and exposing them to sources of environmental interference.

Two examples at contrasting ages are presented in the following paragraphs.

Environmental Dynamics in Old Age

The first example is Langer and Rodin's oft-cited experimental intervention conducted with residents of a New Haven nursing home for the

[7]For example, Pollitt and Gorman (1993) have shown that significant effects of nutritional supplementation would be overlooked if social class were controlled in the standard way, whereas stratifying on socioeconomic status clearly reveals benefits of supplementation for those at lower class levels.

aged (Langer & Rodin, 1976; Rodin & Langer, 1977). The contextual manipulation used in this study is well summarized by Rodin and Langer's following words:

> The hospital administrator gave a talk to residents in the experimental group emphasizing their responsibility for themselves, whereas the communication to a second, comparison group stressed the staff's responsibility for them as patients. To bolster the communication, residents in the experimental group were offered plants to care for, whereas residents in the comparison group were given plants that were watered by the staff. (p. 897)

Residents were assigned at random to either the experimental group or the control group. Data on psychological and health characteristics were collected at three time points: (a) just before the introduction of the experiment, (b) 3 weeks later (when the experiment was formally ended), and (c) in a follow-up study conducted 18 months later.

The substantial effects of intervention found at the end of the experiment (Langer & Rodin, 1976) were still in evidence in the follow-up assessment. To be sure, because the residents were almost a year-and-a-half older, the added age had taken some toll; nevertheless, those in the induced-responsibility group not only significantly surpassed their controls but were appreciably better off, both psychologically and physically, than they had been months earlier before the intervention had begun. For example, in ratings by observers unaware of the experimental conditions, participants in the induced-responsibility group were judged to be more alert, sociable, and vigorous. The most striking results were seen in the comparison of death rates between the two treatment groups. Taking the 18 months before the original intervention as an arbitrary comparison period, in the subsequent 18 months following the intervention, 15% in the induced-responsibility group died, compared with 30% in the control group.

Are all four defining properties of the bioecological model in fact present in the foregoing example? Characteristics of the person were assessed at three points in time, and the two randomly assigned environmental contexts differed only in the instructions read by the hospital administrator, which specified what each group of patients was expected to do.

However, does telling members of a group that they are expected to take care of themselves meet the definition of a proximal process? The excellent documentation provided in Langer and Rodin's (1976) research does not include any systematic information about the frequency and nature of activities in which each group engaged, the extent to which these activities occurred on a fairly regular basis over extended periods of time, or the reports of any behavior that could provide even a proxy measure of proximal processes and their differential occurrence in the experimental and control groups. If such measures were available, they would provide yet another test of the bioecological model in positing proximal processes as primary engines of human development.

Environmental Dynamics in Infancy

A remarkable, independent cross-validation of Langer and Rodin's (1976) principal hypothesis appears in the findings of another intervention experiment (this one almost unknown) that was carried out at about the same time with a sample of 100 9-month-old infants and their mothers in the Dutch city of Nijmegen (Riksen-Walraven, 1978). Although Riksen-Walraven appears not to have been aware of Langer and Rodin's work conducted during the same period, one of the two intervention strategies she used with her sample of infants was similar to that used in the New Haven study of older patients. Mothers randomly assignment to what Riksen-Walraven called the "responsiveness" group were given a "workbook for parents" stressing the idea that "the infant learns most from the effects of its own behavior" (Riksen-Walraven, 1978, p. 113). Specifically,

> caregivers were advised not to direct the child's activities too much, but to give the child opportunity to find out things for himself, to praise him for his efforts, and to respond to his initiations of interaction. (Riksen-Walraven, 1978, p. 113)

By contrast, mothers of infants in the so-called "stimulation" group received a workbook that emphasized the importance of providing the infant with a great variety of perceptual experiences of all kinds, "to point to and name objects and persons," and "to speak a lot to their infants" (Riksen-Walraven, 1978, p. 112).

In the follow-up assessment conducted 3 months later, infants of mothers who had been encouraged to be responsive to their babies' initiatives exhibited higher levels of exploratory behavior and were more likely to prefer a novel object to one that was already familiar. The babies also learned more quickly in a learning contingency task.

Regrettably, in neither of these two investigations did the researchers assess the frequency with which participants actually engaged in the activities that they were encouraged to undertake. In short, there was no measure of what is known as the proximal process. Even in the absence of such measures, however, it is clear that the critical factor accounting for differences in outcome was the contrasting nature of the information initially provided to the participants in each experimental condition. What is the theoretical place and significance of this difference in initial orientation?

Roles as Environmental Forces

The answer to the foregoing question focuses around the concept of *role*. In classical sociology, this concept is typically defined as a set of expectations and behaviors associated with a particular position in society, such as that of mother, baby, friend, employee, and so forth. In a bioecological model of development, the two components of the definition are systematically differentiated. Specifically, *role expectations* are viewed as determined, in the first instance, by the external world. Changes in role expectation, in turn, usually lead to corresponding changes in behavior (i.e., *role performance*), which, if they persist over time, become changes in development. Thus, role expectations constitute dynamic features in the environment that, when altered, can have significant consequences for subsequent development. The extent of the power of role expectations is illustrated not only in the results of the two experimental studies just cited, but also in Sherif's classic Robber's Cave experiment (Sherif, 1956; Sherif, Harvey, Hoyt, Hood, & Sherif, 1961) and in Sticht, Armstrong, Hicks, and Caylor's (1987) study of the effects of providing a military experience for youth cast off from the schools and cast off from employment.

The question arises in what respect the foregoing formulation differs from the familiar concept of role transitions as represented by such events as school entry, graduation, getting a job, marriage, divorce, or retirement. The answer lies in a distinctive characteristic of each of these previously cited examples; namely, roles are not merely normative features of the environment, but also present powerful environmental levels for affecting developmental change.

EFFECTS OF THE PHYSICAL ENVIRONMENT ON PSYCHOLOGICAL DEVELOPMENT

The pioneering work in this sphere has been done by Theodore Wachs. In 1979, he published a seminal paper in which he showed a consistent pattern of relationships between certain features in the physical environment of infants during the first 2 years of life and their cognitive development over this same period. To permit examining effects over time, Wachs grouped his data into successive 3-month blocks. The results are reported in the form of correlations between characteristics of the environment at an earlier time and the developmental status of the infants at a later time.

The findings of the study are quite complex. For present purposes, I focus on those physical features in the environment that were most frequently and strongly associated with various types of cognitive functioning. These included a physically responsive environment, presence of sheltered areas, "the degree to which the physical set-up of the home permits exploration," low level of noise and confusion, and "the degree of temporal regularity" (Wachs, 1979, p. 30).

Regrettably, few researchers have followed the exciting scientific path that Wachs has been the first to chart. Viewed from a theoretical perspective, his original and subsequent work (Wachs, 1986, 1987a, 1987b, 1987c, 1988, 1989, 1990, 1991, 1993; Wachs & Chan, 1986) suggest two contrasting aspects of the environment that are especially worthy of further systematic investigation. The first stimulates and enhances the power of proximal processes, and the second suppresses and undermines them.

In the former domain, Wachs's findings point to aspects of the physical environment that can affect the course of cognitive development: one for better, the other for worse. On the constructive side are areas and objects that invite exploration, whereas the instability, lack of clear structure, and unpredictability of events result in insufficient feedback for proximal processes to be set in motion and sustained.[8] From an ecological perspective, the existence of these countervailing forces in the physical environment leads to a synergistic hypothesis; namely, not only do developmentally instigative features of the surroundings have greater impact in more stable settings, but they also function as a buffer against the disruptive influences of disorganizing environments.

The foregoing considerations introduce an additional component into the research design. As stipulated in Proposition 1, proximal processes involve progressively more complex interaction not only with people, but also with objects and symbols. The question therefore arises to what extent solitary activities involving objects and symbols—such as playing with toys, working at hobbies, reading, or fantasy play—can also foster psychological development? Also, to what degree does involvement in either type of activity produce synergistic developmental effects within or across these domains? The answers to these questions are as yet unknown, but they are now readily discoverable through the use of appropriate designs that differentiate between measures of process and of environmental structure.

However, the most promising *terra incognita* for research on the role of the physical environment in human development may well lie beyond the realm of childhood in the world of adults. A preview of this promise appears in the successive publications of the sociologist Melvin Kohn and his colleagues (for an integrative summary, see Kohn & Slomczynski, 1990;

[8]Especially relevant and important in this regard is a recent article of which Wachs is a coauthor. The article opens with the following statement: "A growing body of research has documented the relevance for children's development of environmental confusion (high levels of noise, crowding, home traffic pattern)" (Matheny, Wachs, Ludwig, & Phillips, 1995, p. 429). The article then describes the psychometric characteristics of an instrument design to assess the degree of "environmental confusion" present in the home. Consistent with requirements of construct validation, the obtained scores are significantly related to observed parental behaviors but "are distinct from socio-demographic measures" (Matheny et al., 1995, p. 429).

see also Schooler, chapter 8, this volume), whose work illustrates the powerful effect of work environments on intellectual development in adulthood. Of particular importance in this regard is the complexity of the task that a given job entails.

BEYOND THE MICROSYSTEM

It is a basic premise of ecological systems theory that development is a function of forces emanating from multiple settings and from the relations between these settings. How can such multiple forces and their interrelations be conceptualized, and what kinds of research designs can be used to measure their combined effects? The first stage in such an expanded model of the environment involves what in ecological systems theory is called a *mesosystem*, defined as comprising the relationships existing between two or more settings; in short, it is a system of two or more microsystems. The nature of mesosystems and their operationalization in a research design is best conveyed through a concrete example.

In a recent study, Steinberg, Darling, and Fletcher (1995) reported on what they described as "an ecological journey." The journey was the consequence of a deliberate decision made at the outset of their research. The initial focus of investigation was on the impact of authoritative parenting on adolescents' academic achievement. They had at their disposal a range of data collected from a large multiethnic, multiclass sample encompassing a variety of family structures. Under these circumstances, they concluded that

> it made no sense at all to control for ethnicity, social class, or household composition in an attempt to isolate "pure" process. No process occurs outside of a context. And if we want to understand context, we need to take it into account, not pretend to control it away. (Steinberg et al., 1995, p. 424)

No sooner had Steinberg et al. (1995) embarked on this unconventional course than they had encountered some unexpected findings. The first of these occurred not in the realm of environmental context, but in that of developmental outcome. When they analyzed adolescents' school performance, they found that, in contrast to European American and Hispanic American youths, African American or Asian American youths did not benefit from authoritative parenting. A first clue to this puzzle emerged when the investigators identified the values held by the different peer crowds (e.g., jocks, brains, nerds, preppies, and druggies) in the nine high schools included in their sample. Their subsequent analysis revealed that "European-American youngsters from authoritative homes are more likely to belong to peer crowds that encourage academic achievement" (Steinberg et al., 1995, p. 445).

On the basis of these and related findings, Steinberg et al. (1995) formulated the following new working hypothesis:

> There is a strong but indirect path between parenting practices and adolescent peer group affiliations . . . by fostering certain traits in their children, parents direct a child toward a particular peer group. Thus to the extent that parents can influence characteristics by which adolescents are associated by peers with a crowd, parents can "control" the type of peer group influences to which their child is exposed. . . . In essence, parents have a direct and primary impact on adolescent behavior patterns—prosocial as well as antisocial. Peer groups serve primarily to reinforce established behavior patterns or dispositions. (pp. 446–447)

However, when Steinberg et al. (1995) put their new hypothesis to the test, they were confronted by yet another unexpected result:

> When we attempted to apply this model to youngsters from minority backgrounds, we were in for a shock. We found that among Black and Asian students, there was no relation between parenting practices and peer crowd membership. (p. 447)

Once again, Steinberg et al.'s (1995) multiple context model paved the way to solving the puzzle:

> Why was there not significant relation between parenting and peer group selection among minority youth? The answer, we discovered, is that models of peer group selection that assume an open system, in which adolescents can select into any number of groups as easily as ordering food off a restaurant menu, fail to take into account the tremendous level of ethnic segregation that characterizes the social structure of most ethnically-mixed high schools in the United States. (pp. 447–448)[9]

As if disappointed at not being confronted with yet another unexpected finding, Steinberg et al. (1995) moved on to extend the ecological

[9]Although not directly related to the primarily theoretical and methodological focus of the present report, Steinberg et al.'s (1995) findings with respect to specific minority groups are of considerable interest. For example,

> Although [Afro-American] parents score highest on our measure of parental involvement in schooling, [Black adolescents] find it much more difficult to join a peer group that encourages the same goal. (p. 449)

By contrast,

> More often than not, Asian-American students have no choice but to belong to a peer group that encourages and rewards academic excellence. . . . Asian-Americans report the highest level of peer support for academic achievement. Interestingly, and in contrast to popular belief, [their] parents are the least involved in their youngsters' schooling. (p. 448)

model to its next-higher systems level—that of the *exosystem*. The formal definition of this environmental structure reads as follows:

> The *exosystem* comprises the linkages and processes taking place between two or more settings, at least one of which does not contain the developing person, but in which events occur that indirectly influence processes within the immediate setting in which the developing person lives. (Bronfenbrenner, 1993, p. 645)

The particular mesosystem that Steinberg et al. (1995) undertook to analyze was "the network of families that develops through the child's peer relationships," more specifically, "the parenting practices of their peers' parents" (p. 450). The analyses led to a series of interrelated findings; here are two examples:

> Adolescents whose friends' parents are authoritative earn higher grades in school, spend more time on homework, . . . have more positive perceptions of their academic competence, and report lower levels of delinquency and substance use. (p. 452)
>
> Adolescents whose parents are already more authoritative appear to benefit more from membership in a peer network with other authoritatively-reared youngsters than do adolescents in similar networks, but from less authoritative homes. It appears that adolescents need certain "home advantages" in order to be able to take advantage of the social capital in their social networks. (pp. 452–453)

Presumably, even an ecological model can only be taken so far, but Steinberg et al. (1995) appear to be trying to push it to its limits—their next analysis moves from the parental network of the adolescent's peers to the level of the *neighborhood*, specifically, its degree of *social integration*. The measure of integration was based on a series of questions about parents' contact with their children's friends, participation in community and school activities, and ties to other families in the neighborhood. An analysis of the data revealed a modest effect of neighborhood integration on adolescent development. However, this finding was qualified in an important way that refocused attention on the key role played by family processes. In the author's words:

> When we reran these analyses separately in neighborhoods characterized by a high proportion of effective versus noneffective parents, we find that . . . **social integration only benefits adolescents whose families live in neighborhoods characterized by good parenting.** Social integration into a neighborhood characterized by a high proportion of bad parents has a harmful effect on adolescents' school performance and behavior. (Steinberg et al., 1995, p. 457)

A subsequent analysis revealed a second, equally critical but not surprising qualifier: "Living in a neighborhood characterized by a high degree of social integration is only beneficial to an individual adolescent if the child's family is also socially integrated" (Steinberg et al., 1995, p. 457).

Steinberg et al.'s (1995) final analysis, at least in this, most recent report, adds psychological substance to social structure. By aggregating information on parenting practices and attitudes within a neighborhood, they were able to calculate a measure of the degree of consensus among parents in a given neighborhood. Once again, the principal finding emerging from the analysis was conditioned by a psychological reality:

> **High neighborhood consensus augments the association between parenting and adolescent outcomes only when the consensus is around good parenting.** . . . In other words, it is what parents agree about, not merely whether they agree, that makes the difference. (Steinberg et al., 1995, p. 458)

So much for environmental process and context as shapers of development. It is time to turn to time.

SPACE THROUGH TIME: ENVIRONMENT IN THE THIRD DIMENSION

Considerations of time and timing as they relate to features of the environment, as opposed to characteristics of the person, have only recently begun to receive systematic attention in developmental research. The principal advances in this regard have been made by sociologists working in the "life course perspective" (e.g., Clausen, 1986, 1993; Elder, 1974, 1998a). In the recent 25th Anniversary Edition of his *Children of the Great Depression*, Elder (1998b, pp. 304–308) discusses in some detail the four basic principles on which his theory of life course development is based. Because of the importance of these principles for developmental theory in general, and their complementary relation to bioecological theory, I take the liberty of summarizing them here.

Life Course Principle 1

According to Life Course Principle 1, the individual's own developmental life course is seen as embedded in and powerfully shaped by conditions and events occurring during the historical period through which the person lives.

In short, history is exploited as an experiment of nature. In the corresponding research design, groups similar in other respects that have been exposed, versus not exposed, to a particular historical event were compared with one another (e.g., Elder's studies of the Great Depression; military service and actual combat in World War II, Korea, and Vietnam; the Iowa

Farm Crisis; and, in his current work [1998b] on youth being sent to the countryside during the Cultural Revolution in China).

Life Course Principle 2

According to Life Course Principle 2, a major factor influencing the course and outcome of human development is the timing of biological and social transitions as they relate to the culturally defined age and role expectations and opportunities through the life course.

The corresponding research design is one that compares early versus late arrivals at a particular transition with respect to their subsequent life course. For example, Elder, Shanahan, and Clipp (1994) have reanalyzed follow-up data on participants from Terman's classic *Genetic Studies of Genius* (1925) [all participants with very high IQs] and were able to show marked differences in subsequent adult development, depending on early versus late entrance into military service during wartime. Here are some of the costs of late entry:

- A higher risk of divorce and separation.
- A work life of disappointment and loss of lifetime income.
- An accelerated decline of physical health, most notably after the age of 50.

On the opposite side:

- For many men, and especially those who entered at an early age, military service was a recasting experience. It provided a bridge to greater opportunity and an impetus for developmental growth up to the middle years.

One is reminded of Brutus's fateful choice in response to Cassius's urgings:

> There is a tide in the affairs of men
> Which, taken at the flood, leads on to fortune;
> Omitted, all the voyage of their life
> Is bound in shallows and in miseries. (William Shakespeare, *Julius Caesar*, Act IV, Lines 218–221)

Life Course Principle 3

According to Life Course Principle 3, the lives of all family members are interdependent. Hence, how each family member reacts to a particular historical event or role transition affects the developmental course of the other family members, both within and across generations.

The basic research design corresponding to this principle involves examining the differential impact of historical events and role transitions on different members of the same family experiencing these same events and transitions. For example, in a study of mother–daughter dyads in the broader historical context of the societal changes in gender roles that have taken place since World War II, Moen and her colleagues (Moen & Erickson, 1995) offered the following concluding comment on the basis of their statistical analysis of data across two generations:

> Conventional mothers embracing traditional gender roles may find themselves with daughters who are in the vanguard of the women's movement, or may even push their daughters to achieve what was impossible for themselves. The fact that mothers and daughters experience historical events and social changes from different vantage points means that their lives are differentially touched and that their perspectives may well diverge. (p. 180)

Life Course Principle 4

According to Life Course Principle 4, within the limits and opportunities afforded by the historical, cultural, and socioeconomic conditions in which they live, human beings themselves influence their own development—for better or for worse—through their own choices and acts.

Concrete examples of this principle, which Elder called "human agency," are often cited in his publications, especially in studies of the Great Depression (Elder, 1974), of the Iowa Farm Crisis (Conger & Elder, 1994; Elder, King, & Conger, 1996), and of military service and actual combat in World War II and Korea (Elder, 1986; Elder et al., 1994). For instance, analyses revealed that youths growing up in the most deprived families were the most likely to volunteer for military service, an experience that then gave them a new start in life (Elder, 1986).

HUMAN DEVELOPMENT AND ENVIRONMENTAL STABILITY

Environmental changes across history and the life course are not the only temporal forces shaping development; changes on a much shorter time scale may be equally consequential. Some of the earliest evidence suggesting this possibility has already been cited. I refer to Wachs's findings (1979) regarding the disruptive developmental effect of environmental instability, lack of clear structure, and unpredictability of events. Since the late 1970s, a growing body of research has pointed in the same direction. For example, many stepparent families appear to be characterized by a lack of parental consistency and clarity of roles (Baumrind, 1989; Hetherington & Clingempeel, 1992; Pasley & Tallman, 1987; Zimiles & Lee, 1991). Moreover, the ultimate sources of such instability often lie in stressful conditions originating in domains outside the family, such as the world of work, the neighborhood, or the society at large. Under such circumstances, the power of proximal processes to enhance psychological development can significantly be undermined.

Perhaps the most comprehensive evidence for such an effect comes from a longitudinal study conducted by the Finnish psychologist Pulkkinen (1982, 1983; Pulkkinen & Saastamoinen, 1986). Pulkkinen and Saastamoinen (1986) examined the influence of environmental stability and change on development between 8 and 20 years of age. Experience of instability over time (e.g., changes in family structure, day care and school arrangements, or parental employment; number of family moves; and frequency of parental absence) was associated with greater psychological insecurity later in life, as well as a higher incidence of problem behaviors such as submissiveness, aggression, early sexual activity, excessive smoking, drinking, and delinquency. These effects could be found within, as well as between, social classes. Moreover, the disruptive impact of environmental instability on developmental outcomes was greater than that of socioeconomic status per se.

Subsequent research has provided more specific evidence that stress and inconsistency within the family, often originating in the external environment, have disruptive effects on children's development. For example, the degree of conflict versus harmony in the marriage influences patterns of parent–child interaction (Belsky & Rovine, 1990), which in turn affect children's school achievement and social behavior in the classroom (Cowan, Cowan, Schulz, & Heming, 1994). At the same time, the quality of the marital relationship has itself been shown to be powerfully affected by extrafamilial factors such as conditions at work (Bolger, DeLongis, Kessler, & Wethington, 1989; Eckenrode & Gore, 1990; Moorehouse, 1991).

In summary, environmental contexts influence proximal processes and developmental outcomes not only in terms of the resources that they make available but also in the degree to which they provide the stability and consistency over time that proximal processes require for their effective functioning.

As the reader will recognize, this principle has been embodied in the first defining property of the bioecological model through the stipulation that, to be effective, proximal processes "must occur on a fairly regular basis over extended periods of *time*."

THE BIOECOLOGICAL MODEL AND THE ENVIRONMENT: IMPLICATIONS FOR MEASUREMENT

As the final topic to be addressed in this chapter, I return to the subtitle of the volume, because from the perspective of a bioecological model the challenge of operational definition is as fundamental as that of theoretical formulation. The term *measurement*, however, is not always interpreted in a way that acknowledges the scientific necessity of this ongoing interdependence. In particular, there is the tendency to think of measurement as pertaining only to variables rather than to the correspondence between the conceptual and operational definitions of a given theoretical model and its constituent hypotheses.

In the present volume, the challenge to achieve such correspondence is further complicated by the necessity to meet a dual demand. The scientific models to be considered are to speak not only to the structure of the environment but also to issues of continuity versus change through the life course. Thus far, I have accorded more attention to the conceptual rather than to the operational aspects of this challenge. I did so for a reason; namely, most of the research designs and methods of measurement currently in use in developmental science are not well-suited for what I have referred to elsewhere as "science in the discovery mode" (Bronfenbrenner & Morris, 1998). To be more specific, these designs and methods are more appropriate for verifying already formulated hypotheses than for the far more critical and more difficult task of developing hypotheses of sufficient explanatory power and precision to warrant being subjected to empirical test.[10]

The present chapter represents an effort toward achieving this goal.

The difficulty of the task, however, does not free the scientist from the necessity of translating evolving hypotheses into corresponding operational form; that is why I have provided some concrete examples of what such operational models might look like. The general strategy that underlies these models is the recognition that the various components of the ecological model cannot all be dealt with in a single analysis; instead, they are examined in smaller combinations that complement one another. Moreover, the most desirable—and at the same time most attainable—result will not be the validation of the model in its present form but in the evolution of a paradigm that may bring researchers closer to the realization of the scientific goals envisioned by the far-seeing editors of this volume. In summary, most of the scientific journey still lies ahead.

REFERENCES

Baumrind, D. (1989). The permanence of change and the impermanence of stability. *Human Development*, *32*, 187–195.

[10]The task is more difficult because it requires a series of progressively more differentiated formulations and corresponding data analyses, with the results at each successive step setting the stage for the next round. A more detailed exposition of this process, with concrete examples, appears in Bronfenbrenner and Morris, 1998.

Belsky, J., & Rovine, M. (1990). Temperament and attachment security in the strange situation. *Child Development, 58,* 787–795.

Bolger, N., DeLongis, A., Kessler, R. C., & Wethington, E. (1989). The contagion of stress along multiple roles. *Journal of Marriage and the Family, 51,* 175–183.

Bronfenbrenner, U. (1958). Socialization and social class through time and space. In E. E. Maccoby, T. M. Newcomb, & E. L. Hartley (Eds.), *Readings in social psychology* (pp. 400–425). New York: Holt, Reinhart & Winston.

Bronfenbrenner, U. (1979). *The ecology of human development: Experiments by nature and design.* Cambridge, MA: Harvard University Press.

Bronfenbrenner, U. (1993). The ecology of cognitive development: Research models and fugitive findings. In R. H. Wozniak & K. Fischer (Eds.), *Scientific environments* (pp. 3–44). Hillsdale, NJ: Erlbaum.

Bronfenbrenner, U. (1994). Ecological models of human development. In T. Husten & T. N. Postlethewaite (Eds.), *International encyclopedia of education* (2nd ed., Vol. 3, pp. 1643–1647). New York: Elsevier Science.

Bronfenbrenner, U. (1995). Developmental ecology through space and time: A future perspective. In P. Moen, G. H. Elder, Jr., & K. Lüscher (Eds.), *Examining lives in context: Perspectives on the ecology of human development* (pp. 619–647). Washington, DC: American Psychological Association.

Bronfenbrenner, U., & Crouter, A. C. (1983). The evolution of environmental models in developmental research. In P. H. Mussen (Vol. Ed.) & W. Kessen (Series Ed.), *Handbook of child psychology: Vol. 1. History, theory, and methods* (4th ed., pp. 357–414). New York: Wiley.

Bronfenbrenner, U., & Morris, P. (1998). The ecology of developmental processes. In R. M. Lerner (Vol. Ed.) & W. Damon (Series Ed.), *Handbook of child psychology Vol. 1: Theoretical models of human development* (5th ed.). New York: Wiley.

Cairns, R., & Cairns, B. D. (1995). Social ecology over time and space. In P. Moen, G. H. Elder, Jr., & K. Lüscher (Eds.), *Examining lives in context: Perspectives on the ecology of human development* (pp. 397–422). Washington, DC: American Psychological Association.

Clausen, J. A. (1986). *The life course.* Englewood Cliffs, NJ: Prentice Hall.

Clausen, J. A. (1993). *American lives: Looking back at the children of the Great Depression.* New York: Free Press.

Conger, R. D., & Elder, G. H., Jr. (1994). *Families in troubled times: Adapting to change in rural America.* Chicago: Aldine-Gruyter Press.

Cowan, P. A., Cowan, C. P., Schulz, M. S., & Heming, G. (1994). Prebirth to preschool family factors in children's adaptation to kindergarten. In R. D. Parke & S. G. Kellam (Eds.), *Exploring family relationships with other social contexts. Family research consortium: Advances in family research* (pp. 75–114), Hillsdale, NJ: Erlbaum.

Drillien, C. M. (1964). *Growth and development of the prematurely born infant.* Edinburgh and London: E. & S. Livingston.

Eckenrode, J., & Gore, S. (1990). *Stress between work and family*. New York: Plenum Press.

Elder, G. H., Jr. (1974). *Children of the Great Depression*. Chicago: University of Chicago Press.

Elder, G. H., Jr. (1986). Military times and turning points in men's lives. *Developmental Psychology, 22*, 233–245.

Elder, G. H., Jr. (1998a). Life course and development. In R. M. Lerner (Ed.) & W. Damon (Series Ed.), *Handbook of child psychology Vol. 1: Theoretical models of human development* (5th ed.), New York: Wiley.

Elder, G. H., Jr. (1998b). *Children of the Great Depression* (25th Anniversary Edition). Boulder, Colorado: Westview Press.

Elder, G. H., Jr., King, V., & Conger, R. D. (1996). International continuity and change in rural lives: Historical and developmental insights. *International Journal of Behavioral Development, 19*, 433–455.

Elder, G. H., Jr., Shanahan, M. J., & Clipp, E. C. (1994). When war comes to men's lives: Life course patterns in family, work, and health. *Psychology and Aging, 9*, 5–16.

Garmezy, N., & Rutter, M. (1983). *Stress, coping, and development in children*. New York: McGraw-Hill.

Hetherington, E. M., & Clingempeel, W. G. (1992). Coping with marital transitions. *Monographs of the Society for Research in Child Development, 57* (Serial Nos. 2–3).

Kohn, M. L., & Slomczynski, K. M. (1990). *Social structure and self-direction: A comparative analysis of the United States and Poland*. Oxford, England: Basil Blackwell.

Langer, E. J., & Rodin, J. (1976). The effects of choice and enhanced personal responsibility for the aged: A field experiment in an institutional setting. *Journal of Personality and Social Psychology, 34*, 191–198.

Lüscher, K., & Jones, G. (1995). The published writings of Urie Bronfenbrenner. In P. Moen, G. H. Elder, Jr., & K. Lüscher (Eds.), *Examining lives in context: Perspectives on the ecology of human development* (pp. 649–676). Washington, DC: American Psychological Association.

Matheny, A. P., Wachs, T. D., Ludwig, J. L., & Phillips, K. (1995). Bringing order out of chaos: Psychometric characteristics of the Confusion, Hubbub, and Order Scale. *Journal of Applied Developmental Psychology, 16*, 429–444.

Moen, P., & Erickson, M. A. (1995). Linked lives: A transgenerational approach to resilience. In P. Moen, G. H. Elder, Jr., & K. Lüscher (Eds.), *Examining lives in context: Perspectives on the ecology of human development* (pp. 169–210). Washington, DC: American Psychological Association.

Moorehouse, M. J. (1991). Linking maternal employment patterns to mother–child activities and children's school performance. *Developmental Psychology, 27*, 295–303.

Pasley, K., & Tallman, M. (1987). The evolution of a field of investigation: Issues and concerns. In K. Pasley & M. Tallman (Eds.), *Remarriage and stepparenting: Current research and theory* (pp. 303–313). New York: Guilford Press.

Pollitt, E., & Gorman, K. S. (1993). Nutrition and development: Considerations for intervention. *Monographs of the Society for Research in Child Development, 58*(7), 116–118.

Pulkkinen, L. (1982). Self control and continuity from childhood to late adolescence. In P. Baltes & O. Brim (Eds.), *Life span development and behavior* (Volume 4, pp. 64–102). San Diego, CA: Academic Press.

Pulkkinen, L. (1983). Finland: The search for alternatives to aggression. In A. P. Goldstein & M. Segall (Eds.), *Aggression in global perspective* (pp. 104–144). New York: Pergamon Press.

Pulkkinen, L., & Saastamoinen, M. (1986). Cross-cultural perspectives on youth violence. In S. J. Apter & A. P. Goldstein (Eds.), *Youth violence: Programs and prospects* (pp. 262–281). New York: Pergamon Press.

Riksen-Walraven, J. M. (1978). Effects of caregiver behavior on habituation rate and self-efficacy in infants. *International Journal of Behavioral Development, 1*, 105–130.

Rodin, J., & Langer, E. J. (1977). Long-term effects of a control-relevant intervention with the institutionalized aged. *Journal of Personality and Social Psychology, 35*, 897–902.

Sherif, M. (1956). *Experiments in group conflicts. Scientific American, 195*, 54–58.

Sherif, M., Harvey, O. J., Hoyt, B. J., Hood, W. R., & Sherif, C. W. (1961). *Intergroup conflict and cooperation: The Robbers Cave experiment*. Norman: University of Oklahoma Book Exchange

Small, S., & Luster, T. (1990, November). *Youth at risk for parenthood.* Paper presented at the Creating Caring Communities Conference, Michigan State University, East Lansing, MI.

Steinberg, L., Darling, N. E., & Fletcher, A. C. (1995). Authoritative parenting and adolescent adjustment: An ecological journey. In P. Moen, G. H. Elder, Jr., & K. Lüscher (Eds.), *Examining lives in context: Perspectives on the ecology of human development* (pp. 423–466). Washington, DC: American Psychological Association.

Sticht, T. G., Armstrong, W. B., Hicks, D. T., & Caylor, J. S. (1987). Cast-off youth: *Policy and training methods from the military experience*. New York: Praeger.

Terman, L. M. (1925). *Genetic studies of genius: Volume 1. Mental and physical traits of a thousand gifted children*. Stanford, California: Stanford University Press.

Wachs, T. D. (1979). Proximal experience and early cognitive intellectual development: The physical environment. *Merrill-Palmer Quarterly, 25*, 3–42.

Wachs, T. D. (1986). Specificity of environmental action, as seen in environmental correlates of infants' communication performance. *Child Development, 57*(6), 1464–1474.

Wachs, T. D. (1987a). Specificity of environmental action as manifest in environmental correlates of infant's mastery motivation. *Developmental Psychology, 23*, 782–790.

Wachs, T. D. (1987b). The short-term stability of aggregated and non-aggregated measures of infant behavior. *Child Development, 58*, 796–797.

Wachs, T. D. (1987c). The relevance of the concept of nonshared environment to the study of environmental influences: A paradigmatic shift or just some gears slipping? *Behavioral and Brain Science, 10*(1), 41–42.

Wachs, T. D. (1988). Relevance of physical environment influences for toddler temperment. *Infant Behavior and Development, 11*(4), 431–445.

Wachs, T. D. (1989). The nature of the physical microenvironment: An expanded classification system. *Merrill-Palmer Quarterly, 35*, 399–402.

Wachs, T. D. (1990). Must the physical environment be mediated by the social environment in order to influence development: A further test. *Journal of Applied Developmental Psychology, 11*, 163–170.

Wachs, T. D. (1991). Environmental considerations in studies with non-extreme groups. In T. D. Wachs & R. Plomin (Eds.), *Conceptualization and measurement of organism–environment interaction* (pp. 44–67). Washington, DC: American Psychological Association.

Wachs, T. D. (1993). "Determinants" of intellectual development: Single-determinant research in a multidetermined universe. *Intelligence, 17*(1), 1–9.

Wachs, T. D., & Chan, A. (1986). Specificity of environmental interactions as seen in physical and social environment correlates of three aspects of 12-month infants' communication performance. *Child Development, 57*, 1464–1475.

Zimiles, H., & Lee, V. E. (1991). Adolescent family structure and educational progress. *Developmental Psychology, 27*, 314–320.

II

AGE-CHARACTERISTIC PROXIMAL ENVIRONMENTS

2

THE HOME ENVIRONMENT

ROBERT H. BRADLEY

For nearly 30 years I have been concerned about the quality of care children receive. My interest in measuring caregiving environments arose in a context of working with parents, training child-care workers, and providing programs for at-risk children. Most of my efforts of the past 20 years have been in partnership with Bettye Caldwell, a long-time friend and colleague. The measures we have constructed and the frameworks we have derived to guide our research reflect an integration of both practical and theoretical perspectives. They are products both inductively and deductively generated. In this chapter, I describe the most commonly used of our measures, the (HOME) Home Observation for Measurement of the Environment Inventory (Caldwell & Bradley, 1984), together with the frameworks we have used to assess children's caregiving environments. Although our research, training, and intervention efforts have included attention to a broad array of family and ecological factors (see Bronfenbrenner, chapter 1, this volume), this chapter is limited to those intimate environments in which children receive care.

ISSUES IN CONSTRUCTING MEASURES OF THE HOME ENVIRONMENT

Those familiar with environmental measurement know that perspectives on the environment vary widely. These varied perspectives lead users to select different measures and to use them in quite different ways. Such diversity is not ideal for coherence in the field of environmental measurement or for consensus on "best practice." Users are often driven by momentary interests such as the following:

- a concern about a particular development period;
- a desire to test a hypothesis that is based on a particular theoretical proposition;
- a concern about a particular developmental problem;
- a need to evaluate a particular program; and
- a need to make a decision about a particular patient, student, or client.

These momentary interests—understandable as they may be—constantly leave the practice of home environment measurement out of balance in its approach to measurement design and use.

How might one go about affecting a better balance, achieving greater coherence in the practical enterprise of measurement? One way is to adopt a more holistic, life-span approach to the process of measurement, an approach consistent with the notion that human beings are phylogenetically advanced, self-constructing organisms constantly transacting with their environments (Ford & Lerner, 1992). Another is to blend theoretical and applied perspectives when constructing measures. The practical needs of educators or social workers or physicians or psychologists may help direct the measurement enterprise in a way that serves validity. Traditionally, evaluation of the validity of home environment measures has been approached in terms of the examination of relationships between scores on the home environment measure and scores (including categorical level scores) on measures of other variables that are thought to be theoretically linked with the environmental construct manifested in that home environment measure. However, theories of human development and human environments do not often provide clear guidance for what the relationships should be. The needs of practice (clinical, educational, therapeutic, legal, etc.), tied as they are to professional (expert) knowledge and insight, may provide a valuable second source of guidance about expected relationships. In effect, neither extant theory nor professional expertise by itself adequately encompasses what is currently understood about human behavior and development. Combining clinical expertise and theory may offer a more productive approach to measurement construction.

Despite their limitations, home environment measures have helped advance an understanding of environment–developed relations and have been useful in applied measurement contexts (e.g., evaluating the effects of parent education programs and identifying homes that may pose a risk for development). The quality of information obtained from home environment measures may be improved by using the following three strategies.

First, and most obviously, is to measure the same environmental phenomenon at several points across time. Wachs (1987) found that repeated measurement of the environment increases reliability. Thirty years ago, Bloom (1964) introduced the concept of a "powerful environment," arguing that a particular aspect of the environment would have a greater influence on children's development if it operated at a *constant* high level across time.

Second, it is often useful to increase the number of indicators of the environmental dimensions included in a measure. It is accepted as axiomatic in the field of psychological measurement that most psychological phenomena are too complex and dense to be clearly manifest in a small number of indicators. Thus, one can generally achieve enhanced reliability by including more indicators of the phenomena. Bloom (1964) also argued that the likelihood that some aspect of the environment would influence the course of development (i.e., it is "powerful") is a function of how *consistent* it is across circumstances. To that I would add that powerful environments are those that manifest themselves in diverse forms. In phylogenetically advanced organisms such as human beings, most psychological phenomena are complex, dynamic, and dense. They derive from a variety of sources, operate at multiple levels, and assume an array of forms. So, too, are most of the environments human beings inhabit. Thus, measures with a greater number and variety of indicators are more likely to capture the phenomena being measured.

A third strategy is to make observations at different times (e.g., early in the morning, around meal time, or after dinner), in different areas of the home (e.g., kitchen, bedroom, or playroom), or with different household members (e.g., mother, father, siblings, or regular visitors). Most measures of the home environment involve relatively brief periods of data collection (rarely more than 2 hours). During such a brief period, an adult may show little communicative responsiveness to a child. Had the observation period been extended, it may have become apparent that the adult does communicate effectively with the child. Similarly, during a short visit to a home, one may not observe a child being disruptive, so the observer sees no displays of parental anger or punishment (as are indexed by such measures as the HOME Inventory). Had the observation been carried on for a longer period, the child may have misbehaved and the parent's normal responses of yelling and spanking may have been noted.

These three strategies are commonly understood means of improving measurement. They involve aggregating data across a greater span of time, a greater variety of circumstances, or a larger array of indicators. If some aspect of the environment is consistent across circumstances, constant across time, and makes its appearance in a variety of ways and in a variety of contexts, its likelihood of effect is great. Thus, any measurement process that (a) taps a dimension at only one point in time, (b) taps a dimension under a small range of conditions, or (c) taps a dimension in only a few of its manifestations may well misestimate the depth or the strength of that dimension for a particular case. Only if it can be assumed that the narrow measure is especially prototypic[1] of the dimension (or central to it) might one feel confident.

Central to fully delineating relations between the home environment and the children's development is the ability to assess continuity in the home environment. No question there is discontinuity in discrete parental behaviors, given the changing developmental tasks and increasing complexity of the growing child. It is less clear whether there is underlying continuity in the quality of the parent–child relationship within particular parent–child domains. Continuity, to the extent that it exists, resides in the organization and meaning of behavior patterns rather than in the stability of discrete parental actions. The discovery of continuity becomes a function of the unit of analysis and the level of abstraction chosen for analysis (Sroufe, 1979). Continuity of meaning may transcend differences in assessment procedures used at different ages. The ability to capture continuity in the environment as the environment pertains to developmental function is to some degree a product of measurement strategy. The use of limited number of indicators assessed in a short time interval will make it difficult to identify environmental continuities because short-term observations of a narrow range of behaviors or events may well be unrepresentative of the broader underlying constructs that they are supposed to characterize. In effect, continuity in the processes by which the environment supports or hinders certain aspects of development may be camouflaged by the use of narrow-band measurement strategies.

Given that none of the existing measures of the home environment fully satisfies the principles of good measurement practice outlined previously, the question remains: How does one choose a measure of the home environment? Part of the answer lies in the goals one has for measurement. If one's goals are clinical, such as identifying homes that pose a risk for development, then a measure that includes a reasonable number of indicators with known relationships to a target developmental problem (e.g., poor school performance, language delay, injury, and behavioral adjustment

[1]If a particular environmental circumstance (e.g., a conversation around the dinner table) can be taken as prototypic of a larger set of circumstance, then the particular circumstance might be a useful indicator of the broader set. However, as I read the literature, particularly the cross-cultural literature, I am increasingly skeptical about any environmental arrangement or circumstance that may be considered to be prototypical.

problems) may be an appropriate choice. The Purdue Home Stimulation Inventory (Wachs, Francis, & McQuiston, 1979), with its extensive coverage of the physical environment, might be a good choice if the goal is to identify homes posing a risk for attention difficulties or injury. Likewise, the Chaos, Hubbub, and Order Scale (CHAOS; Matheny, Wachs, Ludwig, & Phillips, 1995) may be a useful measure to use in studies involving injury and conduct disorders. The HOME Inventory (Caldwell & Bradley, 1984), the Henderson Environmental Learning Process Scale (Henderson, Bergan, and Hurt, 1972), and the Home Environment Questionnaire (Laing & Sines, 1982), because they include items tapping learning materials and enriching learning opportunities, might be useful in identifying homes that pose a risk for poor achievement. If the goal is to identify homes that pose a risk for disrupted attachments, the Parent Behavior Progression Scale (Bromwich, 1976), because it includes items that document parental responsiveness and nurturance, may be useful. A measure that focuses even more intensively on parental sensitivity, such as Ainsworth's (1973) rating scales, may be an even better choice.

STRUCTURE OF THE HOME ENVIRONMENT

During the past half century, there have been a number of efforts to explicate the structure of the home environment. Researchers typically separate elements of the environment into two major categories: social and physical (Casey, Bradley, Nelson, & Whaley, 1988; Wachs, 1989). Some have also identified a third aspect, informational. Thus far, studies of the structure of environmental measures have not been very convincing in terms of identifying a reliable underlying pattern for the total home environment, even including Schaefer's (1959) excellent work on the circumplex model of parent behavior.[2] Techniques such as factor analysis have been used in an attempt to clarify the underlying structure. However, the results are not persuasive because these techniques reflect a limited set of indicators (items) of environmental inputs and because they almost always rely on a single type of data collection methodology (e.g., interview with a parent, observation in a single setting, and ratings).

Some very useful measures of the home environment have derived from conceptions of human behavior and development. These include Williams's (1976) 26-item scale that is based on social learning theory and Marjoribanks's (1972) eight-dimension measure that is based on Murray's (1938) need-press theory. Laing and Sines (1982) also based their 134-item scale on Murray's theory, whereas the Henderson Environmental Learning

[2]It is not the purpose of this chapter to delineate the structure of the home environment fully. Readers are referred to Bronfenbrenner's treatment of the structure of human ecologies in chapter 1 (this volume).

Process Scale (HELPS; Henderson et al., 1972) reflects the ecological analyses of Bloom (1964). Yarrow, Rubenstein, Pedersen, and Jankowski (1975) constructed a four-dimension scale by using information theory, adaptation level theory, operant learning theory, and Piagetian theory. Attachment theory served as the framework for the Parent Behavior Progression developed by Bromwich (1976). However, empirical analyses have not provided strong support for an underlying structure that closely corresponds to these theoretical orientations. Henderson et al. said the following about their attempt at verifying a conceptualized organization of environmental indicators that is representative of the findings extant: "The factors revealed in this analysis did not generally correspond to the hypothesized factors" (p. 189). What may partially account for these discrepancies is that the environment itself is not basically organized in relation to human behavior. The organization of the environment is a function of many, often loosely connected, factors, some of which have little to do with the particular human beings engaging the environment at a given moment.

The search for a generic underlying structure of the home environment has been made more difficult because measures of the same ostensible environmental construct (take, for instance, parental teaching) often measure the construct at different levels of analysis. It is common to find low correlations between measures of an environmental dimension such as responsivity that operationalize the dimension (construct) in an extensive, highly abstract way (such as might be reflected by a single observer rating at the end of hours of observation) and a measure that operationalizes responsivity in a narrower, more concrete way (such as might occur by using microanalytic coding in a brief structured task). In a broad sense, responsivity is appropriately viewed as a facilitator of development (Bornstein, 1989). However, as recent studies by Wachs et al. (1993) have shown, that is quite a different thing from saying that responsivity to distress, responsivity to nondistress, object responsivity, person responsivity, nonvocal responsivity, or vocal responsivity have a positive impact on development.

Cause Versus Effect Indicators

Identification of a clear structure of the home environment has been challenging partly because many of the items in home environment measures are *cause* rather than *effect* indicators. Bollen and Lennox (1991) made the point that part of the motivation for development of factor analysis was the recognition that relatively few latent variables may underlie a large number of indicators. Bollen and Lennox argued, however, that it is critical to determine the direction of causation between latent variables and the indicators designed to measure them. They distinguished cause (formative or induced) indicators from effect (reflective) indicators. For cause indicators, the observed variables are assumed to cause a latent variable. For effect indicators, the latent variable causes the observed variable.

Let us consider the concept of stress (and the indicators used to measure it) to illustrate the difference between cause and effect indicators. Most life stress measures include items that presumably produce stress (e.g., job loss, divorce, and death in the family); that is, they are cause indicators. (See Figure 1.) By contrast, most measures of the phenomenon of stress itself include physiological markers (e.g., sweating and elevated heart rate) or behavioral markers (e.g., observed crying and irritability) as indicators. These indicators are the presumed effects of stress. (See Figure 1.)

Home environment measures typically contain a large percentage of cause indicators. A variety of different acts and conditions results in an environmental phenomenon that a researcher might label *stimulation* or *responsivity* or *organization* or *negative control*. However, stimulation does not cause "stimulating" actions and circumstances to appear. The same might be said of an environmental domain such as control. A variety of different acts and conditions results in control, not the reverse. One of the implications of this distinction is that the underlying structure of many environmental measures may appear less tight and clear than the factor-analytic structures researchers are used to seeing for human traits and characteristics. The latter are more often composed of effect indicators. A trait such as intelligence or gregariousness produces a certain set of reasonably tightly bound actions. The items that index these actions should, correspondingly, hang together reasonably well when they are subjected to factor analysis.

In effect for many environmental dimensions, the indicators may well not derive from the same underlying construct in a causal sense. Broad dimensions, such as stimulation, organization, and responsiveness, may contain indictors emanating from a variety of different causes and, thus, show little evidence of a coherent factor structure. The narrower the dimension, the more likely a "clean" empirical structure may emerge. However, even that can be misleading in that it can represent artifacts of sampling. For example, a measure of communicative responsiveness might

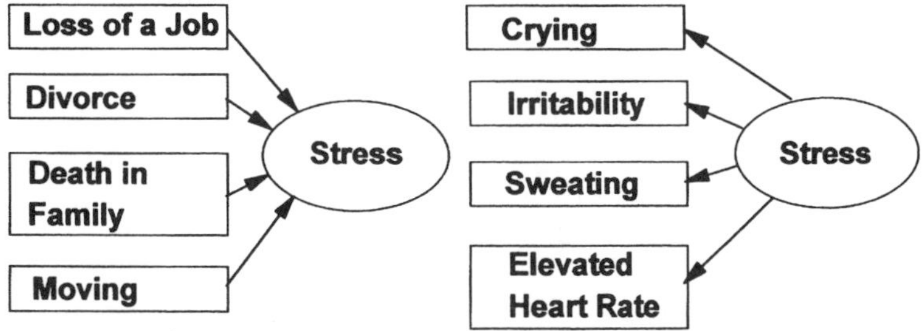

Figure 1. Cause and effect indicators of stress. Left side of figure indicates items that can presumably cause stress. Right side of figure indicates the presumed effects of stress.

show a very tight structure if most of the data are collected from mothers or most of the data are collected in narrow-band situations—even though the measure is intended to provide information about a broader array of circumstances and family members.

With regard to the structure of the home environment, it is not surprising that one does not get convergent findings, given that studies have used a variety of measures with a variety of samples in a variety of contexts. The content of home environment measures varies greatly (both the constructs included and the level of analysis reflected in the items). The measures utilize a variety of different item formats and methods of data collection. The lack of coherence that characterizes the studies aimed at identifying underlying structure not only reflects the direction of the relationship between indicator and construct but also is a function of the types of scaling that is done within the various measures, the kinds of extraction methods used in the studies, and the actual distributions of scores present in particular samples. As I argue later, the environment seems to function at multiple levels in terms of how it affects children, and an elaborate system of classifying environmental elements is needed to integrate what researchers know about how different aspects of the environment affect the course of development.

Three Levels of the Micro Home Environment

There is growing evidence that home environments operate at at least three levels in terms of how they affect the behavior of children. Figure 2 depicts the three levels.

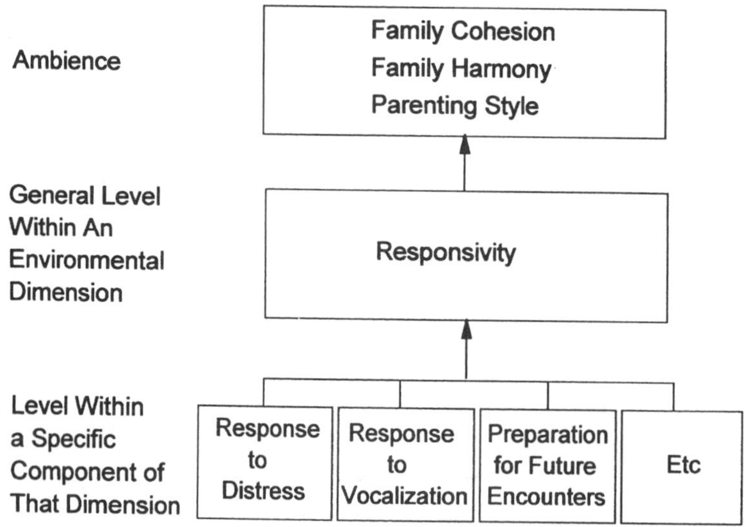

Figure 2. Three levels of the home environment that affect the behavior of children.

First, homes exhibit an ambience (e.g., the overall amount of conflict present, the degree of cohesion in the family, a general style of interaction among family members, and an overall level of organization or harmony; see also Lawton, chapter 4, this volume). As a rule, these pervading conditions are more distal than behaviors aimed directly at the child by other household members present; albeit, there are exceptions such as background noise. Ambient conditions indirectly affect children, and they moderate the effect of direct exchanges between children and those people and objects in the home environment (e.g., a high level of background noise may reduce the effectiveness of parental attempts to teach the child, or a high degree of parental conflict may reduce the effectiveness of parental attempts to nurture the child). Darling and Steinberg (1993) proposed, for example, that parenting style is best viewed as a context that modifies the influence of specific parenting practices. Mink and Nihira (1986) identified three types of family style; for each family type, a different set of relationships between particular parenting behaviors and children's behavioral development emerged. Cummings, Zahn-Waxler, and Radke-Yarrow (1981) observed that toddlers exposed to frequent marital conflict reacted more intensively to later episodes of parental conflict than children who experienced less frequent conflict. Research on noise has indicated that persistent, intensive auditory stimuli has physiological consequences and may be inimical to task performance and interpersonal exchanges (World Health Organization, 1980). Although few aspects of household ambience have intensively been studied, there are likely to be stylistic characteristics of the home that exert an influence on children. The techniques needed to measure most aspects of ambience have yet to be developed or evaluated.

Second, most components of the environment that directly involve the child (e.g., parental responsivity, object stimulation, and structuring of learning opportunities) appear to function at a general level in terms of their influence on behavior. For example, a child's total experience with adult caregivers across a variety of situations may lead the child to conclude that the environment is basically responsive (i.e., at a general level, the environment is responsive). However, the same child's experience with Mom in the area of communication may lead the child to conclude that Mom is not a very responsive communicator (i.e., at a specific level, one adult caregiver is nonresponsive). This third, more specific, level also influences child behavior. If an observer gave an overall responsiveness rating to this home environment, the rating would characterize the environment as responsive, but the same observer would rate Mom's communicative responsiveness as low. Most microanalytic techniques (e.g., Bornstein et al., 1992) focus on highly specific aspects of constructs such as responsiveness. By comparison, measures like the HOME Inventory, the Home Environment Questionnaire, and the HELPS derive scores that are more summative. No wonder scores on such summative measures often correlate only modestly with scores from more microanalytic techniques tapping the same dimension.

As children grow older, they are increasingly able to integrate information from multiple sources within the home and to develop ideas about their meaning. Children construct a generalized set of expectancies and motivational propensities to act in accordance with the general level of responsivity, object stimulation, structured learning opportunities, and the like that are present. Children are also aware of the specific ways that their environments are responsive or not so responsive, stimulating or not so stimulating, and so forth. They can discriminate among the various types of responsivity present, each of which may have different salience for various behavioral systems. Cross-cultural studies of environmental dimensions are especially informative in this regard. Investigators have observed that while broad dimensions such as stimulation or responsiveness may have similar meaning across cultures, the narrower components of these dimensions (verbal stimulation vs. physical contact stimulation and responsivity to vocalization vs. responsivity to exploration) may have different significance (Bornstein, et al., 1992; Wachs, et al., 1992).

There appears to be some independence in the operation of these three levels of the environment that is similar to the independence of the different levels of biological functioning (from organ systems down to the subcellular level). The organization of action is complex: occurring within, between, and across levels. As children get older, and as they are able to comprehend more distal and general conditions, these conditions become more salient for behavioral development.

What does the three-level structure of the home environment imply for environmental measurement? For one thing, it may be advisable to use a measurement battery that includes a broad array of indicators at multiple levels of analysis. Because a dimension like control operates at multiple levels and is produced by a variety of actions, including a wide array of indicators of control should prove useful. It might also be useful to measure certain aspects of the general ambience (e.g., family harmony) and to include some indicators of this ambience as well. Ambience may be best measured by a qualitative judgment or by a summary of representative indicators. As one descends levels of structure, the more useful quantitative approaches to measurement, such as codings of specific behaviors or summations made in narrowly confined situations, are likely to become more useful.

FRAMEWORK FOR MEASURING CAREGIVING WITHIN THE HOME ENVIRONMENT

In the preceding sections of this chapter, the focus was on how to assess the home environment. This section deals with what to measure. I have made assumptions both about what is salient for human development and about how the environment functions to support development. The framework I use to organize information about the environment (or about caregiving wherever it occurs) is based on the systems theory premise that the environment helps to regulate the course of development (Sameroff & Friese, 1991). The framework is elaborate. It allows categorization of actions, objects, and events (the elements composing an environment) by using several dimensions simultaneously. Although potentially useful as a guide for constructing measures of the home environment, it is probably too complex for all its components to be incorporated into a single measurement instrument.

The framework is built upon the notion that caregiving (a facilitative home environment) is best conceived of as a set of regulatory acts and conditions aimed at successful adaptation and at successful exploitation of opportunity structures (Saegert & Winkel, 1990).

The Primary Tasks of a Caregiving System

To promote optimal development, an environmental regulatory system must do four things: (a) *sustain* the child (ensure viability), (b) *stimulate* activity in the child (directed at the child's enhancement), (c) *support* the child's self-sustaining capacities and tendencies, and (d) *control* the amount and pattern of inputs experienced by the child so that there is optimal fit between the child's agenda and the agenda of those systems of which the child is a part. The first three regulatory functions derive from what is known about human needs and arousal systems. For example, Maslow and Murphy (1954) contended that human beings need environments that promote survival, provide information (including enlistment of attention), and affirm worth. The first three regulatory functions map onto the three major domains of organismic functioning, each with its own arousal processes: (a) biological–physical (activity arousal), (b) cognitive (attention arousal), and (c) social–emotional (emotional arousal; Ford & Lerner, 1992). For complex living systems such as human beings, the task of maintaining internal unity is quite complicated because of the large number of component subsystems involved and the elaborateness of their organization (Ford & Lerner, 1992). To deal with the organism's complexity, caregiving systems must perform other functions that are regulatory in a more complete sense (more managerial in nature). These additional functions enable the caregiving environment to most adequately perform its direct service on behalf of the child. The managerial functions of importance are those that enable the environment to engage the child effectively so that organismic integrity is promoted (i.e., operations that increase the likelihood of optimal fit)—thus, the fourth regulatory function, control.

Starting from this basic notation, Bettye Caldwell and I identified five basic kinds of regulatory tasks or functions performed by the caregiving environment: (a) sustenance, (b) stimulation, (c) support, (d) structure, and (e) surveillance. The first three are designed to satisfy the kinds of needs related to the three basic arousal processes described above. The last two are components of the control processes required to optimize fit between the basic needs of humans and the specific requirements for a particular person. These five functions are depicted in Figure 3.

Sustenance

"The growth, health, and functioning of the human body as a physical entity requires the ability to collect and use appropriate material/energy forms and to protect against potentially damaging ones" (Ford & Lerner, 1992, p. 103). Caregiving acts and conditions designed to promote biological integrity are what we called sustenance. The environment must provide adequate nutrients, shelter, and conditions for the maintenance of health to ensure both survival and the level of biological integrity needed for physical and psychological development (Pollitt, 1994). The environment must also protect children from pathogenic conditions such as pollutants, passive cigarette smoke, and exposure to heavy metals (Evans,

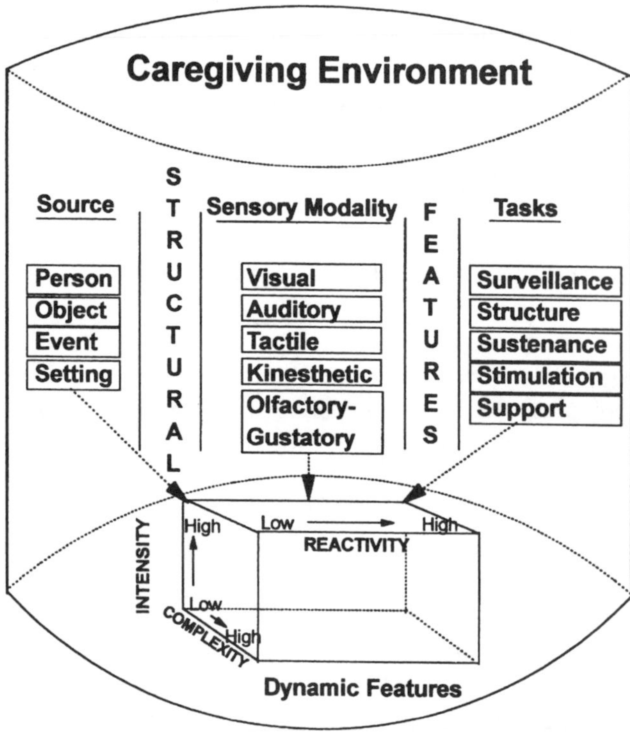

Figure 3. Five basic kinds of regulatory tasks or functions performed by the caregiving environment.

Kliewer, & Martin, 1991; Jacobson, Jacobson, Padgett, Brummitt, & Billings, 1992; Tong & McMichael, 1992).

Stimulation

To ensure cognitive–motivational integrity, the environment must provide sensory data that engage attention and provide information. There is an abundance of both psychological theory and empirical data to buttress the significance of stimulation for cognitive, psychomotor, and social development (Horowitz, 1987). Development in every domain of competency requires a manageable amount of meaningful information (Caldwell, 1968).

Support

Optimal social–emotional development depends on having an environment that responds to human social, and emotional needs (Bretherton & Waters, 1985). Such acts and conditions are what we called support. Some acts of support are given in anticipation of unexpressed needs, and others are given following expressed needs. Emotions function to prepare human beings to take action in their own best interest (Grinker, et al., 1956). The caregiving environment must assist in enlisting and modulating the motivational properties of emotions to help ensure optimal fit with environmental demands.

There also is evidence that children benefit from positive affirmation of worth (Ausubel, 1968; Roberts, 1986). That is, to be supportive, the environment must be reinforcing (in a proactive sense) and responsive (in a reactive sense). How worth is affirmed varies substantially from culture to culture. In some societies, worth is closely tied to individual accomplishments or status; in others, it is more strongly tied to collective commitments and involvement. Finally, a supportive environment is one that provides guidance or direction for adequate functioning in other environments (Pettit, Dodge, & Brown, 1988). At its base, support is motivational preparation for encountering other environments (e.g., in the sense that a secure attachment allows a child to explore the environment more freely; Ainsworth, 1973).

Structure

Although children need sustenance, stimulation, and support for optimal growth and development, there also is evidence that the relation between these inputs and either growth or development is not constant. Receipt of equal amounts of these inputs does not seem to result in equal amounts of "good" growth and development. The arrangement of inputs may be as crucial to development as the amount. In summary, optimal caregiving probably consists not only in ensuring that sufficient amounts of stimulation, sustenance, and support reach a child but also in configuring or structuring a child's encounters with those direct inputs so that "fit" is achieved. What fits one child's needs may not be suitable at all for another child. A good example may be seen in the differential responsiveness of preterm infants and infants prenatally exposed to drugs. Such biologically vulnerable infants are often overwhelmed by levels of stimulation that are quite comfortable for normal babies.

Surveillance

To be effective in the management of inputs to a system, the regulatory apparatus designed to control the system must monitor both the system and its context. This important regulatory function performed by parents (or their proxies) is what we called surveillance. It involves "keeping track of" the whereabouts and activities of the child and the child's surrounding circumstances. Most commonly, surveillance has been thought of as keeping track of the child and of environmental conditions to which the child is exposed so as to protect the child from harm (Darling & Steinberg, 1993; Lozoff, 1989; Patterson, DeBarsyshe, & Ramsey, 1989; Peterson, Ewigman, & Kivlahan, 1993; U.S. Department of Health and Human Services, 1991). However, comprehensive measures of surveillance should also include observations of the child and the environment designed to determine how much the physical and social environment affords the child productive and enjoyable engagements.

Sources of Input and Modalities of Reception

Bettye Caldwell and I identified two other key attributes of environmental actions and conditions that seemed relevant to a broad variety of caregiving episodes and salient for most aspects of development. The first is the *source* of the environmental input. Source was selected as a key characteristic of environmental input because the meaning a person attributes to an act or condition and the reaction a person has to a particular caregiving episode often depends on its source (Kuhn, 1992). The four major sources of input to children are (a) person, (b) object, (c) setting, and (d) event. The person category covers all of the input that a child receives from fellow human beings (e.g., mother, father, siblings, neighbors, teachers, and peers). Failure to act toward a person (e.g., ignoring a child) can also be included under this category (e.g., negative instances). The object category covers all physical phenomena in the child's environment (e.g., toys, clothing, furniture, appliances, and recreational apparatus). Setting pertains to the immediate milieu in which a particular pattern of input is received (e.g., house or apartment, playground, child-care center, or doctor's office). It is a common designation used in ecological psychology, albeit the word *place* is often used rather than the word *setting* (Whiting,

1981). Setting does not just refer to social address but also represents an amalgam of person–object elements that have potential meaning beyond the individual inputs of the people and objects contained therein. The combining of people and objects into a potent and time-limited stimulus is what we label an event. The input from an event often takes on meaning and significance for a person that is not simply the sum of the discrete inputs from the people and objects therein. For example, a fire truck (an object) driven by a man (a person) rushes by en route to a fire next door (a setting). Should the input reach the child, it will be from this tableaux resulting from a particular constellation of people and objects over a limited period of time.

It also seemed useful to us to classify environmental acts in terms of the sensory *modality* through which the input is received. Humans obtain relevant information through a set of sensoriperceptual structures, each capable of collecting different kinds of information that the nervous system can use to construct, maintain, elaborate, and use with respect to different patterns of behavioral functioning (Ford & Lerner, 1992). Although the human neurological system is organized so that it can integrate information from the various sensory modalities, there is evidence that people respond to information from the various modalities differently (Cicchetti & Sroufe, 1976). The proposed system utilizes common designations for this category: (a) visual, (b) auditory, (c) tactile, (d) kinesthetic, and (e) olfactory–gustatory.

The proposed system for classifying environmental elements centers on the idea that the environment performs a number of functions necessary for human development. This conception is offered with no assumption that the environment is actually "out there" ready to serve human development nor that humans are inactive in constructing environments for their own benefit or interest. (See Lerner, 1986.) Rather, the conception is offered as a convenient perspective regarding how the environment can operate to assist or to deter maximum development. This framework allows one to observe the environment (and to measure it) in terms of how the environment regulates development. In summary, to understand how the environment influences human behavior and development, it is important to view the environment not only from the perspective of its observable attributes but also from the perspective that human beings engage their environments in relation to their needs, styles, and capabilities (i.e., the goals of development such as health, joy, and accomplishment of developmental tasks that are appropriate to one's culture).

Finally, this system for classifying the acts and conditions of caregiving is offered as a heuristic framework that may be helpful in identifying key limitations and gaps in measuring the home environment. The dimension of structure illustrates the system's potential usefulness. The importance of structure is widely acknowledged (Matheny et al., 1995), and there is evidence from diverse areas of research (e.g., crowding, environmental design, and parental teaching practices) that support the importance of an orderly, structured environment. Oddly enough, most home environment measures give scant attention to structuring activities and conditions—the CHAOS Scale (Matheny et al., 1995) and the Purdue Home Stimulation Inventory (Wachs, Francis, & McQuiston, 1979) being notable exceptions. Structuring can be accomplished by means of individual caregiving acts, rules, and physical arrangements. The fact is that there are numerous ways in which structure can facilitate or impede the provision of optimal types of sustenance, stimulation, and support. Consider sustenance. The arrangements made regarding meals can be as significant as the amount and type of nutrients consumed. The potential value of stimulation from objects in the environment may be enhanced by a variety of structuring activities, including drawing attention to them, physically arranging them for interest and ease of comprehension, and making them readily accessible. Such activities are often included in measures of classrooms (and child-care centers) but less often in home environment measures. The likelihood of support can also be enhanced by such structuring activities as introducing a child to new adults, bringing children to play groups, and the like.

Engaging the Environment

Description of the environment in terms of its regulatory function, source, and modality through which it is received does not adequately account for the person as transactor with the environment nor does it depict the environment in terms adequate to gauge the likely fit of environmental inputs to human needs. How an environmental element presents itself to a child (stylistic attributes) may be as crucial as what it is (content–function attributes). Fit means a fulfillment of need, and need is a function of both what the child brings to an encounter with the environment (internal motivational states and competencies) and what the environment offers. Thus, we created an "innerlayer" of classificatory dimensions to depict environmental elements with reference to how they present themselves to the child. (See Figure 3.) These dimensions represent dynamic qualities of the home environment.

We chose three particular dynamic attributes of environmental inputs that seem related to a child's likely motivational state on encountering the element and to the child's capability of beneficially assimilating the element: reactivity, intensity, and complexity. The notion of person–environment fit implies that the environment must be responsive to the child. Responsiveness is a difficult quality to define with precision (see Bornstein, 1989, for a treatment of the construct). However, it would seem to imply that an input be (a) sufficient in amount to engage the child and begin the process of need fulfillment; (b) in a form that is assimilable, given the child's capabilities and set; and (c) energizing in the sense that it moves the child out of a given need state toward a state of rest and enjoyment or to the point of being able to deal with a less pressing (higher order) state of need—ascending the hierarchy of needs much like Maslow and Murphy (1954) described them. *Intensity* includes frequency, magnitude, proximity, saturation, or amount of the input. *Complexity* refers to such features as number of parts, number of connections between parts, hierarchical arrangement among parts, and so forth. *Reactivity* refers to latency and inevitability (contingency) of response. The qualities of environmental inputs represented in these three dimensions appear related to a person's adaptability (i.e., they would help determine the ability of the organism to maintain its integrity in the face of demands from the environment) and to a person's capacity to derive advantage from opportunities. Viewed negatively, an environment too intense to be controllable, too complex to be comprehended, or not reactive to a child's attempts to manipulate cannot be considered responsive.

Perhaps nothing so clearly illustrates the basic dilemma of environmental measurement as does our effort to identify dimensions or attributes of the environment that operationalize person–environment transactions and the importance of fit between what a person needs and what the environment affords. Even prolonged observation does not allow the observer to know precisely what a person needs (or, by deduction, to know whether what the environment affords meets those needs). Human beings are too complex and dynamic, and need has to be judged with reference not only to present state but also to goals and anticipated future states as well. Thus, even though the aim of environmental measurement should be to describe environments such that one can estimate the likely fit between person and environment, construction of reliable procedures that include judgments about fit for individual cases is quite difficult. For now, it seems more realistic to describe (and to measure) the environment itself, to do so comprehensively, and to do so using dimensions that help capture more of the nuances of transactions. The information from such measurement approaches can then be integrated with information about the child.

For purposes of integrating information about environment and development, it is also useful to adopt a life-span, cross-cultural perspective. To wit, an apparatus containing only a small number of parts may appear quite complex to a toddler (i.e., it is difficult to comprehend and operate) while appearing quite simple to most adults. A sophisticated piece of technology may not seem complex to those trained in its use or to those generally experienced with advanced technology. However, to those with little technical background or to those from cultures where little advanced technology exists, such equipment may appear exceedingly complex.

The yardsticks used to scale the dynamic dimensions of the classification system should be developed by using a human species view (life span and cross-cultural). Identification of useful yardsticks may not be so difficult for intensity, given that measurement procedures already exist for such things as noise level, color saturation, brightness, and tartness. Acceptable yardsticks may also be achievable for complexity by using consensus judgments of experts in particular areas of content. However, arrival at reliable yardsticks for reactivity may prove a formidable challenge, given that reactivity involves both amenability to change and controllability.

Our scheme for classifying elements of caregiving environments derives from a conception of the environment as a regulator. This conception provides a useful complement to the notion of humans as self-regulating, self-constructing systems reactive to their contexts. This framework is a heuristic or organizational device designed to help guide a measurement strategy, it is not a prescription for a measurement system. The framework is not yet finished; we expect that some classes can usefully be subdivided.

BRIEF REVIEW OF HOME ENVIRONMENT MEASURES

During the past half century, there have been a number of efforts to construct measures of the home environment. The content and format of these measures reflects (a) the research interests (including developmental periods and developmental domains) of the instrument developers, (b) the historical era (even within this past 50 years) during which the measure was constructed (see Wachs, 1992, for a discussion of the evolving conceptions of environment–development relationships), (c) the preferences regarding measurement methodologies, and (d) the feasibility considerations surrounding data gathering. None of these measures assesses the full range of caregiving functions described earlier in this chapter; none was intended to. Even so, these measures offer potentially useful means of gathering data about aspects of the proximal environments of children.

My purpose is not to evaluate these measures critically but to describe them, with a view of illustrating the kinds of instruments currently available. I make a few summarizing comments about the measures, beginning with the following three. First, the type of data collection process used tends to change as children age. Measures for infants frequently include direct observations of parental actions and household objects, whereas measures for older children increasingly rely on parent report. Most of the items in home environment measures designed for young children assess conditions quite proximal to the child. By contrast, measures for older children include indicators of more distal aspects of the environment. Second, most measures have been developed by using quite restricted samples. Their applicability to other groups in not established nor is there useful normative information on most of the measures. Third, most research done with these measures has involved mothers as informants or as the targets of observation. Thus, it is not known how accurately the measures represent the total home environment.

The Fels Longitudinal Study included one of the first detailed assessments of the home environment (Baldwin, Kalhorn, & Breese, 1945). Observations were made by using the Parent Behavior Record (Baldwin et al., 1945). This scale examined parenting behaviors such as intensity of contact, accelerational attempts, babying, hostile detachment, and justification of policy. Although these scales showed high predictive value for many child outcomes in the Fels sample, they were not widely used thereafter (Crandall, Dewey, Katkovsky, & Preston, 1964; McCall, Appelbaum, & Hogarty, 1973).

With the publication of *Stability and Change in Human Characteristics*, Bloom (1964) gave impetus to environmental measurement. Together with his students at the University of Chicago, Dave (1963) and Wolf (1964), Bloom constructed a 63-item rating scale that was based on information collected by interview with the parents. These scales cover such areas as intellectual aspirations for the child, rewards for intellectual accomplishment, quality of language use by parents, availability and encouragement of use of books and learning supplies. The Chicago School was the first to conceptualize the environment as a montage of "presses" or "forces," a notion in keeping with Murray's (1938) concept of need press. Bloom and his students influenced a number of others to develop similar types of home environment measures, including Marjoribanks (1972), whose scale assesses eight environmental forces (e.g., press for achievement, press for independence, press for English, and mother dominance); Keeves (1972), whose scale assesses seven forces (e.g., achievement press, work habits and the press for order, and affiliation in the home and between home); and Mosychuk (1969), whose scale assesses 10 environmental presses (e.g., academic and vocational aspirations and expectations, female dominance in child rearing, harmony in the home, and physical environment). Bloom also influenced Henderson and his colleagues (1972), whose HELPS measure assesses five factors (e.g., extended interests and community involvement, valuing language and school behavior, and attention), and Laing and Sines (1982), whose Home Environment Questionnaire assesses eight environmental presses (e.g., press for achievement, press for aggression, press for change, and press for sociability). These scales have had a rich history in studies of intellectual and academic achievement during middle childhood (Iverson & Walberg, 1979). Most of the items assess direct parenting practices and conditions in the home, but some assess attitudes (particularly involving expectations) and parent status. Not surprisingly, when Williams (1976) factor analyzed Mosychuk's scale, he identified four major factors: a General Stimulus factor reflecting the extent to which parents specifically structure opportunities for the child to interact with people and things, a Parental Dominance factor dealing with the relative dominance of one parent in the rearing process, a Reinforcement factor dealing with the use of physical versus nonphysical punishment, and a Parental Expectations factor.

The approach used by Moore (1968) was somewhat different. He depended more on direct observation of the opportunities for stimulation and the kinds of encouragement to learn in the home. He was also concerned about the level of nurturance provided. So, too, was Radin (1973), whose scales involve observing the extent to which parents meet the needs of their children and the extent to which parents are restrictive. The notion of looking more at what the child needs and what the environment affords to meet those need represents an important conceptual distinction from the concept of environmental forces or presses.

Because of their focus on intrinsic motives, Yarrow et al. (1975) also approached the measurement of home environments somewhat differently. These researchers included items that considered not only the variety of stimulation and nurturance available but also the responsiveness to these as well. As the notion of the child as an active participant in the environment (rather than as a more passive recipient) has emerged strongly in theories of human development, the concept of responsiveness has become increasingly important in the development of home environment measures. Wachs et al. (1979) utilized the concept of responsiveness in constructing the Purdue Home Stimulation Inventory, a comprehensive measure of the physical home environment. This multidimensional measure inventories a large number of physical objects, plus the organization of objects and events. The PHSI also assesses aspects of the physical environment (e.g., noise, and confusion) that tend to interfere with the child's optimal functioning in the home.

The concept of order (or disorganization) has a long history in research about human development. Nonetheless, home environment measures rarely include more than scant attention to arrangements and conditions that produce order (or chaos). The CHAOS (Matheny et al., 1995) attempts to fill this gap. It is a narrowly focused measure that includes items dealing with clutter in the physical environment and the degree of calm and confusion in the social environment. Like a number of recently developed measures, CHAOS is concerned not just with the content of the environment but also with its potential responsiveness to children's needs.

The HOME Inventory

Of all the scientific work I have done, nothing is better known than the research involving the HOME Inventory (Caldwell & Bradley, 1984). This measure has been used in many studies worldwide and by hundreds of agencies offering services to children and families (Bradley, 1994). I would like to briefly describe HOME and present some of the issues I have confronted as a result of my experiences with it.

HOME is designed to assess the quality and quantity of stimulation and support available to children in the home environment. There are four versions of the inventory: The first is designed for children from birth to age 3, the second for children ages 3 to 6, the third for children from 6 to 10, and the fourth for children ages 10 to 14.

The information needed to score the inventories is obtained through a combination of observation and a semistructured interview conducted at home, when both the child and the child's primary caregiver are present. Often there are other family members present during the visit as well.

Exhibit 1 includes a list of subscales from the four inventories, including the one in development. Each inventory assesses several dimensions of the home environment. There are similarities among the four instruments: Each taps such dimensions as parental responsiveness, use of aversive control techniques, objects and materials for learning, enriching experiences to which the child is exposed, and activities of father figures. Each measure taps dimensions of special salience for its age period as well. The Early Childhood HOME, for example, includes items that deal with the teaching of school readiness competencies. Every version, except the one for infants, devotes attention to the safety and appeal of the environment external to the home residence. The Early Adolescent version includes substantial attention to family regulatory and monitoring activities that seem particularly relevant to the increased freedom and competencies characteristic of adolescence and to the new issues and expectations that face adolescents.

Research involving the HOME reveals a number of important characteristics about home environment measures (Bradley, 1994). First, relationships with family status and structure measures such as maternal education, household income, and degree of crowding are generally moderate (.3–.6), but they vary from one sociocultural group to another. For example, the correlation between HOME scores and the occupation of the head of the household for African Americans is low (<.2). Second, relationships with parental characteristics such as maternal IQ, maternal depression, parental substance abuse, attitudes toward child rearing, and the like range from low to moderate, depending on the characteristic. Correlations with parental IQ tend to be strong (around .6). Third, relationships with family ecological factors such as social support and stress are generally low but significant. Fourth, relationships with children's intelligence, achievement, and language scores tend to be moderate (.4–.6), whereas relationships with measures of socioemotional development are generally low to moderate (.2–.4). Significant relations are also noted for health-related factors such as failure to thrive, malnutrition, lead burden, and abuse. Fifth, even though there is a reasonable level of consistency in

EXHIBIT 1
Subscales of the Home Observation for Measurement of the Environment Inventories

Infant Toddler
Parental Responsivity
Acceptance
Organization of the Environment
Learning Materials
Parental Involvement
Variety of Experience
Early Childhood
Learning Materials
Language Stimulation
Physical Environment
Parental Responsivity
Academic Stimulation
Modeling
Variety of Experience
Acceptance
Middle Childhood
Parental Responsivity
Encouragement of Maturity
Acceptance
Learning Materials
Enrichment
Family Companionship
Parental Involvement
Early Adolescent
Physical Environment
Learning Materials
Modeling
Instructional Activities
Regulatory Activities
Variety of Experiences
Acceptance and Responsivity

Note. From *Home Observation for Measurement of the Environment* by B. M. Caldwell and R. H. Bradley, 1984, Little Rock: University of Arkansas at Little Rock.

findings pertaining to the HOME Inventory, our experience with the measure (both personal experience obtained by actual home visits and experience in analyzing information from research studies) shows that what goes on in the homes of children is amazingly varied, even in homes of people living in the same neighborhoods and in homes of people with the same demographic characteristics. Rarely can one account for more than half of the variance in HOME scores by using a combination of family structure and family demographic factors—families have unique reasons for providing the kinds of care and arrangements that they do (Bradley & Caldwell,

1984; Bradley, Mundfrom, Whiteside, Barrett, & Casey, 1994). Correlations between HOME scores and child measures also vary as a function of children's characteristic (e.g., age, temperament, disability, and sex). Finally, there are cultural differences in what parents do with their children and how they provide for their children (Chua, Kong, Wong, & Yoong, 1989; Field, Widmayer, Adler, & DeCubas, 1990; Reis & Hertz, 1987). These differences sometimes result in different patterns of relations between what goes on in the home and children's behavioral development (Bradley et al., 1989; Bradley et al., 1994).

Because the HOME Inventories have been used so widely for research and applied purposes, it has given me an opportunity to grapple firsthand with many of the thorny issues involved in measuring the home environment. In California, for example, it is commonplace for children of divorce to be placed in joint custody; the children spend time living with each of the parents. A long-term user of HOME posed the question: What should researchers consider the home environment of such children to be? A few years ago the state of California initiated a program for drug-dependent women and their children. Many of the children had no stable place of residence—some were even living on the streets. Those charged with the responsibility of evaluating the program asked the question: How should researchers designate and evaluate the home environments of these children? We have run into similar conundrums in our efforts to use home environment measures for atypical children, most specifically children with severe disabilities. What is a good home environment for children whose disabilities markedly constrain their capacity to profit from the conditions that afford most children ample opportunities for good development? Should the items in environmental measures derive from a generic, objective template that represents expert consensus on what is important for development or should the content and structure of items allow for idiosyncratic, subjective perspective of individuals or groups?

Not surprisingly, the issue of group differences has often arisen in situations in which the HOME was to be given to non-White families. There is both cultural and economic bias in the HOME Inventories, but what implications does such bias have for use of the instrument with non-White, especially poor, families? In some cultural groups, it is far less common for a child's father to be present in the household, but does that mean that items dealing with fathers should be eliminated or that items dealing with other adult caregivers should be substituted? Poor families often lack access to medical care, but does that mean that items dealing with how often the parent takes the child in for regular medical care be altered? Likewise, many of the households in rural Chile have no toys or learning materials. Should the items dealing with availability of such materials be eliminated? Should efforts be made to identify substitute items? In effect, what perspective should prevail in the determination of content for measures of the home environment: Cultural? Normative? Individual needs? Although a partial answer to all of these questions devolves from the use one wants to make of the information obtained, fully satisfactory answers are difficult to come by. They depend on one's assumptions and perspectives regarding children's development, one's concepts about the fundamental nature of family and the home environment, and one's philosophy of science as it applies to measurement.

CONCLUSIONS

Thirty years ago the seminal work of Hunt (1961) and Bloom (1964) on the relationship between experience and development catalyzed efforts to develop measures of children's environments. A number of measures have been successfully used in research and applied settings, and these measures have helped further advance knowledge about the forces shaping development. These subsequent advances in theory and research compel a renewal of effort to construct measures of the home environment. Most measures of the home environment do not sufficiently incorporate current beliefs about the environment as a complex, dynamic transactor with individuals in the process of development. They do not reflect the home environment as a complex, dynamic set of interrelated systems that operates at multiple levels to help regulate human behavior. Unfortunately, there is not yet a comprehensive, unifying theory about the environment to guide a new generation of measurement construction efforts (Patterson & Yoerger, 1991). Moreover, much of classic test construction theory is not readily applicable to measurement of the home environment because many home environment measures will not be composed of the type of indicators upon which classical approaches to test construction were built. Thus, future efforts to construct measures of the home environment will have to focus more than ever on construct validity and approaches to reliability other than internal consistency.

REFERENCES

Ainsworth, M. (1973). The development of infant–mother attachment. In B. Caldwell & H. Riccuiti (Eds.), *Review of child development research* (Vol. 3, pp. 1–94). Chicago: University of Chicago Press.

Ausubel, D. (1968). *Educational psychology: A cognitive view*. New York: Holt, Rinehart & Winston.

Baldwin, A. L., Kalhorn, J., & Breese, F. (1945). Patterns of parent behavior. *Psychological Monographs*, 58(No. 3).

Bloom, B. S. (1964). *Stability and change in human characteristics*. New York: Wiley.

Bollen, K. A., & Lennox, R. (1991). Conventional wisdom on measurement: A structural equation perspective. *Psychological Bulletin, 110,* 305–314.

Bornstein, M. H. (1989). *Maternal responsiveness: Characteristics and consequences.* San Francisco: Jossey-Bass.

Bornstein, M. H., Tamis-LeMonda, C. S., Tal, H., Ludemann, P. I., Toda, S., Rahn, C. W., Pecheux, M., Azuma, H., & Vardi, D. (1992). Maternal responsiveness to infants in three societies: The United States, France, and Japan. *Child Development, 63,* 808–821.

Bradley, R. H. (1994). The HOME Inventory: Review and reflections. In H. W. Reese (Ed.), *Advances in child development and behavior* (Vol. 25, pp. 241–288). Orlando, FL: Academic Press.

Bradley, R. H., & Caldwell, B. M. (1984). The HOME Inventory and family demographics. *Developmental Psychology, 20,* 315–320.

Bradley, R. H., & Caldwell, B. M. (1995). Caregiving and the regulation of child growth and development: Describing proximal aspects of caregiving systems. *Developmental Review, 15,* 38–85.

Bradley, R. H., Caldwell, B. M., Rock, S. L., Barnard, K. E., Gray, C., Hammond, M. A., Mitchell, S., Siegel, L. M., Ramey, C. T., Gottfried, A. M., & Johnson, D. L. (1989). Home environment and cognitive development in the first 3 years of life: A collaborative study involving six sites and three ethnic groups in North America. *Developmental Psychology, 28,* 217–235.

Bradley, R. H., Mundfrom, D. J., Whiteside, L., Barrett, K., & Casey, P. H. (1994). A factor analytic study of the infant–toddler and early childhood versions of the HOME Inventory for black, white, and Hispanic Americans. *Child Development, 65,* 880–888.

Bretherton, I., & Waters, E. (1985). Growing points of attachment theory. *Monographs of the Society for Research in Child Development, 50*(1–2, Serial No. 209).

Bromwich, R. (1976). Focus on maternal behavior in intervention. *American Journal of Orthopsychiatry, 46,* 439–446.

Caldwell, B. M. (1968). On designing supplementary environments for early child development. *BAEYC Reports, 10,* 1–11.

Caldwell, B. M., & Bradley, R. H. (1984). *Home observation for measurement of the environment.* Little Rock: University of Arkansas at Little Rock.

Casey, P. H., Bradley, R. H., Nelson, J. Y., & Whaley, S. A. (1988). The clinical assessment of a child's social and physical environment during health visits. *Developmental and Behavioral Pediatrics, 9,* 333–338.

Chua, K. L., Kong, D. S., Wong, S. T., & Yoong, T. (1989). Quality of the home environment of toddlers: A validation study of the HOME Inventory. *Journal of the Singapore Paediatric Society, 31,* 38–45.

Cicchetti, D., & Sroufe, A. (1976). The relationship between affective and cognitive development in Down's syndrome infants. *Child Development, 47,* 920–929.

Crandall, V. J., Dewey, W., Katkovsky, W., & Preston, A. (1964). Parents' attitudes and behaviors and grade school children's achievement development. *Journal of Genetic Psychology, 104*, 53–66.

Cummings, E. M., Zahn-Waxler, C., & Radke-Yarrow, M. (1981). Young children's responses to expressions of anger and affection by others in the family. *Child Development, 52*, 1274–1282.

Darling, N., & Steinberg, L. (1993). Parenting style as context: An integrative model. *Psychological Bulletin, 113*, 487–496.

Dave, R. H. (1963). *The identification and measurement of environmental process variables that are related to educational achievement.* Unpublished doctoral dissertation, University of Chicago.

Evans, G. W., Kliewer, W., & Martin, J. (1991). The role of the physical environment in the health and well-being of children. In H. E. Schroeder (Ed.), *New directions in health psychological assessment* (pp. 127–157). New York: Hemisphere Publishing.

Field, T. M., Widmayer, S. M., Adler, S., & DeCubas, M. (1990). Teenage parenting in different cultures, family constellations, and caregiving environments: Effects on infant development. *Infant Mental Health Journal, 11*, 158–174.

Ford, D. M., & Lerner, R. M. (1992). *Developmental systems theory.* Newbury Park, CA: Sage.

Grinker, R. R., Korshin, S. J., Bosowitz, H., Hamburg, D. A., Sabshin, M., Pershy, H., Chevalier, J. A., & Borad, F. A. (1956). A theoretical and experimental approach to problems of anxiety. *American Medical Association Archives of Neurology and Psychiatry, 76*, 420–431.

Henderson, R. W., Bergan, J. R., & Hurt, M. (1972). Development and validation of the Henderson Environmental Learning Process Scale. *Journal of Social Psychology, 88*, 185–196.

Horowitz, F. (1987). *Exploring developmental theories: Toward a structural/behavioral model of development.* Hillsdale, NJ: Erlbaum.

Hunt, J. M. (1961). *Intelligence and experience.* New York: Ronald Press.

Iverson, B. K., & Walberg, H. J. (1979, April). *Home environment and learning: A quantitative synthesis.* Paper presented at the annual meeting of the American Educational Research Association, San Francisco.

Jacobson, J. L., Jacobson, S. W., Padgett, R. J., Brummitt, G. A., & Billings, R. L. (1992). Effects of prenatal PCB exposure on cognitive processing efficiency and sustained attention. *Development Psychology, 28*, 297–306.

Keeves, J. P. (1972). *Educational environment and school achievement.* Stockholm, Sweden: Almqvist.

Kuhn, D. (1992). Cognitive development. In M. H. Bornstein & M. E. Lamb (Eds.), *Developmental psychology: An advanced textbook* (3rd ed.) (pp. 211–272). Hillsdale, NJ: Erlbaum.

Laing, J. A., & Sines, J. O. (1982). The Home Environment Questionnaire: An instrument for assessing several behaviorally relevant dimensions of children's environments. *Journal of Pediatric Psychology, 7*, 425–449.

Lerner, R. (1986). *On the nature of human plasticity*. New York: Cambridge University Press.

Lozoff, B. (1989). Nutrition and behavior. *American Psychologist, 44*, 231–236.

Marjoribanks, K. (1972). Environment, social class, and mental abilities. *Journal of Educational Psychology, 63*, 103–109.

Maslow, A., & Murphy, G. (1954). *Motivation and personality*. New York: Harper.

Matheny, A. P., Wachs, T. D., Ludwig, J. L., & Phillips, K. (1995). Bringing order out of chaos: Psychometric characteristics of the Chaos, Hubbub, and Order Scale. *Journal of Applied Developmental Psychology, 16*, 429–439.

McCall, R. B., Appelbaum, M., & Hogarty, P. (1973). Developmental change in mental performance. *Monographs of the Society for Research in Child Development, 38*(3, Serial No. 150).

Mink, I. T., & Nihira, K. (1986). Family life-styles and child behaviors: A study of directions of effect. *Developmental Psychology, 22*, 610–616.

Moore, T. (1968). Language and intelligence. A longitudinal study of the first eight years: Part II. Environmental correlates of mental growth. *Human Development, 11*, 1–24.

Mosychuk, H. (1969). Differential home environment and mental ability patterns. Unpublished doctoral dissertation, University of Alberta, Alberta, Canada.

Murray, H. A. (1938). *Explorations in personality*. New York: Oxford University Press.

Patterson, G. R., DeBarsyshe, B. D., & Ramsey, E. (1989). A developmental perspective on antisocial behavior. *American Psychologist, 44*, 329–335.

Patterson, G. R., & Yoerger, K. A. (1991, April). *A model for general parenting is too simple: Mediational models work better*. Paper presented at the biennial meeting of the Society for Research in Child Development, Seattle, WA.

Peterson, L., Ewigman, B., & Kivlahan, C. (1993). Judgments regarding appropriate child supervision to prevent injury: The role of environmental risk and child age. *Child Development, 64*, 934–950.

Pettit, G. S., Dodge, K. A., & Brown, M. M. (1988). Early family experience and social problem solving patterns, and children's social competence. *Child Development, 59*, 107–120.

Pollitt, E. (1994). Poverty and child development: Relevance of rearch in developing countries to the United States. *Child Development, 65*, 283–295.

Radin, N. (1973). Observed paternal behaviors as antecedents of intellectual functioning in young boys. *Developmental Psychology, 8*, 369–376.

Reis, J. S., & Hertz, E. J. (1987). Correlates of adolescent parenting. *Adolescence, 22*, 599–609.

Roberts, W. L. (1986). Nonlinear models of development: An example from the socialization of competence. *Child Development, 57*, 1166–1178.

Saegert, S., & Winkel, G. H. (1990). Environmental psychology. *Annual Review of Psychology, 41*, 441–477.

Sameroff, A. J., & Friese, B. H. (1991). Transactional regulation and early intervention. In S. J. Meisels and J. P. Shonkoff (Eds.), *Handbook of early intervention* (pp. 119–149). Cambridge, England: Cambridge University Press.

Schaefer, E. (1959). A circumplex model for maternal behavior. *Journal of Abnormal and Social Psychology, 59*, 226–235.

Sroufe, A. (1979). The coherence of individual development. *American Psychologist, 34*, 831–841.

Tong, S., & McMichael, A. J. (1992). Maternal smoking and neuropsychological development in childhood: A review of the evidence. *Developmental Medicine and Child Neurology, 34*, 191–197.

U. S. Department of Health and Human Services. (1991). *Healthy people 2000* (DHHS Publication No. PHS 91-50212). Washington, DC: U.S. Government Printing Office.

Wachs, T. D. (1987). Short term stability of aggregated and nonaggregated measures of parent behavior. *Child Development, 58*, 796–797.

Wachs, T. D. (1989). The nature of the physical micro-environment: An expanded classification system. *Merrill-Palmer Quarterly, 35*, 399–402.

Wachs, T. D. (1992). *The nature of nurture*. Newbury Park, CA: Sage.

Wachs, T. D., Bishry, Z., Sobhy, A., McCabe, G., Galal, O., & Shaheen, F. (1993). Relation of rearing environment to adaptive behavior of Egyptian toddlers. *Child Development, 64*, 586–604.

Wachs, T. D., Francis, J., & McQuiston, S. (1979). Psychological dimensions of the infant's physical environment. *Infant Behavior and Development, 2*, 155–161.

Wachs, T. D., Sigman, M., Bishry, Z., Moussa, W., Jerome, N., Neumann, C., Bwibo, N., & McDonald, M. A. (1992). Caregiver child interaction patterns in two cultures in relation to nutritional intake. *International Journal of Behavioral Development, 15*, 1–18.

Whiting, B. B. (1981). Culture and social behavior: A model for the development of social behavior. *Ethos, 8*, 95–116.

Williams, T. (1976). Abilities and environments. In W. H. Sewell, R. M. Hauser, & D. L. Featherman (Eds.), *Schooling and achievement in American society* (pp. 61–101). New York: Academic Press.

Wolf, R. M. (1964). *The identification and measurement of environmental process variables related to intelligence*. Unpublished doctoral dissertation, University of Chicago.

World Health Organization (1980). *Noise: Environmental health criteria 12*. Geneva, Switzerland: Author.

Yarrow, L. J., Rubenstein, J. L., Pedersen, F. A., & Jankowski, J. J. (1975). Dimensions of early stimulation and their differential effects on infant development. *Merrill-Palmer Quarterly, 19*, 205–218.

3

MEASURING THE PEER ENVIRONMENT OF AMERICAN ADOLESCENTS

B. BRADFORD BROWN

Adolescence is, by definition, a period of transition. Individuals during this stage of life are often understood primarily in terms of what they are becoming rather than what they are. Decades ago, the tendency was to portray and interpret adolescence largely in terms of a core set of internal, biological changes: pubertal transformations (Tanner, 1972), insurgence of sexual drives (Freud, 1958), and emergence of new cognitive abilities (Piaget, 1958). Within an "average, expectable environment" (Scarr, 1992), theorists contended, these would unfold in a predictable sequence to create the "essence" of adolescence. Over time, however, it has become increasingly apparent that the meaning or impact of internal or biological changes is heavily contingent on the young person's environment (Petersen, 1993). In American society, one feature of the environment that seems to take center stage at adolescence is the social world of peers. Studies of peer influences and peer relationships during adolescence have been extensive. Yet, the impact of peers on adolescent development (as well as on adolescents' abilities to shape the peer environment) remains unclear, largely because of nagging uncertainties about how best to conceptualize and measure the peer environment. In this chapter I hope to shed some light on these measurement issues by assessing them from the perspective of a new conceptualization of the adolescent peer environment.

The social world of peers among youth in contemporary societies is deceptively complex. This chapter is not intended as an exhaustive review of adolescents' peer environment but as an illustrative analysis of common themes and major methodological challenges in studies of this environment, with some suggestions for future research. I begin with a sampling of the issues investigators have entertained in their studies of the peer context, with special attention to problems they have encountered in measuring this environment. Then, I illustrate how a new conceptual model of the adolescent peer environment can help direct future studies of peer influences on adolescents.

Four points are emphasized. First, the adolescent peer environment is a multilevel, multicontextual phenomenon. It contains a variety of structures and relationships that can be arranged hierarchically into several levels of immediacy or concreteness to the person. Interactions and influence processes are not necessarily equivalent, in form or effect, at each of these levels. Second, the peer environment is nested in a broader set of social and interpersonal contexts, which help to shape the structure of the peer context and its influence on individual adolescents. Third, features of the peer environment are contingent on individual characteristics, many of which change over adolescence. Finally, it is wiser to conceive of the relationship between individuals and the peer environment as reciprocal rather than unidirectional (to consider how individuals and the peer environment influence each other, rather than focusing exclusively on peer influences on adolescents).

SCOPE OF THE ADOLESCENT PEER ENVIRONMENT

Before surveying some common issues in studies of the peer environment among adolescents, it may be useful to describe the scope and substance of that environment. In current American society, adolescents typically enjoy increasing levels of autonomy without necessarily shouldering greater responsibilities in common adult roles. Emotional dependence on family diminishes, as does the young person's reliance on family as the center of social activities (Steinberg, 1990). School commitments rarely venture much beyond 6 hours of class a day, and there is nominal time for homework or an extracurricular activity or two (Thomas, 1993). Involvement in work, caretaking, and other common adult roles is limited, if present at all (Erikson, 1968). This leaves plenty of time and "psychic energy" to invest in peers, which is manifested in increases in time spent with peers rather than with adults (Csikszentmihalyi & Larson, 1984) and in the importance accorded to peer relationships (Brown, Eicher, & Petrie, 1986; J. C. Coleman, 1974).

The form and function of peer relationships expand during this stage of life. Peers continue to provide emotional and instrumental support and to organize leisure activities, as they have in childhood, but they also become a component of sexual gratification and identity development. This introduces new types of relationships or affiliations, most notably romantic partner and crowd member, to the young person's repertoire of peer associations. Indeed, adolescents negotiate a broad array of relationships within the peer environment. Some are formal, or directed by major social institutions such as the school (e.g., lab partners and teammates), the workplace (coworkers), or the church or synagogue (fellow youth group members). Others are informal and range from short-term (e.g., one-time sexual partners) or circumscribed associations ("hiking buddies" vs. "people I party with") to long-term and intimate companions (close friends or steady boyfriend or girlfriend). Researchers often fail to discriminate among this diverse assortment of peer associates; they treat them as equally important and influential in young people's lives. In this chapter I point out the dangers of dealing with the peer environment in this fashion.

COMMON ISSUES IN STUDYING THE PEER ENVIRONMENT

Understandably, in view of the scope of adolescent peer relations, studies of teenagers' peer environment are remarkably diverse, both in the topic of study and in the types of peer associates examined. Generally, however, investigators have focused on three major facets of the peer environment: the *structure* of peer groups, the *content* of peer relationships, and the *processes* of peer interaction and influence. Work in each of these areas is illustrated, with special emphasis on methodological approaches and issues.

Structure of Peer Groups

Some researchers have been preoccupied with how the adolescent peer environment is organized into discernible groups and how (or how effectively) these groups are interrelated. These issues are interesting in their own right, but researchers have also been concerned with the connections between peer group affiliations and a variety of outcomes. For example, one of the strongest correlates of delinquent activity is the degree of delinquency within an adolescent's friendship group (Patterson & Dishion, 1985); there are also substantial differences among members of different sociometric groupings or peer crowds in drug use (Ennett & Bauman, 1993), delinquency (Cusick, 1973), sexual activity (Dolcini & Adler, 1994), and prosocial behaviors such as academic achievement (Brown, Lamborn, Mounts, & Steinberg, 1993; Lesko, 1988). In this work, it is sensible to distinguish between interaction-based groupings of peers, most commonly referred to as *friendship groups* or *cliques*, and the more abstract groupings that emerge in adolescence to reflect individuals' status, image, or reputation among peers.

Friendship Groups

The most classic study of friendship groups is Dunphy's (1969) assessment of peer group structures among Australian youth. Relying heavily on participant observation, Dunphy discovered two levels of peer group organization: the "clique," numbering six to eight adolescents who interacted almost daily and regarded one another as good friends, and the "crowd," comprising several cliques that occasionally combined for major social activities (such as a weekend party). By following groups over the course of an academic year and involving himself in groups of different ages, Dunphy also discerned a developmental sequence to this structure. The isolated, monosexual cliques that dominated early adolescence gave way by middle adolescence to heterosexual crowds, which in turn degenerated into fairly autonomous but mixed sex cliques by the end of adolescence. The primary function of this evolving crowd structure, Dunphy concluded, was to socialize young people into new heterosocial roles and interests (romantic and sexual partner).

Dunphy's (1969) study is noteworthy not only for its interesting findings but also for methodological reasons. The author supplemented his extensive participant observations with individual interviews and diaries that participants kept of daily social activities. Multiple data sources helped Dunphy to discern weaknesses in specific methodologies. In individual interviews, for example, most participants fiercely denied that their groups had leaders, even though, in participant observations, leaders were an obvious and essential feature of the groups.

With the advent of more powerful computers and software, new methodologies have appeared for mapping friendship networks. Some derive the structure of cliques from lists participants provide of their close friends (Ennett & Bauman, 1993; Shrum & Cheek, 1986); others depend on individuals' reports of friendship groupings among peers, which are combined to derive a "social–cognitive map" of the clique structure (Cairns, Perrin, & Cairns, 1985). These approaches are capable of tracking the stability of friendship cliques over time (discussed later) and also of tracing developmental changes in the organization of cliques. Shrum and Cheek, for example, reported that, across adolescence, a pattern of clearly discernible cliques was replaced by a more loose-knit structure in which increasing numbers of teenagers serve as "liaisons," linking two or three cliques by virtue of their friendships with members of more than one group. This is reasonably consistent with Dunphy's (1969) observation of individual cliques combining for larger social activities.

Studies based on these social network programs do have drawbacks, however. Most notably, the programs work well only if 75%–85% of the peer population provides usable data—a daunting task if one wishes to lay out the peer group structure in an average-sized American secondary school.

Reputation-Based Groups

Despite his emphasis on interaction patterns and heterosocial activities, Dunphy (1969) did acknowledge another dynamic in the Australian adolescent peer system: groups identified not so much by interaction patterns (who adolescents hung out with) as by reputation. Behavior patterns, dress and grooming styles, orientations toward authority, and activity choices clearly differentiated a group called the "surfies" from one labeled "rockers." These reputation-based clusters point to another facet of peer group structure. Sometimes researchers use their own conceptual categories to construct these groups (e.g., work on sociometric status); other times they focus on groups that emerge from adolescents' own understanding of the peer context (such as Dunphy's rockers and surfies).

Using a technique developed to study sociometric status among children, investigators have asked adolescents to provide nominations or ratings of peers in a circumscribed setting (usually a classroom) as desirable or undesirable interaction partners. These are used to identify clusters of adolescents who, relative to their peers in this setting, are "popular," "rejected," or "neglected." Efforts are then made to discern characteristics that lead to one or the other of these labels and to the consequences of one's reputational groupings for a variety of outcome measures. The chief drawback of sociometric ratings is that the technique is designed for a small rating pool: 15 to 30 students (about the size of one classroom). Unlike elementary students, who typically stay with one classroom of students for most of the day, secondary students interact with a broader array of peers and may not even know many of their classmates. Confining sociometric ratings to peers in one classroom distorts the nature of the adolescent peer environment; asking adolescents to rate a much broader array of peers becomes an odious task.

More important, adolescents seem to incorporate sociometric status into their own lexicon of major reputation-based groups within the peer context. These groups are referred to by many researchers as *crowds* (Brown, 1990). Some crowd types seem to persist across time and place (e.g., jocks, nerds, populars, and brains), whereas others seem to arise from the specific features of a particular community—Buff's (1970) "dupers"—or historical moment—the smokers of the 1950s, the hippies of the 1960s, and the metal heads of the 1990s. Much of this work is based on ethnographic data (Eder, 1985; Larkin, 1979; Lesko, 1988). Kinney (1993), for example, traced how the peer crowd structure expanded from middle school to high school in one midwestern community, allowing teenagers who had previously been relegated to the masses of "dweebs" to achieve some status as a member of one of the newly emerging crowds in high school. Others have interviewed a small and select cadre of expert informants (prominent members of various crowds), whose "social type ratings" of classmates are combined to ascertain the crowd affiliations of a school's entire student body (Brown, et al., 1993; Schwendinger & Schwendinger, 1985).

Such peer crowd affiliations help establish the more specific context within the broader peer environment in which an individual is located and discern the specific norms or influence processes to which the individual is most likely to be exposed. For example, Clasen and Brown (1985) found that individuals in different crowds (ascertained by social type ratings) perceived markedly different patterns of peer pressure from friends. These observations are affirmed by ethnographers who discuss the different normative climate relative to school achievement or delinquent activity in various crowds (e.g., see Deyhle, 1986; Matute-Bianchi, 1986).

Yet, crowds do not function as isolated entities. Ethnographic studies often trace the alliances and enmities that exist between particular groups, directing and constraining choice of partners in other peer relationships (Eckert, 1989; Eder, 1985; Larkin, 1979). More recently, multidimensional scaling techniques have been used to map the "social distance" among crowds and to identify the major dimensions along which crowds are differentiated in a specific school or community (Brown, Dolcini, & Leventhal, 1997). Social type ratings reveal that many, if not most, adolescents establish an image among peers that straddles two or more crowds, so they may be subjected to influences of multiple peer groups (Brown, 1992).

Ethnography is a particularly useful methodology in studies of peer crowds because it encourages open-minded exploration of the unique features of peer group structures in specific settings. Gaining access and trust within groups, however, is a time-consuming process. Moreover, close association with members of one crowd often compromises one's credibility with another group, so ethnographers are limited in the number of groups that they can explore in-depth. As an alternative, the social type rating system (Schwendinger & Schwendinger, 1985) is appealing: Crowd affiliations for a large group of students can be derived quickly and efficiently from ratings of a small number of informants. However, it is labor intensive and its reliability remains untested. Investigators have not ascertained whether two separate groups of informants classify classmates comparably or whether the rating system is effective in large multiethnic high schools in urban areas, in which students often do not know more than half of their classmates well enough to categorize them into crowds. Peer nomination systems also have yet to be tested in populations of youth that do not contain European Americans. It is unclear just how prominent peer crowds are, for example, in schools with almost exclusively African American, Hispanic, or Native American populations (Kinney, 1995).

Stability of Peer Group Structure

A key factor in the structure of peer groups is their stability: Do adolescents maintain the same friendships for a long time? Does a friendship clique, once formed, manage to stick together, or is there a substantial turnover in membership? Once associated with a particular crowd, do adolescents maintain that reputation? Evidence from the small corpus of longitudinal studies capable of addressing the questions suggests that groups and relationships within the peer environment are relatively fluid. Hogue and Steinberg (1995) asked a sample of high school students to list their five closest friends at two time points 1 year apart; for less than half of the students at least one name from their original list carried over to their follow-up list.

Using the social–cognitive mapping method, Cairns, Leung, Buchanan, and Cairns (1995) found that over a very short period (3 weeks), less than 5% of the cliques named by a sample of 7th graders remained identical, but most cliques (90%) were still recognizable if the criterion was that at least 50% of original clique members were still associated with the group at follow-up. Stability of crowd affiliations has rarely been reported. Brown, Freeman, Huang, and Mounts (1992) found that, over a 2-year period, only 41% of adolescents claimed membership in the same crowd, although the percentage did climb with age—from 34% of 7th graders to 53% of 10th graders.

There is some question, however, about the reliability of stability analyses that are based on self-report data or peer ratings because the participant pool is rarely exactly the same in these longitudinal studies. If the data for calculating friendship networks or crowd affiliations come from even moderately different samples of reporters at the two time points, ostensible changes in group structure or membership could, instead, be a function of rating samples. Information from a more stable and consistent set of observers (teachers, parents, or an ethnographer) might seem more reliable. Yet, this is doubtful because adolescents tend to conduct their peer interactions *away* from the watchful eyes of adults. It does seem clear, however, that peer group affiliations are more stable among central than peripheral group members; central group members are the individuals with the most linkages to other clique members or the adolescents most consistently associated by peers with a given crowd (Cairns et al., 1995). Yet, this is also a potential methodological problem. To the extent that studies are based primarily on central group members (as is often the case, for example, in ethnographic studies), findings may distort the true dynamics of the group and its impact on individual adolescents.

Summary

Efforts to chart the structure of the peer environment have distinguished interaction-based and reputation-based groupings of peers, noting age-related changes and influences from the broader social context in the pattern of relationships among cliques or crowds. Methodologically, ethnography and peer-rating techniques dominate these studies, although each approach has shortcomings that compromise its ability to chart the structure of adolescent peer groups effectively.

Content of Peer Relationships

In addition to issues of peer group structure, researchers have been concerned with the content or character of particular relationships within the peer environment. Three different lines of investigation illustrate research in this domain: studies of youth culture, studies of the features of friendship or romantic relationships in adolescence, and research on the quality of friendship.

Youth Culture

Research on youth culture is predicated on the assumption that, at least in general terms, young people share a common set of values, lifestyles, or a meaning system that is somehow distinctive from the culture of the community, ethnic group, or the broader (and largely adult-controlled) society in which they live. One way of identifying youth culture norms is simply to assess the mean or modal response of adolescents as a whole (or a random sample of the adolescent population) on a particular assessment instrument (e.g., Sebald, 1981). An alternative is to identify the most powerful or prestigious group within the peer environment and to study that group's attitudes and activities. J. S. Coleman (1961), for example, maintained that every secondary school features a "leading crowd" to which most students aspire, and their primary means of gaining membership is to follow the dicta of that crowd. Largely on the basis of survey data among adolescents and their parents, Coleman used students' descriptions of the leading crowd to pinpoint the major conflicts in values and aspirations between adolescents and the adult generation.

A third strategy of exploring the youth culture involves studies of the media used to convey this culture, most notably, rock music. This more anthropological approach assumes that lyrics of popular songs, or the antics of popular rock performers, reveal to young people the essential values and orientations endorsed by their peers, the "normative climate" of the peer environment. To the extent that adolescents are exposed to these messages (or involve themselves in media portrayals of youth culture themes and symbols), they will subscribe—in word and deed—to the basic tenets of that culture (Roe, 1992; Walker, 1988).

Researchers are inclined to portray the youth culture as a major source of influence on individual adolescents' attitudes and behavior. Investigators have been particularly concerned with how youth culture norms differ from those of adult society and how these differences (or the degree of conflict in values) help explain young people's attitudes or behavior—particularly attitudes and behaviors judged deviant by the broader society (J. S. Coleman, 1961; Feueur, 1969; Keniston, 1968). The connection, however, between youth culture and individual behavior is not well established, and it is unclear which of these three research strategies provides the most valid measure of the youth culture. Indeed, the diversity of themes or styles inherent in rock music (Arnett, 1995) and the apparent inattentiveness of many young people to the leading crowd (Cohen, 1976; Eckert, 1989; Larkin, 1979) cast doubt on the image of youth culture as a monolithic force in the peer environment. The role of the youth culture in shaping young people's behavior, as well as its very existence, remains in doubt.

Features of Dyadic Relationships

Studies of the content of peer relationships also focus on specific features of friendships or romantic relationships. Well-known in this area are investigations that trace developmental changes in the characteristics that young people regard as central to close friendships, based primarily on content analyses of responses to open-ended questions about friendship expectations. From an emphasis on sharing activities in childhood, there is a shift in early adolescence toward loyalty, trust, and exclusivity, which in turn gives way by middle or late adolescence to an emphasis on a shared history and respect for the partner's interests and relational needs outside the friendship (Bukowski, Newcomb, & Hoza, 1987; LaGaipa, 1979). In a similar vein, using self-report rating scales, investigators have shown age differences across adolescence in levels of intimacy, conflict, social support, and other particular features of friendships (Buhrmester, 1990; Sharabany, Gershoni, & Hofman, 1981). Such factors highlight the differing bases of adolescents' relationships with peers as opposed to family members, particularly parents (Youniss & Smollar, 1985).

Work on romantic relationships is much less well developed, but there have been enough studies to affirm that the central criteria for these relationships differ across demographic groupings. Girls regard intimacy and companionship as more central than sex in romantic relationships; boys display the opposite ordering (Hendrick & Hendrick, 1994). Dating relationships in early adolescence often appear to be "simple social interchanges," whereas by later adolescence they typically evolve into committed relationships (Feinstein & Ardon, 1973).

Because the norms of friendship and romantic attachments are quite different, one cannot assume (as many investigators do) that asking adolescents about their boyfriend or girlfriend is equivalent to inquiring about their closest relationship with an opposite-sex peer. In fact, with considerable demographic variability in the basic definition of romantic relationships, it is a challenge to word questions about them in such a way that all respondents select the appropriate relationship on which to base answers to questions. The label "boyfriend or girlfriend" is simple and straightforward but inappropriate for samples that include gay youth. Indeed, gathering reliable information about gay romantic relationships is especially challenging because of the social sanctions against such relationships, especially during the teenage years (Savin-Williams, 1994).

Much of an adolescent's relationship with a specific friend or lover is carried out in private. Teenagers are likely to treat or respond to their friend or lover differently in private than in a public setting, such as within the context of the friendship group (Cusick, 1973). This limits the applicability of ethnography or participant observation and forces investigators to rely on self-report data to study the features of friendships and romantic relationships. Investigators rarely attempt to consider perceptions of the relationship among both members of the dyad (but see Shulman, 1993). In fact, respondents are often asked to rate characteristics of their friendships *in general* rather than to specify features of each close associate—a strategy that may obscure the influence of relational features to major outcome variables that researchers want to address (Berndt & Keefe, 1995).

Quality of Relationships

A more specific feature of peer relationships that is gaining attention is the *quality* of the relationship. The impetus for these studies stems from social control theory (Hirschi, 1969), which stipulates that delinquent adolescents engage in deviance because they do not have strong bonds to conventional social institutions and because they are relatively incapable of forming constructive, nurturing relationships with peers. This begs the issue of whether adolescents with deviantly oriented friends engage in more delinquency because of the deviant lifestyles of their friends or because of the poor quality of these friendships. Two methodological approaches are common in these studies: One is to ask adolescents to rate the quality of their friendships on various dimensions (supportiveness, trust, rivalry, and so forth; e.g., see Berndt & Perry, 1986); the other is to videotape a friendship interaction in a laboratory setting, then rate the interaction on the dimensions of interest (Dishion, Andrews, & Crosby, 1995). The latter strategy obviates potential biases of "impression management" in responses to self-report surveys; it also allows comparisons between interactions with close friends, acquaintances, or strangers. Its drawback, of course, is that behavior in a laboratory setting may differ substantially from behavior in the "real" peer environment.

Summary

Studies of the content of peer relationships cover a diverse array of relationship characteristics and span a number of levels of the peer environment—from the youth culture as a whole to the specifics of a particular friendship or romantic attachment. Because of adolescents' increasing autonomy from adults and the intimacy expected in their dyadic relationships, it is no longer easy to observe interactions to assess the content of relationships. Thus, investigators are forced to rely extensively on self-report measures. Some alternative strategies are available, however: anthropological approaches at the level of youth culture and controlled laboratory observations of dyadic interactions. Many issues in this area are still open to debate: whether features of a specific friendship or romantic relationship differ appreciably from features of the friendship group as a whole; which level of relationship is most salient to outcome variables of interest; and whether there is a recognizable, general youth culture, and if so, how it is communicated to individuals. It is also important to extend analyses beyond the middle-class, European American youth who have dominated samples to date; emerging research suggests that characteristics of peer relationships may be quite different among adolescents of different social or ethnic backgrounds (Fordham & Ogbu, 1986; Hamm, 1993; Zisman & Wilson, 1992).

As analyses move from a general (youth culture) to a more specific level (assessment of dyadic attachments), there is greater opportunity to explore reciprocal levels of influence—how adolescents shape and are shaped by the peer environment. In this regard, it is surprising to see so little work on the process of selecting or abandoning particular peer associates. Adolescents are insistent that friendships, and even romantic affiliations, are not carefully planned; they just happen. The same cannot be said about attachments to formal peer groups, however: clubs, church groups, sports teams, and so forth. Adolescents' efforts to shape the content of the peer environment by their selection of these particular affiliations deserve closer scrutiny.

Peer Interaction and Influence Processes

Both the structure and the content of peer relationships clearly affect adolescent development and behavior. Yet, researchers remain most concerned with the processes by which peers influence teenagers. Indeed, investigators have been so preoccupied with charting processes of peer influences that they have grossly neglected the bidirectionality of this process —the fact that individuals make concerted efforts to shape their peer environment, rather than merely being shaped by it. Studies concerning both directions of influence are illustrated.

Peer Influence

Researchers have used a variety of methods to operationalize peer influence on adolescents. One of the earliest grew out of laboratory studies of conformity behavior among college students or adults. In one such study, children and adolescents were seated with a group of unknown peers and were then given a series of problems in which they had to identify which line was the same length as a stimulus line (Costanzo & Shaw, 1966). The other participants, all confederates of the experimenter, always answered before the target respondent and, on prespecified items, gave consistently wrong answers. Costanzo and Shaw found that young people's willingness to conform to peers' incorrect responses declined with age and varied inversely with the strength of their self-concept. Such results, though intriguing, raised several validity-oriented questions: Would youngsters conform to the behavior of close friends (rather than unknown peers) in social situations (rather than an academic task) in which the appropriate (socially sanctioned) response was clear-cut (rather than ambiguous)?

As an alternative strategy that could address these concerns, some investigators administered a self-report instrument with hypothetical situations in which close friends urged the respondent to join in an activity that he or she either felt was wrong (antisocial items) or did not want to do as much as another activity (peer socializing items). Respondents indicated how sure they were that they would or would not conform to their friends' request or demands (e.g., Berndt, 1979). Results with this measure demonstrated an inverted U-shaped developmental curve, with compliance peaking around eighth grade, differing by type of activity (weaker for antisocial items) and by gender within type (boys more conforming than girls to antisocial activities). Scores on this instrument have been linked to a variety of attributes and outcomes among adolescents, but they seem to reflect conformity dispositions rather than behavior, and they still do not assess the amount or type of peer pressure adolescents actually encounter.

To catalog peer pressures actually faced by youth, Clasen and Brown (1985) developed the Peer Pressure Inventory (PPI), measuring the degree and direction of pressure adolescents encountered from friends on a wide assortment of behaviors. The instrument pointed to different domains of peer pressure that featured different developmental trajectories and, in conjunction with conformity disposition as measured by Berndt's (1979) instrument, were significantly associated with antisocial activity and peer socializing (Brown, Clasen, & Eicher, 1986). Yet, low mean scores on the PPI scales raise doubts about its validity; at best, it is a good measure of explicit pressures adolescents face from friends. It does not cover other types of peer influence (Kandel & Andrews, 1987).

Participant observation is a promising alternative to contrived situation or self-report methodologies for assessing peer influences. This technique is especially useful in tracing the sequence of influence strategies to which adolescents are exposed in their "career" as members of a particular clique (Eder, 1985). Drawing from opportunities to observe their own children's interactions with friends, Adler and Adler (1995) cataloged the strategies group leaders used in preadolescence to recruit, retain, and eject members from the popular clique. Similar processes are probably operative in adolescent groups but have not been as carefully examined (but see Eder, 1985, and Kinney, 1993). These strategies are too subtle and dynamic to be easily captured by other methodologies. Yet, it is more difficult for adults to gain access to adolescent groups than to children's groups, and this approach will not work with dyadic relationships because the addition of an observer to one-on-one interactions is much too noticeable and intrusive.

A more straightforward—and by far the most common—approach to measuring peer influence is to correlate an individual's behavior with that of her or his friend, on the assumption that if friends share certain characteristics, it is because an individual has been influenced by the friend. The inadequacy of this approach is obvious, however (Kandel, 1978): Friends are similar to one another, to a large degree, because adolescents choose as friends those peers who have much in common with them. Longitudinal studies charting behavioral or attitudinal change over time in the direction of a friend's level on a particular attribute suggest that friends' influence on teenagers is actually quite modest. This is especially true if the friend's own report of attitudes or behavior is used rather than the target adolescent's perception of the friend's attributes (Fisher & Bauman, 1988; Kandel, 1978).

All of these approaches fall short of capturing a curious reality of peer pressure and peer influence among adolescents: namely, that each adolescent is concurrently the recipient and initiator of influence. Consider, for example, the common assumption that teenagers encounter pressure from their friendship group to behave in a certain way. One could imagine a four-person group in which Alisha is influenced by Betty, Coletta, and Diaz to attend (or stay away from) a party. To be conceptually consistent, however, one must also regard Alisha as part of the influence (along with Coletta and Diaz) on Betty in regards to the party. How can one consider the influence of the friendship group on Alisha's actions without concurrently considering Alisha's role in influencing each other peer in the group? Researchers' predilection is to simply pick one girl as the target, treat the rest of the group as an influencing agent, and approach the issue in a strictly linear fashion. Results of these studies fall well short of capturing the complex dynamics of influence processes in the peer environment.

Impression Management

In contrast to the extensive work on how peers pressure or influence adolescents, there is only a smattering of studies on how individuals influence their peers, especially peers' impression of the self (impression management). For example, Juvonen and Murdock (1995) presented fourth, sixth, and eighth graders with hypothetical situations in which they had done either poorly or really well on an exam, then asked respondents to indicate how they would explain their performance to a teacher and to the popular peers in the class. There was a decrease across age groups in respondents' willingness to convey to peers that they had worked hard when they succeeded on the exam—even though respondents were consistently likely to convey this message to teachers. Furthermore, eighth graders were more likely to assert that strong effort on school work would damage a student's reputation among popular peers. Studies such as this reveal adolescents' efforts to "read" and respond to norms and pressures within the peer group, to essentially influence the influencers. Of course, the young people's behavior was still more reactive than proactive: They were responding to subtle, unspoken peer pressures not to work hard at school, rather than trying to shape peer norms about academic effort.

A better perspective on the cycle of influence within the peer environment comes from ethnographic studies. Eder (1985) recounted the efforts of middle school girls attempting to gain entry into the popular clique. By maintaining friendly relations with all of their peers, making the cheerleading squad, or being a good friend of one of the popular girls, several students were accepted into the popular clique. Once in, however, they encountered new pressures to snub peers outside of the group to maintain their status. Thus, they found themselves trapped between pressures from their new group and pressures from their old friends. At the other end of the status hierarchy is Merten's (1996) 2-year ethnographic study of a group of rejected middle school boys, labeled *mels*. Merten cataloged the ways in which peers established the rejected status of these boys: assigning them to the mel crowd, teasing them, forcing them to sit at the front of the bus, and so on. He then followed the efforts of several boys to cope with their undesirable status, including the successful efforts of one boy to break out of the mel crowd by so egregiously violating its norms (the behavior expected of mels) that peers were forced to reevaluate his crowd status. An important component of these "norm violations" was the boy's efforts to reshape his social network by ending relationships with fellow mels, cultivating friendships with students in the popular crowd, and joining formal groups (e.g., sports teams) that were atypical of mels.

Summary

Short-term and longitudinal ethnographic studies that track adolescents' efforts to mold peers' impression of self and respond to peer group norms and pressures come much closer to revealing the "give and take" in peer influence processes than studies based on other methodologies. Yet, self-report methodologies can be effective in charting the diversity of peer group norms and pressures that adolescents encounter and the variety of strategies they use to cope with or, perhaps, even shape these modes of peer influence. Of course, it is likely that peer influence operates at multiple levels. Most studies have focused on responses to pressures from close friends, but peer influences also emanate from the friendship group or clique, the crowd, and even the broader youth culture. Dynamics within formal peer groups (adult-sponsored youth groups, athletic teams, and so on) have routinely been ignored by investigators—even though these are ideal settings for participant observations. In short, there is much left to learn about how adolescents encounter, contribute to, and respond to influence processes in each of these segments of the peer environment.

Integrating Structure, Content, and Process

Investigators have explored a host of other factors in the adolescent peer environment beyond those illustrated previously. Moreover, some work intersects the three broad categories in which I have presented research. Both Eder (1985) and Eckert (1989) described how the features of friendships (content) differ among individuals in different peer crowds (structure). Feldman, Rosenthal, Brown, and Canning (1995) traced the different processes leading youngsters from different sociometric status groups (structure) into extensive sexual activity by middle adolescence. Berndt and Keefe (1995) examined the joint effects of the quality of friendships (content) and friends' efforts to support or undermine academic achievement (process) on adolescents' adjustment to school.

Nevertheless, the task of tying all this work together into a comprehensive portrait of the peer environment and its effects on adolescents seems overwhelming, as does the task of recommending which measurement strategies are most suitable for future work, or what lingering measurement problems are most important to resolve. To address these issues, it first seems necessary to understand how the various strands of research fit within the peer environment as a whole and how this environment is connected to other major social contexts for adolescents. In the next section I present a conceptual framework for understanding the adolescent peer environment and then suggest how it may guide decisions about future work in this area.

RECONCEPTUALIZING THE PEER ENVIRONMENT

Researchers have been inclined to treat the peer environment as a unified entity, a simple microsystem (see Bronfenbrenner, chapter 1, this volume). Thus, there seems to be little concern about the specific facet of this environment that is tapped for measurement. Assessment of peer crowd norms, perceived pressures from the friendship group, and levels of similarity between friendship dyads are commonly viewed as equivalent operationalizations of peer influence. As is clear from the preceding discussion, the peer environment is actually a more complex social ecology, influenced by historical and developmental forces and embedded in other social contexts of teenagers' lives. What follows is a more comprehensive and differentiated conceptualization of the social ecology of adolescent peer relationships.

A Model of the Peer Environment

The peer environment is most commonly perceived as a network of dyadic and small-group relationships. At adolescence, it becomes more obviously *contextual* as well as relational. That is, in addition to continuing relationships with friends, activity mates, and classmates, peer contexts emerge in the form of interest groups, peer groups, or crowds—or at a more abstract level, the youth culture. To some extent these contexts are behavioral and observable: The drama club hangs out in the auditorium, gang members wear their hats a certain way, and so on. In other respects, they are more *cognitive* or phenomenological. Dunphy (1969), for example, found that adolescents readily used terms such as "surfie" and "rocker" but had difficulty articulating what differentiated the groups or determined membership. "It's not just the clothes they wear," one respondent said (Dunphy, 1969, p. 114), "it's personality—a surfie and a rocker are two different things. It's hard to say what it is." "The term surfie was an emotional one," Dunphy (1969, p. 114) explains, "Its value to the group lay in its very vagueness." A model of the peer environment must incorporate both the immediate, concrete relationships adolescents engage in as well as this more abstract, phenomenological level of peer associations and interactions.

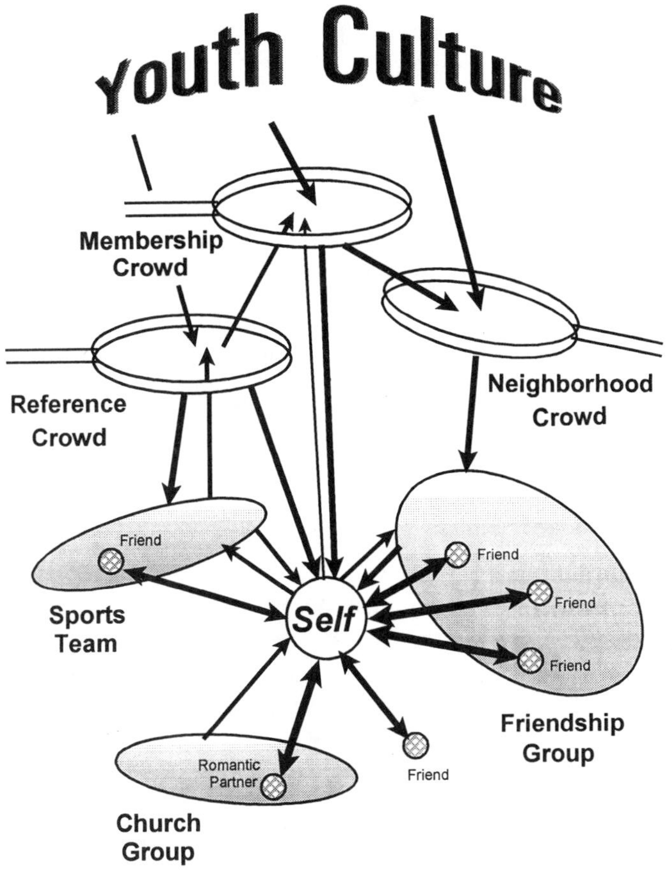

Figure 1. Conceptual model of the adolescent peer environment. Arrows indicate influence of one entity on another; thickness of arrow indicates magnitude of influence. Bent arrows indicate influence is filtered through intervening entity.

Figure 1 portrays this complex, multilevel peer ecology. Arrows represent influences between one component and another. The thickness of the arrow represents the degree of influence. Some arrows are bent to indicate that the influence of one entity on the individual is "filtered" through another entity.

Dyadic Relationships and Small-Group Interactions

At the heart of the peer ecology are an adolescent's one-on-one relationships with a close friend or romantic partner. These can be conceptualized as fully reciprocal because each partner has extensive input into the initiation, nurture, and dissolution of the relationship. Adolescents also exercise considerable influence over small-group relationships, mostly in their freedom to select or opt out of formal groups and friendship cliques.

Yet, teenagers have only limited control over such groups' memberships and activities because they are only one of many voices. Of course, an individual's level of influence on the group will depend on the person's status within the group (Adler & Adler, 1995; Savin-Williams, 1987); this model does not depict this individual variability very effectively.

The groups to which teenagers belong have their own pattern of relationships. A friendship clique may emerge from athletic teammates; one group of friends may share a strong antipathy toward another friendship group. Thus, one could easily conceive of each small group as a microsystem that manifests a constellation of goals and objectives operating norms, schedules of interactions, and temporal history and duration. Relations and interactions among the groups to which an adolescent belongs could be approached as a mesosystems analysis (Bronfenbrenner, 1986).

Crowd Contexts

At a higher level of abstraction are peer crowds. These are less concrete and interactional than microsystem peer groupings. Yet, like these groupings, they can be either formal (based on an individual's school, neighborhood, or community membership) or informal (reflecting an individual's abilities, interests, or belief systems). The crowd reflects an adolescent's reputation or image among peers. Though adolescents may endeavor earnestly to be affiliated with a particular crowd, or with none at all, to a great extent they are at the mercy of their neighborhood or ethnic origins or peers' opinions of them to determine the crowds with which they are associated (Eckert, 1989; Eder, 1985; Ianni, 1989; Schwendinger & Schwendinger, 1985). Thus, influence is much stronger from crowd to individual than from individual to crowd, although a crowd's influence may be buffeted by the interaction-based groups to which someone belongs. Crowds can also influence one another. One crowd may emulate the characteristics of a higher status crowd (J. S. Coleman, 1961; Eder, 1985). On the other hand, animosities can develop between crowds, such that members of one group consciously cultivate attitudes and activities that are precisely the opposite of identifying features of the other group (Dunphy, 1969; Eckert, 1989).

It is tempting to liken the crowd to Bronfenbrenner's (1986) description of an exosystem, but it does not meet the definition of this type of system because it quite clearly does include some of the individuals whom it affects. Instead, Bradley's (chapter 2, this volume) concept of the "ambience" of the family or Lawton's (chapter 4, this volume) discussion of "environmental mosaic" is applicable here. The crowd provides normative guideposts from which to interpret the attitudes and activities of self and others. In addition, the crowd provides some directives on attending to and interpreting messages from the broader youth culture. It is common for adolescents to have a "split image" among peers—that is, to be associated with one crowd by some peers and with another crowd by others (Brown, 1992). Thus, they may be affected by the norm, values, and pressures of multiple groups—particularly in late adolescence as the barriers between groups begin to dissipate (Brown, Mory, & Kinney, 1994).

Youth Culture

An even more abstract layer of the peer environment, equivalent in many ways to Bronfenbrenner's (chapter 1, this volume) macrosystem, is the youth culture, which is the essential values and orientations of adolescents as a whole—the mood and message of a generation, if you will. Because change is an inherent feature of adolescence, macrosystems in the teenage peer environment are not nearly as permanent as their equivalent in the broader social ecology of the United States. Indeed, the evanescence of macrosystems reveals one facet of the final layer of the peer environment, the chronosystem (Bronfenbrenner, 1986), in which historical shifts in peer cultural norms or generational aspirations can be recorded. Individual time is also reflected in the chronosystem, in that one may observe developmental or maturational changes in the structure or function of the peer system.

In Figure 1, the influence of the youth culture on individuals is portrayed as indirect (through crowds and small groups) and unidirectional. Some, however, might argue that individuals can influence youth culture through their selection of specific media and music, their allegiance to particular rock performers, and so on (Arnett, 1995).

Historical and Developmental Forces

The intensity of friendships, the snobbishness and cliquishness of the popular crowd, and the evanescence of romantic attachments are all considered timeless features of adolescent peer relations. To be sure, some characteristics of the peer environment are replicated across generations. Yet, historical forces can shape this environment in important ways as well. Shifts in sexual mores will alter dating patterns and the course of romantic relationships. Efforts to desegregate schools will alter opportunities for and acceptance of cross-race friendships. Legislation to equalize extracurricular opportunities for the sexes will introduce new formal peer groups (e.g., women's sports teams). Peer crowds will appear and disappear in response to historically bound social movements: hippies give way to Valley girls; smokers are transformed into druggies and headbangers.

Because history cannot be anticipated, it is not feasible to work historical change into the design of most studies. Yet, there are several ways to explore historical effects on the peer environment. Some investigators have taken advantage of archival data sets to assess the role of history in shaping adolescence (e.g., Elder, 1974). Others have replicated earlier studies to deduce how intervening historical events may have altered peer group norms or values (e.g., Eitzen, 1975); still others have seized on special opportunities to examine how ongoing historical circumstances may affect the dynamics of peer or cross-generational relationships (e.g., Keniston, 1968). Even when historical forces are not examined directly, investigators can acknowledge them indirectly by resisting bold generalizations about the applicability of their findings across time and place.

Studies have also revealed a number of significant developmental shifts in adolescents' orientations toward peers. With age, friendships are transformed into more stable and multiplex relationships (LaGaipa, 1979). There is also an increase across adolescence in levels of intimacy in peer relationships, especially with opposite-sex peers (Sharabany et al., 1981). The timing of this trend differs for boys and girls; it may also differ by social class or ethnicity, but such factors have not yet been studied. Conformity to peers seems to decline steadily (Costanzo & Shaw, 1966), whereas susceptibility to antisocial peer pressures follows an inverted U-shaped trajectory across childhood and adolescence (Berndt, 1979).

Perceptions of the dynamics of interaction in microsystems peer groups also change curvilinearily across adolescence. Gavin and Furman (1989) reported that, compared with early and late adolescents, individuals between 7th and 10th grade placed more importance on being popular, were more aware of a status hierarchy within their group, and found group interactions more negative in tone. On the other hand, conformity to group norms was perceived to diminish with age across adolescence, whereas group permeability (openness to outsiders) increased steadily. O'Brien and Bierman (1988) found linear developmental shifts in the basis for identifying or defining peer groups. With age, group descriptions based on overt behavior patterns diminished in favor of more frequent descriptions based on attitudes or group processes. In other words, older adolescents viewed peer groups in more abstract terms.

Such developmental patterns should prompt investigators to think carefully about age or stage in the sample selection process. Developmental status must also be considered routinely in data analyses and interpretations of results. The capacity of individuals to engage in successful impression management or influence of friends, cliques, and even crowds (the thickness of arrows from self to other entities in Figure 1) may change considerably across adolescence. Such changes have only begun to be charted.

Embeddedness

Researchers should not be so preoccupied with the multiple levels or layers of the peer environment that they lose sight of the fact that this environment is embedded in the broader social ecology of adolescents' lives. At all levels, the peer environment is affected by the other major social contexts or microsystems in which adolescents operate, most notably the family, school, neighborhood or community, and workplace. These contexts, in turn, are affected by the structure and dynamics of peer relationships. Like the peer environment, these other contexts are complex social systems with multiple levels and a variety of relationships. Mapping these contexts and their connections to various features of the peer context is an important task, but beyond the scope of this chapter. Yet, there is a wealth of research that has moved investigators in this direction. Sometimes the peer environment is conceptualized as a competitor with these other contexts for an adolescent's allegiance and orientation (Brittain, 1963). Sometimes it is seen as an outcome of the dynamics of family relationships (Brown et al., 1993; Eckert, 1989; Oetting & Beauvais, 1987; Patterson & Dishion, 1985) or of community norms or resources (McLaughlin, 1993; Peshkin, 1991). In other cases, peer relationships are regarded as primary forces shaping adolescents' experiences in other contexts, especially in school (J. S. Coleman, 1961; Fordham & Ogbu, 1986; Matute-Bianchi, 1986). These studies reflect the full array of conceptual and methodological challenges that have already been mentioned in this chapter.

Summary

Two important missions are accomplished by this conceptualization of the adolescent peer environment. First, it arranges the types of peer associations to which teenagers are routinely exposed into a hierarchy of levels, clarifying the interconnections between the types and their relationship to individual adolescents. Second, the model emphasizes the interactional nature of peer group influences, or what Stokols (1988; also see chapter 11, this volume) refers to as a *transactional* approach to the environment. Rather than viewing the environment and an individual's behavior as independent and dependent variables, respectively, this approach focuses on the enduring qualities of interdependence between people and settings. Human behavior is also assumed to be embedded in and markedly influenced by social contexts (in this case, friendship and formal peer groups as well as peer crowds, not to mention other contexts such as school and family to which the peer environment is closely related). An especially important feature of this approach is that relationships between people and environments are viewed as reciprocal rather than unidirectional, so that people shape environments as well as being shaped by them. Finally, person–environment relationships are to be viewed as dynamic (constantly changing) rather than as static.

To illustrate the advantages of this approach, let us reconsider Alisha and her friendship group. This approach not only acknowledges that Alisha is the recipient of as well as contributor to peer pressures of the friendship group but also insists on seeing peer influence as reciprocal. The features of embeddedness and change encourage researchers also to attend to ways in which the friendship group as a whole is influenced or pressured by other facets of the peer ecology, by developmental and historical factors, and by other contexts that affect and are affected by the peer environment. Researchers are still free to study the friendship group's influence on Alisha, so long as they realize that they are examining only one part of a bidirectional, multifaceted influence process.

STUDYING THE PEER ENVIRONMENT: RECOMMENDATIONS AND CAUTIONS

Obviously, it is impossible to incorporate all of the levels and dynamics of the peer environment, let alone the connections to other social contexts, into a single study. Thus, Figure 1 should not be regarded as a blueprint for all future research in this area. It is more sensible to treat it as an overall "battle plan" that can help guide the selection of samples, methods, variables, and levels of analysis that underlie studies of specific issues related to peer influences on adolescents. In this final section of the chapter, I want to illustrate this approach with reference to two persistent issues that have preoccupied researchers of adolescent peer culture in the United States: the role of peers in teenage drug use and in academic achievement.

Peer Influences on Drug Use

There is extensive and consistent evidence that peers affect adolescent drug use, but efforts to specify peer influences have been remarkably diverse and, for the most part, fragmented. Researchers have operationalized peer influence by cataloging the drug-oriented messages in mass media consumed by teenagers, comparing drug usage of adolescents in different peer crowds (Dolcini & Adler, 1994; Mosbach & Leventhal, 1988), determining the strength of an adolescent's association with drug-using peer groups (Oetting & Beauvais, 1987), ascertaining drug use patterns or attitudes of close friends (Kandel & Andrews, 1987), assessing adolescents' "peer orientation" (Condry & Simon, 1974), examining adolescents' perceptions of peer pressure to use drugs (Clasen & Brown, 1985), and many other ways. Are these all equally valid and appropriate measures of peer influence? If so, is it appropriate to aggregate these measures into a superordinate indicator?

The conceptual model presented in this chapter (Figure 1) suggests that the various levels of the peer environment, which could be regarded as multiple sources of influence, do not have equal and direct paths of influence on the individual nor are they equally vulnerable to reciprocal influences from the adolescent. This undermines the sensibility of a simple, additive composite measure. Kandel and Andrews (1987) drew interesting distinctions between three different processes of peer influence: normative influence, modeling, and direct pressure. To take these distinctions a step further, investigators should carefully consider the type of influence that predominates in each level or type of relationship within the peer environment. Normative influence is most likely to be manifest in peer crowds or, at a more distant level, in youth culture. Modeling should be especially apparent in interaction-based groups (friendship cliques, clubs, sports teams, etc.). Direct pressure should be strongest in a dyadic relationship but is probably strong in friendship cliques as well. The task, then, is to design suitable measures of each process within the appropriate level or type of peer relationship. Preferred measurement strategies are likely to arise from this Process × Level interaction. For example, modeling in interaction-based groups is more reliably measured by ethnographic or participant observation approaches than by self-report. Crowd norms, on the other hand, are experienced more phenomenologically than behaviorally. That is, they are most powerful in terms of what adolescents perceive them to be rather than what they really are among crowd members; thus, a self-report measure of perceptions of crowd norms should be more telling than participant observation data or information from each crowd member.

The thicker the arrow leading from self to another facet of the peer environment in Figure 1, the more pressing is the need to examine reciprocal influences. Laboratory studies of interaction processes (e.g., Dishion et al., 1995) or analyses of self-report data from both members of a dyadic relationship are effective alternatives to self-report data on friends' influence. Assessments of an individual's influence on the group (e.g., Savin-Williams, 1987) or consideration of the personal salience of groups to which an adolescent belongs can become moderating variables in analyses of interaction group influences on adolescent drug use. Studies that consider both crowd and interaction group affiliations can explore the filtering process that affects peer influence and the higher levels of the peer environment.

It is very difficult to measure multiple processes of influence across variable levels of the peer environment. How does one choose the most appropriate level to investigate? The conceptual model provides no clear answer to this question. Rather, as a battle plan, it condones different studies of different levels, so long as measurement strategies are suitable to the nature of peer influence at each level in question, and so long as there is an effort to build these studies into a comprehensive corpus of findings.

Studies that do examine multiple levels are potentially quite insightful. Urberg (1992), for example, gathered data on students' crowd affiliation and drug usage in their friendship network to determine which of these two were more strongly predictive of the adolescents' own drug use patterns. Variables based on friends' use were significant predictors of individual drug use; crowd affiliation was not a factor. This is consistent with the conceptual model, which suggests that crowd influences will be filtered through friendship networks. Yet, significant crowd influences may have been masked in this study by the way in which crowd and friend influences were conceptualized. By contrast, Huang (1992) considered crowds as contexts in which the process (more specifically, the magnitude) of friend influence might differ. Adolescents grouped by peer-rated crowd affiliation were compared for the degree to which drug use levels reported by close friends were associated with the adolescents' own use and short-term changes in use. In this study, friends' level of drug use was a strong predictor of drug use among populars, brains, normals, and the Hispanic crowd but not among druggies or nerds.

In addition to improperly equating peer variables across different levels of the peer environment, there is the problem of ignoring salient peer variables within levels. Studies of peer group influences on adolescent drug use concentrate almost exclusively on the friendship group. Admittedly, this is likely to be the most influential interaction-level peer group, and the most expedient to measure, because virtually all adolescents can identify one. Still, interesting dynamics are overlooked by failing to inquire about other groups to which the teenager belongs: church or community youth groups, school- or community-sponsored extracurricular activities, and so on. Gathering data on these diverse groups should provide a more adequate measure of peer influence (modeling, direct pressure, or whatever). It may be desirable to create an aggregate score from measures of influence in these various groups, although investigators should consider weighting the scores from each group by the adolescents' psychological or temporal investment in the group. As I have already said, such a weighting scheme would show sensitivity to the reciprocity of influence; in this case, the notion is that peer groups will influence the teenager most strongly when she or he is clearly committed to the group.

Peer Influences on Academic Achievement

In recent years, educators and scholars have been dismayed by the low performance of American adolescents, in comparison to their counterparts in other industrialized nations, on measures of academic effort, interest, and achievement (Tomlinson, 1993). Several continue the decades-old tradition (J. S. Coleman, 1961) of placing much of the blame on peers, but others emphasize the potential of other social contexts—especially family and workplace—to contribute to adolescents' low academic commitment. Which of these environments is most to blame—or more generally, how does each setting contribute to student achievement? Answers to this question require comparisons of the peer environment to other social contexts. In other words, in addition to intracontextual analyses addressed in the previous section, there are important research questions that call for intercontextual assessments.

The conceptual model implies that peer influences may intersect with family or work or school or community influences at a number of different levels. The school structure may influence the peer group structure, as when school tracking systems crystallize normative differences among crowds and obstruct intercrowd interaction (Ball, 1981; Schwartz, 1981): The brains, who are defined in part by their steady diet of advanced placement courses, may rarely encounter druggies or hoods, who populate remedial track courses. Parent–child interaction seems to provide a model that is replicated in features of peer friendships (Cooper, Carlson, Keller, Kock, & Spradling, 1991). Community norms can fuel or diffuse enmities that are likely to arise among ethnically based peer crowds (Ianni, 1989; Peshkin, 1991). How does one determine the appropriate variables to draw from each context for these comparisons? Although each of these social contexts is a rich and complex environment, these contexts are not likely to share the same arrangement of components, as is stipulated in Figure 1. Contexts are more likely, however, to share the differentiation among structure, content, and process that was articulated for the peer environment earlier in this chapter. By comparing variables in the same category across environments (e.g., family structure vs. peer group structure), investigators can minimize the "method error" that often accompanies studies that draw variables from different facets of each environment. Comparisons of conflict management styles in parent–adolescent and adolescent–friend relationships provide a good illustration of this approach (Laursen, 1993; Youniss & Smollar, 1985).

Interestingly, the direction of peer influence, as well as the capacity of peers to override or undermine family influences on school achievement, is not consistent across ethnic groups (Steinberg, Dornbusch, & Brown, 1992). Certainly, it is important to continue the trend toward drawing samples that are diverse or "unusual" (i.e., not primarily European American) in ethnic composition. More specifically, however, investigators should strive for more programmatic sampling. That might involve sampling on a series of key individual difference variables thought to affect peer relations. Matute-Bianchi's (1986) examination of differences in peer norms among immigrant, first-generation, and second-generation Mexican/Mexican American adolescents could be viewed as the first step in such a research program. Or programmatic sampling could involve assessments of peer environments in a series of clearly specifiable social contexts, such as Ianni's (1989) comparison of peer relationships in urban and suburban communities. The general objective is to select a succession of samples that permit careful, programmatic analyses of specific components of the general conceptual model of the peer environment. This should help refocus researchers' understanding of the adolescent peer environment on a contextually based rather than on a generic or Eurocentric model.

In a similar fashion, investigators need to be attentive to the settings from which their samples are drawn. J. S. Coleman (1961), for example, demonstrated that community orientations toward education clearly affected the salience of academic achievement as a criterion of peer status in different high schools. Samples drawn from a single school or community should carefully examine how that context shapes (or is shaped by) the specifics of the peer environment. Multiple-school or multiple-community studies should be guided by efforts to sample identifiably different contexts rather than simply to increase sample size.

Even within a school or community, setting is an important consideration. Ratings of sociometric status made by peers in an advanced physics class are unlikely to be the same as ratings in a health class taken by a broader cross-section of classmates. Confining analyses of friends to school classmates—though expedient for locating and gathering data from friends of respondents—may seriously misrepresent characteristics of a teenager's actual friendship group, especially among urban minority adolescents (DuBois & Hirsch, 1990).

The most insightful intercontextual (as well as intracontextual) analyses involving the peer environment are likely to be those that incorporate variables across the domains of structure, content, and process of relationships. For such work, Bronfenbrenner's process–person–context–time model (see Bronfenbrenner, chapter 1, this volume) may be an especially effective organizational scheme. Steinberg et al. (1992) speculated that parenting styles (process) do not seem to have the same effect on achievement outcomes of adolescents from various ethnic groups (person) because adolescents in these ethnic groups do not have equal access to peer crowds (context) that reinforce or undermine school achievement. Of course, access to peer crowds is likely to vary across adolescence (developmental time) and be influenced by historical circumstances such as the acceptability of segregated schools and communities (historical time). Thus, it is easy to transform and expand Steinberg et al.'s speculations into the PPCT formulation.

Bronfenbrenner's (chapter 1, this volume) approach provides a sensible strategy for a coordinated set of analyses that systematically assesses the major components of the peer environment that I have identified: structure, content, and process of peer relations that change developmentally, are embedded in historical context, and are related to social contexts of adolescents' lives. Although it lends itself to linear, cause–effect (rather than to reciprocal effects) analyses, this approach can help investigators design studies to capture the multifaceted nature of the adolescent peer environment.

CONCLUSION

Wachs (1992) noted that although it is common to speak about and measure environmental influences as if they were direct, they are often indirect. The effects of one environmental factor will be contingent on another environmental factor and will be further moderated by individual variables. In this chapter I have offered a conceptual scheme that acknowledges the multidimensionality of the peer environment; its embeddedness in other social environments; and its capacity to affect and be affected by individual, developmental, and historical factors. Although this makes measurement of the peer environment more complex, it provides a mechanism for dealing with that complexity in a sensible and systematic fashion. Researchers appear to be ready to move beyond simple cause–effect models to more interactional approaches of multiple contingencies. Measures and measurement strategies must proceed in the same direction. Only then can researchers hope to appreciate the intriguing intricacies of the peer environment at this stage of the life cycle.

REFERENCES

Adler, P. A., & Adler, P. (1995). Dynamics of inclusion and exclusion in preadolescent cliques. *Social Psychology Quarterly, 58*, 145–162.

Arnett, J. J. (1995). Adolescents' use of media for self-socialization. *Journal of Youth and Adolescence, 24*, 519–533.

Ball, S. J. (1981). *Beachside comprehensive*. Cambridge, England: Cambridge University Press.

Berndt, T. J. (1979). Developmental changes in conformity to peers and parents. *Developmental Psychology, 15*, 606–616.

Berndt, T. J., & Keefe, K. (1995). Friends' influence on adolescents' adjustment to school. *Child Development, 66*, 1312–1329.

Berndt, T. J., & Perry, T. B. (1986). Children's perceptions of friendships as supportive relationships. *Developmental Psychology, 22*, 640–648.

Brittain, C. V. (1963). Adolescent choices and parent–peer cross-pressures. *American Sociological Review, 28*, 385–391.

Bronfenbrenner, U. (1986). Ecology of the family as a context for human development: Research perspectives. *Developmental Psychology, 22*, 723–742.

Brown, B. B. (1990). Peer groups and peer cultures. In S. S. Feldman & G. R. Elliott (Eds.), *At the threshold: The developing adolescent* (pp. 171–196). Cambridge, MA: Harvard University Press.

Brown, B. B. (1992). The measurement and meaning of adolescent peer groups. *SRA (Society for Research on Adolescent) Newsletter*, 6(1), 6–8.

Brown, B. B., Clasen, D. R., & Eicher, S. A. (1986). Perceptions of peer pressure, peer conformity dispositions, and self-reported behavior among adolescents. *Developmental Psychology, 22*, 521–530.

Brown, B. B., Dolcini, M. M., & Leventhal, A. (1997). Transformations in peer relationships at adolescence: Implications for health-related behavior. In J. Schulenberg, J. L. Maggs, & K. Hurrelmann (Eds.), *Health risks and developmental transitions during adolescence* (pp. 161–189). Cambridge, England: Cambridge University Press.

Brown, B. B., Eicher, S. A., & Petrie, S. (1986). The importance of peer group ("crowd") affiliation in adolescence. *Journal of Adolescence, 9*, 73–96.

Brown, B. B., Freeman, H., Huang, B. H., & Mounts, N. S. (1992, March). *"Crowd hopping": Incidents, correlates, and consequences of change in crowd affiliation during adolescence.* Paper presented at the biennial meeting of the Society for Research in Adolescence, Washington, DC.

Brown, B. B., Lamborn, S. L., Mounts, N. S., & Steinberg, L. (1993). Parenting practices and peer group affiliation in adolescence. *Child Development, 64*, 467–482.

Brown, B. B., Mory, M., & Kinney, D. A. (1994). Casting adolescent crowds in relational perspective: Caricature, channel, and context. In R. Montemayor, G. R. Adams, & T. P. Gullotta (Eds.), *Advances in adolescent development: Vol. 6, Personal relationships during adolescence* (pp. 123–167). Newbury Park, CA: Sage.

Buff, S. A. (1970). Greasers, dupers, and hippies: Three responses to the adult world. In L. Howe (Ed.), *The white majority* (pp. 60–77). New York: Random House.

Buhrmester, D. (1990). Intimacy of friendship, interpersonal competence, and adjustment during preadolescence and adolescence. *Child Development, 61*, 1101–1111.

Bukowski, W. M., Newcomb, A. F., & Hoza, B. (1987). Friendship conceptions among early adolescents: A longitudinal study of stability and change. *Journal of Early Adolescence, 7*, 143–152.

Cairns, R. B., Leung, B.-C., Buchanan, L., & Cairns, B. D. (1995). Friendships and social networks in childhood and adolescence: Fluidity, reliability, and interrelations. *Child Development, 66*, 1330–1345.

Cairns, R. B., Perrin, J. E., & Cairns, B. D. (1985). Social structure and social cognition in early adolescence: Affiliative patterns. *Journal of Early Adolescence, 5*, 339–355.

Clasen, D. R., & Brown, B. B. (1985). The multidimensionality of peer pressure in adolescence. *Journal of Youth and Adolescence, 14*, 451–468.

Cohen, J. (1976). The impact of the leading crowd on high school change: A reassessment. *Adolescence, 11*, 373–381.

Coleman, J. C. (1974). *Relationships in adolescence*. Boston: Routledge and Kegan Paul.

Coleman, J. S. (1961). *The adolescent society*. New York: Free Press.

Condry, J., & Simon, M. L. (1974). Characteristics of peer- and parent-oriented children. *Journal of Marriage and the Family, 36*, 543–554.

Cooper, C. R., Carlson, C. I., Keller, J., Kock, P., & Spradling, V. (1991, April). Conflict negotiation in early adolescence: Links between family and peer relational patterns. In B. B. Brown (Chair), *From family to peer: Family influences on peer relations from early childhood through adolescence*. Symposium conducted at the biennial meetings of the Society for Research in Child Development, Seattle, WA.

Costanzo, P. R., & Shaw, M. E. (1966). Conformity as a function of age level. *Child Development, 37*, 967–975.

Csikszentmihalyi, M., & Larson, R. (1984). *Being adolescent*. New York: Basic Books.

Cusick, P. A. (1973). *Inside high school*. New York: Holt, Rinehart & Winston.

Deyhle, D. (1986). Break dancing and breaking out: Anglos, Utes, and Navajos in a border reservation high school. *Anthropology and Education Quarterly, 17*, 111–127.

Dishion, T. J., Andrews, D. W., & Crosby, L. (1995). Antisocial boys and their friends in early adolescence: Relationship characteristics, quality, and interactional process. *Child Development*, 66, 139–151.

Dolcini, M. M., & Adler, N. E. (1994). Perceived competencies, peer group affiliation, and risk behavior among early adolescents. *Health Psychology, 13*, 496–506.

DuBois, D. I., & Hirsch, B. J. (1990). School and neighborhood friendship patterns of blacks and whites in early adolescence. *Child Development, 61*, 524–536

Dunphy, D. C. (1969). *Cliques, crowds, and gangs*. Melbourne, Australia: Chesire.

Eckert, P. (1989). *Jocks and burnouts: Social categories and identity in the high school*. New York: Teachers College Press.

Eder, D. (1985). The cycle of popularity: Interpersonal relations among female adolescence. *Sociology of Education*, 58, 154–165.

Eitzen, D. S. (1975). Athletics in the status system of male adolescents: A replication of Coleman's *The adolescent society*. *Adolescence, 10*, 267–276.

Elder, G. H. (1974). *Children of the Great Depression*. Chicago: University of Chicago Press.

Ennett, S. T., & Bauman, K. E. (1993). Peer group structure and adolescent cigarette smoking: A social network analysis. *Journal of Health and Social Behavior, 34*, 226–236.

Erikson, E. H. (1968). *Identity, youth, and crisis*. New York: Norton.

Feinstein, S. C., & Ardon, M. S. (1973). Trends in dating patterns and adolescent development. *Journal of Youth and Adolescence, 2*, 157–166.

Feldman, S. S., Rosenthal, D. R., Brown, N. L., & Canning, R. D. (1995). Predicting sexual experience in adolescent boys from peer rejection and acceptance during childhood. *Journal of Research in Adolescence, 5*, 387–411.

Feueur, L. S. (1969). *Conflict of generations*. New York: Basic Books.

Fisher, L. A., & Bauman, K. E. (1988). Influence and selection in the friend–adolescent relationship: Findings from studies of adolescent smoking and drinking. *Journal of Applied Social Psychology, 18*, 289–314.

Fordham, S., & Ogbu, J. U. (1986). Black students' school success: Coping with the burden of "acting white." *Urban Review, 18*, 176–206.

Freud, A. (1958). Adolescence. *Psychoanalytic Study of the Child, 13*, 255–278.

Gavin, L. A., & Furman, W. (1989). Age differences in adolescents' perceptions of their peer groups. *Developmental Psychology, 25*, 827–834.

Hamm, J. V. (1993, March). *African-American, Asian-American, and Hispanic-American adolescents' perceived crowd affiliations in multi-ethnic high schools*. Paper presented at the biennial meetings of the Society for Research in Child Development, New Orleans, LA.

Hendrick, S., & Hendrick, C. (1994, February). *Gender, sexuality, and close relationships*. Paper presented at the biennial meetings of the Society for Research in Adolescence, San Diego, CA.

Hirschi, T. (1969). *Causes of delinquency*. Berkeley: University of California Press.

Hogue, A., & Steinberg, L. (1995). Homophily of internalized distress in adolescent peer groups. *Developmental Psychology, 31*, 897–906.

Huang, B. H. (1992, March). *Parent and peer influences on adolescent deviance revisited: Impact of crowd affiliation*. Paper presented at the biennial meetings of the Society for Research in Adolescence, Washington, DC.

Ianni, F. A. J. (1989). *The search for structure*. New York: Free Press.

Juvonen, J., & Murdock, T. B. (1995). Grade-level differences in the social value of effort: Implications for self-presentation tactics of early adolescents. *Child Development, 66*, 1694–1705.

Kandel, D. B. (1978). Homophily, selection, and socialization. *American Journal of Sociology, 84*, 427–438.

Kandel, D. B., & Andrews, K. (1987). Processes of adolescent socialization by parents and peers. *International Journal of the Addictions, 22*, 319–342.

Keniston, K. (1968). *Young radicals*. New York: Harcourt, Brace, and World.

Kinney, D. A. (1993). From "nerds" to "normals": Adolescent identity recovery within a changing social system. *Sociology of Education, 66*, 21–40.

Kinney, D. A. (1995, April). From at-risk to resilient: Examining the role of extracurricular activities for urban high school students. In D. Mekos & G. H. Elder, Jr. (Chairs), *Developmental perspectives on adolescent extracurricular involvement*. Symposium conducted at the biennial meetings of the Society for Research in Child Development, Indianapolis, IN.

LaGaipa, J. J. (1979). A developmental study of the meaning of friendship in adolescence. *Journal of Adolescence, 2*, 201–213.

Larkin, R. W. (1979). *Suburban youth in cultural crisis*. New York: Oxford University Press.

Laursen, B. (1993). The perceived impact of conflict on adolescent relationships. *Merrill-Palmer Quarterly, 39*, 535–550.

Lesko, N. (1988). *Symbolizing society: Stories, rites, and structure in a Catholic high school*. Philadelphia: Falmer Press.

Matute-Bianchi, M. E. (1986). Ethnic identities and patterns of school success and failure among Mexican-Descent and Japanese-American students in a California high school: An ethnographic analysis. *American Journal of Education, 95*, 233–255.

McLaughlin, M. W. (1993). Embedded identities. In S. B. Heath & M. W. McLaughlin (Eds.), *Identity and inner city youth: Beyond ethnicity and gender* (pp. 36–68). New York: Teachers College Press.

Merten, D. (1996). Vulnerability and visibility: Responses to a stigmatized identity. *Journal of Early Adolescence, 16*, 5–26.

Mosbach, P., & Leventhal, H. (1988). Peer group identification and smoking: Implications for intervention. *Journal of Abnormal Psychology, 97*, 238–245.

O'Brien, S. F., & Bierman, K. L. (1988). Conceptions and perceived influence of peer groups: Interviews with preadolescents and adolescents. *Child Development, 59*, 1360–1365.

Oetting, E. R., & Beauvais, F. (1987). Peer cluster theory, socialization theory, and adolescent drug use: A path analysis. *Journal of Counseling Psychology, 34*, 205–213.

Patterson, G. R., & Dishion, T. J. (1985). Contributions of families and peers to delinquency. *Criminology, 23*, 63–79.

Peshkin, A. (1991). *The color of strangers, the color of friends*. Chicago: University of Chicago Press.

Petersen, A. C. (1993). Creating adolescents: The role of context and process in developmental trajectories. *Journal of Research on Adolescence, 3*, 1–18.

Piaget, J. (1958). *The growth in logical thinking from childhood to adolescence*. New York: Basic Books.

Roe, K. (1992). Different destinies, different melodies: School achievement, anticipated status, and adolescents' taste in music. *European Journal of Communication, 7*, 335–357.

Savin-Williams, R. C. (1987). *Adolescence: An ethological perspective*. New York: Springer-Verlag.

Savin-Williams, R. C. (1994). Dating those you can't love and loving those you can't date. In R. Montemayor, G. R. Adams, & T. P. Gullatta (Eds.), *Advances in adolescent development: Vol. 6. Personal relationships during adolescence* (pp. 168–195). Thousand Oaks, CA: Sage.

Sebald, H. (1981). Adolescents' concept of popularity and unpopularity: Comparing 1960 with 1976. *Adolescence, 16*, 187–193.

Scarr, S. (1992). Developmental theories for the 1990's: Development and individual differences. *Child Development, 63,* 1–19.

Schwartz, F. (1981). Supporting or subverting learning?: Peer group patterns in four tracked high schools. *Anthropology and Education Quarterly, 12,* 99–121.

Schwendinger, H., & Schwendinger, J. S. (1985). *Adolescent subcultures and delinquency.* New York: Praeger.

Sharabany, R., Gershoni, R., & Hofman, J. (1981). Girlfriend, boyfriend: Age and sex differences in intimate friendship. *Developmental Psychology, 17,* 800–808.

Shrum, W., & Cheek, N. H. (1986). Social structure during the school years: Onset of the degrouping process. *American Sociological Review, 52,* 218–223.

Shulman, S. (1993). Close friends in early and middle adolescence: Typology and friendship reasoning. In B. Laursen (Ed.), *Close friendships in adolescence* (pp. 55–71). San Francisco: Jossey-Bass.

Steinberg, L. (1990). Autonomy, conflict, and harmony in the family relationship. In S. S. Feldman & G. R. Elliott (Eds.), *At the threshold: The developing adolescent* (pp. 255–276). Cambridge, MA: Harvard University Press.

Steinberg, L., Dornbusch, S. M., & Brown, B. B. (1992). Ethnic differences in adolescent achievement: An ecological perspective. *American Psychologist, 47,* 723–729.

Stokols, D. (1988). Transformational processes in people–environment relations. In J. E. McGrath (Ed.), *The social psychology of time: New perspectives* (pp. 233–252). Newbury Park, CA: Sage.

Tanner, J. M. (1972). Sequence, tempo, and individual variation in growth and development of boys and girls aged twelve to sixteen. In J. Kagan & R. Coles (Eds.), *Twelve to sixteen: Early adolescence* (pp. 1–24). New York: Norton.

Thomas, J. W. (1993). Expectations and effort: Course demands, students's study practices, and academic achievement. In T. M. Tomlinson (Ed.), *Motivating students to learn* (pp. 139–176). Berkeley, CA: McCutchan.

Tomlinson, T. M. (Ed.). (1993). *Motivating students to learn.* Berkeley, CA: McCutchan.

Urberg, K. A. (1992). Locus of peer influence: Social crowd and best friend. *Journal of Youth and Adolescence, 21,* 439–450.

Wachs, T. D. (1992). *The nature of nurture.* Newbury Park, CA: Sage.

Walker, J. C. (1988). *Louts and legends: Male youth culture in an inner-city school.* Concord, MA: Allen & Unwin.

Youniss, J., & Smollar, J. (1985). *Adolescent relations with mothers, fathers, and friends.* Chicago: University of Chicago Press.

Zisman, P., & Wilson, V. (1992). Table hopping in the cafeteria: An exploration of "racial" integration in early adolescent social groups. *Anthropology and Education Quarterly, 23,* 199–220.

4

ENVIRONMENTAL TAXONOMY: GENERALIZATIONS FROM RESEARCH WITH OLDER ADULTS

M. POWELL LAWTON

Much of the research in person–environment relations has been performed in contexts that are very user specific, such as mental hospitals; residences for mentally impaired individuals; schools; offices; and various settings for children, adolescents, and the aged. Theory in person–environment relations has been, as it should be, less user-group bound. Although in this chapter I deal with the particular perspective of older people, wherever possible, application to all user groups is sought in the discussion of concepts and measures. I make the assertion that generic structures for assessment can be identified. I then argue that the technology of environmental assessment can be improved in a way that utilizes universal dimensions but is still flexible enough to allow instrument versions or modules for user-specific content. Another view of environmental assessment issues in gerontology may be found in Carp (1994).

This presentation begins with a brief depiction of the ecological model (Lawton & Nahemow, 1973), in which I attempt to specify some concepts in the person–environment transaction. These concepts require further differentiation and operationalization. Several strategies for environmental assessment are described and illustrated with findings from research in environmental psychology and gerontology. It is suggested that an environmental taxonomy can lead to better assessment, in which the dimensions are universal but the content is user-group specific. A beginning classification, which is congruent with the constructs used by other authors in this volume, is outlined, with suggestions for further development. Specifically, environmental classes, objective versus subjective dimensions, and nonmutually exclusive attributes are suggested as the basis for such a taxonomy.

THE ECOLOGICAL MODEL

In contrast to the transactional view that asserts the indivisible nature of person and environment (Ittelson, 1973), Lawton and Nahemow (1973) argued that for heuristic purposes, these two components of the ecology of human action must be measured separately and their varying relationships determined empirically, at least until satisfactory units combining person and environment can evolve. Keeping person and environment separate is necessary despite the fact that cause and effect are often a less adequate representation of reality than is the idea of system-wide processes of mutual change or stability.

Borrowing in obvious ways from Lewin (1935), Murray (1938), White (1959), and Helson (1964), Nahemow and I (Lawton & Nahemow, 1973) posited a model of adaptation that would predict outcomes (adaptive behavior and affect) associated with the interaction between a person, characterized in terms of competence, and an environment of a given level of press (Murray's term for environmental demand). Competence was meant to be indexed in terms of biological health, sensory and motor skills, and cognitive function, viewed as relatively stable capacities but clearly changeable in trajectories of illness and health. Environmental press was characterized as Murray did, in terms of "alpha press" (objective, externally observable criteria) and "beta press" (demand as perceived by the person). The surface of Figure 1 represents outcomes of individuals of varying levels of competence interacting with environmental press of differing intensities. Broadly, the outcomes are depicted as surface areas of adaptive response (the inner area enclosed by diagonals), maladaptive or stressful (to right of diagonal), and maladaptive in the sense of underchallenge or atrophy (to left of diagonal). The points around which the interactions vary represent adaptation level (Helson, 1964), in which environmental demand is congruent with competence. In fact, adaptive outcomes may occur anywhere within the limits of the challenge range (zone of maximum performance potential) or the mildly understimulated range (zone of maximum comfort).

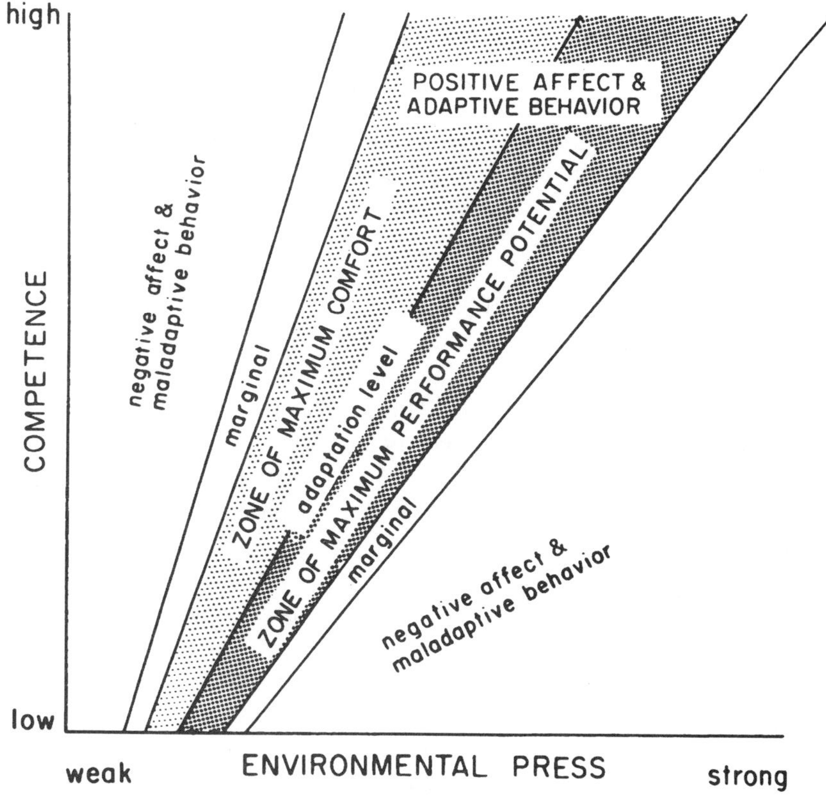

Figure 1. Outcomes of competence interacting with environmental press of differing intensities.

This representation suggested the environment docility hypothesis: The less competent the person, the greater the influence of the environment on the outcome of behavior (Lawton & Simon, 1968). This is depicted in the diverging diagonals, so that the same absolute change in environmental press level has a major impact on the adaptive quality of a low-competent individual's behavior or affect but has a much smaller impact in the case of the more competent individual.

This model was suggested by research on the determinants of friendships in a study of planned housing for older people (Lawton & Simon, 1968). For healthy older adults, friends were chosen from many locations in the building, facilitating choices made on the basis of shared qualities. For the less healthy, geographic proximity was a much stronger determinant of friendship choice. The environmental barrier of distance between apartments thus limited the choice of less competent tenants more than it did for the more competent ones.

This model was articulated on the basis of research findings from a sample of older people. From the beginning, however, we saw it as applying to anyone with a limitation in personal competence—the mentally ill; disabled; or, with only slight extensions of definitions, to groups such as children, the poor, or those whose options were limited by factors such as racism. The concepts underlying this model were thus clearly not intrinsic to old age.

My colleagues Frances and Abraham Carp, however, pointed out that this model was applicable primarily to the segments of any population in which its competence ranged from average to low (Carp & Carp, 1984). Although our scale of competence theoretically had no cap, the ecological model did not account well for above-average performance. They rightly noted that in the case of older adults, for example, only 20% had major limitations on their ability to perform everyday tasks of daily living (National Center for Health Statistics, 1987). They also noted that the relevance of environment for the competent segment of the population was more as a "resource center" than as a controller of behavior and affect. These criticisms, and other research on personal control (Baltes & Baltes, 1986), led then to the formulation of the environmental proactivity hypothesis (Lawton, 1985). This hypothesis suggested that the higher the competence of the person, the better able the person would be to utilize the resources of any environment in the service of personal needs. In the person–environment interaction, this hypothesis acknowledges the reciprocal nature of the interaction—that is, that older people, like all others, choose, alter, and create environments. The dual mechanisms of docility and proactivity are consistent with the phenomena discussed by Bronfenbrenner (chapter 1, this volume), in which the influence of positive environmental processes (a parent) was most effective in reducing dysfunction for environmentally deprived children. By contrast, such an effect is evidenced only in enhancing higher levels of competence for children in privileged environments.

These dual hypotheses were then incorporated into a view of environmental action as a dialectic between security and autonomy, in which each person has a characteristic preferred mix of the two (Lawton, 1985; Parmelee & Lawton, 1990). The mix expresses a personal style, but the mix varies also with such factors as life stage, family cycle, health, occupation, and other influences.

This brief summary of the genesis of a set of grouped constructs is provided here to illustrate that despite the logical applicability of such a model to person–environment interactions other than those of older people, this approach has rarely been applied outside gerontology. The next topic links the question of why the model has not been generally applied to the other major topic of this book, the measurement issue.

OPERATIONALIZING THE ECOLOGICAL MODEL

The ecological model (Lawton & Nahemow, 1973), despite a number of empirical confirmations, has not led to very productive operationalizations of environmental press. Demand can be translated into such terms as a physical barrier like a change of level, a home in which the upkeep demands physical energy, or a neighborhood with a high crime rate. Concrete examples such as these are easy to use in research studies in which the purposes are, respectively, environmental negotiability for the handicapped, a frail person who lives alone "aging in place" (Tillson, 1990), or the quality of life of tenants in public housing. Such single-variable research has, in fact, characterized most environmental research in aging. The generation of new knowledge requires measurement to develop within a conceptual framework, however. Our model has contributed relatively little to such a search, a fate shared also by most research in gerontology.

The original articulation of the ecological model also suggested a beginning for a taxonomy of environment, which is shown in Table 1. As indicated and defined, environment was conceived as physical, divisible into classes of personal, small-group, suprapersonal, and megasocial environments. Each class may also have indicators that are objective or subjective. This classification, how it fits into other possible taxonomies, and how it leads into assessment is discussed later in this chapter. Before that discussion, I provide an overview of environmental assessment in gerontology. As a beginning, measurement can be viewed in terms of tesserae, collections of tesserae, and mosaics.

THE TESSERAE OF ENVIRONMENTAL MEASUREMENT: THE BOTTOM-UP APPROACH

Roger Barker (1963, 1968) contrasted his transactional ecological psychology that wedded people and environment into indivisible units called "behavior settings" with the fractionating approach in which person and environment were measured separately and in cataloging detail. He termed the units of the traditional fractionated approach as the "tesserae" of person and environment. The tessera is a convenient metaphor for each of a very long list of highly specific aspects of the environment that cannot be ignored in the real world of environmental planning and design. The environmental psychology of later life has accepted environmental tesserae as core independent variables. Examples are single versus shared rooms in a nursing home (Lawton & Bader, 1970), number of dwelling units in a development (Lawton, Nahemow, & Teaff, 1975), high rise versus low rise (Nahemow, Lawton, & Howell, 1977), presence of a nursing unit and other on-site services in a housing environment (Lawton, 1976), rented versus owner-occupied unit (Lawton, 1981), size of community (Lawton & Nahemow, 1979a), proximity of shopping (Newcomer, 1976), square footage of a residence and amount of counter space in a kitchen (Lawton &

TABLE 1
Classes of Environment

Class	Definition	Example
Physical environment	Objective (alpha press): what can be counted, measured in centimeters, grams, and seconds or consensually evaluated; Subjective (beta press): personally ascribed meaning, salience, or evaluation of the objective environment.	Housing deficits, amount of seating space, distance from amenity to domicile, ecological characteristics such as vacancy rate and demolition rate; Satisfaction with kitchen, satisfaction with neighborhood, perceived safety, and importance of physical amenities.
Personal environment	One-on-one relationships; friends, family, and support networks.	Number of close friends, number of children, relationship to household occupants, and presence of confidant.
Small-group environment	The dynamics that determine the mutual relationships among people in a small group in which all members have some one-on-one relationship or interaction.	Residents of a small-group home, employees of a small business, or a small affinity group.
Suprapersonal environment	Modal characteristics of people in geographic proximity to the subject (as in social area analysis).	Age mix of a high-rise building, range of health of residents in a nursing home unit, and ecological characteristics of residential block (age, race, income, crime rate, etc.).
Social (megasocial) environment	Organizational character, social norms, cultural values, legal system, regulations, political ideology, and psychosocial milieu.	The "total institution": dress code, self-sufficiency norm, white-collar versus blue-collar justice, Americans With Disabilities Act, liberal capitalism, and cohesion versus conflict.

Note. Each class may have an objective or subjective aspect. Such possibilities are spelled out here only for the physical environment class.

Nahemow, 1979b), and many aspects of institutional design (Calkins, 1988; Hiatt, 1991; Koncelik, 1976). Clearly this list could go on.

The subjective aspect of environment also encompasses tesserae. The most usual way of eliciting such judgments is through the preference question, which is much used in market research: Would you rather have a tub or just a shower stall? Do you prefer a doorknob or a lever? If you were going to move, would you like to live in a high-rise building or a garden apartment? However, there are obvious problems with such direct attempts to elicit preferences. (See Lawton, 1987, for a review of sources of error and suggestions for bettering the quality of such data.)

Designers nurture the myth that social scientists can provide ready answers to questions regarding the design of tesserae. The big problem with environmental tesserae is that their number and variety are limitless. One obvious way to move beyond the single-item tessera is to combine these items into composite indexes.

COLLECTIONS OF TESSERAE

Obvious dimensions like housing deficiencies allow straightforward indexes of housing quality to be developed (Christensen, Carp, Cranz, & Wiley, 1992; Lawton, 1980; Struyk & Turner, 1984). A number of checklists designed to evaluate the usability of ordinary dwelling units by older adults have been designed (American Association of Retired Persons, 1985; Canada Mortgage and Housing Corporation, 1989; Olsen, Ehrenkrantz, & Hutchings, 1993; Pynoos, Cohen, Davis, & Bernhardt, 1987).

Other similar efforts have been developed to assess the environmental quality of residential facilities for older adults. The most developed measure is the Therapeutic Environment Screening Scale (TESS) (Sloane & Mathew, 1990), which is used in special units for patients with Alzheimer's disease. The TESS requires an observer to walk through a unit and note a broad variety of purely descriptive (e.g., square footage and number of chairs occupied) and presumed quality indicators (e.g., percentage of rooms with personalized features and quality of views from bedroom windows).

These checklists, and others to be described later in this section, begin with very specific design features, most gleaned from the qualitative literature to represent putatively desirable features for older adults. Collections of tesserae are intended to represent environmental dimensions that are more general than those of the individual tessera. Some dimensions like housing deficits or aggregate of distances of a residence from neighborhood amenities are "accretive," with clear meaning and relatively unidimensional structure. Nonetheless, these dimensions suffer from being both atheoretical and insufficiently focused on behavioral goals.

One alternative to the simple collection of items is the use of factor analysis as a way of defining meaningful categories from a large collection of empirical environmental measures. Frances and Abraham Carp have made the most systematic efforts to impose meaning on collections of tesserae by factor-analytic methods. Domains to which these methods were applied included "neighborhood technical assessment indices" (Carp & Carp, 1982a) and need-relevant physical characteristics of housing (Christensen & Carp, 1983). Such objectively defined clusters of tesserae were then correlated with subjective aspects of the environment. Table 2 shows concretely some of the results from their program of research (Carp & Carp, 1982b; Carp & Christensen, 1986a, 1986b; Christensen et al., 1992). Table 2 shows items with significant beta weights for predicting meal-preparation satisfaction from physical housing indexes and the items composing an index of perceived neighborhood quality. It should be noted that theoretically based judgments were made by Carp and Carp (1984) in constituting the types of collections of tesserae to be factored and the correlates of the factors, thus giving a substantial top-down emphasis to the derivation of these indexes.

ENVIRONMENTAL MOSAICS: THE TOP-DOWN APPROACH

The third approach is called a "mosaic" because the ideal goal is to define major dimensions that explain broader phenomena than tesserae while still maintaining close ties to observable reality. Almost by definition, the attempt to capture environment and its elusive essences requires the opposite approach, which is to begin with the global and then search for the components—the top-down approach. These explanatory dimensions have usually been articulated first, followed by their elaboration in terms of selective tesserae presumed or demonstrated to be indicators of the dimension.

An example of top-down thinking is provided by the application of behavioral knowledge to the design of nursing homes and other residences. Table 3 shows some of the major design categories that several authors have suggested for older adult's residential environments. Each of these lists was derived from an a priori judgment of how the major needs, goals, or deficit-counteracting measures of users might be served by each environmental dimension.

How inclusive and salient is any set of such rational attempts to characterize basic dimensions? Those suggested for dementia care units (Calkins, 1988; Weisman, Lawton, Sloan, Calkins, & Norris-Baker, 1996) have had the advantage of successive improvement with the addition of new researchers in this area. It is possible to locate all aspects of Weisman et al.'s categories in more inclusive models of behavioral competence and quality of life (Lawton, 1983). There appears to be considerable congruence

TABLE 2
Technical Environmental Quality for Meal Preparation and Perceived Neighborhood Quality Indexes

Index	Standard/rating
Technical environmental quality for meal preparation	
Volume of storage space below 2 feet from the floor	Cubic feet
Adequate hot water pressure	Presence or absence (at least 1/4 cup per s.)
Electric sockets in kitchen area	Number of
Kitchen/dining/living room combination	Presence or absence
Water temperature deviation from 110°F	After 30 s.
One foot and 5 in. of counter space on both sides of kitchen sink	Presence or absence
Indicator lights for electric stove burners	Presence or absence
Lever type faucet handles in kitchen	Presence or absence
One foot and 5 in. of counter space on at least one side of kitchen sink	Presence or absence
Stove controls at front	Presence or absence
Perceived neighborhood quality	
Feelings about local area	One of the worst in Oakland or one of the best in Oakland
Feelings about block	One of the worst in this part of town or one of the best in this part of town
Rating of local area compared to the ideal	Very bad, the worst or ideal, perfect
Kind of local area respondent deserves and ought to have	Much better than this one or a lot worse than this one
Satisfaction with local area as a place to live	Not at all satisfied or completely satisfied
Living in local area makes respondent feel	Unhappy or happy
Living in local area makes respondent feel	Ashamed or proud
Living in local area makes respondent feel	Angry or peaceful
Living in local area makes respondent feel	A second-class citizen or a first-class citizen
Living in local area makes respondent feel	Powerless or powerful
Living in local area makes respondent feel	Discontented or contented
Living in local area makes respondent feel	Neglected or cared for

Note. From "A Role for Technical Assessment in Perceptions of Environmental Quality of Well-Being," by F. M. Carp and A. Carp, 1982, *Journal of Environmental Psychology, 2,* p. 281. Copyright 1982 by Sage Publications.

TABLE 3
Suggested Design Categories for Older Adults' Residential Environments

Authors	Environment	Goals
Marlow (1973)	Mental hospitals and nursing homes	Autonomy, personalization, warmth, social integration, resources, constructive activity, community integration, physical appeal, succorance, and tolerance for deviation.
Lawton (1986)	Nursing homes	Safety, negotiability, orientation, autonomy, personalization, social integration, and aesthetics.
Regnier (1987)	Housing	Resident satisfaction, social interaction, management, sensory aspects, physiological constraints, and wayfinding.
Calkins (1988)	Design for dementia	Wayfinding/orientation, privacy versus socialization, personalization, safety/security, and competence.
Weisman, Lawton, Sloane, Calkins, and Norris-Baker (1996)	Dementia special care units	Maximize safety and security; maximize awareness and orientation; support functional abilities; sensory stimulation (regulation); sensory stimulation (quality); facilitation of social contact; opportunities for personal control; ties to the healthy, the familiar, and the continuity of self; and privacy.

among the dimensions shown in Table 3. Better specification of the mosaics will require new concepts and new measures that can be more generally relevant beyond the dementia care unit. Two necessary next steps have already begun: one that links the mosaic with the tesserae and one that does its part to link the physical with the nonphysical.

Linking the Mosaic With the Tesserae

It was mentioned earlier that empirical clusterings of tesserae through the use of methods such as factor analysis might have some hope of leading to the specification of basic environmental components (bottom-up). Conversely, a necessary complementary direction of research activity is to move from the mosaic to the tesserae (top-down). In fact, Marlowe (1973; see also Lieberman & Tobin, 1983), Calkins (1988), and Weisman et al. (1996) took that path by articulating an a priori group of indicators for each dimension. For example, Marlowe's resources category was indexed by a checklist of observable resources, such as private telephones, magazines, game equipment, and so forth.

Carp and Carp (1984) used top-down methods to link neighborhood and housing tesserae to some of the personal needs identified by Murray (1938). They sought physical dwelling-unit characteristics that could serve as indicators of the ability of the unit to satisfy such needs as Harm, Avoidance, Order, and Affiliation (from Murray's list). Regression analysis of a global measure of housing satisfaction served as validation of the relevance of many tesserae to the larger satisfaction dimension and also to more general psychological well-being (Carp & Christensen, 1986a, 1986b). Both Marlowe's (1973) and Carp and Carp's (1984) research demonstrated substantial relationships between both the tesserae and the mosaic, on the one hand, and person outcomes, on the other. Unfortunately neither has been sufficiently recognized in the general literature or has been developed into an easily available evaluation form.

Such a top-down linkage offers the opportunity to test empirically a large number of item indicators, at least insofar as determining their prevalence. Determination of their validity is another matter. One step in this direction is being taken right now. The Physical Environment Assessment Protocol (PEAP; Weisman et al., 1996) seeks expert ratings of the nine goals (as indicated in Table 3) by using conceptual definitions and a small number of illustrative indicators. These nine dimensions are in an item analysis of the TESS (Sloane & Mathew, 1990) to determine the correlates of each global goal (Weisman et al., 1996).

Linking the Physical and the Nonphysical

Near the beginning of this chapter I suggested that I would deal especially with the conceptual and measurement problems of the physical environment. Although this is useful for heuristic purposes, it is obvious that such a separation between the physical and other aspects of environment really does not work very well. The mere names of many of the dimensions in Table 3 convey concepts that are not limited to the physical environment. A brief mention of three research accomplishments in environmental gerontology illustrates how socially oriented mosaics, in turn, often invoke the need for physical cognates.

Kahana (Kahana, 1982; Kahana, Liang, & Felton, 1980) has made major conceptual and empirical contributions to the literature on environment and aging. Although her approach is consistent with the Lawton and Nahemow (1973) position, she has detailed the concept of person–environment congruence as an independent variable in determining a variety of outcomes in the psychological realm. Following French, Rodgers, and Cobb (1974), Kahana and her collaborators chose dimensions that could be measured in both person and environment: segregation, congregation, institutional control, structure, stimulation, affect, and impulse control (see Table 4). These seven dimensions were construed on the person side as needs and operationalized as multi-item preference scales—that is, residents' preferences for environments in which the features facilitated the satisfaction of each need. In analogous fashion, environmental rating scales of the same dimensions were completed by staff members in a number of nursing homes. These scales characterized nursing home environments by the same dimensions. (Consensual, or mean, ratings by multiple staff members served as the environmental indicators.) With such an array of person–environment pairs, congruence was measured by standardized score formulas that could denote three types of congruence or incongruence: nondirectional incongruence (simple unsigned deviation, reflecting the hypothesis that any departure from exact balance would be associated with ill-being), positive incongruence (environmental oversupply), and negative incongruence (environmental undersupply). Nondirectional incongruence represents all situations except those in which the environment's ability to satisfy a need is about equal to the strength of that need. Incongruence is posited to erode well-being, whether the mechanism is too much or too little of the need-satisfying resource in the environment. For example, if the person's need for

TABLE 4
Dimensions of Person–Environment Congruence

Dimension	Description
Segregate	Homogeneity versus heterogeneity of residents, staff, and physical design; changeability versus sameness of activities, stimuli, and people; and continuity versus discontinuity with the past in activities, possessions, and social contacts.
Congregate	Private versus public quality of behavior, individual versus categorical treatment or application of rules, and individual versus group quality of activities.
Institutional control	Staff versus resident control over behavior, valuation of conformity versus individuality in institutional norms, and dependence versus independence.
Structure	Tolerance versus intolerance of ambiguity and order versus tolerance for disorder.
Stimulation	Simplicity versus complexity of sensory and social environment and encouragement of activity versus passivity.
Affect	Encouragement versus discouragement of affect expression and level of affective stimulation in institutional environment.
Impulse–control	Motor control versus discharge of tension, immediate versus delayed need gratification, and impulsiveness versus deliberation.

Note. From "A Congruence Model of Person Environment Interaction," by E. Kahana, 1982, in M. P. Lawton, P. G. Windley, and T. O. Byerts, *Aging and The Environment: Theoretical Approaches* (pp. 104–106), New York: Springer. Copyright 1982 by Springer Publishing. Adapted with permission.

order is either greater or lesser than that of the context, the result would be lower psychological well-being. An oversupply hypothesis would suggest that only an excess of the resource (e.g., too much noise) would lead to a poorer outcome, whereas too little would be neutral. An undersupply hypothesis would apply to other resources in which negative outcomes occur with deprivation (e.g., too little social support), but the relationship to well-being disappears above some threshold level. Kahana's (1982; Kahana et al., 1980) research demonstrated that congruence in congregation, impulse control, and segregation contributed to well-being over and above the separate measures of person and environment on these dimensions. It also showed a complex pattern of differential associations, depending on congruence type.

In Kahana's (1982) conceptualization of environment, however, the items defining environmental dimensions are primarily in the realm of what might be called "psychosocial milieu indicators" (e.g., care practices, organizational routines, staff characteristics, and collective behaviors of residents). A strength of this approach is that all facets of environment may be included in each dimension, resulting in true mosaic structures. A weakness is that research using these mosaic-level dimensions generates relatively little knowledge that is useful in designing the details of the physical environment.

The Multiphasic Environment Assessment Procedure (MEAP; Moos & Lemke, 1994, 1996) for residential environments for older adults measures separate dimensions of social climate, suprapersonal factors, policy and program, and physical–architectural factors, as depicted in Table 5. Moos began with a larger mosaic applicable to all user groups that defined context in terms of three metadimensions referred to as relationship, personal growth, and system maintenance and change. The measured dimensions of the MEAP flowed from the metadimensions but are not exactly aligned with them. The Physical and Architectural Features Checklist and the Policy and Program Information Form data are obtained from direct observation, interview, or both, with a key informant. The Resident and Staff Information Form (representing the suprapersonal environment, as shown in Table 1 and discussed later) is obtained primarily from archival or specially generated aggregate data. The Sheltered Care Environment Scale scores (social climate factors) are the means (with the intention of representing relative consensus) of multiple staff or resident ratings.

The MEAP (Moos & Lemke, 1984, 1994, 1996) metadimensions are descriptive rather than evaluative. Working from all MEAP indicators, Lemke and Moos (1986) abstracted a different set of dimensions from those shown in Table 5 that were hypothesized to represent four types of broad environmental goals: resources, autonomy, privacy/identity, and psychosocial relationship quality. From these general goals, researcher judges sorted 33 individual MEAP indexes into quality indicators, which were comfort, security, staff richness, services, autonomy, control, and rapport (plus the single item, staff:resident ratio). Significant and varied patterns

TABLE 5
Dimensions of the Multiphasic Environmental Assessment Procedure

Physical and architectural features	Policy and program features	Suprapersonal factors	Social climate factors
Physical amenities	Selectivity	Residents' social resources	Cohesion
Social–recreational aids	Expectations for functioning	Resident heterogeneity	Conflict
Prosthetic aids	Tolerance for deviance	Resident functional abilities	Independence
Orientational aids	Policy clarity	Resident activity level	Self-exploration
Safety features	Policy choice	Resident community integration	Organization
Architectural choice	Resident control	Staff richness	Resident influence
Space availability	Provisions for privacy		Physical comfort
Staff facilities	Availability of health services	Utilization of health services	
Community accessibility	Availability of daily living assistance	Utilization of daily living assistance	
	Availability of social–recreational activities	Utilization of social–recreational activities	

Note. From "Supportive Residential Settings for Older People," by R. H. Moos and S. Lemke, 1984, in I. Altman, J. Wohlwill, and M. P. Lawton, *Human Behavior and the Environment: The Elderly and the Physical Environment* (p. 167), New York: Plenum Press. Copyright 1984 by Plenum Press. Reprinted with permission.

of relationships between these indicators of quality and residential type, ownership, and size were reported.

The MEAP (Moos & Lemke, 1994, 1996) is the most complete existing battery for assessing the range of environments for older adults that includes nursing homes, assisted living, board and care, and congregate housing. It should be noted, however, that the MEAP is not suited for unplanned community housing or for planned housing for older adults that serves independent older people.

Lieberman and Tobin (1983) generated a set of quality-relevant psychosocial context descriptors (progenitors of Marlowe's [1973] list as shown in Table 3) to describe a broad range of residential environments of older adults, ranging from mental hospital ward to private residence: achievement fostering, individuation, dependency fostering, warmth, affiliation fostering, recognition, stimulation, physical attractiveness, cue richness, and tolerance for deviancy. These dimensions, rated by an expert observer, were used to predict outcomes for both an institutional relocation study and a mental hospital shutdown study. The quality of the relocation environment was often a more potent determinant of outcome than were either personal variables or psychopathology indicators. Like Kahana's (1982; Kahana et al., 1980) measures, the items defining these environmental dimensions mix many different types of attributes, including social, physical, and program characteristics.

The research of Kahana (1982; Kahana et al., 1980), Moos and Lemke (1994; 1996), and Lieberman and Tobin (1983), exemplifying the mosaic and the top-down approach, comes closest to dealing with the global concept of milieu of any environmental research in gerontology. *Ambience* is another global term for environmental quality, which is suggested to characterize (a) an entire complex environment (such as housing, institution, or school) in relatively abstract terms with (b) a strong affective component. These terms are discussed again following the discussion of a possible environmental taxonomy.

In summary, with the exception of Carp and Carp's (1984) research, the linking of physical and nonphysical environmental factors in defining the mosaic has been unsystematic. Further research that attempts to derive parallel dimensions for person and environment in the Kahana (1982; Kahana et al., 1980) style or in carefully chosen need-press pairs as Carp and Carp (1984) began to do is recommended.

ENVIRONMENTAL TAXONOMY: A SUGGESTED BEGINNING

I originally suggested that there are five broad classes of environment (see Table 1): the physical environment, the personal environment, the small-group environment, the suprapersonal environment, and the social environment (Lawton, 1970, 1982). A second orthogonal dimension is the objective versus subjective dimension. These two dimensions are illustrated in Table 1. A third dimension, environmental attributes, consists of descriptors by which the cells formed by the classes and the objective–subjective dimensions may be characterized. The discussion that follows elaborates on the five broad classes and illustrates how gerontological research has utilized each class in objective and subjective terms. A discussion of how environmental attributes complete the prototaxonomy then follows.

The Physical Environment

The objective physical environment is all that lies outside the skin of the participant, is inanimate, and may be specified by counting or by measuring in centimeters, grams, or seconds. Theoretically, everything in this class is observable and potentially capable of exact measurement. In the subjective physical environmental realm, an element of the objective physical environment is transformed cognitively or affectively by the participant, endowed with personal meaning or functional significance for the individual. Although common cultural definitions may move some such subjective assessments toward consensus, a person's view of the physical environment by definition remains unique and unknowable from the outside.

There are many examples in the gerontology literature demonstrating the ability of purely physically defined environmental features to account for outcomes in the psychological domain. For example, with personal characteristics controlled, older adults who lived in higher buildings (Lawton et al., 1975) or who lived on higher floors (Nahemow et al., 1977) were less satisfied with their housing and less frequently left the building. In another survey, a number of physical characteristics of subsidized dwelling units designed for older adults were assessed. Among the relationships confirmed, housing satisfaction was greater for those with larger kitchens, more kitchen counter space, and heating that could be controlled by the apartment occupant (Lawton & Nahemow, 1979b). As described earlier, a number of presumably desirable physically defined attributes of neighborhoods were measured by Carp and Carp (1982a) and were found to make substantial contributions to neighborhood satisfaction, psychological well-being, and a variety of subjective neighborhood characteristics such as noise, air quality, neighborhood safety, and municipal maintenance quality.

Among the contributors to this volume, a clear place for physical environment is noted by a majority, although only a few attempt to specify the physical environment conceptually (see Wachs, 1989). Nonetheless, the major emphasis of the sum of the contributions is on the nonphysical environment.

The Personal Environment

The personal environment represents the significant other. To characterize the important dyadic relationships of a person as a part of the environment simply makes explicit what is assumed in most discussions of interpersonal relationships: Important people such as parents, love objects, friends, enemies, coworkers, and so on may be construed in terms of both their objective qualities and their subjective qualities. The measured statuses, personality, behavior, or other attributes of another person who has a one-on-one relationship with the participant may be seen as an element of the participant's objective personal environment. How the participant characterizes, evaluates, or feels about the significant other constitutes the subjective personal environment. The objective and subjective personal environment make up a major portion of all that has been traditionally thought to represent the important influences on personal development, as well as of the environment construed by many authors in this volume (see later discussion in this chapter).

As operationalized in gerontological research, the objective personal environment is easily represented by marital status; presence, frequency of contact with, and geographical proximity of family members; household structure; and characteristics of these individuals whose relationship to the participant is definable by observable criteria. The social network typically describes such attributes (Rook, 1994). Assistance with everyday tasks is a salient feature for many older adults in poor health. Such measures inquire about help actually received in a specified window of time. For example, the Arizona Social Support Inventory Schedule (Barrera, 1986) asks about six types of assistance, such as material aid or physical assistance. For older adults in nursing homes, interactions with nursing staff may well represent their most important person-to-person contact. A stream of research by Baltes (Baltes, Neumann, & Zanks, 1994; Baltes & Zerbe, 1976) has demonstrated how dependent behavior is regularly reinforced by nursing staff, whereas independent behavior is ignored. For these people, the reward–contingency patterns of nursing home staff thus are a highly influential aspect of the personal environment.

Many important instances of the personal environment are difficult to define objectively, however. Such designations as friend, confidant, potential helper, or perhaps even a love object are intrinsically defined by the subjective evaluation of the perceiver. The greatest portion of the personal environment research in gerontology thus concerns the subjective personal environment. A classic and frequently replicated finding concerns the stress-buffering effect exerted by possessing a confidant (Lowenthal &

Haven, 1968). The participant must provide the information that there is a confidant, which is a subjective judgment. A frequently used approach to identifying people who belong in this personal environment category is the "bullseye" technique, in which concentric circles are used to place people judged to be successively more distant from the participant in the center (Kahn & Antonucci, 1980). Closeness is the subjective construct used by Kahn and Antonucci. Once identified, the attributes of the named individuals may then be used to specify further the characteristics of the personal environment. Because they are screened by the initial subjective characterization in terms of closeness, however, these aspects remain in the subjective personal environmental realm.

In my own terms, virtually every author in this book placed the individuals of the personal environment in the primary position among environmental objects. Parents, teachers, child-care workers, supervisors, spouses, and friends are the usual members whose effects on the participant are studied. Such individuals' demographic characteristics, personality, behavior, values, affects, social roles, and interactions with the participant are among the specific facets of the personal environment discussed by one or more authors. Because the actions of people in the personal environment are conducted in close proximity and in time-extended manner, to the subject, Bronfenbrenner (see chapter 1, this volume) refers to this type of personal influence as *proximal process*. He suggests that this type of external influence is stronger than are more *distal* influences such as environmental context. (The proximal–distal distinction is discussed at greater length later.)

The Small-Group Environment

The small-group environment is defined by groups of people (minimum size 3, up to 12 or 15) who fulfill two criteria: Each individual has some one-on-one interaction with the participant and, in addition, has such person-to-person relationships with at least half of the others in the small group. Such small groups may be defined by kinship, friendship choice, or proximity, as in work or residential groups. The objective–subjective distinction is less clear than in the case of the physical or personal environment because some subjective judgment (e.g., a sociometric survey or personally selected interactive behavior) is often necessary to define the group. Some small groups may be defined objectively, as in the case of the residents of a small housing facility, a small club, or a work unit. Nevertheless, once defined, the characteristics of the small group may be defined independently of the subject (number, relationship to subject, multiplexity, shared interests or values, etc.) or characterized subjectively (e.g., ratings made by the subject of "my closest friends," the estimated attitudes of a work group, or the closeness one feels toward other residents in one's building).

The small-group environment is also likely to figure in most authors' conceptions of environment, for example, as a peer group, or "friendship clique," in Brown's terms (see chapter 3, this volume). Household members may be viewed as small groups in addition to their personal environmental function with respect to the participant.

The Suprapersonal Environment

Lawton (1970) defined the suprapersonal environment as the modal characteristics of the other people in close proximity to the participant. Although some may be known personally by the participant, this is not a necessary condition, and the majority often have no one-on-one relationship with the participant. The behavior-activating aspect of the suprapersonal environment is likely to result from the participant's comparison (not necessarily a conscious comparison) of one's own status to that of the aggregate of others within one's own visual environment—the age, sex, race, or apparent health of others. In the subjective realm, judgments are often made of attributes such as the attractiveness, political ideology, manners, or other subjectively evaluated characteristics of the people in one's proximal environment.

The prototype of the objective suprapersonal environment are the social-area characteristics of one's residence, often based on block (Rosenberg, 1970), enumeration-district (Lawton, Nahemow, & Yeh, 1980), or census-tract aggregate measures such as population, age mix, family income, racial mix, and any other features ascertainable from the decennial census or other aggregate data. Although such gross indicators are often proxy measures for other attributes (for example, crime rate and housing-deficiency rate are probably consequences of income), they represent visible features to which the person is exposed regularly, as well as features that have some probabilistic likelihood of being behavior or cognition activating to some residents of the area. On a smaller level, a higher age mix within an apartment building has been shown repeatedly to be associated with higher levels of social interaction and sometimes psychological well-being (Rosow, 1967; Teaff, Lawton, Nahemow, & Carlson, 1978). The extent to which visibly disabled or physically ill people are present in planned housing is associated with objective behaviors. For example, poor health of older residents in a facility may discourage potential applicants from seeking admission to the housing (Lawton, Greenbaum, & Liebowitz, 1980); the social and psychological well-being of tenants in the housing was shown to vary between housing designed for the semiindependent versus fully independent older adults (Lawton, 1976).

The subjective aspects of the suprapersonal environment have been infrequently considered. One example was seen when older adults in a large national survey were asked to estimate the age density of their local neighborhoods; analysis of these results showed the same favorable association between high age density and social–psychological outcomes that was demonstrated when using census data (Lawton, Moss, & Moles, 1984).

In this volume, a concept analogous to the suprapersonal environment is Brown's (see chapter 3, this volume) concept of "the crowd" and its subjective dynamic component, "reputation." Bronfenbrenner (chapter 1, this volume) develops this theme in depth in terms of the nested social–environmental features, whereby the ethos of the parents of the crowd (roughly equivalent to a neighborhood suprapersonal characteristic) constitutes a significant influence on the participant. The class (see Talbert & McLaughlin, chapter 7, this volume) and the work group (see Schooler, chapter 8, this volume) may, depending on their size and the density of one-on-one relationships, be considered either small-group or suprapersonal environments.

Bronfenbrenner (1986) used the term *megasystem* to refer to structural aspects of society and culture that have a behavior-activating effect on the individual, independent of the particular individuals who represent the structure. Social norms, cultural values, social statuses, organizational structures, rules, practices, laws, and other social institutions are examples of what Lawton (1970) originally termed the *social environment*. At this point, because *social* has been used so frequently to refer to relationships at the personal and small-group level, the term *megasocial* seems more desirable and is used hereafter. To give a single term to this immense class of influences surely represents the limited knowledge of a psychologist when attempting to conceive of a large domain in which the internal structure is not part of his or her expertise. Assignment of such a broad range of phenomena to a single class is not intended in any way to diminish their significance. The interest in this chapter is simply to make certain that these phenomena are included as *environmental* classes.

It seems pointless to cite typical research findings documenting the importance of the megasocial environment to older people. Suffice it simply to mention the large amounts of research devoted to topics such as age prejudice (ageism; Butler, 1969), which has been measured by surveying the age attitudes of a population sample (National Council on the Aging, 1975). A large body of research has been devoted to income supports, the health system, and the structures that define entitlements and service provisions (Minkler & Estes, 1991) and the national and cultural norms that determine the propensity of older adults to live alone or with adult children (Lawton, 1992). Yet another example is research on the covert social norms that determine the positioning of older people versus younger people in informal conversational situations (Ryan, Giles, Bartolucci, & Henwood, 1986).

The distinction between objective and subjective aspects of the megasocial environment is often tenuous. Even when there are regulations, laws, or practices, judgments are often required to translate these indicators into variables of use in quantitative research. On the other hand, "perceptions" of megasocial phenomena are often used in research (e.g., personal satisfaction with services or social systems).

Just as prevalent as the personal environment in other author's presentations are many features of the macrosocial environment. Bronfenbrenner's nested systems (see chapter 1, this volume) and Talbert and McLaughlin's (see chapter 7, this volume) embedded systems model illustrate the hierarchical nature of the macrosocial environment. Examples of macrosocial environmental objects discussed in this volume include social status, job routinization and bureaucratization (see Schooler, chapter 8, this volume), child-care regulations and subsidies, school goals, school district, and state and federal educational systems (see Talbert & McLaughlin, chapter 7, this volume).

The distinction between objective and subjective environment appears accepted by all chapter authors in this volume who mention this duality. Even those authors who do not identify this duality explicitly still utilize constructs easily assigned to the objective or subjective realm.

ENVIRONMENTAL ATTRIBUTES

Unlike the five classes and the objective–subjective dimensions into which all environments may be classed, attributes consist of features that may describe some environments and not others. Their number is large and open ended. Combination of the fine classes, the objective and subjective perspective, and the attributes affords the opportunity to characterize environments in their great diversity while still providing a uniform structure into which other investigators may locate the specific environments of concern in their research.

Environmental attributes are seen as descriptive and evaluative. (See Table 6.) *Descriptive attributes* are construed as quantitative, structural, and contextual. Descriptive attributes are those with presumed effects on behavioral outcome but that are not necessarily associated with obvious positive or negative outcomes. *Evaluative attributes*, defined by individual judgment, empirical evidence, or consensus, connote behavioral or affective outcomes that fall on a good-to-bad continuum. Table 6 depicts the organization of the attributes as rows and the five classes in objective and subjective terms as columns. Choice of the attributes to be suggested here derives from the substantial literature in environment and behavior of the past 35 years.

TABLE 6
Three Dimensions of Environment: Classes, Objective Versus Subjective, and Attributes

Attribute	Physical Environment		Personal Environment		Small Group Environment		Suprapersonal Environment		Macrosocial Environment	
	Obj.	Subj.	Obj.	Subj.	Obj.	Subj.	Obj.	Subj.	Obj.	Subj.
Descriptive										
Quantitative										
Scale										
Intensity										
Temporal quality										
Structural										
Proximal vs. distal										
Predictability										
Diversity										
Complexity										
Patterned vs. random										
Contextual										
Interactive quality										
Responsiveness										
Activity vs. passivity										
Novelty vs. familiarity										
Evaluative										
Satisfaction										
Preference										
Affective quality										
General quality										

Note. Obj. = objective; Subj. = subjective.

Descriptive Attributes: Quantitative

The quantitative attributes describe the "how much" of the environmental characteristic. *Environmental scale* is one of the most frequently used attributes. One frequently cited use of scale is the residential continuum that ranges from personal space to room to dwelling to block to neighborhood, and so on. Scale is mentioned or implied by many authors; an example from the educational system is described in the continuum of student, class, school system, community, national educational environment, and total social environment (see Talbert & McLaughlin, chapter 7, this volume). *Intensity* of stimulation is a familiar concept in psychophysics (Brunswick, 1952), no less than in personality research (Murray's [1938], concept of press strength), environmental psychology (see Evans, chapter 9, this volume or Glass and Singer's [1972], classic study of noise), and developmental environmental psychology (Wachs, 1989). Bronfenbrenner's (see chapter 1, this volume) hypothesis regarding the strength of proximal process effects speaks to intensity as one of the attributes involved in this effect. Duration and frequency are facets of *temporal quality*. All of the quantitative attributes have the ability to be measured either in physical units or by subjective judgments. Extension in time is the cornerstone of Bronfenbrenner's proximal process hypothesis, and temporality figures prominently in the discussions of the authors of most of the other chapters.

Structural Attributes

Attributes referred to as structural provide behaviorally relevant information to the participant, particularly in terms that relate the disparate aspects of the environment to one another and thereby convey meaning. The proximal versus distal distinction is less a unit of physical distance than one that refers to the psychological separation of the environment from the person. In Brunswik's (1952) view, the distal environment was the object itself, whereas the proximal environment consisted of the light rays or other physical energy impinging on the sensory end organs. Bronfenbrenner's (chapter 1, this volume) use is less restrictive, viewing this attribute as one that distinguishes figure from ground in that the proximal, one-on-one effects of people in the personal environment represent the focal influence on the child. Wachs's (1989) distinctions between the focal versus background represents one of his major physical–environmental classifications. Environmental stability, or *predictability*, is an important attribute. Dohrenwend and Dohrenwend (1974), for example, found that life events that were unpredictable were more stressful than those that might be predicted. A similar view of the developmental course saw even such a traumatic event as widowhood being less disruptive when it occurred "on time," that is, during later life (Neugarten, 1973). Predictability and lack of stability are noted in a number of the chapters in this volume. *Diversity* is the range of different objects of the environment. In a rough way, a residence in the community is more diverse than that of a nursing home. Schooler's (see chapter 8, this volume) characterization of routinization in work acknowledges the absence of diversity, whereas Talbert and McLaughlin (see chapter 7, this volume) note diversity in the social background of students and others note diversity in the home environment as major attributes. *Complexity* is related to diversity, but internal cognitive structure as well enters into the definition of complexity. In printed medication instructions for very frail older adults, for example, conditional clauses and number of enumerated instances both add to complexity in undesirable ways. Complexity is thought to have a curvilinear relationship to outcome, so that moderate levels have more favorable outcomes than either very low- or very high-complexity environments (Wohlwill, 1968). Schooler's (chapter 8, this volume) research demonstrates many favorable associations with work complexity, and he extends these findings to home activities and leisure. Another classic attribute is the *patterned* versus *random* quality of the environment. Such a continuum in a nursing home setting might run from total quiet except for one resident's moaning, to a focused music therapy session, to the cacophony of multiple television sounds with staff and residents calling loudly. Amount of structure appears to be another term for patterning. This attribute is seen as an important descriptor by other authors: Talbert and McLaughlin (see chapter 7, this volume) note coherence in schools, Bradley (chapter 2, this volume) notes it in the home, and Wachs (chapter 12, this volume) notes it in parenting.

Contextual Attributes

This group of attributes specifies the relationships between the participant and the environment. Contextual attributes are thus the essence of transactionalism, the proof that the participant and environment really are, at some levels, indivisible. *Interactive quality* is the core contextual attribute, one in which the participant's and the environment's interactions are reciprocal, and "the environment" could rarely be specified in the absence of the interchange with the participant. An example is a friend; the body of the other exists independently of the participant, but being a friend demands bidirectional exchanges. Reciprocity (Wachs, 1989) has been shown to be an important feature of the child-care environment. *Environmental responsiveness* is also an interactive phenomenon, but one in which the emphasis is placed on how much the environment "gives." Wachs (1989) defined responsiveness as "feedback to the child which is contingent on the child's action" (p. 405). The environment is made more responsive to a blind person by the use of a cane for wayfinding. Responsiveness, or flexibility, is noted by many of this volume's authors as a desirable characteristic of people in the personal environment and the physical environment. A person–environment interaction may also be described in terms of the degree of *activity* versus *passivity* of the participant in relation to the environment. For example, a home may be given to, selected by, or uniquely created and shaped by the occupant. As an environmental descriptor, this attribute would refer to the extent to which the environment inserts barriers to the behavior, decisions, or general proactivity of the person. The Dutch study cited by Bronfenbrenner (Riksen-Walraven, 1978; see chapter 1, this volume) uses such an example, when the mother's input to the child (personal environment) was manipulated to be opportunity providing (enhancement of proactivity) as contrasted with stimulation producing (environmental docility). *Novelty* versus *familiarity* is interactive because this attribute is definable only in terms of the user's experience, or, perhaps, the collective experience of groups of people. Novelty in the environment is related to the activity–passivity attribute because novelty does provide opportunities for interaction and enrichment. Poverty reduces such opportunities, whereas it increases other types of novelty such as exposure to crime or substance abuse.

Evaluative Attributes

The second group of attributes is relatively easy to define and operationalize because the criterion of desirability is either expressed overtly by the user or judged consensually through social norms and cultural values. One of the most ubiquitous attributes reported in environmental research is *environmental satisfaction*. Judgments of liking, degree of need satisfaction, or closeness to the ideal are often the basis for arraying a group of environmental objects. Related to satisfaction but implying a wishful stance is *environmental preference*, the judgment that something is enjoyed or prized, whether or not present. An environmentally oriented survey of potential users of a planned retirement housing reported by Regnier (1987) succeeded in ranking 36 amenities in order of preference. For example, an infirmary, a pharmacy, and security were among the top 10, whereas adult education, maid service, and swimming pool were among the 10 least desired. Environments are known to elicit emotion; this process is implied in the attribute of *affective quality*. Russell and Lanius (1984), in fact, found that participants had no difficulty rating a series of environments in terms of an affect checklist; the results, in fact, reproduced exactly the two-factor circumplex structure of affect that is found in self-ratings of affect states.

By contrast with the descriptive attributes, the evaluative attributes were infrequently introduced by other authors. Although Vandell and Posner (see chapter 6, this volume) refer to the importance of children's feelings about after-school activities and experiences, for the most part authors are silent about measurement of these evaluative and affective aspects of environment. It is possible that children may be less able to evaluate in terms acceptable to researchers the cognitive and affective aspects of environment. Such a limitation does not explain the lack of attempt to assess the evaluative attributes by observation. Further research thus seems especially desirable in this realm.

Integrative Views of Environment

Both the search for the mosaic to describe an entire milieu and its ambience and the complex three-dimensional structure depicted in Table 6 are attempts to capture the complex, multilayered system of person–environment relations. The inadequacies of such endeavors are only too obvious. The cells of Table 6, even if all provided with excellent measuring instruments, would still not describe the system in any way that would represent the reality. Other elaborations are designed to improve the representation of the complexity, which bring together better the components of environmental milieu: the first in the concept of a *blend* across the environmental classes. The real environments studied by Kahana (1982; Kahana et al., 1980) consist, in fact, of all environmental classes: in her case, the *physical* furnishings of the nursing care unit, the *personal environment* of a roommate or nursing assistant, the *small-group environment* of residents who share a sitting room at the end of the corridor, the *suprapersonal* environment (the old and frail adults with visible signs of limitations such as unsteady gait, wheelchairs, and confusion), and the *megasocial environment* (social norms regarding the appropriateness of having a relative in a nursing home, the reimbursement mechanisms that dictate care practices). An example from an earlier developmental period is the concept of the "social address," a complex category that connotes many different aspects of child-care environments (see Vandell & Posner, chapter 6, this volume). In noting the need to disaggregate this category, Vandell and Posner call attention to the fact that the social address of after-school care is a blend with physical, personal, small-group, and probably megasocial environmental components.

A second integrative perspective deserves in-depth attention but can only be briefly mentioned here and that is the *linkages* across environmental classes. Linkages are mentioned explicitly by Bronfenbrenner (see chapter 1, this volume) in his invoking of the need to explain the mechanisms for influence of one system on another (the mesosystem and the exosystem). Culture is transmitted through social norms, institutions, organizations, and individuals at the personal–environmental level. Still needed is a way of incorporating the linkages between each of the several pairs of the environmental classes. Thus, there are several sources of the fuzzy set of status of environmental dimensions:

- Objective and subjective environment as a continuum, with very unclear or mixed areas of objective and subjective features.
- Blends of environmental classes almost always being necessary to describe real environments.
- Mechanisms of influences across environmental elements that are presently poorly conceptualized.
- Attributes that are many, often correlated with one another, and unequally represented across environmental classes.

Although there is no obvious way to resolve all such ambiguities, several suggestions may put environmental research ahead. First, the researcher would do well to organize research plans around the specification of the constructs and the measures in terms of the three major dimensions and their components. Second, there are conditions in which it is desirable to measure such dimensions separately and treat as an empirical question the extent to which they are correlated. Third, it is desirable to view the measurement of milieu as a profile of separately measured dimensions, in any combination of the classes. Finally, ambience is a holistic, subjective term for characterizing entire environments, a process about which too little is known. Ambience subsumes highly abstracted cognitive and affective schemata that do not lend themselves to decomposition in terms of discrete environmental dimensions. Yet, the relationships among dimensions, milieu, and ambience should be determined empirically.

AGE-NEUTRAL AND AGE-SPECIFIC ENVIRONMENTAL ASSESSMENT

As the technology of psychological assessment of the person has developed, it has become clear that different tests were appropriate for neonates, infants, children, and adolescents. Although the necessity for age-specific tests for adults and those in the oldest stages of life is not established, the norm is to strive to produce age-specific tests. Despite this trend in the content of tests, there is surprisingly good consensus on the dimensions that such tests should assess: intelligence, motor skill, sensory and perceptual functions, work performance, social behavior, attitudes, emotion, and psychopathology. Although the list of dimensions for assessment is long, the notable fact is that the dimensions themselves are generic (i.e., age neutral). In contrast to the age neutrality of the dimensions, there are two main reasons for the content of tests being age specific. First, there is such a phenomenon as cognitive and personality development, which requires that the range over which a test can discriminate among individuals be appropriate to the modal phase of development of the group to be tested. Floor and ceiling effects make differentiation impossible if content is not matched to the group being assessed. Second, cohort-specific content is required if within-group discrimination is to be maximized. For example, in a study of memory for figures, Howell (1972) found that the old-age deficit diminished greatly when the stimuli were objects from a 1910 Sears Roebuck catalog rather than abstract geometric figures,

Does the generic quality of the dimension, coupled with the age-specific content of individual tests, convey any useful analogy for assessment of the environment? In many ways, the research directions pursued by Moos (1974, 1975, 1978; Finney & Moos, 1984; Moos & Lemke, 1994) exhibit a similar pattern. The common thread among most of Moos's environmental assessment schemes is the use of the same three dimensions —relationship, personal growth, and system maintenance and change—as the armature, whether the focus is the mental hospital (Moos, 1974), schools (Moos, 1978), community agencies (Moos, 1975), programs for alcoholic participants (Finney & Moos, 1984), or residences for older adults (Moos & Lemke, 1994). In the larger body of research, however, one looks in vain for consistency across reported research findings in using these three, or any other, environmental dimensions. Therefore, the search for a common dimensionality would seem to be an appropriate starting point. Can researchers identify environmental dimensions that are conceptually relevant to any human-action setting, dimensions that point to a more efficient search for measurement content? Returning to the example of psychometric study of individual differences, the structural features of the person that are the focus of psychological assessment do not derive from any formally articulated taxonomy of individuals. Rather, they represent the prototypes of how individuals vary, as developed from the common language of psychology and other disciplines. The common language of person–environment relations has not yet produced any such set of consensual dimensions. A workable taxonomy should make the task of deciding what in the environment to assess much easier and, in turn, may lead to instruments in which the content may be tailored to the specific user group or setting of interest.

It is clear that there are arguments for user-group-specific assessments and universal assessment schemes. One possible solution is to develop a core set of assessments that applies to all users. Specific user-group modules would then serve users' unique needs but would be structured around universal dimensions, but not universal content.

The structure of a taxonomy would almost by definition be age neutral. Like the dimensions that describe individual psychological differences, however, appropriate measurement would have to define a range of variation across which the attribute would be expected to vary for the targeted participant. Some attributes would be invariant across users, especially objective physical environmental characteristics (e.g., single- versus multiple-occupancy housing). Other attributes would utilize quite different ranges of an attribute for different user groups, for example, the complexity of signage to be used in a museum as compared with the signage in a nursing home unit for residents with Alzheimer's disease. The nature of measurement would clearly have to vary also with the environmental attribute being assessed. For example, environmental responsiveness may be a dimension applicable to all users, but its manifestations would be quite different for different user groups. One manifestation might be the extent to which a working toy lends itself to use by a 2-year-old; another is the responsiveness of nursing staff in adjusting the reinforcements they administer for dependent and independent behavior. Despite such broad subject and context variations, the appearance of responsiveness in a prototaxonomy of environmental dimensions in itself will lead investigators to think about its relevance to highly specific person–environment transactions and to devise assessment forms that tap the phenomenon.

CONCLUSION

Some approaches to research with older people in their typical environmental contexts have been reviewed in a way that highlights issues of measurement. Measurement in environmental gerontology had demonstrated the need for both bottom-up and top-down approaches. The complementary truths that derive from the two approaches illustrate the mutual advantage to both theory and practice that would be gained by developing an environmental taxonomy. The physical environment, the personal environment, the small-group environment, the suprapersonal environment, and the megasocial environment are classes of relevance to every person. Each of these classes may be viewed and measured objectively and subjectively. A third class of environmental attributes is suggested. The taxonomy would lead directly to assessment: The elements and attributes of the taxonomy each imply a family of possible objects to be assessed and dimensions along which they might be assessed. The taxonomy should be generic, not tied to any particular user group or environmental context. Such person- and context-specific considerations would be reflected in the content of the assessment.

REFERENCES

American Association of Retired Persons. (1985). *The do-able renewable home.* Washington, DC: Author.

Baltes, M. M., Neumann, E.-M., & Zanks, S. (1994). Maintenance and rehabilitation of independence in old age: An intervention program for staff. *Psychology and Aging*, 9, 179–188.

Baltes, M. M., & Zerbe, M. B. (1976). Independence training in nursing home residents. *The Gerontologist*, 16, 428–432.

Baltes, P. B., & Baltes, M. (Ed.). (1986). *The psychology of control and aging*. Hillsdale, NJ: Erlbaum.

Barker, R. G. (Ed.). (1963). *The stream of behavior*. New York: Appleton-Century-Crofts.

Barker, R. G. (1968). *Ecological psychology*. Stanford, CA: Stanford University Press.

Barrera, M. (1986). Distinctions between social support concepts, measures, and models. *American Journal of Community Psychology*, *14*, 413–446.

Bronfenbrenner, U. (1986). Ecology of the family as a context for human development. *Developmental Psychology*, 22, 723–742.

Brunswik, E. (1952). *The conceptual framework of psychology*. Chicago: University of Chicago Press.

Butler, R. N. (1969). Age-ism: Another form of bigotry. *Gerontologist*, 9, 243–246.

Calkins, M. (1988). *Design for dementia*. Owings Mills, MD: National Health.

Canada Mortgage and Housing Corporation. (1989). *Maintaining seniors' independence: A guide to home adaptations*. Montreal, Quebec, Canada: Author.

Carp, F. M. (1994). Assessing the environment. In M. P. Lawton & J. S. Teresi (Eds.), *Annual review of gerontology and geriatrics* (Vol. 14, pp. 302–323). New York: Springer.

Carp, F. M. & Carp, A. (1982a). A role for technical assessment in perceptions of environmental quality of well-being. *Journal of Environmental Psychology*, 2, 171–191.

Carp, F., & Carp, A. (1982b). Perceived environmental quality of neighborhoods. *Journal of Environmental Psychology*, 2, 4–22.

Carp, F., & Carp, A. (1984). A complementary congruence model of well-being on mental health for the community elderly. In I. Altman, M. P. Lawton, & J. F. Wohlwill (Eds.), *Elderly people and their environment* (pp. 279–336). New York: Plenum Press.

Carp, F. M., & Christensen, D. L. (1986a). Technical environmental assessment predictors of residential satisfaction. *Research on Aging*, 8, 269–286.

Carp, F. M., & Christensen, D. L. (1986b). Older women living along: Technical environmental assessment of psychological well-being. *Research on Aging*, 8, 407–425.

Christensen, D., & Carp, F. M. (1983, November). *Objective measures of residential quality for community living elderly*. Paper presented at the annual meeting of the Gerontological Society of America, San Francisco.

Christensen, D. L., Carp, F. M., Cranz, G. L., & Wiley, J. A. (1992). Objective housing indicators as predictors of the subjective evaluation of elderly residents. *Journal of Environmental Psychology, 12,* 225–236.

Dohrenwend, B. S., & Dohrenwend, B. P. (1974). *Stressful life events: Their nature and effects.* New York: Wiley.

Finney, J. W., & Moos, R. H. (1984). Environmental assessment and evaluation research: Examples from mental health and substance abuse programs. *Evaluation and Program Planning, 7,* 151–167.

French, J. P. R., Rodgers, W., & Cobb, S. (1974). Adjustment as person–environment fit. In G. V. Coelho, D. A. Hamburg, & J. E. Adams (Eds.), *Coping and adaptation* (pp. 316–333). New York: Basic Books.

Glass, D. C., & Singer, J. E. (1972). *Urban stress: Experiments in noise.* New York: Academic Press.

Helson, H. (1964). *Adaptation-level theory.* New York: Harper & Row.

Hiatt, L. G. (1991). *Nursing home renovation designed for reform.* Boston: Butterworth Architecture.

Howell, S. C. (1972). Familiarity and complexity in perceptual recognition. *Journal of Gerontology, 27,* 364–371.

Ittelson, W. H. (1973). Environmental perception and contemporary perceptual theory. In W. H. Ittelson (Ed.), *Environment and cognition* (pp. 51–59). New York: Seminar Press.

Kahana, E. (1982). A congruence model of person environment interaction. In M. P. Lawton, P. G. Windley, & T. O. Byerts (Eds.), *Aging and the environment: Theoretical approaches* (pp. 97–121). New York: Springer.

Kahana, E., Liang, J., & Felton, B. J. (1980). Alternative models of person–environment fit: Prediction of morale in three homes for the aged. *Journal of Gerontology, 35,* 584–595.

Kahn, R. L., & Antonucci, T. C. (1980). Convoys over the life course. In P. B. Baltes & O. Brim (Eds.), *Life span development and behavior* (Vol. 3, pp. 254–286). New York: Academic Press.

Koncelik, J. (1976). *Designing the open nursing home.* Stroudsburg, PA: Dowden, Hutchinson & Ross.

Lawton, M. P. (1970). Ecology and aging. In L. A. Pastalan & D. H. Carson (Eds.), *Spatial behavior of older people* (pp. 40–67). Ann Arbor: University of Michigan, Institute of Gerontology.

Lawton, M. P. (1976). The relative impact of congregate and traditional housing on elderly tenants. *Gerontologist, 16,* 237–242.

Lawton, M. P. (1980). Residential quality and residential satisfaction among the elderly. *Research on Aging, 2,* 309–328.

Lawton, M. P. (1981). An ecological view of living arrangements. *The Gerontologist, 21,* 59–66.

Lawton, M. P. (1982). Competence, environmental press, and the adaptation of older people. In M. P. Lawton, P. G. Windley, & T. O. Byerts (Eds.), *Aging and the environment: Theoretical approaches* (pp. 33–59). New York: Springer.

Lawton, M. P. (1983). Environment and other determinants of well-being in older people. *The Gerontologist, 23*, 349–357.

Lawton, M. P. (1985). The elderly in context: Perspectives from environmental psychology and gerontology. *Environment and Behavior, 17*, 501–519.

Lawton, M. P. (1987). Methods in environmental research with older people. In R. Bechtel, R. Marans, & W. Michelson (Eds.), *Behavioral research methods in environmental design* (pp. 337–360). New York: Van Nostrand Reinhold.

Lawton, M. P. (1992). Generational interdependence: Living arrangements and housing programmes. *South African Journal of Gerontology, 1*, 1–4.

Lawton, M. P., & Bader, J. (1970). Wish for privacy among young and old. *Journal of Gerontology, 25*, 48–54.

Lawton, M. P., Greenbaum, M., & Liebowitz, B. (1980). The lifespan of housing environments for the aging. *The Gerontologist, 20*, 56–64.

Lawton, M. P., Moss, M. S., & Moles, E. (1984). The suprapersonal neighborhood context of older people. *Environment and Behavior, 16*, 84–109.

Lawton, M. P., & Nahemow, L. (1973). Ecology and the aging process. In C. Eisdorfer & M. P. Lawton (Eds.), *Psychology of adult development and aging* (pp. 619–674). Washington, DC: American Psychological Association.

Lawton, M. P., & Nahemow, L. (1979a). Social areas and the well-being of tenants in planned housing for the elderly. *Multivariate Behavioral Research, 14*, 463–484.

Lawton, M. P., & Nahemow, L. (1979b). Social science methods for evaluating the quality of housing for the elderly. *Journal of Architectural Research, 7*, 5–11.

Lawton, M. P., Nahemow, L., & Teaff, J. (1975). Housing characteristics and the well-being of elderly tenants in federally-assisted housing. *Journal of Gerontology, 30*, 601–607.

Lawton, M. P., Nahemow, L., & Yeh, T.-M. (1980). Neighborhood environment and the well being of older tenants in planned housing. *International Journal of Aging and Human Development, 11*, 211–227.

Lawton, M. P., & Simon, B. (1968). The ecology of social relationships in housing for the elderly. *The Gerontologist, 8*, 108–115.

Lemke, S., & Moos, R. H. (1986). Quality of residential settings for elderly adults. *Journal of Gerontology, 41*, 268–276.

Lewin, K. (1935). *Dynamics theory of personality*. New York: McGraw-Hill.

Lieberman, M. A., & Tobin, S. S. (1983). *The experience of old age*. New York: Basic Books.

Lowenthal, M. F., & Haven, C. (1968). Interaction and isolation: Intimacy as a critical variable. *American Sociological Review, 33*, 20–30.

Marlowe, R. A. (1973, May). *Effects of environment on elderly state hospital relocates.*

Paper presented at annual meetings of the Pacific Sociological Association, Scottsdale, AZ.

Minkler, M., & Estes, C. L. (Ed.). (1991). *Critical perspectives on aging*. Amityville, NY: Baywood Publishing Co.

Moos, R. H. (1974). *Evaluating treatment environments: A social ecological approach*. New York: Wiley.

Moos, R. (1975). *Evaluating correctional and community settings*. New York: Wiley-Interscience.

Moos, R. H. (1978). *Evaluating educational environments*. San Francisco: Jossey-Bass.

Moos, R. H., & Lemke, S. (1984). Supportive residential settings for older people. In I. Altman, J. Wohlwill, & M. P. Lawton (Eds.), *Human behavior and the environment: The elderly and the physical environment* (pp. 159–190). New York: Plenum Press.

Moos, R. H., & Lemke, S. (1994). *Group residences for older adults*. New York: Oxford University Press.

Moos, R. H., & Lemke, S. (1996). *Evaluating residential facilities: The Multiphasic environmental assessment procedures*. Thousand Oaks, CA: Sage.

Murray, H. A. (1938). *Explorations in personality*. New York: Oxford University Press.

Nahemow, L., Lawton, M. P., & Howell, S. C. (1977). Elderly people in tall buildings: A nationwide study. In D. J. Conway (Ed.), *Human response to tall buildings* (pp. 175–181). Stroudsburg, PA: Dowden, Hutchinson, & Ross.

National Center for Health Statistics. (1987). Aging in the eighties: Functional limitations of individuals age 65 years and over. *Advance Data* (No. 133). Hyattsville, MD: Public Health Service.

National Council on the Aging. (1975). *The myth and reality of aging in America*. Washington, DC: Author.

Neugarten, B. L. (1973). Personality change in late life: A developmental perspective. In C. Eisdorfer & M. P. Lawton (Eds.), *Psychology of adult development and aging* (pp. 311–335). Washington, DC: American Psychological Association.

Newcomer, R. J. (1976). An evaluation of neighborhood service convenience for elderly housing project residents. In P. Suedfeld & J. A. Russell (Eds.), *The behavioral basis of design* (Vol. 1, pp. 301–307). Stroudsburg, PA: Dowden, Hutchinson, & Ross.

Olsen, R. V., Ehrenkrantz, E., & Hutchings, B. (1993). *Homes that help: Advice from caregivers for creating a supportive home*. Newark: New Jersey Institute of Technology Press.

Parmelee, P., & Lawton, M. P. (1990). The design of special environments for the aged. In J. E. Birren & K. W. Schaie (Eds.), *Handbook of the psychology of aging* (3rd ed., pp. 464–487). New York: Academic Press.

Pynoos, J., Cohen, E., Davis, L. J., & Bernhardt, S. (1987). Home modifications. In V. Regnier & J. Pynoos (Eds.), *Housing the aged* (pp. 277–304). New York: Elsevier.

Regnier, V. (1987). Programming congregate housing: The preferences of upper income elderly. In V. Regnier & J. Pynoos (Eds.), *Housing the aged* (pp. 207–226). New York: Elsevier.

Riksen-Walraven, J. M. (1978). Effects of caregiver behavior on habitation rate and self-efficacy in infants. *International Journal of Behavior Development, 1,* 105–130.

Rook, K. S. (1994). Assessing the health-related dimensions of older adults' social relationships. In M. P. Lawton & J. A. Teresi (Eds.), *Annual review of gerontology and geriatrics* (Vol. 14, pp. 142–181). New York: Springer.

Rosenberg, G. S. (1970). *The worker grows older.* San Francisco: Jossey-Bass.

Rosow, I. (1967). *Social integration of the aged.* New York: Free Press.

Russell, J. A., & Lanius, U. F. (1984). Adaptation level and the affective appraisal of environments. *Journal of Environmental Psychology, 4,* 119–135.

Ryan, E. B., Giles, H., Bartolucci, G., & Henwood, K. (1986). Psycholinguistic and social psychological components of communication by and with the elderly. *Language and Communication, 6,* 1–24.

Sloane, P. D., & Mathew, L. J. (1990). The Therapeutic Environment Screening Scale. *The American Journal of Alzheimers and Related Disorders, 5,* 22–26.

Struyk, R. J., & Turner, M. (1984). Changes in the housing situation of the elderly: 1974–1979. *Journal of Housing for the Elderly, 2,* 3–20.

Teaff, J. D., Lawton, M. P., Nahemow, L., & Carlson, D. (1978). Impact of age integration on the well being of elderly tenants in public housing. *Journal of Gerontology, 33,* 126–133.

Tillson, D. (Ed.). (1990). *Aging in place.* Glenview, IL: Scott-Foresman.

Wachs, T. D. (1989). The nature of the physical microenvironment: An expanded classification system. *Merrill-Palmer Quarterly, 35,* 339–419.

Weisman, G., Lawton, M. P., Sloane, P. D., Calkins, M. P., & Norris-Baker, L. (1996). *Professional Environmental Assessment Protocol (PEAP): A standardized method of expert evaluation of dementia special care units.* Milwaukee: University of Wisconsin at Milwaukee, School of Architecture.

White, R. W. (1959). Motivation reconsidered: The concept of competence. *Psychological Review, 66,* 297–333.

Wohlwill, J. F. (1968). Amount of stimulus exploration and preference as differential functions of stimulus complexity. *Perception & Psychophysics, 4,* 307–312.

III

ORGANIZATIONAL SETTINGS

5

THE CHILD-CARE ENVIRONMENT: CONCEPTUALIZATIONS, ASSESSMENTS, AND ISSUES

SARAH L. FRIEDMAN AND JO-ANN AMADEO

This chapter is about the assessment of child care. We start by laying out all of the aspects of child care that can be assessed and then move on to a description of existing instruments, while emphasizing the aspects of child care that they assess and those that they do not. We then discuss issues pertaining to the validity of existing instruments and of individual child-care variables. We also tackle the difficult questions of how to choose among the many aspects of child care that can be evaluated and how to choose among the different indexes of these aspects. We conclude with recommendations for future directions for theory and research about the assessment of child care.

CHARACTERISTICS OF THE CHILD-CARE ENVIRONMENT

The child-care environment is a place and a social milieu in which children spend time on a regular basis when their mother is unavailable. Such unavailability is usually due to the mother's employment or to her engagement in other daily activities that preclude face-to-face caring of her child. However, child care is not only an environment but also an experience that children have while away from their mothers. That experience, in turn, is an index of the quality of the environment. Last, but not least, the child-care environment is a workplace for the providers of care. As such, its administration has implications for the experiences of both the providers and the children in their care. Therefore, to assess the child-care environment, one needs to determine who provides the care, who is cared for, where the care is provided, and how the care is provided. In addition, the experience of child care may be measured in terms of the interactions the child has with the provider, peers, and objects in the child-care environment. The child-care environment can also be measured in terms of duration (number of hours) per week or duration over months and years. The stability of exposure to (a) parallel care arrangements, (b) sequentially ordered arrangements, and (c) providers and peers within a setting are also important aspects of the child-care experience. Most of these aspects of care can be assessed at multiple levels. Let us consider them one by one.

Who Provides Care?

One can give information related to the identity of the providers or in terms of their characteristics. For example, the providers' identity can be described as nonmother, relative, specific relative (e.g., father or grandparent), or nonrelative. The characteristics of the providers may be described in terms of their ethnicity, sex, education, child-care experience, attitudes toward child rearing and providing child care, relationship to the child's parents, income, and their behavior toward the child or children in their care.

Where Is Care Provided?

The location of care can be described simply as in the child's home or away from it. On the other hand, one can be more specific and classify child-care arrangements as in the child's home, another's home, a family day care (in which a nonrelative takes care of children), or a child-care center. The more formal arrangements such as family day care and child-care centers can be described in terms of conforming to state regulations or accreditation criteria or in terms of being nonprofit or for profit. Child-care centers can also be described by their auspices (i.e., whether they are independent, part of a chain, or affiliated with a church). Finally, the "where" of child care can be described by criteria that cut across locations, such as administration of the child-care setting, indoor and outdoor space available, furnishings, safety, hygiene, and cost per family.

Who Receives Care?

Child-care settings vary in a number of ways, including the age of the children receiving care (infants, toddlers, and preschool age children) as well as their ethnicity, temperament, socioeconomic background, health status, developmental status, and age at which they were first enrolled in care. The recipient of care can be one child or a group of children. If the recipient is an individual child, the child's age, sex, ethnicity, and psychological characteristics can be described. If the recipient is a group, then the age mix of the group and other information about the number and proportion of children with certain personal characteristics may be important to assess. One can also describe the number of children who are sharing one or more providers (i.e., adult:child ratio).

How Is Care Provided?

Here one would want to measure the extent to which the care setting is generally sensitive and responsive in an age-appropriate way to the nutritional, health, emotional, social, and cognitive needs of children. This aspect overlaps with "who providers care," because one could describe the individual provider in terms of his or her sensitivity and responsiveness. The category of "how care is provided" emphasizes matters of forethought, process, and style that characterize the setting, regardless of the specific identity or the number of providers or children. It should be noted that not all children experience the care given in a particular setting in the same way.

Experiential Aspects of Care

Children who differ in temperament, attractiveness, and developmental level may experience the same setting and the same providers in different ways. Therefore, in addition to the description of how care is provided, one needs to describe how care is experienced.

Interactions of the Child in Care With the Provider, Peers, and Objects

Here one could note the extent to which the interactions experienced by a specific child occur with positive or negative affect and the extent to which the child, the provider, or a peer initiated the interactions. One could also note the extent to which the interactions experienced by the specific child are educational (involving language, reading, and singing); the extent to which the provider is sensitive to a specific child's emotional state, cognitive or social developmental status, or immediate needs; and the extent to which the child plays alone or with others.

Extent of Exposure to Child Care

Extent of exposure can be measured for any child-care arrangement at a given time. In other words, how many hours per week is the child spending in a particular child-care arrangement? Or, how many hours per week does a child spend in any child care? (Nine percent of children have multiple, concurrent arrangements; Hofferth, 1996.) Extent of exposure to child care may also be measured in terms of weeks, months, or years since entry into child care or in terms of total hours spent in child care since entry into any care arrangement.

Stability of Exposure to Child Care

The stability of exposure to child-care arrangements at a given period of time and over time represents an important aspect of the child-care experience. Here the description can be at the level of stable versus unstable care experience or at a level that describes patterns of transition in care arrangements.

This way of characterizing measurable aspects of the child-care environment is one of several possible ways of thinking about the child-care environment. Another way, which is frequently used by researchers, refers to the distal and proximal characteristics of the environment. Assessments of the child-care environment have been placed on a continuum based on Bronfenbrenner's (1988; also see chapter 1, this volume) characterization of the environment—from those that capture aspects of the physical or social environment (or both) that can be or are experienced directly by the child to those that influence the child's experience indirectly. Those aspects that can directly be experienced by the child have been referred to as *proximal*, whereas those that can indirectly influence the child's experiences have been referred to as *distal*. For example, the child directly experiences the manner in which he or she is responded to or talked to, the availability of toys, or the availability of peers. Thus, measures that tap these aspects of the environment were considered proximal. On the other hand, the salary or education of the provider is not directly experienced by the child but nonetheless can still influence the behavior of the provider toward the child. Such descriptive, easy-to-assess, and verifiable measures are mostly focused on distal aspects of the environment. The conceptual justification for the use of distal measures is articulated in terms of their creating conditions that lead to more optimal interactions between providers and children (e.g., Phillips & Howes, 1987). For example, the more training providers have in child development, the more likely they are to have positive and cognitively stimulating interactions with children. On the other hand, the creation of proximal measures of provider–child interaction has conceptually been justified by the scientific literature demonstrating the positive effects of specific aspects of mother–child interactions on the cognitive and social development of children. Therefore, it has been hypothesized that similar interactions between providers and children will lead to similar outcomes (e.g., Clarke-Stewart, Gruber, & Fitzgerald, 1994; National Institutes of Child Health and Human Development [NICHD] Early Child Care Research Network, 1996).

The previous description of the rationale for choosing distal and proximal measures introduces the idea that the goals of measurement determine, at least to an extent, the characteristics of the environment that are measured. Other examples help to emphasize the importance of this idea. Suppose the goal of child care is acculturation of children of immigrants, as it was in the United States at the turn of the 20th century. With this goal in mind, one would want to measure child care in terms of its ability to transmit cultural values. However, if the goal is custodial care, as it was at the time of World War II (Phillips & Zigler, 1987), then the assessment would probably focus on the safety and hygiene of the setting. When the goal is to prepare children for social and academic adjustment in school, as it has been toward the end of the 20th century, assessments are more likely to focus on social and cognitive conditions that prepare children toward such adjustment. Conceptualization of such conditions would determine the aspects of the child-care environment that would need to be measured, and available methods of assessment would determine the way in which assessment would be carried out. In general, the goals of assessment, the conceptualization framework underlying it, and the methods of assessment that are known have always determined the aspects of child care that were focused on and the level of detail at which measurement was done.

In this chapter, we organized the information around three assessment goals: licensing, accreditation, and research. First, we report about measures that have been developed in the service of these goals. We then review what is known about the validity of the different assessments and about the relationships between measures within and across categories (i.e., the aspects of child care described earlier). In addition, we address the question of how one chooses among measures that are positively correlated or among measures that are similarly predictive of the developmental outcomes for children in care. The chapter closes with suggestions for future research.

ASSESSMENT MEASURES AND INSTRUMENTS OF THE CHILD-CARE ENVIRONMENT: CLASSIFICATION BY GOALS

Existing measures of the child-care environment are associated with three practical assessment goals and the conceptualizations associated with these. As stated earlier, the goals are (a) state licensing, (b) accreditation, and (c) research to evaluate the effects of child care on the psychological development of children. We later describe measures and assessment instruments that were either developed or used primarily for the purpose of licensing, accreditation, or research.

Table 1 provides an overview of our classification of measures of the child-care environment in terms of the aspects of care they focus on and the goals for which they were used. Because valid and reliable assessment depends on both the availability of appropriate measures (or instruments) and the qualified users of these, when information is available, we mention the requirements assessors must meet.

ASSESSMENT FOR LICENSING

States regulate the nonparental care of children. In this context, nonparental care refers to care provided for in a group setting such as a child-care center or a family day-care home under private, nonprofit, proprietary, public, or religious auspices. Licensing is aimed at holding providers to minimum standards of health, safety, and quality of care, thereby protecting children from harm (Kandall & Walker, 1984; Morgan, 1980; Young & Zigler, 1986). Phillips, Lande, and Goldberg (1990) and Kontos (1991) referred to licensing criteria as providing the floor of quality. Licensing criteria are clear-cut (i.e., a provider either meets the criteria or does not). Aspects of family day care that are regulated, when these child-care arrangements are not exempt, typically pertain to the provider of care (minimum age, training, and criminal background check), the children that are cared for (immunization before enrollment and number of children per adult), and the rights of parents (to visit during the operation hours of the facility). Centers generally are regulated by the same criteria as family day-care arrangements plus others, such as the number of children allowed per group (Hofferth, 1996). Although the aspects of care that are regulated by states (e.g., provider characteristics and children characteristics) are similar across states, states vary in terms of the specific conditions that they consider as markers of acceptable standards. For variations among states on their requirement for staff:child ratio, group size, enrollment limitation, and staff training, see Phillips et al. (1990).

Fiene and Nixon (1985) described two tools that provide a methodology for monitoring interviews and site visits to day-care programs. The first system assigns weights to the questions on licensing forms so that scores reflect the relative importance of state regulations. The second system is a checklist consisting of selected predictive items from longer comprehensive instruments for checking compliance with state regulations. In Pennsylvania, West Virginia, and California and in New York City, such items have been shown to be effective in discriminating between providers

TABLE 1
Measures of Child-Care Environment Classified by Aspects of the Care Environment and by Goals of Measurement

	Goals of measurement		
Aspects of the environment	Licensing	Accreditation	Research
Who provides care? provider's identity and characteristics	Age and training	Age, education, training, and experience (CECPR, NAEYC, and WHO)	Age, education, training, experience, wages, and benefits
Where? location, facilities, type, auspices, licensing, administration, and cost	Space available (indoors and outdoors), furnishing, safety, and hygiene	Space, furnishing, safety, hygiene, administration, and working conditions for personnel (NAEYC and WHO)	Type of care (center, family care home, etc.), auspices, licensing, administration, space organization, cost, furnishings, safety, hygiene, and working conditions (ECERS, FDCRS, ITERS, PROFILE, CDPE, and HOME)
Care recipient: individual characteristics (age of first enrollment, ethnicity, and special limitations), group, age(s), age mix, and child:adult ratio	Adult:child ratio and group size	Adult:child ratio and group size (NAEYC and WHO)	Adult:child ratio, group size, age of children, and age mix
How? forethought, process, and style of care provision	Activities that promote development of children's skills, self-esteem, positive self-identity, and choice of activities (e.g., CDPE-IC)	NAEYC, WHO, and CECPR	ECERS, FDCRS, ITERS, CDPE (CLS, PQS, and COFAS) PROFILE, ECCO, DCEI, ORCE, Caregiver Interaction Scale, Adult Involvement Scale, and HOME
Child's experiences in care: interactions, extent of care, and stability			DCEI, ORCE, HOME, COFAS, interactive measures in small to medium studies, provider turnover, stability of care, and extent of care (concurrent and overtime)

Note. CDPE = Child Development Program Evaluation Scales; CECPR = Council for Early Childhood Professional Recognition; CLS = Center Licensing Scales; COFAS = Caregiver Observation Form and Scale; DCEI = Day Care Environmental Inventory; ECERS = Early Childhood Environment Rating Scale; FDCRS = Family Day Care Rating Scale; HOME = Home Observation for Measurement of the Environment; ITERS = Infant/Toddler Environment Rating Scale; NAEYC = National Association for the Education of Young Children; ORCE = Observation Rating of the Caregiving Environment; PQS = Program Quality Scale; WHO = World Health Organization.

who typically receive high overall scores on the licensing comprehensive instrument and providers who typically receive low overall scores. These specific items are compliance with group size and adult:child ratios; compliance with minimum space requirements; equipment that is easily accessible to children; vehicles that are equipped with age-appropriate safety carriers; inaccessibility of cleaning materials to children; periodic health appraisals of staff; and activities that promote development of children's skills, self-esteem, positive self-identity, and choice of activities.

A comparison between the aspects of care that states regulate and those described in the introductory section of the chapter shows that states regulate characteristics of the provider and of the recipients of care. Not regulated are the types of care arrangements that children of certain ages or health characteristics should attend (center, family day care, etc.), the extent of exposure to care, the stability of care, and how care is provided or experienced. The range of specific characteristics of the child-care environment that are regulated is frequently limited. For example, although states regulate some provider characteristics, other characteristics such as income and attitudes toward child rearing are not regulated.

For the most part, the literature on state licensing does not include information about the training of inspectors. However, it is clear that inspectors need to be familiar with the state regulations and must collect all of the evidence required by the regulations.

Assessment for Professional Accreditation

Professional accreditation criteria were developed to facilitate the professional development of interested providers and to improve the quality of the physical, social, and educational environment that they provide children. Accreditation criteria represent very high standards of quality as construed by educators and developmental scientists. Providers can be accredited through national systems, such as the Council for Early Childhood Professional Recognition, which confers the title of Child Development Associate, and the National Academy of Early Childhood Programs (of the National Association for the Education of Young Children [NAEYC]).

Accreditation by the Council for Early Childhood Professional Recognition

The Council for Early Childhood Professional Recognition confers accreditation on individuals, not on centers or child-care homes. Furthermore, accreditation is specific to the setting in which an individual works. The settings can be either center-based programs (such as infant–toddler and preschool programs) or family child-care programs. Individuals who seek accreditation must already have child-care work experience in combination with some training in early childhood education. Candidates first meet eligibility requirements, and, once eligible, candidates provide required documentation of their skill as caregivers.

Eligibility requirements pertain to age (>18 years), formal general education (high school diploma or equivalent), experience (480 hours) working with children within the last 5 years, and formal education and training (120 hours) in child care within the past 5 years. After submitting an application, the candidate is interviewed, administered a written assessment, and observed while working with children. In addition, formal documentation of the caregiver's competence is required, including documentation provided by the parents of the children for whom the provider cares.

The evaluation interviews, observations, and written documentation are collected by a representative of The Council for Early Childhood Professional Recognition and are later evaluated by a Council Commission, which makes the decision about accreditation. Accreditation is dependent on the candidate meeting six competency goals: (a) establishing and maintaining a safe, healthy learning environment; (b) advancing physical and intellectual competence; (c) supporting social and emotional development and providing positive guidance and discipline; (d) establishing positive and productive relationships with families; (e) ensuring a well-run, purposeful program responsive to participant needs; and (f) maintaining a commitment to professionalism.

This accreditation focuses on the individual characteristics of the provider, including age, education, and relevant training and experience. It does not focus on the physical environment and its furnishing, on the child-care setting as a workplace, or on the direct experience of the children in care.

Accreditation by the National Academy of Early Childhood Programs

In addition to the accreditation to individual providers, centers also have the option of seeking accreditation. The National Academy of Early Childhood Programs offers a center accreditation system based on criteria developed for the NAEYC's program (1991) that were derived from a literature review and a review of evaluation documents. Content validity of this system was assessed by early childhood specialists. The criteria need to be verified by observation because half of the criteria relate specifically to the experiences of the child in the child-care setting. Consequently, the Early Childhood Classroom Observation (ECOS) was developed and field tested (Bredekamp, 1986). The accreditation system evaluates many aspects of child care in great depth. The following is an attempt to highlight some of the details of the system as these fit the aspects of care described in this chapter.

Who provides care? Accredited programs need to be efficient and carried out with attention to the needs and desires of children, parents, and staff. The staff qualification accreditation criteria call for the providers to be adults who understand child development; who recognize and provide for children's needs; and who demonstrate a positive, courteous, and flexible manner. The providers musts be 18 years of age or older and must be trained in early childhood education and child development. The amount of training required depends on the level of professional responsibility of the provider. In addition, to obtain accreditation, the program must employ an early childhood specialist to direct the educational program. Finally, the program must provide the staff with regular training opportunities to improve its skills in working with children and families.

Where is care provided? For a program to be accredited, the physical settings, the furnishings, and the resources must be in the service of the needs of the children and the providers. The indoor and outdoor physical environments should foster growth and development through opportunities for exploration and learning. The space and its furnishing should be designed to protect the health and safety of the children and the adults in the program. In addition, accredited programs must have the resources to meet the nutritional needs of the children and the adults in the program in a manner that promotes physical, social, emotional, and cognitive development.

Who receives care? Accredited programs provide care to groups of children. A group is defined as the number of children assigned to a staff member or to a team of staff members. The group size and the adult:child ratio must not exceed recommended standards. Recommended child:staff ratios vary by group size and by the children's ages. They also vary depending on the type of activity, whether it is indoors or outdoors, inclusion of children with special needs, and other factors.

How is care provided? Accredited providers follow a carefully planned, age-appropriate, and individualized curriculum by using developmentally appropriate materials and activities. They work at interacting with the children in a manner that provides opportunities for children to develop an understanding of self and others. The interactions between provider and child are characterized by warmth, personal respect, individuality, positive support, and responsiveness. In addition, accredited providers are expected to facilitate interactions among children to provide opportunities for development of self-esteem, social competence, and intellectual growth. Accredited providers also need to demonstrate sensitivity in their interactions with parents, both by keeping the parents informed and by welcoming parents as observers and contributors to the program.

Interactions of the child with providers, peers, and objects. This aspect is not measured for individual children in the program, even though the assessments of the environment require that the interactions that all children experience should be of the highest quality standards that lead to conversation, laughter, and excitement rather than harsh, stressful noise or enforced quiet. The aspect of extent and stability of exposure to child care is also not tapped by accreditation criteria because this aspect, while important, is not under the control of the providers, even though it may, to some extent, be influenced by their practices.

Evaluation of the program is done through a minimum of one full-day visit to a program with up to 60 children. The visitor or validator is a qualified early childhood professional. Validators' qualifications include experience in working directly with children in group programs and in administering such programs; a college degree in early childhood education, child development, or the equivalent; and demonstrated objectivity, good communication skills, and professionalism. The validators are trained in the validation procedures and tasks. The visit to the program includes an initial meeting with the director, a tour of the facility, observations of several classrooms, interviews with care providers whose classrooms are observed, a sampling of records and written policies, and an in-depth discussion of the entire validation with the director.

Accreditation by the World Health Organization (WHO) Child Care Facility Schedule

Although it does not confer accreditation on either providers or centers, the World Health Organization (WHO) Child Care Facility Schedule is based on an established accreditation system and is thus included in this section. The WHO, interested in the mental health implications of child care, designed a screening instrument that could be used in multiple, diverse settings. Specifically, the WHO Child Care Facility Schedule (Caldwell et al., 1990) was developed to describe conditions in group child-care settings that provide services to infants, toddlers, preschool age children, and school age children. The intention of the schedule was to provide an instrument that was easy to use, quick, and helpful to policymakers interested in setting child-care standards. To that end, the developers of the procedure first studied the accreditation criteria and procedures of the National Academy of Early Childhood Programs (first published in 1984 by the NAEYC). In addition, consultants recommended by the WHO suggested items based on observations in different countries in which the schedule might be used. Following a process by which advice was sought from child-care and child development specialists around the world, the WHO finalized the schedule with 74 items, each making a simple declarative statement of conditions. All of these can easily be observed and categorized as present or absent on a visit to a center or otherwise can be scored on the basis of nonsensitive information gathered in a brief interview. The items cover seven important areas of care: physical environment, health and safety, nutrition and food service, administration, staff–family interaction, and observable child behavior and curriculum. The 10 items pertaining to the physical environment describe the indoor and outdoor environments of the facility in which the program operates as well as the teaching and play materials. The 10 health and safety items describe conditions and practices that are essential for promoting and maintaining good health and for ensuring that no safety hazards exist in the facility. The 4 nutrition and food service items pertain to nutrition and sanitary conditions in the food services. The 22 items pertaining to the administration and management of the program cover areas of hiring, training, personnel, official relations with parents, fiscal practices, and decisions about group size and provider:child ratio. The 10 items about staff–family interactions pertain to the relationships between staff and parents and between staff and children. The 6 items of observable child behavior describe the behaviors of the children in the center at the time that the center is evaluated. They describe the children's individual behavior and interactions with other children and adults. Finally, the 10 items regarding the curriculum refer to the formulation of language objectives; the selection and preparation of learning materials; the arrangement of the learning environment; and the planning of teaching activities aimed at facilitating the socioemotional, cognitive, and motor development of the children.

In addition, information is collected about the ownership of the center, sources of funding, availability of a board of directors, its composition, the length of time the center has been in operation, whether parents pay, admission policy, and type of facility (private for profit, private nonprofit, public, corporate–business sponsored, church affiliated, or otherwise affiliated). Information is also collected on the number of children enrolled and their ages, whether they are full time or part time, the number of staff members (full time and part time), and the level of education of the child-care providers.

In summary, the WHO schedule (Caldwell et al., 1990) provides information about who provides care, where care is provided, who receives care, and how care is provided. It does not provide information about the experience of specific children or about the extent or stability of care that specific children have experienced. There are no eligibility criteria for users of the schedule, but the manual mentions that the schedule should be useful for researchers, advocates, and personnel in child-care centers.

Assessment for Research

In general, researchers are interested in the relationship between aspects of the child-care environment and the development of children. The assessments of the environment that have been used by researchers can be classified into four types (Phillips & Howes, 1987; Zaslow, 1991).

Details and examples of these four types are offered in the sections that follow.

Descriptive, Easy-to-Measure or -Verify Aspects of the Environment

These aspects of the environment include space available, group size, provider:child ratio, equipment, cost, and administrative aspects such as auspices. First, aspects of the physical and social environment that are experienced directly by the children are frequently used to assess the child-care environment. These aspects include amount of indoor and outdoor space available, division of space into areas by function (sleeping area, reading area, play area, and area with tables for meals and for "work"), group size (e.g., Allhusen, 1992), ages of children in the group, adult:child ratio (e.g., Ruopp, Travers, Glantz, & Coelen, 1979), provider turnover (e.g., Benn, 1986; NAEYC, 1991), and turnover of children in the setting.

One example of a comprehensive observational instrument for measuring the physical space of child-care centers and homes is the Observation Schedule for Physical Space developed by Prescott, Kritchevsky, and Jones (1972). The information coded on this instrument pertains to the number of children per session, the number of groups per session, the teacher:child ratio, the number of rooms available, and the amount of outdoor space. Other criteria for describing the environment include the potential for seclusion, the "softness" of the setting, and the school policies regarding space use.

Child care as an adult work environment is a second descriptive measure of the child-care environment. Examples include the wages, benefits (health, sick leave, retirement, cost of living adjustments, merit increases, and reduced fee for child care), and working conditions (e.g., ongoing continuing education and career ladder) of the child-care providers. For more details, see Whitebook, Howes, and Phillips, 1989.

A third descriptive measure comes under the heading of child-care auspices. That is, child-care environments are examined in terms of whether they are independent, for-profit, nonprofit, chain, or church sponsored (Whitebook et al., 1989).

Finally, the extent to which child-care settings meet quality standards is a fourth descriptive measure. Examples of quality standards used for assessment include state standards, standards of the Federal Interagency Day Care Requirements, and accreditation standards such as those of the National Association for the Education of Young Children (Whitebook et al., 1989).

Most of the previously indicated measures of child-care relate to where care is provided. The exceptions are measures of group size, ages of children, and number of children cared for by one adult (adult:child ratio), which are descriptors of the recipients of care.

Provider Characteristics

These characteristics include the provider's age, education, work experience, and psychological characteristics. Psychological characteristics include psychological well-being (e.g., self-efficacy, depression, or professional self-esteem) as well as attitudes about child rearing and child care. The provider's education level (e.g., high school diploma or less, some college, BA or BS, or graduate education) has been measured in several studies (Berk, 1985; Clarke-Stewart, et al., 1994). Similarly, the provider's training in child development or in early childhood education (Arnett, 1989; Howes, 1983; Stallings & Porter, 1980) and the provider's experience in caring for young children (e.g., Howes, 1983; Kontos & Fiene, 1987) have also been measured.

The provider's attitude toward child rearing also falls into this category. For example, in the NICHD Study of Early Child Care (1994, 1996), at 6, 15, 24, 36, and 56 months, providers were given the Parental Modernity Scale (Schaefer & Edgerton, 1985) to examine their ideas about raising children. The questionnaire includes 30 statements, and the provider rates each statement on a 5-point scale, with responses ranging from *strongly disagree* to *strongly agree*. The scores differentiate a provider with an authoritarian attitude from one with an authoritative attitude.

Finally, the provider's psychological adjustment (e.g., depression; measured in the NICHD Study of Early Child Care, in which a modified version of the Center for Epidemiological Studies—Depression (CES-D) Scale is used; Radloff, 1977) is an example of this type of assessment.

The previously indicated measures obviously map on the category of variables describing who provides care. This category was mentioned in the opening section of the chapter.

Global or Summary Measures of the Quality of the Environment

The summary measures are based on instruments that evaluate many aspects of the environment and that provide a summary score of the total quality of the environment. Further details about specific global measures can be found in Table 2.

Early Childhood Environment Rating Scale (ECERS; Harms & Clifford, 1980). Environment, as defined by this scale, is the optimal use of space, materials, and experience to enhance the development, daily schedules, and supervision of the children. The instrument includes seven subscales, with each item in the subscale rated on a 7-point scale. Six subscales focus on resources and practices that promote the well-being and healthy development of children, whereas one subscale focuses on the well-being of the providers and parents.

The ECERS (Harms & Clifford, 1980) is focused primarily on the

TABLE 2
Measures Used to Assess Caregiving Environment

Measures	Citation	Type of Assessment	Subscale	Type of Setting
Observation Schedule for Physical Space	Prescott, Kritchevsky, & Jones (1972)	Descriptive	Number of groups, number of children, teacher:child ratio, number of rooms, available outdoor space	Center and family day care
Early Childhood Environment Rating Scale (ECERS)	Harms & Clifford (1980)	Global	Personal care routines, Furnishing, Language, Motor Activities, Creative Activities, Social Development, and Adult Needs	Center
Family Day Care Rating Scale (FDCRS)	Harms & Clifford (1984)	Global	Space, Basic Care, Language, Learning Activities, Social Development, and Adult Needs	Family day care
Infant/Toddler Environment Rating Scale (ITERS)	Harms, Cryer, & Clifford (1990)	Global	Furnishing, Personal Care Routines, Listening and Talking, Learning Activities, Interaction Program Structure, and Adult Needs	Center
Child Development Program Evaluation (CDPE)	Fiene (1984)	Global	Center Licensing Scales, Program Quality Scales, and Caregiver Observation Form and Scale	Center
PROFILE	Abbott-Shim & Sibley (1987)	Global	Safety and Health, Nutrition, Learning Environment, Interacting, Individualizing, Scheduling, and Curriculum	Infant programs, preschool programs, and day-care homes
Caregiver Interaction Scale	Arnett (1989)	Global	None	All
Home Observation for Measurement of the Environment (HOME)	Caldwell & Bradley (1984)	Global	Responsivity, Acceptance, Organization, Learning, and Involvement Variety	Family day care, in-home provider, and relative care
Adult Involvement Scale	Howes & Stewart (1987)	Global	None	All
Day Care Environmental Inventory	Prescott, Kritchevsky, & Jones (1972)	Experiential	None	Center and family day care
Observation Rating of the Caregiving Environment (ORCE)	NICHD Child Care Research Network (1994)	Experiential	Frequency and ratings	All

Note. NICHD = National Institute of Child Health and Human Development.

physical resources in the care environment for both the children and the adults as well as on how care is provided. In addition, there is some emphasis on who receives care. For example, some scale items have one version for infant care and a different version for care arrangements for older children. Also, the program is evaluated for the extent to which it accommodates children with special needs. There is no emphasis on the identity, credentials, or attitudes of the providers or on the experiences of individual children in care in terms of extent of child-care experiences, stability of care, or interactive experiences. As with the accreditation instruments we reviewed, the emphasis here is on the experiences of all children; ignoring the possibility that the same care arrangement may provide different experiences for different children.

Family Day Care Rating Scale (FDCRS) and the Infant/Toddler Environment Rating Scale (ITERS). The FDCRS (Harms & Clifford, 1984) is an adaptation of the Early Childhood Environment Rating Scale (Harms & Clifford, 1980). As its name suggests, it was designed to give an assessment of the quality of care provided in family day-care settings. Similarly, the ITERS (Harms, Cryer, & Clifford, 1990) is an adaptation of the Early Childhood Environment Rating Scale (Harms & Clifford, 1980) and the FDCRS (Harms & Clifford, 1984).

Child Development Program Evaluation Scales (CDPE). The Child Development Program Evaluation Scales (Fiene, 1984) consist of two scales: (a) the Center Licensing Scale and (b) the Program Quality Scale. The latter also includes an observational scheme called the Caregiver Observation Form and Scale. The CDPE is a comprehensive scale measuring administration, environmental safety, curriculum, health, nutrition, social services, and parental involvement. The 37 items of the scale were selected from 900 items found in different state instruments assessing compliance with state regulations. These compliance instruments have been extensively field tested and implemented. The selected items have been shown to predict statistically overall compliance with state requirements.

PROFILE. The PROFILE (Abbot-Shim & Sibley, 1987) is a cluster of similarly constructed instruments originally designed for early childhood programs. It includes instruments for: (a) focusing on the administration of early childhood programs; (b) assessing programs for preschool age children; (c) assessing programs for infants; and (d) assessing programs for school age children. The PROFILE was developed for the self-evaluation of programs and providers but was also used for research purposes. Later, a research version was developed for early childhood programs (Abbot-Shim, Sibley, & Neel, 1992). Unlike the original nonresearch instrument, the research version is the same for early childhood programs, infant programs, preschool programs, and school age programs. Also, the research version for early childhood programs does not include all of the subscales found in the original self-evaluation version. Another research version was developed for day-care homes with young children (Abbot-Shim & Sibley, 1993).

Each PROFILE instrument (Abbot-Shim & Sibley, 1987) consists of subscales that are organized around a particular domain. For example, the Administration PROFILE includes subscales related to physical facilities, food service, program management, and personnel and program development. Each subscale contains specific items that are coded dichotomously as present or absent. Data are collected in three ways: (a) through observation (preferred), (b) from a review of documents, and (c) from discussion with the director or caregiver. The total number of criteria that was scored yes on a given dimension is plotted on a profile sheet that is marked to show the percentage of criteria that was scored positively.

Caregiver Interaction Scale. Arnett (1989) developed the Caregiver Interaction Scale, which is a 26-item global rating system focusing on various socialization practices identified in the research on parenting. The items measure the degree to which the provider encourages children to try new experiences and is enthusiastic about children's activities and efforts. The Caregiver Interaction Scale also examines the amount of time the provider spends in activities that do not involve interaction with the children, whether the provider reprimands children when they misbehave, and the degree to which the provider seems harsh when scolding or prohibiting children. The scale yields four factors that are conceptually meaningful: positive interaction, punitiveness, permissiveness, and detachment. The measure was used in two recent large-scale studies: the Study of Children in Family Child Care and Relative Care (Galinsky, Howes, Kontos, & Shinn, 1994) and the study of Cost, Quality and Child Outcomes in Child Care Centers (Helburn, 1995).

Adult Involvement Scale. The Adult Involvement Scale was developed by Howes and Stewart (1987) and was used in the Study of Children in Family Child Care and Relative Care (Galinsky et al., 1994) and the Cost, Quality and Child Outcomes in Child Care Centers study (Helburn, 1995). The caregiver's interaction with the child is rated every 20 seconds during two 15-minute observation periods, leading to a total of 90 ratings per child. The provider's behavior is rated in terms of six possible types of behavior ranging from no interaction to intense interaction.

Home Observation for Measurement of the Environment (HOME) Inventory—infant/toddler version. This instrument is based on the HOME Inventory for home settings and was adapted by the original authors (Caldwell & Bradley, 1984) for use in the NICHD Study of Early Child Care. According to Caldwell and Bradley, this version of the HOME Inventory is designed to measure the quality and quantity of stimulation and support available to a child in the child-care environment. Because the emphasis is on the child as a recipient of input from objects, events, and social transactions, the environment is assessed for the extent to which it provides the types of input that Caldwell and Bradley deemed necessary for the well-being and development of the child.

Experiential Measures

Experiential measures of the child-care environment include measures related to the extent and the stability of care received by the child and measures of the provider's interaction with the child and the child's interactions with peers. Extent of care can be measured both in terms of hours of care per week and hours of care over the child's lifetime. Stability is measured by the number of care arrangements experienced by the child at any one time and over time. Also, stability can be measured by turnover of the provider with primary responsibility for the child and by peer turnover in the child-care setting.

The experience of the child in child care can be measured indirectly through characterizing the child-care environment in the ways captured by subscales of the global measures that we have reviewed. To the extent that the environment is characterized by developmentally appropriate resources and by caregivers who are trained to provide sensitive, responsive, and cognitively stimulating care, the child is very likely to be the target of the positive ministrations of the providers.

Many of the global ratings are based on judgments that trained observers make on the basis of their immersion in a given program for some reasonable length of time (e.g., at a minimum an hour or two and frequently longer). However, some researchers feel that they can get more objective and valid data by using a quantitative technique frequently used in research on mother–child interaction. In this line of research, the investigator specifies caregiver and child behaviors that are of interest and notes every time these behaviors are observed. Frequently, the observation period is divided into short time segments (e.g., 15 or 30 seconds) for observation and short time segments for recording the target behaviors. Such time-intensive methods have several methodological advantages. First, as already stated, they provide quantifiable, valid data. Second, they permit testing the possibility that the frequency of providers' engagement in specific behaviors is associated with variations in specific outcomes for children. Third, within a child-care setting, children's experiences will vary. This could be due to the age, health, attractiveness, race, or personality characteristics of the child. For example, children who are more demanding of interaction may be getting more of it than those who are less demanding. Similarly, children who respond with more positive affect may reward providers who interact with them, thereby increasing the probability of such interactions. For such reasons, there is an advantage of characterizing the child-care environment in terms of the experiences that specific children have. Such information allows the researcher to explore the effects of child care that are due to an interaction between child care and child.

At the same time, the method is not without limitations and critics. It has been argued that time sampling overestimates behaviors, relies on the assumption that all behaviors are "equal," and limits the kinds of behaviors that are recorded; that is, simultaneous, sequenced behaviors are often not recorded (Mann, Ten Have, Plunkett, & Meisels, 1991).

There are only a few instruments that assess the experiential aspects of the environment (listed in Table 2). An example of one such instrument is the Observation Rating of the Caregiving Environment (ORCE; NICHD Early Child Care Research Network, 1996).

ORCE. The NICHD Early Child Care Research Network (1994) developed a complex instrument for recording caregiver behavior toward a specific child (target child) and the behaviors of the specific child during the same time periods. The instrument combines an objective and quantitative sampling and recording of caregiver and child behaviors during narrow time windows as well as ratings of caregiving and child behavior. These ratings are based on observations taken over large units of time. The method was first described by NICHD Early Child Care Research Network (1996).

In addition to the ORCE (NICHD Early Child Care Research Network, 1996), several studies have used detailed observational assessment of providers' behavior toward children. For example, McCartney (1984) used an observational coding system to measure the function and quantity of verbal interactions between children and providers and children and peers. Caregiver and peer utterances directed at the observed children were coded for four functions: control, expressive, representational, and social. The language environment of each center was observed continuously for 8 hours, over all activities except nap time. McCartney's goal was to characterize the language environment in the center, not the experiences of specific children. Therefore, only a few children were observed per center, and their experience was used as a predictor for the language development of all children in the center.

This is one example of a study that assessed providers' behaviors and children's experiences. There are several other studies of this type: Clarke-Stewart et al. (1994); Howes and Rubenstein (1985); and Rubenstein, Pedersen, and Yarrow (1977).

To summarize the section on assessment for research, Table 2 offers an overview of some of the more widely used or more complex measures described earlier. It provides the reader with the title of the assessment, a citation, the type of assessment, its subscales, and the child-care settings for which it was designed.

TOWARD THE VALIDATION OF MEASURES

To be worthwhile, assessments must be valid. That is, measures of the child-care environment obviously must measure accurately whatever it is that they are designed to assess, but they need to do more than that. The specific aspects of the environment that are measured are supposed to be indexes of the quality of the child-care environment. According to current conceptualizations of the goals of child care, a high-quality environment is one in which children thrive and are helped to develop optimally. Therefore, to be valid, measures of the child-care environment need to capture those conditions that discriminate between high- and low-quality environments.

Some of the authors of instruments for assessing the child-care environment have reported information about the validation of their instruments. For example, the validity of the ECERS (Harms & Clifford, 1980) was verified through two procedures. First, nationally recognized experts in the day-care and early childhood fields were asked to rate each item on the scale in terms of its importance to early childhood programs. Overall, 78% of the ratings indicated high importance, whereas only 1% indicated low importance. On the basis of this information, minor modifications to this scale were made. The second validation procedure checked the extent to which the scale could distinguish between programs varying in quality as determined by trainers who had been working with the staff in these programs. The rank order correlation between ratings of 18 programs and their ECERS scores was .74. The PROFILE was validated (Abbot-Shim et al., 1992) by early childhood professionals, by a cross-reference against the accreditation criteria of the NAEYC, and by a study of 53 preschool classrooms evaluated by both the PROFILE (Abbot-Shim & Sibley, 1987) and the ECERS (Harms & Clifford, 1980).

Another method for evaluating the validity of measures of the child-care environment is verifying the extent to which the developmental outcomes of children in high-quality programs (as evaluated by the measure under scrutiny) are more favorable than the developmental outcomes of children in low-quality programs. The initial steps toward this type of validation are provided by the research literature related to the effects of child care on child development (as reviewed by Phillips and Howes, 1987, and by Lamb, 1997). Of course, when using such a validation strategy, one needs to be aware of the fact that what is gleaned from the scientific literature is constrained by the interests of the investigators who conducted the studies. First, there may be aspects of the child-care environment that were never measured. For example, for reasons stemming from theory or from cultural beliefs, assessments may fail to focus on the extent or regularity of exposing young children to accomplished works of visual art or to high-quality music. On the side of the dependent variables, because no investigator was interested in the effects of characteristics of child care on health and injury, the extant scientific literature cannot instruct researchers about the validity of the measures of the child-care environment as they relate to the health of children. In addition, one needs to be aware of the fact that in most studies conducted to date, child-care effects are confounded with family effects. That is, unless one covaries the effects of variables like family income, parental education, or maternal behaviors toward the child, the developmental outcome may be due to family or to the interaction of family and child-care influences, not to child-care influences alone. This is the case because family characteristics and child-care characteristics are not independent: Family characteristics influence (if not determine) the child care that families arrange for their children (NICHD Early Child Care Research Network, 1997a). Indeed, studies that have investigated the relative effects of family and child-care variables or covaried the effects of family when studying the effects of child care suggest that effects of family circumstances and characteristics are greater than child-care effects (e.g., Clarke-Stewart, Gruber, & Fitzergerald, 1994; Goelman & Pence, 1987; Kontos & Fiene, 1987; NICHD Early Child Care Research Network, 1997b, 1997c, 1998). Child-care effects could also covary with children's biological and psychological characteristics. The age, sex, health status, or temperament of the child could very well be related to the child-care effects.

Table 3 presents examples of available knowledge about the relation between specific measures of the child-care environment and developmental outcomes to which they predict. Many studies cluster data from specific environmental variables or combine data from specific environmental variables with data from global instruments measuring the environment. The results are then reported in terms of the effects of the cluster on measures of children's development. We did not make references to such clusters. The table focuses on examples of studies that show relations between specific environmental variables or specific instruments and specific developmental outcomes for the children who are cared for in the measured environments. The developmental outcomes are reported at the level presented in the reviewed papers. For example, if the author reports about the play level of the children, we report about the same, rather than subsume it under the term *cognitive outcome*. In the service of simplicity, we did not note the age of the children studied or the type of care arrangement in which observations were made (i.e., center and family day care). Although both variables are very important, we were interested in highlighting whether specific measures have been shown to predict outcomes, regardless of the age of the children studied or the specific type of care.

Although Table 3 reveals much about what is already known concerning the predictive validity of measures of the child-care environment, it also reminds us of many unknowns. As can be seen, for cases in which global instruments are used (mostly because subscales were found to be

TABLE 3
Measures of the Child-Care Environment and Experience: Prediction to Child Outcome

Predictor	Child outcome	Source
Organization (+)/division of space (+)	Competence (+)	Clarke-Stewart (1987)
Neatness of setting (+)	Cognitive performance (+)	Clarke-Stewart, Gruber, & Fitzgerald (1994)[a]
Group size (+)	Social competence (−)	Holloway & Reichart-Erikson (1989)[a]
	Preschoolers: cooperation and involvement in tasks (−), verbal initiative (−), gain in cognitive test scores (−), reflective/innovative behavior (−), hostility and conflict (+)	Ruopp, Travers, Glantz, & Coelen (1979)
	Infants: distress and apathy (+) and potentially harmful behavior (+)	
	Social knowledge and social competence (−) when groups exceed 5	Clarke-Stewart (1987)
Heterogeneity of children (age, SES, and ethnicity) (+)	Children's competence (cognitive competence enhanced when other children are older, no effect of SES and ethnicity)	Clarke-Stewart (1987)
Age at first enrollment (+)	Insecure attachment (+)	Benn (1986); Lamb, Sternberg, & Prodromidis (1992)
	No effects on percentage of children securely attached to their mothers	NICHD Study of Early Child Care (1997b)
	Achievement (+)	Caughy, DiPietro, & Strobino (1994)
Adult:child ratio (+)	No effect	Holloway & Reichart-Erikson (1989)[a]
	Social competence (−)	Clarke-Stewart (1987)
	Infants: apathy (−), potentially harmful behavior (−), and infant cognitive development (+)	Ruopp et al. (1979)
	Socially defiant behavior (−)	Dunn (1993)[a]

	Play/talk (+)	Howes & Rubenstein (1985)
	Considerateness (+) and anxiety (+)	Phillips, McCartney, & Scarr (1987)[a]
	Children's likelihood of playing with objects (+)	Galinsky, Howes, Kontos, & Shinn (1994)[a]
	Cognitively complex play (+), social play complexity (+), adaptive language scores (+), security of attachment to providers (+), and behavior problems (aggression, anxiety, and hyperactivity) (−)	Howes, et al. (1998)
Accreditation (for care arrangement or provider) (+)	Cognitively complex play (+) and social play complexity (+), adaptive language scores (+), security of attachment to providers (+), and behavior problems (aggression, anxiety, and hyperactivity) (−)	Howes et al. (1998)
Provider education (+)	Social competence (+), cognitive development (+), and expressive language (+)	Clarke-Stewart (1987) Ruopp et al. (1979) Burchinal, Roberts, Nabors, & Bryant (1996)[a]
Director or provider experience (+)	Sociability (−) and intelligence (−)	Dunn (1993)[a]
	Social competence (−) and social adjustment (+)	Phillips, Scarr, & McCartney (1987)[a]
Director experience (+)	Aggression (+), hyperactivity (+), and anxiety (−)	Phillips, McCartney, & Scarr (1987)[a]
Provider training (+)	Cooperation and persistence in tasks and activities (+) and gains in cognitive test scores (+)	Roupp et al. (1979)
	Cognitive competence (+) and social competence (−)	Clarke-Stewart (1987)
Provider attitudes (+)	Social competence (+)	Clarke-Stewart, Gruber, & Fitzgerald (1994)[a]
ECERS (+)	Social development (+), language development (+), and children's anxiety (possibly curvilinear)	Phillips (1987); Phillips, McCartney, & Scarr (1987)
	Intellectual, language, and social development (no effect)	Kontos & Fiene (1987)[a]
	Security of attachment to provider (+)	Galinsky et al. (1994)[a]
	No relationship to children's play with other children	Galinsky, Howes, Kontos & Shinn (1994)[a]
ITERS (+)	Cognitive outcomes (+)	Burchinal et al. (1996)[a]

Table continues

TABLE 3 (*Continued*)

Predictor	Child outcome	Source
FDCRS (+)	Likelihood of being securely attached to provider (+)	Galinsky et al. (1994)[a]
Caregiver Interaction Scale (taps sensitivity) (+) (Arnett, 1989)	Likelihood of children's being securely attached to their provider (+)	Galinsky et al. (1994)[a]
	No relationship to children's play with other children	Galinsky et al. (1994)[a]
Adult Involvement Scale (Howes & Stewart, 1987) (taps responsiveness) (+)	Likelihood of children being securely attached to their provider (+), play with objects (+), and engage in higher levels or more complex play with objects (+)	Galinsky et al. (1994)[a]
	No relationship to children's play with other children	Galinsky et al. (1994)[a]
ORCE (+)	Interactions of maternal sensitivity with ORCE quality	NICHD Study of Early Child Care (1997b)[a]
	Children's engagement during interactions with their mothers (+)	NICHD Study of Early Child Care (1997c)[a]
	Cognitive and language competence (+)	NICHD Study of Early Child Care (1997c)[a]
	Problem behaviors (−)	NICHD Study of Early Child Care (1998)[a]
Interactions and behaviors of provider and child (+) (small to medium studies)	Cognitive competence (+), social competence (+), interactions with friend (+), negative behavior with unfamiliar peer (−), and aggression (−)	Clarke-Stewart et al. (1994)[a]
	Considerateness, sociability, intelligence and task orientation (+)	Phillips et al. (1987)[a]
	Intellectual competence (+)	Clarke-Stewart (1987)
Hours per week in daycare (+)	Interaction with gender/in interaction with maternal sensitivity: percentage of children insecurely attached (+)	NICHD Study of Early Child Care (1997b)[a]
	Child engagement with mother (−)	NICHD Study of Early Child Care (1997c)[a]
	Likelihood of avoidance of attachment figure (−)	Blanchard & Main (1979)
	Percentage of infants securely attached (−)	Belsky & Rovine (1988)

Provider turnover (+)	Play with peers (−) and PPVT scores (−)	Whitebook, Howes, & Phillips (1990)
	Dependence, sociability, anxiety, and language (+)	Phillips et al. (1987)[a]
Stability of care (+)	Interaction of starts (+) of new care arrangements and maternal sensitivity (−) associated with higher percentage of insecurely attached children	NICHD Study of Early Child Care (1997b)[a]
	Children likely to play with objects (+)	Galinsky et al. (1994)[a]
	Cognitive performance (+) for privileged children.	Pierrehumbert, Ramstein, & Karmaniola (1995)[a]

Note. A plus sign signifies high levels of a characteristic, and a minus sign indicates a low level of a characteristic. Sources given are not exhaustive, merely examples. SES = Socioeconomic status; NICHD = National Institute of Child Health and Human Development; ECERS = Early Childhood Environment Rating Scale; ITERS = Infant/Toddler Environment Rating Scale; FDCRS = Family Day Care Rating Scale; ORCE = Observation Rating of the Caregiving Environment; PPVT = Peabody Picture Vocabulary Test.
[a]Indicates child-care effects were identified after controlling for family effects.

highly correlated, as reported by Phillips, McCartney, and Scarr, 1987, and by Scarr, Eisenberg, and Deater-Deckard, 1994), we do not know how the subscales predict to relevant outcomes. Nor is it known how generalizable the results of the referenced studies are for child-care settings catering to children of different age levels, different maturational status (e.g., children with special educational needs), or different ethnic or cultural backgrounds.

RELATIONS AMONG MEASURES OF THE CHILD-CARE ENVIRONMENT

For this section of the chapter, we report about associations found in the literature among the various measures. Our review of this literature is meant to provide examples rather than to be comprehensive. We provide references to small studies and to a few large studies. In the category of large studies, we reviewed three studies of center-based care: National Child Care Staffing Study (Whitebook et al., 1990), the Cost, Quality and Child Outcomes in Child Care Centers (Helburn, 1995), and the Florida Child Care Quality Improvement Study (Howes et al., 1998). We also reviewed the Study of Children in Family Child Care and Relative Care (Galinsky et al., 1994), the Family Child Care Training Study (Galinsky, Howes, & Kontos, 1995), and the results about infant care from the NICHD Study of Early Child Care (NICHD Early Child Care Research Network, 1996). For the purpose of organizing the findings, we used our classification of aspects of care in terms of who provides care, where care is provided, who are the care recipients, how care is provided, and the child's experiences in care. Table 4 focuses on an important subset of the findings based on our review of the literature.

There are several uses for the information about the relation among the different measures. First, it shows which easy-to-collect information is predictive of complex measures of quality of care. Second, it is useful when considering the possibility of creating cluster measures that are not redundant. Third, the information can be used for selecting measures to introduce into the research design or into the data analysis process. Some further elaboration about the importance of studying information about the relations among measures is presented in the following paragraphs.

Identifying Predictors of Difficult-to-Measure Aspects of Quality

The measures describing the furnishing of the child-care environment, how care is provided, and how it is experienced by children are conceptually the most important among the measures we have described. This statement is based on scientific theory and empirical evidence indicating that physical and social environments influence humans from infancy onward through the interactions human beings have with both physical and social aspects of their environment (Bronfenbrenner, 1988; Piaget & Inhelder, 1969; Vygotsky, 1934; Wertsch, 1985). Yet, at the same time that the details of the physical and social environments that impinge on the child are important, the measurement of social interactions is very complex and time intensive. Consequently, it is important to find index measures (i.e., measures that are easy to collect and that are predictive of the complex and detailed measures). Determination of what such index measures are and the extent to which these measures are predictive of the complex measures would greatly facilitate routine assessment of the child-care environment by parents (for the purpose of selecting child-care settings), by states (for the purpose of regulation), and by researchers. The search for such measures is in process and has already led to the identification of predictors of quality that one can obtain by interviewing the director of a child-care setting, the provider, or both. These include measures such as the adult:child ratio, group size, cost per child, provider education, provider training, accreditation, and financial and security benefits for the provider (e.g., see Phillips & Howes, 1987). Such findings have led researchers to propose a model describing the way in which the easy-to-measure indexes are theoretically and empirically associated with variations in the quality of interactive care and with developmental outcomes (Howes, Phillips, & Whitebook, 1992).

Identifying Independent Measures of the Child-Care Environment

Because the measures of the child-care environment are quite diverse, some are likely to be highly correlated (e.g., provider education and provider training in child care), whereas others may be statistically independent (provider education and benefits the provider receives as an employee). Knowledge about the actual statistical associations in different types of child care (e.g., center care, day-care homes, and relative care) is useful for those interested in constructing clusters of measures. For example, one may want to use in a cluster a representative from each set of highly correlated measures. For similar reasons, one may want to know the relation between different global measures. Are findings based on the ECERS (Harms & Clifford, 1980) and on the PROFILE (Abbot-Shim & Sibley, 1987) highly correlated? If they are, there is no point in using both in the same research project.

Knowledge about the relation among measures within and across the distal and proximal divide is useful when investigators are faced with the task of selecting predictors to be entered into a regression model that considers the effects of distal and proximal aspects of child care on the developmental outcomes. For example, if the adult:child ratio has been shown in the literature to be a sizable, reliable, and consistent predictor of

TABLE 4
Relations Among Measures of the Environment

Who provides care and how care is provided	Where care is provided and how care is provided	Who receives care and how care is provided
Providers' education (+) and providers' training (+) in centers and in family day care are associated with encouragement (+), guidance (+), restrictiveness (−), promotion of verbal expression and skills (+), and generally good care (+). But some studies did not find an association	Providers in nonprofit centers are more likely to engage in appropriate caregiving; providers in independent, for-profit centers are more harsh and less sensitive than teachers in other programs; and for-profit centers in a state with relaxed licensing criteria provided poor-quality care	SES (−) or minority status associated with quality of care (−)
Providers' experience (+) is predictive of better proximal quality of care, of worse quality of care, and sometimes is not predictive of quality of care	Being regulated is associated with sensitivity (+) and planning activities for children (+) and center accreditation status (+) associated with quality (+)	Group size (+) is associated with provider stimulation (−) and responsiveness (−) in center care and in family day care and with affect (−) in family day care
Providers' sensitivity (+) is associated with overall quality of care (+)	In centers complying with Federal Interagency Day Care requirements (ratio, group size, and provider training), provider behavior is less harsh and more appropriate	Group size (+) is associated with provider responsiveness (−)
Providers' nonauthoritarian beliefs (+) are associated with quality of care (+)	Centers with higher expended costs and total revenue per child hour, with more donated resources and less dependence on parents' fees, have better overall quality. Higher quality is costly but not necessarily associated with much higher costs	There are studies that find no association between group size and quality of care
	Space organization (+) and varied materials (+) are associated with care stimulation (+)	Better adult:child ratio is associated with providers spending less time in management of infants and toddlers
		Better ratios in center care are associated with provider sensitivity (+), arrangement of appropriate behaviors for children (+), harshness (−), and detachment (−). Ratio is found to be the best predictor of center quality
		In family day care and in relative care, a somewhat higher number of children per adult predicts better overall quality

TABLE 4 (*Continued*)

Who provides care and child's experiences in care	Where is care is provided and child's experiences in care	Who receives care and child's experiences in care
Providers' experience (−) is associated with provider turnover (−), providers' detached behavior (+) is associated with provider turnover (+), and providers' nonauthoritarian attitudes (+) are associated with positive interactions with infants and preschool children (+)	Nonprofit centers had more teachers in a class at any given time and were more likely to have overlapping shifts of staff. Both are experienced directly by children For-profit status; lower wages for providers; and noncompliance with Federal Interagency standards of ratio, group size, and provider training are associated with greater staff turnover (which is a negative experience for children) Nonprofit status of centers is associated with adult:child ratios (+) and with provider turnover (−) Church affiliation of center is associated with adult:child ratios (−) Safe, uncluttered child-care settings with age-appropriate materials are associated with providers' behaviors toward target children (+)	Better ratio (+) is associated with positive (+) and individualized (+) care for toddlers in second year of life Adult:child ratios (+) and group size (−) are associated with more sensitive, warm, and responsive care for 6-month-old infants One comprehensive study did not find an association between ratio and quality of young children's experience in care

Note. A positive sign indicates high levels of the variable, and a negative sign indicates low levels. Relations reported here are based on a review of the literature. SES = Socioeconomic status.

the proximal or overall quality of care (as measured by a global measure, such as the ECERS; Harms & Clifford, 1980), the justification for the use of both a measure of the adult:child ratio and a measure of proximal characteristics of the quality of care in the same regression model would be limited.

CHOOSING AMONG MEASURES

We started this chapter by stating that the child-care environment is a place, a social milieu, an experience, and an employment setting. We presented a comprehensive array of dimensions of the child-care environment that pertains to who provides the care, where the care is provided, who receives the care, how the care is delivered, and how the care is experienced. Each of these dimensions, we argued, has multiple facets or levels, each of which can be measured. We then described the measures that have been used in the service of three different goals: licensing, accreditation, and research. We showed how different, frequently used research measures of the environment are predictive of developmental outcomes for children in care, and we reviewed knowledge about the relation among many of the available measures. We now turn to a discussion of the choice among the many measures.

Our presentation of the aspects of the child-care environment suggests that, under ideal circumstances, to provide a comprehensive evaluation of the child-care environment, all aspects of that environment need to be assessed. That is, even when measures of who provides care, who receives care, where care is provided, how it is provided, and how it is experienced are positively correlated, these dimensions merit independent assessment. This is the case because the different aspects are interconnected in a system in which a small change in one of the aspects may lead to no change, a small change, or a large change in some of the others. These possible interdependencies are not yet understood. For example, the effects of variations in provider training, type of care, or cost of care and of variations in child ethnicity, health and developmental status on peer interactions, or cognitive gains are not known. These relations may be different in settings that vary in terms of structure, physical setting, or adult:child ratio.

The scheme we presented shows that each aspect of the environment can be assessed by different criteria. These criteria are theoretically independent of one another. When it is known that care is provided in a center, the amount of indoor or outdoor space available, the age appropriateness of furnishings, or the details about the administration of the center are not necessarily known. This suggests that when engaging in an ideal comprehensive assessment, one would want to characterize the different aspects of the environment in terms of multiple aspects that are conceptually independent of one another.

Several comprehensive systems for evaluating the child-care environment have been devised and briefly described in this chapter. The CDPE, the NAEYC accreditation system, and the WHO system, which is based on the NAEYC system, come close to providing a comprehensive assessment of day-care centers. Some states have very comprehensive assessments for licensing (e.g., Maryland). Some large-scale studies are also quite comprehensive in terms of the measurement of different aspects of the environment (Galinsky et al., 1994; Helburn, 1995; Whitebook et al., 1989). The NICHD Study of Early Child Care (NICHD Early Child Care Research Network, 1994) is the most comprehensive to date in terms of its measurement of the child-care environment. The interest in assessing most or all of the multiple aspects of the child-care environment is relatively recent. One reason for this may be that comprehensive assessment is costly when done right.

The expense of valid assessments is only one reason for the fact that investigators shied away from comprehensive assessments. Another reason is that evaluators of child-care environments have been guided by a conceptual model that places more value on some aspects of the environment than on others. Developmental psychologists and early childhood education experts are guided by research showing that effects of the environment on child development are mediated primarily by proximal aspects of the environment (i.e., by how care is provided and by how it is experienced by the target children). In this framework, the responsiveness and sensitivity of providers to children in their care are considered critical elements of the quality of care. The language and cognitive stimulation that are transmitted in the child-care environment are other critical elements. This conceptualization has led some investigators to think of the conditions that facilitate or support sensitivity, responsiveness, and cognitive–linguistic stimulation as environmental aspects that are of secondary interest or proxies for the really important aspects. Consequently, the critical elements of sensitivity, responsiveness, and cognitive stimulation are the centerpiece of several of the global and experiential measures that we reviewed in this chapter (e.g., caregiver interaction, adult involvement, and the ECERS; Harms & Clifford, 1980).

When resources for evaluating the child-care environment are limited, the research literature can serve as a guide for choice of measures that are relatively easy to collect while predictive of the quality of care and the outcomes for children in care. For example, by reviewing existing knowledge, the parent would know that providers who are better educated and who have training in child development are likely to provide better quality care (e.g., Burchinal, Roberts, Nabors, & Bryant, 1996; Clarke-Stewart, 1987; Ruopp et al., 1979). In addition, the developmental outcomes for the child are likely to be better under the care of such providers and under optimal conditions of the adult:child ratio (e.g., see Dunn, 1993; Galinsky et al., 1994; Holloway & Reichart-Erikson, 1989; Phillips et al., 1987). Research also suggests that for infants, one-on-one relations or one-on-two relations between number of providers to number of children are a very important predictor of quality of care (NICHD Early Child Care Research Network, 1996). The well-informed parent of an infant will also look at a care setting that is physically well organized and appropriate for the care of young children (Clarke-Stewart et al., 1994; NICHD Early Child Care Research Network, 1996). In addition, parents should aim at identifying a setting in which provider turnover is either unexpected or very low (Phillips et al., 1987; Whitebook et al., 1989). They should also do their best to find a setting that is accredited or where the child's provider is accredited (Howes et al., 1998). Research also shows that it is important for parents to limit the number of different arrangements they place their children in. This is the case because transitions from one care setting to the next are hard on children (Galinsky et al., 1994; NICHD Early Child Care Research Network, 1997b).

When the goal of assessment is research, one may want to use the available knowledge to identify information that is currently missing. This would serve as a first step toward the development of new research to answer questions that are still open. It is quite clear that we do not know the relation among all existing measures, nor do we know how all measures of the child-care environment are associated with developmental outcomes. For example, we did not find research articles with information about the relation between provider wages, benefits, working conditions, and children's outcomes. Similarly, we could not find information about relations between the auspices of care or the setting's overall compliance with federal standards and their effects on children's outcomes. Moreover, one could determine that there are developmental outcomes of interest that are believed to be predicted by characteristics of the child-care environment that are yet to be measured. For example, it could be argued that the more continuity between the child-care environment and the family environment, the happier the children would be during their stay in care and the less upset they would be during daily transitions. (This, of course, would not be the case for children from disorganized, chaotic, or unloving homes.) This point of view would suggest that practices like having parents visit in the child-care setting regularly, having pictures of the parents in the child-care setting, having special time to share stories about the children's families, and having the provider visit children's families would all enhance children's affect and their readiness to spend time at the child-care settings. To evaluate this hypothesis, one would need to assess the aspects of care that build bridges between the child-care setting and children's homes. Another area that could be explored is that of the relation between variation in the hygiene of the child-care environment and nutrition provided there and variation in children's health outcomes.

From all of this, it is quite clear that to determine which of the available measures of the environment would be best in terms of one's own goals, one would need to consider the following: (a) why one wants to assess the child-care environment (e.g., licensing, accreditation, finding an arrangement for one's child, and research), (b) one's resources (time available, funds available, and personnel), (c) measures that have been developed and used by others, and (d) research findings about the available measures. When the goal is that of conducting research about the child-care environment, one needs to consider two other points: (a) the need for new information about existing measures and (b) the need for measures that are not yet available.

FUTURE DIRECTIONS FOR THEORY AND RESEARCH

Given that much of the assessment of child care is focused on the quality of care, researchers certainly need more theoretical work about what is meant by quality. Is quality an overall construct that predicts all positive developmental outcomes for children in care, or are there different aspects of quality that map onto specific child outcomes? The development of the global measures of quality seems to be based on the assumption that it does not matter which aspects of quality are met, only that a certain overall level is met. Scarr, Eisenberg, and Deater-Deckard (1994) found support for this assumption. Their study shows that a small subset of PROFILE (Abbot-Shim & Sibley, 1987) items, drawn randomly, provides an acceptable measure of quality of care. Yet, one might expect that specific aspects of quality will predict specific outcomes and will not have an effect on outcomes to which they are not conceptually related.

At this time, it is not clear to what extent certain aspects of the child-care environment operate the same in different types of care. Are adult:child ratio, group size, age mix, and provider education operating the same way in relative care, in family day care, and in center-based care? When research findings validate one of these measures in one setting, do the findings generalize to other settings? Similarly, it is not clear if knowledge based on providers or children from one ethnic group generalize to providers or children from other ethnic groups. It has been argued that relations between environmental factors and child development may vary across ecological settings (Bronfenbrenner, 1988; Ogbu, 1981; Rogoff, 1990).

The distinction between distal and proximal measures is frequently associated with the distinction between reported and observed measures, so that the distal measures are more likely to be garnered from existing documents or reported by mothers or care providers than directly observed by the investigators or by members of their teams. Although there is ample information about the reliability and validity of direct observation, there is scant information, if any, about the reliability and validity of information provided by care providers, center directors, and parents. Creating such a body of knowledge is important. If parents can provide valid information about the child-care setting, the furnishing, and the child-care providers as well as the adult:child ratio and group size, the ease of doing child-care research would increase, and the cost of such research would decrease.

Child-care research has come into being because of concern about the effects of historical changes affecting mothers and families on the development of children. As the number of mothers of young children who have joined the workforce has increased, so has the interest in the quality of the care that children are receiving (Hayes, Palmer, & Zaslow, 1990). History pertaining to maternal employment, child care, and child development has not come to a halt. Just recently there has been welfare reform legislation that limits the availability of welfare and requires that people formerly eligible for welfare, including mothers of infants and young children, find employment. This change of policy has tremendous implications for child care. Where will child care be provided and by whom? How will it be provided and how will it be experienced? Most of the information researchers currently have about child care and its effects is about care for children who are no longer infants and about settings that are formal (licensed). Also, the information is mostly about more affluent children, not the children of the poor (income-to-needs ratio less than 1.0), the near poor, or the working poor. Consequently, there is tremendous need and pressure to evaluate the child care that children of the working poor will be receiving, and such evaluations must focus not only on the availability and affordability of such care but also on its quality.

REFERENCES

Abbott-Shim, M., & Sibley, A. (1987). *Assessment profile for early childhood programs.* Atlanta, GA: Quality Assist.

Abbott-Shim, M., & Sibley, A. (1993). *Assessment profile for homes with young children—research version.* Atlanta, GA: Quality Assist.

Abbott-Shim, M., Sibley, A., & Neel, J. (1992). *Assessment profile for early childhood programs—research version.* Atlanta, GA: Quality Assist.

Allhusen, V. D. (1992). *Differences in day care experiences of infants in three different teacher–child ratio groups: Variations in caregiving quality.* Unpublished doctoral dissertation, Cornell University.

Arnett, J. (1989). Caregivers in day-care centers: Does training matter? *Journal of Applied Developmental Psychology, 10,* 541–552.

Benn, R. (1986). Factors promoting secure attachment relationships between mothers and their sons. *Child Development, 57,* 1224–1231.

Berk, L. E. (1985). Relationship of caregiver education to child-oriented attitudes, job satisfaction, and behaviors toward children. *Child Care Quarterly, 14,* 103–129.

Belsky, J., & Rovine, M. J. (1988). Nonmaternal care in the first year of life and the security of infant–parent attachment. *Child Development, 59,* 157–167.

Blanchard, M., & Main, M. (1979). Avoidance of the attachment figure and social–emotional adjustment in day-care infants. *Developmental Psychology, 15*(4), 444–446.

Bredekamp, S. (1986). The reliability and validity of the Early Childhood Observation Scale for accrediting early childhood programs. *Early Childhood Research Quarterly, 1,* 103–118.

Bronfenbrenner, U. (1988). Interacting systems in human development. *Persons in context: Developmental processes* (pp. 25–49). New York: Cambridge University Press.

Burchinal, M. R., Roberts, J. E., Nabors, L. A., & Bryant, D. M. (1996). Quality of center child care and infant cognitive and language development. *Child Development, 67,* 606–620.

Caldwell, B. M., & Bradley, R. H. (1984). *Home observations for measurement of the environment.* Little Rock: University of Arkansas at Little Rock.

Caldwell, B. M., Sartorius, N., Orley, J., Banaag, C. J., Hardeman, W. J., Jegede, R. O., & Tsiantis, J. (1990). *WHO Child Care Facility Schedule.* Unpublished manuscript, University of Arkansas at Little Rock.

Caughy, M. O., DiPietro, J., & Strobino, D. M. (1994). Day care participation as a protective factor in the cognitive development of low income children: Children and poverty [special issue]. *Child Development, 65,* 457–471.

Clarke-Stewart, K. A. (1987). Predicting child development from child care forms and features: The Chicago study. In D. A. Phillips (Ed.), *Quality in child care: What does research tell us?* (pp. 21–42). Washington, DC: National Association for the Education of Young Children.

Clarke-Stewart, K. A., Gruber, C. P., & Fitzgerald, L. M. (1994). *Children at home and in day care.* Hillsdale, NJ: Erlbaum.

Dunn, L. (1993). Proximal and distal features of day care quality and children's development. *Early Childhood Research Quarterly,* 8, 167–192.

Fiene, R. J. (1984). *Child Development Program Evaluation Scale.* Washington, DC: Children's Services Monitoring Consortium.

Fiene, R., & Nixon, M. (1985). The instrument based program monitoring information system and the indicator checklist for child care. *Child Care Quarterly, 14,* 198–214.

Galinsky, E., Howes, C., & Kontos, S. (1995). *The Family Child Care Training Study: Highlights of findings.* New York: Families and Work Institute.

Galinsky, E., Howes, C., Kontos, S., & Shinn, M. (1994). *The study of children in family child care and relative care.* New York: Families and Work Institute.

Goelman, H., & Pence, A. (1987). Effects of child care, family, and individual characteristics on children's language development: The Victoria Day Care Research Project. In D. A. Phillips (Ed.), *Quality in child care: What does research tell us?* (pp. 89–104). Washington, DC: National Association for the Education of Young Children.

Harms, T., & Clifford, R. (1980). *Early childhood environmental rating scale*. New York: Teachers College Press, Columbia University.

Harms, T., & Clifford, R. (1984). *The family day care rating scale*. New York: Teacher's College Press, Columbia University.

Harms, T., Cryer, D., & Clifford, R. (1990). *The infant/toddler environment rating scale*. New York: Teachers College Press, Columbia University.

Hayes, C. D., Palmer, J. L., & Zaslow, M. J. (1990). *Who cares for America's children?* Washington, DC: National Academy Press.

Helburn, S. W. (Ed.). (1995). *Cost, quality and child outcomes in child care centers* (Tech. Rep.). Denver: University of Colorado at Denver, Center for Research in Economic and Social Policy, Department of Economics.

Hofferth, S. L. (1996). Child care in the United States today. *The Future of Children* (Summer/Fall) 6(2), 41–61.

Holloway, S. D., & Reichart-Erikson, M. (1989). Child-care quality, family structure, and maternal expectations: Relationship to preschool children's peer relations. *Journal of Applied Developmental Psychology, 10*, 281–298.

Howes, C. (1983). Caregiver behavior in center and family day care. *Journal of Applied Developmental Psychology, 4*, 99–107.

Howes, C., Galinsky, E., Shinn, M., Gulcur, L., Clements, M., Sibley, A., Abbott-Shim, M., & McCarthy, J. (1998). *The Florida Child Care Quality Improvement Study: 1996 report*. New York: Families and Work Institute.

Howes, C., & Rubenstein, J. L. (1985). Determinants of toddlers' experience in day care: Age of entry and quality of setting. *Child Care Quarterly, 14*, 140–151.

Howes, C., & Stewart, P. (1987). Child's play with adults, toys, and peers: An examination of family and child-care influences. *Developmental Psychology, 23*, 423–430.

Howes, C., Phillips, D., & Whitebook, M. (1992). Thresholds of quality: Implications for the development of children in center-based child care. *Child Development, 63*, 449–460.

Kandall, E. D., & Walker, L. H. (1984). Day care licensing: The eroding regulations. *Child Care Quarterly, 13*, 278–290.

Kontos, S. J. (1991). Child care quality, family background, and children's development. *Early Childhood Research Quarterly, 6*, 249–262.

Kontos, S. J., & Fiene, R. J. (1987). Child care quality, compliance with regulations, and children's development: The Pennsylvania Study. In D. A. Phillips (Ed.), *Quality of child care: What does research tell us?* (pp. 57–80). Washington, DC: National Association for the Education of Young Children.

Lamb, M. E. (1997). Nonparental child care: Context, quality, correlates, and consequences. In I. E. Sigel & K. A. Renninger (Vol. Eds.) & W. Damon (Series Ed.), *Handbook of child psychology: Child psychology in practice* (4th ed., pp. 783–915). New York: Wiley.

Lamb, M. E., Sternberg, K. J., & Prodromidis, M. (1992). Nonmaternal care and the security of infant–mother attachment: A reanalysis of the data. *Infant Behavior and Development, 15,* 71–83.

Mann, J., Ten Have, T., Plunkett, J. W., & Meisels, S. J. (1991). Time sampling: A methodological critique. *Child Development, 62,* 227–241.

McCartney, K. (1984). Effect of quality of day care environment on children's language development. *Developmental Psychology, 20,* 244–260.

Morgan, G. (1980). Federal day care requirements: One more round. *Day Care and Early Education, 8,* 26–30.

National Association for the Education of Young Children (NAEYC). (1991). *Accreditation criteria and procedures.* Washington, DC: Author.

National Institutes of Child Health and Human Development Early Child Care Research Network. (1994). Child care and child development: The NICHD study of early child care. In S. L. Friedman & H. C. Haywood (Eds.), *Developmental follow-up: Concepts, domains, and methods* (pp. 377–396). San Diego, CA: Academic Press.

National Institutes of Child Health and Human Development Early Child Care Research Network. (1996). Characteristics of infant care: Factors contributing to positive caregiving. *Early Childhood Research Quarterly, 11,* 269–306.

National Institutes of Child Health and Human Development Early Child Care Research Network. (1997a). Familial factors associated with characteristics of nonmaternal care for infants. *Journal of Marriage and the Family, 59,* 389–408.

National Institutes of Child Health and Human Development Early Child Care Research Network. (1997b). The effects of infant child care on infant–mother attachment security: Results from the NICHD Study of Early Child Care. *Child Development, 68,* 860–879.

National Institutes of Child Health and Human Development Early Child Care Research Network. (1997c, April). *Mother–child interaction and cognitive outcomes associated with early child care: Results from the NICHD Study.* Poster presented at the biennial meeting of the Society for Research in Child Development, Washington, DC.

National Institutes of Child Health and Human Development Early Child Care Research Network. (1998). Early child care and self-control, compliance, and problem behavior at 24 and 36 months. *Child Development, 69,* 1145–1170.

Ogbu, J. (1981). Origins of human competence: A cultural–ecological perspective. *Child Development, 52,* 413–429.

Phillips, D. A. (Ed.). (1987). Quality in child care: What does the research show us? (Vol. 1). Washington, DC: National Association for the Education of Young Children.

Phillips, D. A., & Howes, C. (1987). Indicators of quality in child care: Review of research. In D. A. Phillips (Ed.), *Quality in child care: What does the research show us?* (pp. 1–19). Washington, DC: National Association for the Education of Young Children.

Phillips, D. A., Lande, J., & Goldberg, M. (1990). The state of child care regulation: A comparative analysis. *Early Childhood Research Quarterly, 5*, 151–179.

Phillips, D., McCartney, K., & Scarr, S. (1987). Child-care quality and children's social development. *Developmental Psychology, 23*, 537–543.

Phillips, D. A., Scarr, S., & McCartney, K. (1987). Dimensions and effects of child care quality: The Bermuda Study. In D. A. Phillips (Ed.), *Quality in child care: What does research tell us?* (pp. 43–56). Washington, DC: National Association for the Education of Young Children.

Phillips, D. A., & Zigler, E. E. (1987). The checkered history of federal child care regulation. In E. Rothkopf (Ed.), *Review of research in education* (Vol. 14, pp. 3–41). Washington, DC: American Educational Research Association.

Piaget, J., & Inhelder, B. (1969). *The psychology of the child.* New York: Basic Books.

Pierrehumbert, B., Ramstein, T., & Karmaniola, A. (1995). Bebes a partager [Babies to share]. In M. Robin, I. Casti, & D. Candilis-Huisman (Eds.), *La construction es liens familiaux pendant la premiere enfance [The construction of family ties in infancy]* (pp. 107–128). Paris: Presses Universitaires de France.

Prescott, E., Kritchevsky, S., & Jones, E. (1972). *The daycare environmental inventory* (Rep. No. OCD-R-219-C6). Pasadena, CA: Pacific Oaks College. (ERIC Document Reproduction Service No. ED 076 228)

Radloff, L. (1977). The CES-D Scale: A self-report depression scale for research in the general population. *Applied Psychological Measurement, 1*, 385–401.

Rogoff, B. (1990). *Apprenticeship in thinking: Cognitive development in social context.* New York: Oxford University Press.

Rubenstein, J. L., Pedersen, F. A., & Yarrow, L. J. (1977). What happens when mother is away: A comparison of mothers and substitute caregivers. *Developmental Psychology, 13*, 529–530.

Ruopp, R., Travers, J., Glantz, F., & Coelen, C. (1979). *Children at the center: Final results of the National Day Care Study.* Cambridge, MA: Abt Associates.

Scarr, S., Eisenberg, M., & Deater-Deckard, K. (1994). Measurement of quality in child care centers. *Early Childhood Research Quarterly*, 9, 131–151.

Schaefer, E. S., & Edgerton, M. (1985). Parental and child correlates of parental modernity. In I. E. Sigel (Ed.), *Parental belief systems: The psychological consequences for children* (pp. 287–318). Hillsdale, NJ: Erlbaum.

Stallings, J., & Porter, A. (1980). *National day care home study.* Washington, DC: Department of Health, Education, and Welfare.

Vygotsky, V. (1934). *Thought and language.* Cambridge, MA: MIT Press.

Wertsch, J. V. (1985). *Vygotsky and the social formation of mind.* Cambridge, MA: Harvard University Press.

Whitebook, M., Howes, C., & Phillips, D. A. (1989). *Who cares? Child care teachers and the quality of care in America* (Final report, National Child Care Staffing Study). Oakland, CA: Child Care Employee Project.

Young, K. T., & Zigler, E. (1986). Infant and toddler day care: Regulation and policy implications. *American Journal of Orthopsychiatry, 56*, 43–55.

Zaslow, M. J. (1991). Variation in child care quality and its implications for children. *Journal of Social Issues, 47*, 125–138.

6

CONCEPTUALIZATION AND MEASUREMENT OF CHILDREN'S AFTER-SCHOOL ENVIRONMENTS

DEBORAH LOWE VANDELL AND JILL K. POSNER

Kate and Jack are in the third grade. Each day after school, they walk from their classrooms to the school cafeteria, where an after-school program is conducted until 6:00 p.m. Most afternoons they spend some time outside playing soccer or chase, some time completing homework, and some time working on a craft project. Kate's best friends are enrolled in the program, and she spends most of her time with them. Jack's friends go home after school, and he wishes that he could go home as well. He thinks the after-school program is boring and that the teachers are mean.

Sam is in the fourth grade. Two days a week he goes home from school, makes himself a snack, and watches television or plays computer games until his father gets home from work at about 5:30 p.m. His parents have clearly laid out after-school rules, and Sam calls his mom as soon as

This research was supported by grants from the Spencer Foundation and the National Institute of Child Health and Human Development (HD30587-02). We are grateful to our colleagues Kim Pierce, Robert Rosenthal, Lee Shumow, and Kyungseok Kang for their insights, advice, and hard work on research projects in which children's after-school arrangements are studied.

he gets home. Two afternoons, Sam goes to play at a neighbor's house until his father gets home. One day a week Sam's father comes home early to take him to karate lessons.

Christine is in the first grade. She returns home after school. Her mother is usually there because she has been unable to find employment. Their family income is below that specified by federal poverty guidelines. Christine spends most of her time in the apartment watching television because she and her mother are frightened of some of the people who hang out in their neighborhood.

These brief descriptions reflect some of the diversity that characterizes children's after-school environments. They also illustrate some of the challenges facing researchers who seek to study these environments. These challenges include identifying the salient aspects of children's experiences after school, determining how to measure these experiences, and ascertaining how these experiences are affected by other environmental contexts. Until recently, there has been remarkably little research on children's after-school environments. Perhaps the assumption was that children return home to their families at the end of the school day, making the study of after-school care redundant with the study of homes and families. Both demographic (Hofferth, Brayfield, Deich, & Holcomb, 1991) and observational (Posner & Vandell, 1994; Rubin, 1983) data, however, indicate that this assumption is not warranted (if it ever was). In the United States, over 60% of mothers of school-aged children are employed, which means that many families must adopt forms of after-school care beyond mother care. According to one national survey (Hofferth et al., 1991), these after-school arrangements include care by fathers, in-home providers, other-home providers, formal after-school programs, and self-care (sometimes referred to as *latchkey care*).

Features within these arrangements vary widely. Some arrangements are highly stable, with children going to the same place each afternoon. Other arrangements vary by the day, week, and season of the year. Some settings afford children opportunities to interact with other children and with adults, whereas other settings are socially restricted, as when children are left alone. Some settings are rich in the provision of activities and materials that are of interest to children; others are bereft of such materials. Also, as the opening vignettes suggest, the after-school environment includes psychological dimensions that are reflected in children's feelings about and perception of the setting. Children may feel safe, comfortable, and happy about their after-school arrangements, or they may experience ambivalence, fear, or vague discontentment. Variations also occur in children's roles in decision making about after-school care. Some children are forced by circumstances into arrangements they dislike or fear, whereas other children wholeheartedly embrace their after-school care. It seems likely that each of these factors can have a marked impact on how the after-school environment affects children's development. A critical task is to identify and measure these variations in after-school experiences so that effects on children's social, emotional, and academic adjustment can be ascertained.

In addition, as the opening paragraphs suggest, after-school care does not exist in isolation. Rather, it occurs within a broader context of family, school, and community. This broader context affects which particular after-school environments are available to children. For example, affluent families are more likely to pay for their children to participate in enrichment "lessons" after school, and they are more likely to pay for the use of formal school-aged child-care programs than are less affluent families (Rubin, 1983). The broader context is also instrumental in framing the after-school experience. Self-care in a suburban neighborhood with a supportive neighbor nearby affords different opportunities and experiences than self-care in an urban neighborhood that has a high crime rate (Howard, Broquest, & Farrell, 1991). What children are permitted to do in these self-care settings varies widely, as do children's feelings about these experiences. Finally, as the opening vignettes describe, after school-care occurs within a developmental context. The same after-school environment undoubtedly affects 6-year-olds and 14-year-olds differently. For example, a formal program with activities designed for young grade school children does not appeal to most 14-year-olds (Halpern, 1992). What is unclear are the specific effects of developmentally inappropriate after-school care on children's social and academic adjustment.

AFTER SCHOOL: THE PERSPECTIVE OF ECOLOGICAL SYSTEMS THEORY

How, then, should researchers approach the formidable task of studying the after-school environment? One goal of this chapter is to present a conceptual framework for studying variations in the after-school environment. Figure 1 graphically portrays an ecological systems approach to the after-school environment. Drawing on ecological systems theory (Bronfenbrenner, 1979, 1989, chapter 1, this volume), the after-school environment is viewed as a microsystem consisting of "a pattern of activities, roles, interpersonal relations experienced by the developing person in a given setting with particular physical and material characteristics" (Bronfenbrenner, 1979, p. 22). Within this framework, after-school settings are examined for the potential they afford children for interacting with parents, siblings, other adults, and peers. Specific activities within the setting (some growth enhancing and some detrimental to development) are measured

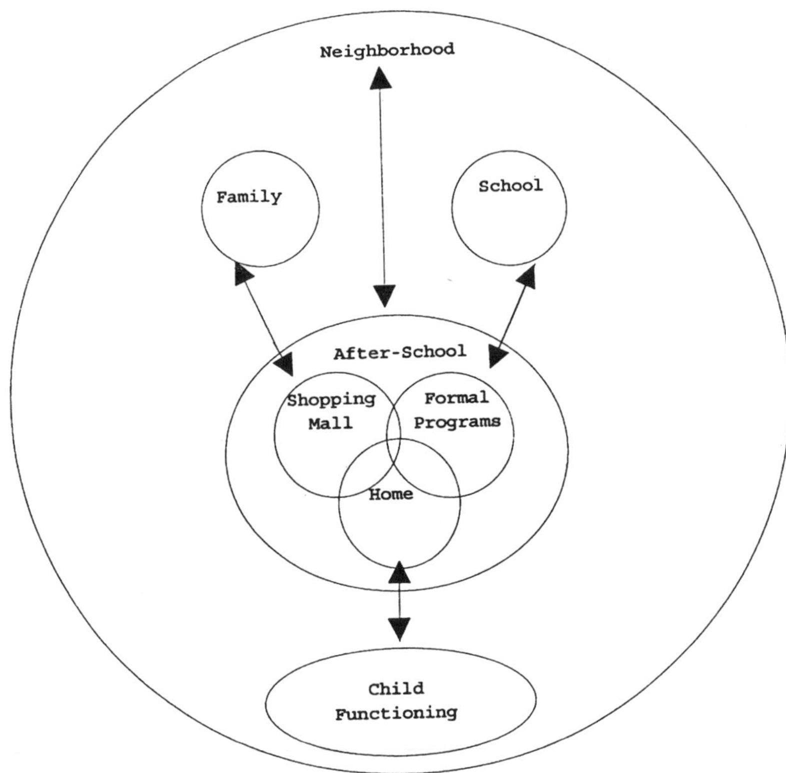

Figure 1. A conceptual model of the after-school environment: Relations among systems can occur concurrently and over time. Some arrows, such as those designating relations between family and child or between child or family and school, are omitted to highlight the focus of the current model on the after-school environment.

along with children's and parents' perceptions of these experiences. A child who is in an after-school arrangement because he or she wants to be is expected to interpret the experience differently than a child who has the arrangement forced on him or her. An important component of the proposed research agenda is the articulation and description of the diversity of after-school microsystems.

As Figure 1 illustrates, children's after-school environments can actually consist of a series of microsystems because many children do not experience a single setting. Rather, their time after school is composed of a series of settings that is experienced across the afternoon, week, and year. Figure 1 suggests some of the multiplicity of after-school settings that individual children may experience. Children may go home, go to the shopping mall, go to a friend's house, or hang out on the street. Within each setting, there is a potential array of social partners, roles, and activities. A critical task is to determine how to conceptualize and measure this multiplicity of settings. When these settings are considered in combination, researchers may determine that studying the after-school environment will make studying children's home environments seem relatively simple.

The conceptual model presented in Figure 1 also illustrates the placement of the after-school environment within a broader social–ecological context. Children's experiences after school and in their families are linked in several ways. First of all, families differ in their likelihood of utilizing different after-school options. For instance, children whose mothers are employed are more likely to be enrolled in after-school programs than children whose mothers are not employed (Hofferth et al., 1991; Seligson, 1991). African American families are more likely than European American families to have children cared for by extended family after school (Hofferth et al., 1991; Posner & Vandell, 1994). Families with greater financial resources are more likely to utilize paid enrichment lessons after school. Children's nonrandom assignment in after-school arrangements has important implications for studies of the effects of after-school care because these putative effects may actually be artifacts of differences in family characteristics.

In addition to affecting children's placement in after-school care, family characteristics may moderate the impact of after-school experiences. For example, there is evidence that children respond differently to self-care experiences when their families distally monitor these experiences than when the children are left to hang out without parental supervision (Galambos & Maggs, 1991; Steinberg, 1986). Yet another link between family environment and children's after-school experiences is reflected in changes in family interactions over time as a result of the children's after-school experiences. Galambos and Maggs, for example, found that time in self-care was associated with girls having more conflicts with their parents over time.

Figure 1 also illustrates another example of mesosystem (or cross-system) relationships experienced by children: linkages between school and after-school settings. Some formal programs occur at elementary schools and are viewed as part of an extended school day (Vandell & Posner, 1995). In these cases, the connection between school and after school is obvious. More commonly, however, after-school experiences are not aligned formally to what children do at school. This lack of a formal link does not mean, however, that the school environment does not influence children's after-school experiences, or vice versa. There is the potential for significant continuities (and discontinuities) between these microsystems of school and after school. Because many elementary schools offer structured days with minimal opportunities for children to make choices, to select activities, or to be alone or to interact with peers, children's time after school must be evaluated within the context of that school experience. There has been speculation (Rosenthal & Vandell, 1996) that highly structured after-school programs, in conjunction with highly structured classroom experiences, deprive children of the time needed for independent activities, physical activity, or "down time." If this is the case, children's school performance may negatively be affected as children turn off to structured academic activities.

Also reflected in the conceptual model portrayed in Figure 1 is the placement of the after-school microsystem within the broader context of neighborhood and community. Children's after-school experiences occur in neighborhoods that vary in terms of the availability of supportive adults and peers, objective measures of crime and of city services, and residents' subjective impressions of their neighborhoods. These features result in differential usage of some forms of after-school care. For example, self-care is more common in suburban and rural areas in comparison to urban areas (Hofferth et al., 1991). Within urban communities, parents are more likely to use self-care when they and their children believe the neighborhood is safer (Rubin, 1983; Vandell, Posner, Shumow, & Kang, 1995).

The effects of the after-school setting also appear to vary as a function of the neighborhood context. Formal after-school programs can serve as a safe haven within neighborhoods in which crime rates are high and the time after school exposes youngsters to deviant peers, illegal activities, and violence (Halpern, 1992; Posner & Vandell, 1994). Formal after-school programs may have a different meaning for children in suburban or rural neighborhoods (Belle, 1988; Vandell & Corasaniti, 1988), where some children believe that program participation deprives them of opportunities to participate in team sports, join clubs, or play with friends.

Although the description of after-school arrangements and their interface with the school, family, and community is a formidable task, consideration of these factors alone is not sufficient for understanding the effects of the after-school environment. As illustrated in Figure 1, the after-school environment must be placed within a developmental framework. The meaning and effects of after-school experiences are expected to vary with children's developmental status and maturity. For example, being left alone has been observed to have more negative effects on third graders' emotional well-being than on fifth graders' well-being (Vandell et al., 1995). Participation in supervised formal programs has been associated with better academic achievement for early elementary school children, but not for older children (Halpern, 1992; Vandell & Posner, 1995).

Other individual characteristics related to children's gender and temperament must be incorporated within an ecological model of after-school care. For example, there is evidence that girls are more negatively affected by self-care than boys (Galambos & Maggs, 1991; Woods, 1972). Children who are fearful about being left alone are less likely to be left alone (Vandell et al., 1995). Thus, an ecological systems approach to the after-school environment must consider how individual children's characteristics influence after-school placement and moderate the effects of that experience.

Although findings from various after-school studies are consistent with an ecological systems framework, comprehensive programmatic tests of the model outlined in Figure 1 have not been conducted. In the pages that follow, additional issues that need to be considered within this framework are discussed. First, the adequacy of a simple social address approach is examined, followed by a more differentiated view of the after-school environment. We then turn to some specific strategies for (a) classifying and quantifying after-school arrangements, (b) contrasting different arrangements, and (c) examining variations within a single type of arrangement. Then, the chapter turns to consideration of aspects of the family, school, and neighborhood that may prove particularly relevant for the study of the after-school environmental. Finally, child characteristics such as developmental status, gender, and temperament are considered as they pertain to an ecological model of after-school care.

CLASSIFYING AND QUANTIFYING AFTER-SCHOOL CARE

After-School Care as a Social Address

In contrast to the study of other environmental contexts such as home and school, relatively little research has examined children's after-school environments. For the most part, empirical research has appeared only since the mid-1980s, although there were some early studies of after-school care (e.g., Zucker, 1944). Most of the early studies (e.g., Long & Long, 1983; Rodman, Pratto, & Nelson, 1985; Zucker, 1944) adopted a social address approach in which children in different types of after-school arrangements were compared in terms of their developmental outcomes. Results from these studies were contradictory. Some studies have found that self-care children have more problematic development than supervised children, including being more fearful (Long & Long, 1983), lonely (Long & Long, 1983), and antisocial (Posner & Vandell, 1994; Vandell & Ramanan, 1991), as well as having more academic problems (Woods, 1972), using more alcohol and drugs (Richardson et al., 1989), and engaging in more sexual activities (Howard et al., 1991). Others (Rodman et al., 1985; Steinberg, 1986; Vandell & Corasaniti, 1988; Woods, 1972), however, reported no overall differences between the developmental outcomes of self-care and other-care children.

Research findings from studies examining the effects of attending formal after-school programs are also contradictory. On the one hand, some (Howes, Olenick, & Der-Kiureghian, 1987; Mayesky, 1980; Posner & Vandell, 1994) have identified beneficial effects associated with attending formal after-school programs, whereas others (Vandell & Corasaniti, 1988) have found problematic development associated with program attendance.

Are these different findings inexplicable random effects? Are they really contradictory findings? Or, do these different findings represent meaningful results that can be explained within an ecological systems framework? Examination of the specific features of the studies suggest that these differences are meaningful and that they are related to (a) the specific aspects of the after-school settings, (b) the families and neighborhoods in which the care is situated, and (c) the developmental and individual characteristics of the children utilizing the care. In the sections that follow, these features are described in more detail as we move beyond the simple social address.

Issues of Definition: How to Ask the Question

Although the identification of after-school arrangements might seem a straightforward task in which one asks parents (or children) to report what kinds of care are used after school, identification of these arrangements can be accomplished in several ways. In our research (Posner & Vandell, 1994; Vandell & Posner, 1995), a variety of techniques have been used to identify after-school arrangements. One technique was to ask a custodial parent to report if his or her child had a "regular" after-school arrangement. "Regular" was defined as care used for 3 days a week or more. Several types of arrangements were provided as choices: care by mother, care by another adult, care by a sibling less than 14 years old, care by an adolescent, self-care, and attendance at an after-school program. Some large-scale surveys (Hofferth et al., 1991; Vandell & Ramanan, 1991) have made similar requests in which parents were asked to report their "primary" after-school care arrangement, in which similar response options were used. One advantage of this global or primary report is that it evens out some sporadic variations in child care. For example, a child who usually stays with the grandmother but occasionally plays at a friend's house is scored as being in relative care. Using this classification scheme, Vandell and Posner examined the after-school arrangements of 236 low-income urban children. In third grade, 56% were cared for by the mother after school, and 21% were cared for by other adults; 7% were in self-care, and 16% were in formal programs. In fifth grade, 62% were cared for by the mother, 15% were supervised by other adults, 9% were in self-care, and 13% were in formal programs. Interestingly, these reports are consistent with the figures reported in a national data set examining child-care choices among low-income families (Vandell & Ramanan, 1991), in which 7% of the third to fifth graders were in self-care and 63% were in mother care after school.

Vandell and Posner (1995) also asked the children and research staff (who knew the children well) to report the children's regular after-school arrangement. Good agreement between parents and researchers was found. For children in the third, fourth, and fifth grades, parents and researchers were in agreement in 87%, 92%, and 91% of the cases, respectively. Agreement between parents and children was more modest but improved with child age: There was 70% agreement between parents and children in third grade and 79% agreement between parents and children in fifth grade. These comparisons suggest that parents are reliable respondents about children's modal after-school arrangements and that children become more reliable with age.

Global reports of primary arrangements have been shown to be associated with children's developmental outcomes. Posner and Vandell (1994) reported that third-grade children who attended formal programs 3 or more days per week performed better academically than children who used mother care, self-care, or other-adult care as their primary after-school arrangement. Vandell and Ramanan (1991) found that mother care after school was associated with children's behavior problems in some circumstances: Returning home to mother in single-parent households was associated with lower Peabody Picture Vocabulary Test (PPVT) scores and higher ratings for antisocial behavior, anxiety, and peer conflict.

Although a categorical approach to identifying primary arrangements has been used successfully, it suffers from the limitations of all categorical approaches in that it masks some variability in after-school experiences. Children who attend a program 3 days a week and who are in self-care 2 days a week are categorized as *program children*, with no indication of time in self-care. As a result, Vandell and Posner (1995) also asked parents to report on their children's "typical" arrangement for each weekday. From these reports, participation scores for each arrangement were constructed, ranging from 0 to 5, indicating how many days in a typical week a particular arrangement was used. Vandell and Posner also asked if children "occasionally" or "never" used self-care. This approach is similar to the 5-point rating scale used by Todd and Mayberry (1991) to quantify self-care usage. From these quantitative reports, a more differentiated view of self-care emerged. Although relatively few children were reported to use self-care as a primary arrangement, these numbers increased when occasional, 1-day-a-week, and 2-days-a-week designations were reported. In their study of middle-class third and fourth graders, Todd and Mayberry found that 10% were left alone "regularly." This figure increased to 21% when daily reports were examined. Similarly, Vandell and Posner found that the number of children participating in formal programs increased when "by-day" reports rather than primary arrangements were recorded, because these by-day figures included children who attended programs for 1 day or 2 days per week. These more differentiated reports of self-care and formal program utilization were better predictors of child adjustment than was the categorical designation of only the primary arrangement.

A further refinement of these parental or child reports was to break the afternoon into time units so that it was possible for the child to be recorded as using more than one arrangement during a single day. For these daily reports, Vandell and Posner (1995) telephoned children during the evening and asked them to report, in 15-minute time blocks, (a) who they were with, (b) where they were, and (c) what they were doing from the time school ended until 6:00 p.m. If children did not have telephones, they were interviewed at school the following day. During third grade, children were interviewed three times during the school year. During both the fourth and the fifth grades, children completed four or five time-use interviews across the school year. the accuracy of the children's recollections was assessed against spot-check phone calls made during the afternoons and against observations conducted in the formal settings. From these reports, it was possible to determine the amount of time (per day) that children were engaged in different activities in different settings and the amount of time that they were without adult supervision. "Without adult supervision" included the time a child was (a) alone, (b) with a sibling less than 14 years old, (c) with an adolescent, or (d) with unsupervised peers. A notable increase in the number of children spending some part of the afternoon without adult supervision was found across grades. The phone calls revealed that 75% of the children in third grade, 87% of the children in fourth grade, and 92% of the children in fifth grade were without adult supervision at some point during the afternoon. The mean amount of time spent unsupervised did not change from third to fifth grade, averaging about 30 minutes per day. At the same time, there was substantial variation across children in the amount of time in self-care, ranging from always being supervised after school to almost 3 hours per day without supervision.

From these reports of after-school arrangements, additional measures of children's after-school environments can be obtained. When reports are obtained over time, it is possible to develop estimates of (a) age of entry into and exit from different types of after-school care, (b) cumulative amounts of time in different types of care, and (c) the stability and continuity of after-school care. Each of these aspects of after-school care may contribute differentially to children's development.

Assessing Age of Entry and of Exit

Although newspaper and magazine stories sometimes offer parents advice about the appropriate timing of after-school experiences, there has been little research on which to base this advice. Questions about timing are salient for three arrangements: self-care, formal programs, and informally supervised settings. It can be asked, for example, at what age (and under what conditions) do children enter self-care with minimal developmental risk. Similarly, it can be asked at what age (and under what conditions) do children leave formal programs without negative repercussions. Finally, the age at which children transition out of formal programs to informally supervised care can be considered.

Todd, Albrecht, and Coleman (1990) have proposed a developmental model in which adult supervision is portrayed as lying along a continuum ranging from full adult supervision to no adult supervision. Adult supervision with a high degree of accountability occurs when children are cared for by parents, sitters, or formal programs in which adults directly supervise children and have full responsibility for their welfare. Next along the continuum is adult supervision with some accountability such as that provided by library programs, clubs, and sports teams. Adults monitor activities, but children have greater choice about attending and participating in the activities. Neighborhood check-in programs and self-care with parental monitoring by telephone typify a third point on the continuum in that some distal supervision is offered. In these cases, children have major responsibility for their own care, but adults are aware of where the children are, what they are doing, and who they are with. A final point on the continuum reflects a complete lack of supervision, typified by little or no contact with responsible adults. The effects of age of entry (into self-care) and exit (from formal programs and informal settings) might be expected to vary, depending on where the arrangements lie in terms of this supervision continuum.

Vandell et al. (1995) explored the issue of timing of self-care in a longitudinal examination of 196 low-income children living in Milwaukee, Wisconsin. In this study, unsupervised time alone for children in the third grade was associated with the children having more behavior problems, whereas unsupervised time alone for children in the fifth grade did not show a similar association, suggesting that third graders were more vulnerable to this form of self-care. Further support for this timing hypothesis was the finding that the third-grade behavior problems did not appear to be transitory. Unsupervised time alone for children in the third grade even continued to be associated with behavior problems when the children were assessed in fifth grade.

Assessing Cumulative Quantity of Care

Another way of operationalizing the after-school environment is assessing the amount of time that children spend in a setting at a given point in time and over time. A study by Richardson et al. (1989) suggests that quantity of time in particular after-school environments is an important issue, even in adolescence. After controlling for social class, gender, race, family stress, and participation in extracurricular activities, Richardson et al. found that urban eighth graders who were in self-care for more than 10 hours per week were twice as likely to engage in problem behaviors such as smoking cigarettes, drinking alcohol, and smoking marijuana as those who experienced less unsupervised time. Furthermore, adolescents in self-care between 5 and 10 hours per week displayed higher rates of these activities than those with fewer than 5 hours per week in self-care. Vandell et al. (1995) found a similar linear relationship between amount of time per week in self-care and behavior problems in grade school children: In third grade, the more time in self-care, the more behavior problems.

Quantity can be conceptualized by examining it cumulatively as well. In this case, amount of time in a given arrangement is summed over time rather than relying on quantity measured at a single point in time. Vandell et al. (1995) observed cumulative effects of unsupervised time when information from third, fourth, and fifth grades was considered jointly. Behavior problems were more common and school achievement was lower when children spent more unsupervised time with peers over a 3-year period.

Assessing Stability and Consistency

Within the infant and preschool child-care literature, there is evidence that consistency or stability of care arrangements is beneficial for children's development. For example, Howes and her colleagues (Howes, 1988; Howes & Olenick, 1986; Howes & Stewart, 1987) reported that instability of care, measured as the number of changes in arrangements, had both concurrent and long-term negative effects on children's social competence and academic performance. In addition, stability of individual caregivers has been found to be important. The more teachers that children experience as preschoolers, the less gregarious and the more socially withdrawn the children appear to be (Howes & Hamilton, 1993).

Similar issues pertaining to stability and consistency have not been investigated with respect to children's after-school environments. Such studies present special challenges. One challenge is to define what is meant by stability and consistency. School-aged children's lives are complicated (Bryant, 1989; Medrich, Roizen, Rubin, & Buckley, 1982). Within a single afternoon, children can experience more than one after-school setting, as when a child is taken by a parent from home to a piano lesson or the child rides her bike from an after-school program to baseball practice. In addition, within a single week, children can participate in multiple arrangements. For example, a child may spend 1 day at a neighbor's house, 2 days at an after-school program, and 2 days with his or her own parents. Do children experience these predictable but multiple arrangements as stable or unstable? Should these arrangements be distinguished from situations in which children experience breaks in arrangements, such as stopping one arrangement and beginning another one? In assessing stability of after-school care, it may prove important to distinguish between daily and weekly patterns that are consistent but include multiple arrangements as opposed to breaks in arrangements (such as moving from one after-school program to another or changing from one sitter to another). We suspect that these different types of inconsistency will have different developmental implications.

Inspection of the data from the Milwaukee After-School Study (Vandell & Posner, 1995), which was collected over a 3-year period, reveals that all of these situations were common. From parent interviews obtained in the fall and spring of each school year, it appeared that many children experienced changes in their primary arrangements. For example, 31% of the mothers of fourth graders reported using a different type of primary arrangement in the fall and spring, and 29% of the fifth graders were listed as being in different types of arrangements in the fall and spring. Given the good agreement between parental and researcher concurrent reports, these discrepancies in parental reports likely reflect real changes in after-school care over the course of the year, rather than measurement error.

The fluidity of after-school arrangements was further underscored when patterns from third through fifth grades were examined. Of the 193 children for whom data from third to fifth grade were available, 41% experienced at least one major change in their regular after-school arrangement. The most stable arrangement occurred for children who were cared for by the mother after school (41% of the sample were in mother care across the 3 years). Seventeen children (9%) were in formal programs and 14 children (7%) were in informal adult-supervised arrangements for all 3 years. Very few children (1.5% of the sample) were reported to be in self-care for all 3 years.

Inspection of daily reports and time-use interviews revealed that children often experienced several after-school environments during a given week. Some attended formal programs and then returned home to their parents in the late afternoon. Other children were in self-care right after school and then moved into parental care. Other children experienced changes across the week as they went to a community center one day and stayed with neighbors on other days. Belle's (1988) detailed qualitative interviews with parents and children and Hofferth et al.'s (1991) national phone surveys also underscore the need to address this issue of multiple after-school arrangements.

Future examination of the effects of consistency and stability of care arrangements on children's developmental outcomes will need to discriminate among these different types of consistency. The possibility of nonlinear effects should also be considered. Experiencing some variations in after-school settings and activities may be developmentally appropriate for school-aged children. Bryant (1989), for example, argued that school-aged children benefit from a balance of activities that can provide emotional and instrumental support from adults on the one hand and autonomy and independence on the other. Bryant found that children whose mothers were not employed (and who were presumed to be more available to supervise their children) showed social benefits of free time off with peers, whereas children whose mothers were employed (who were presumed to offer less intense supervision) appeared to benefit from supplementary involvement with other adults in the form of formal programs, lessons, and clubs. Drawing from Bryant's data, one might hypothesize that after-school experiences that afford children with opportunities for different activities and broader social networks are more beneficial than those environments that offer only restricted activities, roles, and partners day in and day out.

ASSESSMENTS ACROSS AND WITHIN SETTINGS

After-School Care as a Microsystem

Identifying settings and assessing quantity, onset, and stability alone do not tell researchers why after-school environments are associated with children's developmental outcomes. Participation in stable arrangements may have positive or negative effects, depending on the quality and age appropriateness of those stable arrangements. The effects of hours of self-care may depend, in part, on the children's activities and feelings when they are alone. We contend that understanding why after-school environments affect development requires an examination of psychological processes, activities, roles, and experiences that occur within the settings. The identification of these experiences will be instrumental in resolving seemingly discrepant findings regarding the effects of after-school care.

Comparisons Across Settings

To investigate the hypothesis that children's development is affected by the after-school environment, investigators may want to conduct some assessments that can be applied across settings. With these measures, it is possible to contrast the extent to which different settings afford opportunities that are either beneficial or detrimental to child development. Researchers examining the effects of early child-care experiences have faced a similar task. Like older children, infants and preschoolers participate in various child-care arrangements, including day-care centers, family day care, and in-home sitters. To contrast children's experiences in these different settings, investigators (Clarke-Stewart, Gruber, & Fitzgerald, 1994; Howes, 1983; National Institute of Child Health and Human Development [NICHD] Early Child Care Research Network, 1996) have developed observational assessments that focus on children's interactions with caregivers, peers, and objects that can occur in all of the settings.

A similar strategy can be followed to describe school-aged children's experiences in different after-school settings. There are notable difficulties in designing such assessments. One problem is that school-aged children's sensitivity to the observers' presence may seriously influence their behavior, especially if the observers are intrusive. Recent playground-based studies (Asher & Gabriel, 1993; Ladd & Price, 1993; Sheldon, 1990) suggest the feasibility of conducting such field-based research by using a variety of strategies, including wireless microphones. These researchers succeeded in recording a range of peer interactions on playgrounds.

A second difficulty of conducting observations in diverse after-school settings pertains to the mobility of school-aged children. To send observers with children about their neighborhoods is a challenge, although once again some investigators (Barker & Wright, 1955; Whiting, 1980) have been successful in observing children as they move about their communities. Even if observational measures are adapted successfully for formal programs, playgrounds, and public settings, one important after-school setting, self-care, is not amenable to observation. The introduction of observers into self-care settings fundamentally transforms the setting to one in which adult supervision is occurring. In response to the difficulties with conducting observations in after-school settings (especially self-care), other techniques for obtaining information about after-school microsystems have been developed. Reports of children's time use by using beepers, phone interviews, and written diaries represent ways of obtaining information about where a child is, who the child is with, and what the child's activities are (Bryant, 1989; Duckett, Raffaelli, & Richards, 1989; Medrich et al., 1982; Posner & Vandell, 1994; Vandell & Posner, 1995). Using beepers, Csikszentmihalyi and Larson (1984) were able to document high school students' activities. Medrich used phone interviews to record school-aged children's after-school time. In both cases, the obtained information directly corresponds to Bronfenbrenner's (1979, 1989) specification of the key features of a microsystem.

Posner and Vandell (1994) used telephone interviews with children about their after-school activities to contrast four after-school microsystems (mother care, formal programs, self-care, and informal adult supervision). Six activities were found to occupy 5% or more of the after-school time of low-income urban third graders, with considerable variability across children: watching television (M = 19%; range = 0%–64%), transit (M = 15%; range 0%–45%), homework or other academic activities (M = 11%; range = 0%–58%), outside unorganized activities (M = 11%; range = 0%–61%), eating (M = 9%; range = 0%–30%), and indoor unstructured activities (M = 6%; range = 0%–36%). Comparisons across settings (mother care, self-care, other-adult supervision, and formal programs) revealed significant differences. Children who attended formal programs spent more time in academic activities (M = 23%) and enrichment lessons

(M = 5%) than children in other types of care, who did not differ from one another (M = 9% for academics and 0% for enrichment lessons). Children in self-care (M = 26%) and informal adult supervision (M = 20%) watched more television than did children who attended formal programs (M = 10%). Children in self-care (M = 11%), informal adult supervision (M = 14%), and mother care (M = 11%) spent more time playing outside while unsupervised than did children who attended programs (M = 5%). Settings also differed in terms of adults, siblings, and peers being present and in amount of time others were actively engaged with the child. Children who attended formal programs were more actively involved with adults (57% of the time) and peers (63% of the time) in contrast to children in self-care (29% and 43%, respectively) or informal adult supervision (34% and 38%, respectively).

It is important to note that the time spent in these activities was related to children's development (Posner & Vandell, 1994). Children who spent more time in unorganized outdoor activities had poorer academic grades, work habits, and emotional adjustment. Children who spent more time in enrichment activities such as music and gymnastics lessons had better grades, work habits, emotional adjustment, and peer relationships. Time spent working with adults on academic activities was positively associated with academic and conduct grades. Each of these relations between time use and child adjustment was obtained for the sample as a whole as well as for analyses conducted within the four types of care. Thus, it appears that the children's activities and social partners were salient, regardless of the particular care setting, even though some settings afforded more opportunities for some activities. There was, however, one notable exception to this consistent pattern across settings. Time spent with peers after school was associated with increased antisocial behavior for children who were in self-care but was associated with fewer antisocial behaviors for children who attended formal programs. Peer activities appeared to have a different meaning under supervised and nonsupervised conditions.

In a follow-up study of these same children in fourth and fifth grades, Posner and Vandell (1995) found similar setting differences associated with television watching, academics, outside unstructured activities, and enrichment lessons. In addition, they examined the effects of gender and family composition on after-school experiences. Boys spent more time than girls playing informal sports and inside structural games (e.g., Nintendo). Girls spent more time after school socializing, doing homework, and engaging in personal care activities. Children in two-parent households were more likely to participate in enrichment lessons, whereas children in single-parent households spent more time in outdoor unstructured activities. Interestingly, these time-use differences associated with gender and family structure corresponded to those reported for middle-class children's after-school time (Carpenter, Huston, & Spera, 1989; Duckett et al., 1989; Timmer, Eccles, & O'Brien, 1985).

Although time-use reports offer a useful perspective of children's after-school environments, some limitations to this methodology must be considered. The feasibility of obtaining accurate, detailed time-use reports has not been established for children before third grade, although some researchers (Marshall, 1991) have been successful in having children as young as first graders report more globally about their after-school activities. A second limitation is that time-use reports do not focus on the quality of children's experiences with others. They do not inform researchers about how sensitive or warm the available adults are, nor do they tell researchers about the kinds of interactions the children are having with their peers. A final limitation of this method is that children's feelings or thoughts about their activities, roles, and partners are not typically incorporated into the time-use reports.

Consequently, researchers may need to consider additional assessments that examine children's subjective evaluation of their after-school experiences. In this regard, children can be asked about how they feel during the after-school hours. To date, children's reports of their feelings about self-care (Long & Long, 1983; Todd & Mayberry, 1991; Williams & Fosarelli, 1987) and formal programs (Halpern, 1992) have been presented. Systematic comparisons across care settings have not been made. A final perspective that can be applied across after-school settings can be provided by parents. Parents' satisfaction with the arrangement, their perceptions of their children's experiences in the setting, and their view of alternative arrangements can be obtained. A 10-item parental satisfaction questionnaire developed by Rosenthal and Vandell (1996) illustrates this approach. Rosenthal and Vandell asked parents about their children's reactions to formal after-school programs as well as their own impressions of the programs. These parental reports were related to child reports of program climate and to observers' ratings of the programs.

Within-Setting Variations

During the past 10 years, researchers (e.g., Clarke-Stewart et al., 1994; NICHD Early Child Care Research Network, 1996; Howes, Phillips, & Whitebook, 1992) examining infant and preschool child care have documented substantial within-setting variations. Day-care centers, for example, vary widely in structural features such as child:adult ratio and group size, as well as in caregiver training and beliefs. Substantial variation has also been recorded in family day-care homes and in in-home care. There is no reason to believe that there is less within-setting variation in after-school settings. In the section that follows, aspects of within-setting variations are described.

Variations in Self-Care Experiences

A widespread concern (Erikson, 1988; Harris & Associates, 1987; Long & Long, 1983; Seligson, 1991) is that self-care has detrimental effects on children's development. Unfortunately, much of the research investigating self-care has failed to distinguish among different types of self-care. (See Belle, 1988, for a thoughtful discussion of this issue.) In fact, self-care experiences can vary substantially (Belle, 1988; Steinberg, 1986; Vandell et al., 1995). Children can be *alone* (no one else present). They can be with a *sibling*, who may be younger or older than they are. They can be with older *adolescents*, who serve as responsible care providers, or they can be with adolescents who may introduce them to health-endangering activities. Children can also be with unsupervised *peers*. Vandell et al. examined some of these variations. The percentages of children who were alone after school increased from 26% of the children in third grade to 54% of the children in fifth grade. Forty-three percent of the children spent some unsupervised time with peers in third grade; 60% of the fifth graders spent some time with peers that was unsupervised. The proportions of children spending unsupervised time with siblings also increased from third to fifth grade (23% to 38%), as did the proportions of children spending unsupervised time with adolescents (12% to 20%).

Vandell et al. (1995) found that these different types of self-care were differentially associated with children's third- and fifth-grade adjustment. Amounts of unsupervised time with adolescents and siblings were not associated with behavior problems, whereas amount of time alone predicted behavior problems in third grade (but not in fifth grade). Amount of unsupervised time with peers was associated with behavior problems in both third and fifth grades. Galambos and Maggs (1991) have also found that a more differentiated view of self-care is needed. In a study of middle-class sixth graders, no differences in socioemotional adjustment were found when children were supervised by adults after school or were in self-care in their own homes. Problem behaviors and contact with deviant peers were more likely only when self-care consisted of hanging out with unsupervised peers.

Variations in School-Aged Child-Care Programs

In contrast to the extensive research literature examining preschoolers' experiences in formal programs, there has been little research examining children's experiences within school-aged child care (SACC) programs. Instead, practitioners and policymakers (Erikson, 1988; Seligson, 1991) have assumed that factors associated with high-quality preschool programs are pertinent for after-school programs. These features include domains that are amenable to regulation, such as child:staff ratios, classroom size, and staff education and training. Aspects of the physical environment identified in the preschool literature, such as amount of space, arrangement of the space, availability of materials, and health and safety provisions are also assumed to be important. In addition, there may be other issues that are salient for school-aged children that are not emphasized with younger children. Drawing on the developmental literature during middle childhood, the SACC professional community (Seligson, 1991) has argued that provisions for autonomy, child choice, and privacy are critical. Children's interest in organized sports and performance arts suggests that these activities are another necessary component of school-aged programs.

One of the first systematic examinations of school-aged child care programs is represented by the National Study of Before and After School Programs (RMC Research Corporation, 1993). Phone interviews were conducted with a nationally representative sample of 1,304 after-school providers. From this survey, it appears that after-school programs vary substantially in terms of teacher characteristics, physical setting, and provision of activities. Unfortunately, this study did not examine relations between these program characteristics, nor were associations between program variations and children's developmental outcomes investigated. An important task for future research is the systematic examination of these issues.

Rosenthal and Vandell's (1996) research represents an initial attempt to examine these additional issues. Observations were conducted in 30 school-aged programs that were selected to reflect the diversity of programs available in and around Madison, Wisconsin. Each program was observed for two afternoons. Regulatable features such as total enrollment, child:staff ratio, and staff education were assessed by director report. Observers recorded positive–neutral and negative staff–child interactions, and they rated programs in terms of flexibility and age appropriateness. Negative staff–child interactions were more frequent when child:staff ratios were larger and when staff had less formal education. Director reports of the number of different program activities were positively associated with observers' reports of more frequent positive or neutral staff–child interactions and higher ratings of program flexibility and age appropriateness.

Evidence that these program experiences were meaningful for children and parents was apparent in parents' own reports about the after-school programs. Rosenthal and Vandell (1996) asked 180 third-, fourth-, and fifth-grade children to complete a 36-item questionnaire about their experiences in the programs. Items focused on the children's relationships with the adult staff, children's relationships with other children in the program, children's feelings that their needs for autonomy and privacy were being met, and children's overall feelings about the program. These child reports of the program climate were related to the observers' reports. Children reported poor program climate when programs had larger enrollments and when observers recorded more frequent negative staff–child interactions. Parental perceptions were also related to program quality: Parents had more positive perceptions of the programs when child:staff ratios were smaller and when their children reported more positive climates.

Research examining the effects of these variations in formal programs on children's social, emotional, and academic development has not been completed. The extensive research involving preschool child care has documented short- and long-term effects associated with program quality (Howes, 1990; Howes et al., 1992; McCartney, 1984; Vandell, Henderson, & Wilson, 1988). Whether similar effects will be found for school-aged child care is an unanswered question.

AFTER-SCHOOL CARE WITHIN A BROADER ECOLOGICAL CONTEXT

Even if children's specific experiences within the after-school microsystem are fully articulated, this articulation is not sufficient for understanding the developmental implications of after-school experiences for children's adjustment because after-school care occurs within a broader context of family, school, and community. These factors influence not only the particular after-school arrangements that children utilize but also the impact of the after-school experience on children's development. In the sections that follow, these selection effects and moderated effects are considered as they pertain to family, school, and neighborhood and community.

After-School Care in a Family Context

Families differ in their utilization of after-school care. In an analysis of U.S. census data, Cain and Hofferth (1989) found that European American families and families with more income were more likely to use self-care than were minority race or less affluent families. Similar demographic differences have been reported in other national data sets in which more educated mothers and employed mothers were more likely to use self-care for their school-aged children (Coleman, Robinson, & Rowland, 1990; Hofferth et al., 1991; Vandell & Ramanan, 1991). Families also differed in their utilization of formal programs. Children from low-income families were more likely to attend community centers, whereas children from more affluent families were more likely to attend for-profit programs and enrichment lessons. Family goals and expectations for programs also differed. As family income declined, parents preferred programs that emphasize academic preparation (Hofferth et al., 1991); as incomes increased, parents were more likely to endorse arrangements that emphasize the arts and cultural appreciation. Psychological characteristics of the family also appear to serve as selection effects. Families who endorse firm or strict disciplinary strategies were less likely to use self-care for their children than were families who were more permissive (Vandell et al., 1995). These and other family selection effects are important to consider because they illustrate the larger context in which decisions about after-school care occur. After-school care is not randomly distributed across families but reflects family resources and beliefs. These family selection effects must be considered in analyses of after-school effects. Otherwise, ostensible effects of after-school care may be artifacts of those preexisting family differences.

In addition, researchers need to be aware that families may change, over time, as a result of children's after-school experience. Siblings may be closer and more supportive as a result of increased time together in self-care, or this time together may result in increased conflict. Marital relationships may be enhanced when mothers respond positively to fathers adjusting their work schedules to care for their children during the after school hours. Alternatively, marriages may be stressed when parents are unable to construct workable after-school arrangements for their children. To date, researchers have not examined how families respond to after-school care, but the emerging literature involving younger children (Mason & Duberstein, 1992; Vandell, Hyde, Plant, & Essex, 1997) suggests that such effects may be found.

Another reason that it is necessary to consider family characteristics is that these characteristics may moderate the influence of the after-school environment. Steinberg (1986), for example, found that teenagers reported being more susceptible to negative peer influences only when self-care was paired with minimal parental monitoring. Negative peer influences were not reported when self-care occurred in the context of authoritative parenting. Another example of family characteristics moderating after-school experiences was evident in Vandell and Ramanan's (1991) analysis of mother care after school. Mother care was associated with more peer conflicts and antisocial behaviors, and lower PPVT scores, when the families were single-parent households living in poverty. Mother care after school was not associated with problematic development in the context of two-parent households with more economic resources, perhaps because these families were also found to offer more emotionally and cognitively supportive home environments.

Future research should examine other ways in which family characteristics such as income and stress interact with after-school experiences. One hypothesis to be tested is that low-income children may derive greater benefit from high-quality after-school programs than middle-income children because the after-school programs provide enrichment activities that are otherwise unavailable.

These interfaces between family and after-school environment present researchers with challenging data analytic issues. What analytic strategies might researchers used to identify (a) under what conditions does after-school care influence children's development over and above family experiences, (b) under what conditions does after-school care contribute to family functioning, and (c) under which conditions do the joint circumstances created by families and after-school settings support or undermine children's development? As Bronfenbrenner (1989, 1993) noted, some of the most frequently used statistical techniques are not appropriate for addressing questions from an ecological framework. Simply relying on statistical partialling as a "control" for selection effects, for example, may mask the very phenomenon of interest. Such statistical controls assume that variables or factors are acting in isolation, which they often do not. Bronfenbrenner also worried that such attempts at control take the phenomenon out of context and undermine efforts to identify moderating influences.

It is necessary to consider other analytic approaches. One promising strategy that Bronfenbrenner (1989, 1993) proposed is to examine development within and across different ecological niches. In the case of after-school research, for example, researchers might examine the impact of participation in different types of after-school programs for boys and girls whose families are living in urban poverty. (See Vandell & Pierce, 1996, for such a study.) Other important ecological niches may be represented by dual-earner households who live in suburban neighborhoods and families who live in rural communities that vary in their availability of supportive adults. Bronfenbrenner recommended that researchers include more than one ecological niche within their studies as a way of illuminating the features of development in context.

Further understanding of after-school experiences within these ecological niches is made possible by comprehensive examinations of person–context–process interactions over time. As researchers follow children's movements across and between after-school environments over time, they have observations that are suggestive of natural experiments. For example, the configurations of family and after-school conditions under which improved child well-being is observed over time can be determined. Likewise, the family and after-school conditions that compromise children's well-being over time can be identified. Within these analyses, researchers can ascertain if changes in children's well-being are associated with changes in after-school experiences, as they occur within different ecological niches. As will become apparent in the sections that follow, it may be necessary to incorporate into the analytic strategy a consideration of school and neighborhood factors as salient aspects of the ecological niche in which children experience their after-school care.

After-School Care in a School Context

There has been little research examining linkages between after-school settings and children's school experiences. There are some suggestions, however, as to what some of these salient linkages might be. Similar to the family/after-school linkages that were just described, school features can serve as both selection effects and moderators of the after-school environment. In the Milwaukee After-School Study (Vandell & Posner, 1995), a school/after-school link was apparent in children's use of time. Schools varied in their dismissal times, with some schools dismissing children at 2:30 p.m. and other schools dismissing children at 3:30 p.m. Earlier dismissal was associated with children spending more time in self-care and more time watching television. Another school-related difference was evident in the time that children spent in transit. The desegregation plan in the Milwaukee schools resulted in African American children spending more time in transit (on school buses) than European American children in the sample. In both of these examples, the range and types of experiences available to children varied as a result of school policies.

Another link between school and after-school environments can occur at the curricular or programming level. Because classrooms and school days for many children are highly structured, with minimal opportunities to exercise choices and autonomy, an important aspect of the after-school setting is the extent to which it also is highly structured. Informal surveys (Erikson, 1988) suggest that a major reason that children press their parents to move into self-care is because of the children's desire for greater freedom and autonomy after school. An issue for subsequent research is a determination of whether children's press to move into self-care occurs later if the school curriculum includes opportunities for small-group and individual child–initiated activities.

Another direction for research is the determination of how children's after-school experiences interact with school experiences. The impact of participating in or attending a highly structured after-school programs may be dependent on how highly structured the regular school-day program is. Highly structured after-school programs may be detrimental to children's growing needs for some independence and autonomy only when it is coupled with highly structured school days. Another potential interactive effect that might be tested in future research is the possibility that high-quality after-school programs offset the effects of poor-quality classroom experiences.

The dynamics of classrooms and overall school climate may also change as a result of after-school programs. Howes et al. (1987), for example, found that children who participated in an extended-day after-school program were more competent in their kindergarten classrooms than were children who did not participate in the program. Although not explicitly examined by Howes et al., one might suspect that the classrooms as a whole might have changed to reflect the changing competencies within the class. Another way in which after-school care may influence is in the development of teacher-led after-school programs. Posner and Vandell (1994) found that some of the programs that they had observed that served low-income families were organized and lead by teachers. To our knowledge, no researchers have examined the impact of such programs on the teachers or on the regular school curriculum, although the impact of such programs may be substantial.

After-School Care Within a Neighborhood Context

The after-school environment must be examined within a framework of children's neighborhoods or communities. Salient aspects of the neighborhood include demographic distinctions such as urban/suburban/rural as well as proportions of households in the neighborhood who live in poverty, have single parents, or contain adults without high school diplomas. These features provide one type of summary of the resources and models that are potentially available to children (Shumow, Vandell, & Posner, 1998). Crime rates and adults' and children's psychological perceptions of neighborhood safety are other aspects of neighborhoods that may affect children's and adults' sense of well-being. Finally, children's and parents' perceived support from individuals within the community may be salient to understanding the after-school environment.

There is evidence that each of these neighborhood indicators influences choices in after-school care. These neighborhood-level selection effects are consistent with the view that self-care is more likely when neighborhoods are viewed as safer. Self-care is less likely to be used in urban settings than suburban or rural settings (Cain & Hofferth, 1989). It is less likely when parents and children perceive their neighborhoods as being unsafe (Vandell et al., 1995). Although no single study has contrasted the effects of self-care versus supervised care in rural, suburban, and urban settings, cross-study comparisons suggest that the effects of self-care may be moderated by community setting. Self-care has not been associated with developmental problems when children live in rural and suburban settings (Rodman et al., 1985; Vandell & Corasaniti, 1988), but it has been associated with problems in academic achievement (Woods, 1972); use of alcohol, cigarettes, and marijuana (Richardson et al., 1989); and children's feelings of fear and loneliness (Long & Long, 1983) in urban settings. There also are cross-study suggestions that neighborhood characteristics may moderate the effects of attending formal programs (Posner & Vandell, 1994; Vandell & Corasaniti, 1988): Children who live in low-income urban neighborhoods may derive greater benefits from attending formal programs than children who live in suburban neighborhoods. Also, just as children's after-school experiences may affect their families and their schools, after-school arrangements (or their absence) can affect neighborhoods. For example, some funds from recent federal anticrime legislation were targeted to after-school programs in high-crime neighborhoods (Vandell & Pierce, 1996). The assumption underlying this allocation of funds is that the programs provide youth with positive alternative activities and that neighborhood crime will be reduced. Additional research is clearly to test systematically these associations between neighborhoods and after-school care.

AFTER-SCHOOL CARE AND INDIVIDUAL CHILD CHARACTERISTICS

In addition to examining after-school care within the context of family, school, and neighborhood, it is necessary to consider the after-school environment in relation to children's developmental status and psychological functioning. There is clear evidence that children's characteristics influence placement into difference after-school settings (Hofferth et al., 1991; Vandell & Posner, 1995). The use of self-care, formal programs, and informal adult supervision varies with child age, for example. Using the National Child Care Survey, Hofferth et al. reported that only 1% of the 5-year-olds were in self-care as a primary child-care management, whereas 14% of the 13-year-olds were in self-care as their primary arrangement. When self-care was assessed as a secondary or additional arrangement, proportions increased substantially for each age, although the linear age increase in usage was maintained. Child-care surveys also document developmental changes in the use of formal programs. Formal after-school programs are more likely to be used by children in the early elementary grades. By fourth grade, a marked decline in the number of children in formal after-school programs occurs (Hofferth et al., 1991). Informal after-school supervision by neighbors and friends also declines during grade school.

These normative patterns have implications for examining the effects of the after-school environment. One question pertains to how children who deviate from these normative patterns differ from other children. One would suspect that children who are placed in self-care as 5-year-olds are at substantially higher risk than those who move into self-care during adolescence, all other factors being equal. It is less clear what happens if children remain in formal programs longer than their classmates. On the one hand, children may be stigmatized by their peers as being in a program for "babies" (Vandell & Corasaniti, 1988). Because the program activities may be geared to younger children, there may not be opportunities to participate in activities that are developmentally appropriate for them. On the other hand, children who remain in the programs may be those children who continue to need supervised arrangements. These children may be placed at risk if they leave programs. In this regard, Vandell and Posner (1995) found that children who remained in formal programs at fifth grade were more likely than their classmates who had left the programs to have displayed school and behavioral problems as third graders. These children continued to display more behavioral problems as fifth graders. As unanswered question is what would have occurred if children with academic or adjustment problems leave formal programs along with their classmates.

CONCLUSION

This chapter describes some of the challenges associated with studying children's after-school environments. These challenges include recognizing the multiplicity of after-school settings experienced by children, identifying the salient aspects of these settings, and developing methods that can be applied within and across after-school settings. Several different research methodologies appear promising. Parent and child reports can provide general information about primary and secondary arrangements, but it is necessary to move beyond these reports if researchers are to understand after-school care as a microsystem. These approaches include observations of children's experiences in formal programs and informal settings and time-use interviews that describe activities, partners, and roles during the after-school hours. School-aged children are also able to describe their experiences within their after-school settings and the extent to which they perceive the emotional climate as supportive or hostile.

It is clear that the study of after-school environments cannot occur in isolation. Other environmental contexts such as the family, school, and neighborhood are closely linked with children's after-school experiences. Children are not randomly assigned to after-school experiences. Systematic associations between after-school care and children's family, school, and neighborhood have been observed. Family, school, and neighborhood features also serve as moderators of after-school experiences for children. The study of after-school care is further complicated because families, schools, and neighborhoods may change as a function of what children are doing after school. Finally, it is clear that the study of after-school environments must occur within a developmental framework because children's developmental status affects placement into after-school settings and contributes to the effects of the setting on child adjustment.

Documenting and explicating these complex relationships represents a substantial analytic challenge. Using statistical controls or simply partialling variances assumes an independence of factors that is probably not the case. A more promising approach may be to examine after-school care within different ecological niches. Such an approach may be particularly powerful when applied longitudinally.

In conclusion, the ecological systems theory provides a useful conceptual framework for organizing the existing literature and for suggesting directions for future research. Seemingly contradictory findings regarding self-care, formal after-school programs, and informal after-school settings can be integrated by considering the after-school environment as a microsystem characterized by different activities, interaction partners, roles, and experiences. Further resolution of discrepant findings is possible when associations between after-school settings and other environmental contexts are taken into account.

REFERENCES

Asher, S. R., & Gabriel, S. W. (1993). Using a wireless transmission system to observe conversation and social interaction on the playground. In C. H. Hart (Ed.), *Children on playgrounds: Research perspectives and applications* (pp. 184–209). Albany: State University of New York Press.

Barker, R. G., & Wright, H. F. (1955). *Midwest and its children: The psychological ecology of an American town*. New York: Row, Peterson.

Belle, D. (1988). *Social support processes among latchkey and adult supervised children*. Unpublished report, Boston University.

Bronfenbrenner, U. (1979). *The ecology of human development*. Cambridge, MA: Harvard University Press.

Bronfenbrenner, U. (1989). Ecological systems theory. In R. Vasa (Ed.), *Annals of child development* (pp. 187–249). Greenwich, CT: JABI Press.

Bronfenbrenner, U. (1993). The ecology of cognitive development research models and fugitive findings. In R. H. Wozniak & K. W. Fischer (Eds.), *Development in context: Acting and thinking in specific environments* (pp. 3–44). Hillsdale, NJ: Erlbaum.

Bryant, B. (1989). The need for support in relation to the need for autonomy. In D. Belle (Ed.), *Children's social networks and social supports* (pp. 332–351). New York: Wiley.

Cain, V. S., & Hofferth, S. L. (1989). Parental choice of self care for school age children. *Journal of Marriage of the Family, 51*, 65–77.

Carpenter, C. J., Huston, A., & Spera, L. (1989). Children's use of time in their everyday activities during middle childhood. In M. Block & A. Pellegrini (Eds.), *The ecological context of children's play* (pp. 165–190). Norwood, NJ: Ablex.

Clarke-Stewart, K. A., Gruber, C. P., & Fitzgerald, M. M. (1994). *Children at home and in day care*. Hillsdale, NJ: Erlbaum.

Coleman, M., Robinson, B. E., & Rowland, B. H. (1990). *Children and youth services review, 12*, 327–339.

Csikszentmihalyi, M., & Larson, R. (1984). *Being adolescent: Conflict and growth in the teenage years*. New York: Basic Books.

Duckett, E., Raffaelli, M., & Richards, M. H. (1989). "Taking care": Maintaining the self and the home in early adolescence. *Journal of Youth and Adolescence, 18*, 549–565.

Erikson, J. B. (1988). Real American children: The challenge for after-school programs. *Child and Youth Care Quarterly, 17*, 86–103.

Galambos, N. L., & Maggs, J. L. (1991). Out-of-school care of young adolescents and self-reported behavior. *Developmental Psychology, 27*, 644–655.

Halpern, R. (1992). The role of after-school programs in the lives of inner-city children: A study of the "urban youth network." *Child Welfare League of America, LXXI*(3), 215–230.

Harris and Associates, Inc. (1987). *The American teacher, 1987: Strengthening links between home and school* (Metropolitan Life Survey). New York: Author.

Hofferth, S. L., Brayfield, A., Deich, S., & Holcomb, P. (1991). *National child care survey, 1990*. Washington, DC: Urban Institute Press.

Howard, C. W., Broquest, A. J., & Farrell, A. D. (1991, April). *The impact of after-school context and supervision on urban middle school youth's prosocial and problem behaviors*. Paper presented at the biennial meeting of the Society for Research in Child Development, Seattle, WA.

Howes, C. (1983). Caregiver behavior in centers and family day care. *Journal of Applied Developmental Psychology, 4*, 99–107.

Howes, C. (1988). Relations between early child care and schooling. *Developmental Psychology, 24*, 53–57.

Howes, C. (1990). Can the age of entry and the quality of infant child care predict adjustment in kindergarten? *Developmental Psychology, 26*, 252–263.

Howes, C., & Hamilton, C. E. (1993). The changing experience of child care: Changes in teachers and in teacher–child relationships and children's social competence with peers. *Early Childhood Research Quarterly, 8*, 15–32.

Howes, C., & Olenick, M. (1986). Family and child care influences on toddlers' compliance. *Child Development, 65*, 202–216.

Howes, C., & Stewart, P. (1987). Child's play with adults, toys, and peers: An examination of family and child care influences. *Child Care Quarterly, 14*, 140–151.

Howes, C., Olenick, M., & Der-Kiureghian, T. (1987). After school child care in an elementary school: Social development and continuity and complementarity of programs. *The Elementary School Journal, 88*, 93–103.

Howes, C., Phillips, D. A., & Whitebook, M. (1992). Thresholds of quality: Implications for the social development of children in center-based child care. *Child Development, 63*, 449–460.

Ladd, G. W., & Price, J. M. (1993). Playstyles of peer-accepted and peer-rejected children on the playground. In C. H. Hart (Ed.), *Children on playgrounds: Research perspectives and applications* (pp. 130–161). Albany: State University of New York Press.

Long, T. J., & Long, L. (1983). *The handbook for latchkey children and their parents*. New York: Arbor House.

Marshall, N. L. (1991, April). *Empowering low-income parents: The role of child care.* Poster session presented at the biennial meeting of the Society for Research in Child Development, Seattle, WA.

Mason, K. O., & Duberstein, L. (1992). Consequences of child care for parents' well-being. In A. Booth (Ed.), *Child care in the 1990s: Trends and consequences* (pp. 127–158). Hillsdale, NJ: Erlbaum.

Mayesky, M. E. (1980). A study of academic effectiveness in a public school day care program. *Phi Delta Kappan, 62,* 284–285.

McCartney, K. (1984). Effects of quality of day care environment on children's language development. *Developmental Psychology, 20,* 244–260.

Medrich, E. A., Roizen, J. A., Rubin, V., & Buckley, S. (1982). *The serious business of growing up: A study of children's lives outside school.* Berkeley: University of California Press.

National Institute of Child Health and Human Development Early Child Care Research Network. (1996). Characteristics of infant child care: Factors contributing to positive caregiving. *Early Childhood Research Quarterly, 11,* 269–306.

Posner, J. K., & Vandell, D. L. (1994). Low-income children's after school care: Are there beneficial effects of after school programs? *Child Development, 65,* 440–456.

Richardson, J., Dwyer, K., McGuigan, K., Hansen, W., Dent, C., Johnson, C. A., Sussman, S., & Brannon, B. (1989). Substance use among eighth graders who take care of themselves after school. *Pediatrics, 84,* 556–566.

RMC Research Corporation. (1993). *National study of before and after school programs* (Report to the Office of Policy and Planning, U.S. Department of Education, Contract No. LC89051001). Portsmouth, NH: Author.

Rodman, H., Pratto, D. J., & Nelson, R. S. (1985). Child care arrangements and children's functioning: A comparison of self-care and adult-care children. *Developmental Psychology, 21,* 413–418.

Rosenthal, R., & Vandell, D. L. (1996). Quality of care at school-aged child care programs: Regulatable features, observed experiences, child perspectives, and parent perspectives. *Child Development, 67,* 2434–2445.

Rubin, V. (1983). Family work patterns and community resources: An analysis of children's access to support and services outside school. In C. D. Hayes & S. B. Kamerman (Eds.), *Children of working parents: Experiences and outcomes* (pp. 73–99). Washington, DC: National Academy Press.

Seligson, M. (1991). Models of school-aged child care: A review of current research on implications for women and their children. *Women's Studies International Forum, 14*(6), 577–584.

Sheldon, A. (1990). Pickle fights: Gendered talk in preschool dispute. *Discourse Processes, 13,* 5–31.

Shumow, L., Vandell, D. L., & Posner, J. K. (1998). Harsh, firm, and permissive parenting in low-income families: Relations to children's academic achievement and behavioral adjustment. *Journal of Family Issues, 19,* 483–507.

Steinberg, L. (1986). Latchkey children and susceptibility to peer pressure: An ecological analysis. *Developmental Psychology, 22*, 433–439.

Timmer, S. G., Eccles, J., & O'Brien, K. (1985). How children use time. In F. T. Juster & F. P. Stafford (Eds.), *Time, goods and well-being* (pp. 353–381). Ann Arbor: University of Michigan, Institute for Social Research.

Todd, C. M., Albrecht, K. M., & Coleman, M. (1990, Spring). School-age child care: A continuum of options. *Journal of Home Economics, 82*, 46–52.

Todd, C. M., & Mayberry, A. K. (1991, April). *Urban and rural children's responses to self care*. Paper presented at the biennial meeting of the Society for Research in Child Development, Seattle, WA.

Vandell, D. L., & Corasaniti, M. A. (1988). The relation between third graders' after-school care and social, academic, and emotional functioning. *Child Development, 59*, 868–875.

Vandell, D. L., & Pierce, K. (1996). *Safe Haven program evaluation (1994–95)* (Report prepared for the City of Madison and the Madison Metropolitan School District).

Vandell, D. L., & Posner, J. (1995). *An ecological analysis of the effects of after school care* (Report to the Spencer Foundation).

Vandell, D. L., Henderson, V. K., & Wilson, K. S. (1988). A longitudinal study of children with day care experiences of varying quality. *Child Development, 59*, 1286–1292.

Vandell, D. L., Hyde, J. S., Plant, E. A., & Essex, M. J. (1997). Fathers and "others" as infant care providers: Predictors of parents' emotional well-being and marital relationships. *Merrill-Palmer Quarterly, 43*, 361–385.

Vandell, D. L., Posner, J., Shumow, L., & Kang, K. (1995, March). *Concurrent, short term, and long term effects of self care*. Poster session presented at the biennial meeting of the Society for Research in Child Development, Indianapolis, IN.

Vandell, D. L., & Ramanan, J. (1991). Children of the National Longitudinal Survey of Youth: Choices in after school care and child development. *Developmental Psychology, 27*, 637–644.

Whiting, B. (1980). Culture and social behavior: A model for the development of social behavior. *Ethos, 8*, 95–116.

Williams, R. L., & Fosarelli, P. D. (1987). Telephone call-in services for children in self-care. *American Journal for Diseases of Children, 141*, 965–968.

Woods, M. B. (1972). The unsupervised child of the working mother. *Developmental Psychology, 6*(1), 14–25.

Zucker, H. L. (1944). Working parents and latchkey children. *Annals of the American Academy*, 43–50.

7

ASSESSING THE SCHOOL ENVIRONMENT: EMBEDDED CONTEXTS AND BOTTOM-UP RESEARCH STRATEGIES

JOAN E. TALBERT AND MILBREY W. MCLAUGHLIN

Social scientists who study school effects on individuals' development and life chances tend to specialize on one or another level or on one kind of education context and, within one of these, in particular lines of theory and research. Some study classroom structure and processes in lines of work on, for example, the social organization of the classroom or classroom discourse. Others concentrate on the school organization environment, working in research traditions on student tracking or school ethos, for example. Other researchers analyze conditions such as governance structures or policy cultures at the district, state, or federal levels of the school system. Some researchers look outside the formal school system at, for example, the parent community, teachers' professional organizations, and higher education institutions to assess their interface with school processes and student outcomes.

Crosscutting these levels and lines of school-context research are methodological traditions that further specialize knowledge about how school environments shape individual development. *Quantitative researchers* generally estimate the average effect of a particular variable across a large number of cases and seek to isolate its effect from confounding context and individual variables. Causal importance of a context variable is judged by the size of its independent effect. In contrast, *qualitative researchers* tend to conceptualize school context as the syndrome of conditions that describe a particular case. The significance of an environment condition is judged in terms of its meaning and effects in a particular context; interdependence among environment conditions is assumed. Each methodological tradition has its shortcomings: main-effects quantitative research decontextualizes relationships, and case study methods afford little opportunity to examine diversity across contexts or to specify interaction effects among particular context variables.

In this chapter, we sketch rudiments of an integrative paradigm for school-effects research. Our conception of the school environment embraces multiple system levels and multiple theoretical perspectives on the school environment. We assume that students' educational experiences and outcomes are situated in school settings that are embedded in multiple system levels and broader education environments. Students' realities in school, then, are inherently multilevel. The relevance and power of particular environment conditions vary across class and school settings. For example, new professional standards for mathematics instruction are relevant just to math lessons and classes, and their effects on classroom processes depend on how teachers and schools respond to them.

With this general conception of school effects, the analyst's task is to explain differences in students' realities across school settings in terms of multiple and interactive environment conditions. What contexts shape the character of proximal processes in schools (Bronfenbrenner, chapter 1, this volume), or the quality of a sustained interactions among students, teachers, and subject matter?

We describe a bottom-up research strategy for measuring school effects—a strategy that begins with students' educational experiences (the dependent variable) and works upward to identify which and how multiple school contexts shape a phenomenon of interest. The relevance of a particular level of context, or unit of analysis, is treated as an empirical question. In bottom-up analyses, the researcher asks, for instance, How much does students' agency vary between particular kinds of school contexts (e.g., classes, schools, social classes, policy systems, and subject areas)? and What particular conditions combine or interact to generate these differences? Like other contributors to this volume, we reject simple main-effects views of environment effects on individual development.

Our research on the school environment has focused mainly on the *exosystem* of the ecological model (Bronfenbrenner, 1993, p. 24), or the interface between proximal processes in classrooms and schools and higher level school contexts. On theoretical and empirical grounds, we emphasize the role of adults in school settings, and particularly teachers' professional communities, to translate school-context conditions into action. How teachers and administrators perceive and respond to myriad local and remote conditions of schooling, including the students' own social and academic resources, significantly shapes students' school experiences. A key interest in our research, then, is to measure how school-context variables interact with teaching cultures to affect classroom processes.

We begin this chapter with a brief critique of two common genres of research on the school environment: *social-address/main-effects research* and *research on school cultures*. We then describe our conception of the embedded contexts of schooling and research strategies suitable for assessing their effects on students' educational experiences and outcomes. Finally, we illustrate a bottom-up analysis of school environment effects, using students' efforts in mathematics classes as the criterion.

CRITIQUE OF SCHOOL-EFFECTS RESEARCH

Prominent approaches to assessing the school environment include analyses of social-address variables with large-scale survey databases and field studies of school effectiveness. In the first genre, researchers assess school effects on student outcomes in terms of specific nominal or structural descriptors of the school environment, such as school sector (private vs. public) or school size. The effective-schools research examines aspects of life inside schools, most particularly the strength and character of school community, that relate to students' educational outcomes. Each has particular strengths and limitations in its conception and measurement of the school environment that inform our efforts to develop an integrative research paradigm.

Social-Address/Main-Effects Research

This research genre uses measures of students' locations in the education system, and their position in the socioeconomic system, as indicators of environmental factors thought to influence student outcomes. Principal lines of research have estimated consequences of *school sector* (private or public) and *course track assignment* for student learning and educational attainment.

Research on school sector uses national longitudinal surveys of secondary-school students to estimate effects of private versus public schools on learning outcomes and persistence in schooling, while controlling statistically for a variety of individual background variables.[1] A few highly publicized studies in which the researchers used these databases reached the conclusion that private schools do better than public schools to promote students' academic achievement, after other variables relevant to educational success have been controlled (see Chubb & Moe, 1990; Coleman & Hoffer, 1987; Coleman, Hoffer, & Kilgore, 1982).

Research on student tracking estimates effects of an individual's placement in academic versus general versus remedial courses in high school on his or her educational attainment (the *allocation effects* of tracking) or on his or her cognitive achievements (the *socialization effects* of tracking).[2] In general, this line of work finds that students assigned to low-track classes achieve at lower rates than do their peers assigned to high-track classes, after prior academic performance has been taken into account.

These prominent lines of research use information on the individual's location in the educational system or in the school curricular structure as the central measure of his or her school environment. These researchers commonly aim to isolate effects of the social address on educational outcomes by statistically controlling for prior educational achievements and confounded variables such as the student's social class background. By design, social-address research strives to simplify measurement and explanation through *ceteris paribus*, or all else equal, assumptions about environments inside and outside of the school.

Problems With Social-Address Research

As an explanation of relations between educational environment and student outcomes, social-address research is highly limited. One problem is the small size of effects found by much of this research. Although simplicity of social-address research satisfies the standard for social science and education policy research to isolate effects of particular variables, main-effects models often mistake statistical for substantive significance. For example, the statistically significant differences in student achievement out-

[1]Three generations of longitudinal education surveys are being conducted by the National Center for Education Statistics. They include the National Longitudinal Survey of the Class of 1972 (NLS:72), the High School and Beyond (HS&B) Survey, and the National Education Longitudinal Survey of 1988 (NELS:88). Each began with a nationally representative sample of students in particular grade cohorts: NLS:72 sampled high school seniors in 1972, HS&B sampled 10th and 12th graders in 1980, and NELS:88 sampled eighth graders in 1988. Both the HS&B and the NELS:88 programs have supported considerable social science research estimating effects on student achievement of school sector and other social-address variables. For additional information about the development of these surveys, technical information, final reports, and user manuals, contact the National Center for Education Statistics, U.S. Department of Education, Office of Educational Research and Improvement, Washington, DC 20208.

[2]Research on the consequences of students' track assignment is a long-standing tradition in the sociology of education (cf. Alexander, Cook, & McDill, 1978; Hallinan, 1990; Jencks et al., 1972; Rosenbaum, 1976).

comes reported by Chubb and Moe (1990), which were the basis for their conclusion that private schools were more effective educational settings than public schools, represented differences of only two test items on a reading assessment—a difference few teachers would consider meaningful in terms of learning.

Weak effect sizes found in social-address studies are symptomatic of a more fundamental problem: Such measures of the school environment mask enormous diversity in conditions within the address categories. For instance, private schools are quite diverse in their governance structures and in their missions (cf. Bryk, Lee, & Holland, 1993), and public schools range from college-preparatory academies in elite suburbs to career academies in large urban districts to poorly equipped and poorly staffed urban and rural schools.

A second limitation of main-effects models of social-address variables is that researchers cannot say how or why observed effects occur. Such research cannot determine conditions or processes that interpret the structural effects on student outcomes. Is the lower achievement observed for lower track students a direct outcome of track placement, as this research suggests, or does it reflect other factors that covary with track assignment? Is it the "privateness" of private schools that supports higher student achievement, or is some other factor at work?

Research that shows educational effects of a particular kind of social-address variable, at best, sets the stage for field studies of school processes. Process-focused research on student tracking, for example, documented differences in the average quality and character of instruction between academic and general classes in the high school curriculum (cf. Gamoran, 1986, 1987; Oakes, 1985). Many teachers believe that low-achieving students are "behind" and need to catch up before going on to the material and skills being mastered by high-achieving peers (Oakes, 1985; Rosenbaum, 1976; Wilson & Schmits, 1978).[3] Thus, some researchers have shown that instruction in low-track classes emphasized rote memory of facts and highly structured assignments, whereas high-track classes emphasized complex tasks that required analytic thinking (Hargreaves, 1967; Metz, 1978; Oakes, 1985). Students assigned to lower tracks, in other words, perform relatively poorly because they are offered less.

Furthermore, causality in social-address models is problematic. Did school governance structures "cause" differences in student achievement, or did the types of students and families enrolling in an independent school generate the outcomes or the particular governance arrangements? In terms

[3]Teachers are generally unaware of evidence from cognitive research that basic and higher order tasks have their own inherent demands and that mastery of one type of task does not necessarily lead to proficiency on the other (see Becker & Gerstein, 1982; Brown & Campione, 1977, 1980; Greeno, 1991; Greeno, Smith, & Moore, 1991; Mayer & Greeno, 1972).

of standards for this research paradigm, how adequate are the controls for clientele differences? In tracking research, how much of the track effects on learning outcomes are due to patterns of teacher assignment, as opposed to effects of the structural arrangement? In fact, research has shown that teachers relatively weak in their subjects are more likely than are well-prepared colleagues to be assigned to low-track classes (Ball & Lacey, 1984; Finley, 1984; Lacey, 1970; Rosenbaum, 1976) and to be marginal in their school community (Finley, 1984; Talbert, 1990).

Main-effects models with social-address measures of the school environment are useful in directing researchers to further investigate issues of process and causality. However, such studies provide little insight regarding differences in the character of school settings or in the relationships between the settings and students' experiences. (For further review and critique, see Talbert, McLaughlin, & Rowan, 1993.)

Effective-Schools Research

Another line of research considers internal school organization and culture as sources of variation in students' educational success. An early and influential study conducted by Rutter, Maughan, Mortimore, Outson, and Smith (1979) in inner-city English schools used the term *school ethos* to describe the syndrome of values and beliefs conducive to high achievement. Their work highlighted the cultural underpinnings of schools' success in promoting or inhibiting student learning and engagement in school.

In the United States, a significant tradition of research on school effectiveness developed during the late 1970s and early 1980s. Research on "effective schools" sought to identify school policies, norms, and processes that distinguished relatively successful from relatively unsuccessful schools (see Purkey & Smith, 1983, for review). The criterion of school effectiveness in most studies was the mean of students' scores on a standardized achievement test. Research in this genre isolated such school-level factors as principal leadership, goal consensus and collegiality, high faculty expectations for student success, and extended teacher roles (extraclassroom interaction with students) as correlates of average student achievement.

Problems With Effective-Schools Research

Although this line of work addresses some of the shortcomings of the social-address models and actually gets inside schools to consider organizational processes, how it represents relations between educational settings and student outcomes is also problematic. The reliance of these studies on average test scores as criteria of school effectiveness ignores variation in students' experiences and success within a school. Researchers know that within-school variance on academic achievement is much greater than between-schools variance (cf. Jencks et al., 1972).

The tracking literature, for example, also shows that "school" is different for students situated in advanced placement and remedial classes. Conceptions and measures of the school environment that are bounded by school walls, and that ignore differences in the microcultures of classrooms or tracks or grade levels or subject areas, are limited for capturing students' school experiences and educational outcomes. In our research, we found that even within the same high school and same curricular track, students encountered very different learning environments within their different classes, depending on teachers' ideas about students' role and academic potential (McLaughlin & Talbert, 1993b). In short, substantial within-school variation in teachers' professional cultures and in students' academic performance argues against the monolithic view of school community embraced in the school-effects literature.

AN EMBEDDED-CONTEXTS VIEW OF THE SCHOOL ENVIRONMENT

Our conception of the school environment places the classroom at the core of multiple embedded contexts of schooling. The model illustrated in Figure 1 represents three kinds of school environments and analytic lenses for assessing environment effects on students' educational experiences. We distinguish between school settings and proximal education processes, administrative system units and structures, and institutional contexts and cultures.

The classroom core of our embedded-context model is the primary *school setting*—the locus of regular and sustained interactions of students and teachers around subject matter. Other kinds of school settings, or sites for ongoing adult–student interaction or interactions among school adults, can be defined beyond classroom boundaries. Most common among them are extracurricular activities in secondary schools, such as clubs and sports teams; homerooms or other kinds of classes not framed by educational content; and subject departments and other curricular units that can be important settings for teacher interaction and community.

Social systems theory provides a general analytic framework and research literature that focus inquiry on proximal processes within school settings. This perspective considers social norms as a powerful source of differences in teaching and learning between classrooms, for example. It highlights the role of school communities to define and enforce particular values and norms for teaching and learning.

With this notion of embedded contexts, we posit that the meaning and effects of school-context conditions are embedded in individual and

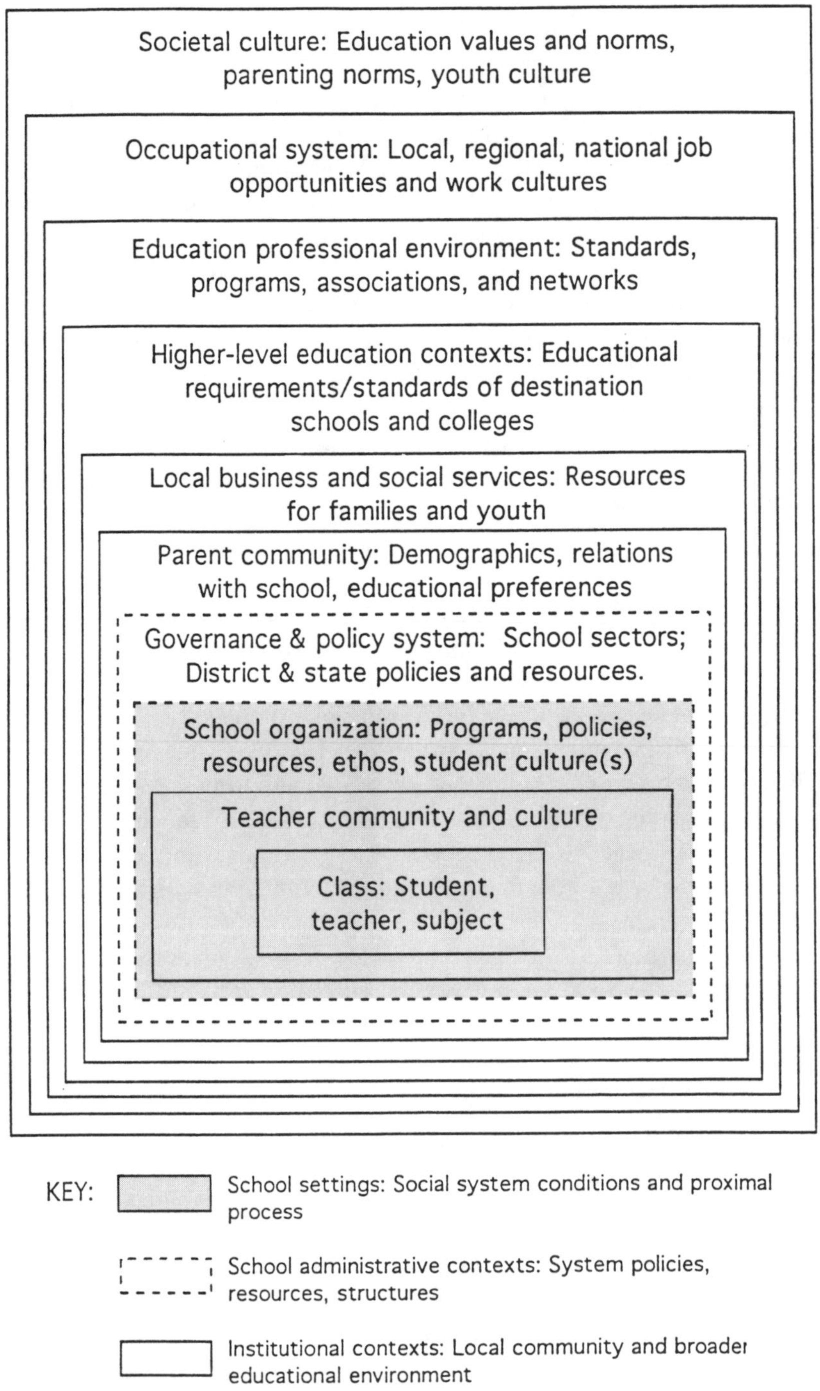

Societal culture: Education values and norms, parenting norms, youth culture

Occupational system: Local, regional, national job opportunities and work cultures

Education professional environment: Standards, programs, associations, and networks

Higher-level education contexts: Educational requirements/standards of destination schools and colleges

Local business and social services: Resources for families and youth

Parent community: Demographics, relations with school, educational preferences

Governance & policy system: School sectors; District & state policies and resources.

School organization: Programs, policies, resources, ethos, student culture(s)

Teacher community and culture

Class: Student, teacher, subject

KEY:

School settings: Social system conditions and proximal process

School administrative contexts: System policies, resources, structures

Institutional contexts: Local community and broader educational environment

Figure 1. **Multiple and embedded settings and contexts of schooling.**

community values, beliefs, and standards for teaching and learning. A social systems perspective on the school environment challenges a view of school contexts as nested, highlighting the interaction between proximate professional norms and context variables.

School administrative contexts are levels or official units in the school organization system. Administrative contexts are what researchers generally consider when they evaluate school effects on student outcomes. We distinguish among sector, state, district, and school policy systems. Within secondary schools, the subject department is another part of the formal organization system. As shown in Figure 1, we regard school and department settings as both administrative units and potential boundaries for distinct teacher communities and cultures.

The theoretical lens of rational organization theory describes these contexts in terms of educational policies, resource levels and allocation patterns, and program and governance structures. Although the structural hierarchy of the school administrative system presents a nested model of school organization, the policy system does not operate in a linear and hierarchical manner. In other words, lower level policies are not predicated on high-level policies; furthermore, higher level policies can have effects on practice that are not mediated by middle-level policies of the system. For example, a district policy on science instruction can determine texts and assessments, regardless of school action; a failed bond issue can demoralize teachers in a district, even in a strong school community. Regardless of a district's nested organization structure, administrative conditions are not necessarily mediated by lower system units.

Institutional contexts in our model refer to education environments outside of the school system, such as the traditions and norms particular to different subject areas' cultures, higher education institutions, and labor markets. The institutional environment of K–12 (kindergarten through grade 12) schooling, shown as outer layers of our schema, frames the work of teachers and students in ways quite independent of official school policies and community preferences. The relevance of particular institutional contexts can vary across classroom settings. For example, academic and nonacademic classes within the same high school are situated in different environments. In academic classes, features of the higher education arena frame teachers' and students' work; in vocational and general track classes, local labor markets and economic conditions can be important contexts of schooling.

The theoretical model of schools as institutional organizations frames much of what goes on in schools as efforts to obtain legitimacy by adhering to organizing rules in the broader environment. For example, John Meyer and Brian Rowan (1977) analyzed school organization structure as "rationalized myth," as ritual conformity to rules of effective organization embraced by economic organizations in the institutional environment. Extending this perspective to teachers' roles, we consider contexts and avenues through which institutional rules or values, in the education environment and in the broader cultural arena, can affect classroom processes. Potential institutional effects come from, for example, conceptions of subject matter and student learning process in disciplinary cultures (Grossman & Stodolsky, 1994), subject reform initiatives outside of the school system (e.g., the National Council of Teachers of Mathematics, 1989, 1991, 1995), and parent preferences for programs or pedagogy. Our embedded-contexts model assumes that teaching is permeated by conditions in the institutional environment of K–12 schooling.

In summary, our notion of embedded school contexts refers to coexisting kinds of school contexts that combine in nonlinear ways to shape classrooms processes. First, institutional environments permeate school settings and teachers' work; they are not mediated by formal school policy. Second, school administrative policies do not directly affect lower levels of the system, nor do their effects on teaching and learning depend on a "chain of command." Third, school and teacher communities interpret and mediate effects of conditions in their institutional and administrative environments—students' experiences of the broader school contexts depend on the variable ways in which adults in their classroom and school respond to those conditions.

The embedded-contexts model challenges assumptions of additivity implicit in much policy-oriented research on schooling and routines of estimating average effects of a particular context variable on student outcomes. It also requires going beyond typical case study designs. Our conception of the school environment calls for research designs that enable comparative analysis of embedded school contexts. Furthermore, bottom-up measurement of school-context effects on students' educational experiences is essential because school settings are situated in particular combinations of relevant contexts and because their effects are mediated by educators and school communities.

STRATEGIES FOR ASSESSING EMBEDDED SCHOOL ENVIRONMENTS

Research compatible with our conceptual framework aims to describe the interplay of multiple levels of the school environment as they shape students' educational experiences and outcomes. Fundamental to embedded-context research are questions of which and how different levels or units of analysis are relevant to particular school settings and kinds of students' experiences and outcomes. For example, the school unit might be the appropriate setting for studies of students' social integration in school or of peer subcultures, whereas the classroom and subject department units would be central in studies of academic outcomes.

The empirical issue of where differences in students' experiences are greatest is a starting place in our bottom-up analysis strategy. Although some school-effects studies have advanced strong theoretical arguments with weak statistical support, we recommend first locating levels that show strong between-unit variance and then using theory and prior research to identify variables that could account for the variance.

In our model, contexts of analysis will also differ according to the research problem. For example, parent cultures might be important contexts for research on student tracking, whereas local teacher networks would be more important contexts for studies of subject teaching reforms. Detecting which contexts and conditions matter for a particular student outcome or classroom environment for learning depends on the strategic choices in sampling as well as on a bottom-up approach to measurement and analysis. As available, prior research focuses on particular context levels and variables and sets sampling parameters.

Sampling Design

A sampling design consistent with our conceptions of the school environment defies prescriptions for both survey and ethnographic research. Survey research standards call for independent case sampling. The more unrelated the cases, the better. The large, nationally representative samples of students and schools established for national longitudinal studies in education maximize dispersion of school environments and are considered by many to be ideal for estimating context effects on student outcomes, even if they obtain only superficial measures of context conditions. These samples provide good estimates of population parameters for U.S. students and schools on measured variables. However, in our view, the standard of independent sampling constrains the opportunity to study how environments of schooling affect teaching and learning. This is because context variables under analysis have been extracted from their own contexts.

Ethnographic research standards call for samples of students or schools small enough to afford intensive and sustained case analyses. These in-depth case studies provide rich descriptions of behavior within syndromes of context conditions. However, they provide little opportunity to isolate effects of particular embedded contexts of the case.

We recommend a sampling design that aims to represent both diversity across school environments and capacity to conduct in-depth, multilevel analyses of embedded school contexts. Design choices are guided by prior research and the aim to represent important contrasts at any level of the embedded-context model. Apart from typical resource constraints, researchers are constrained to sample few enough contrasts to enable embedded-context analyses.

What kind of embedded-context sample provides the best opportunities to understand context effects on teaching and learning? How many and what kinds of cases are needed in particular school settings and contexts?

Relatively large numbers of students and their teachers at proximate levels of the school environment are needed to produce reliable measures of variation across classroom, department, and school settings. It is this variation that broader context analysis seeks to explain. Depending on school boundaries for analysis, at least five individuals randomly sampled from each unit is recommended. Whole-school samples of teachers are recommended for measuring department or grade-level subcultures of teaching. Samples of at least five students per class are needed to measure students' experiences of this setting, and samples of at least five classes per student are needed to assess class effects on student outcomes.

The question of numbers of higher level cases depends on contrasts that are important for the scope of inquiry. Given limited degrees of freedom, the selection of contrasts to represent in an embedded-context study is a core issue for theory and design. Selection of higher level cases seeks to represent contrasts on context variables of theoretical and practical interest, such as student characteristics and state policy cultures. Contrasts represented in the sample design need to be few enough to allow for quantitative and qualitative data collection at all levels of the embedded sample.

In our (McLaughlin, 1993; McLaughlin & Talbert, 1993a, 1993b; Talbert & McLaughlin, 1994) longitudinal research program on secondary education, a sample size of 16 high schools represented contrasts at multiple context levels:

- state contrasts on centralization and reform activity: California, a centralized state and leader in K–12 systemic reform throughout the 1980s, and Michigan, a decentralized, nonreform state during the period of our research;
- within each state, two metropolitan areas that contrast on economic conditions;
- within each metropolitan area, one urban school district and one suburban school district or one independent school;
- within each urban school district, "typical" schools within relatively middle-class and relatively poor neighborhoods;
- within each school, all teachers for surveys and most teachers for interviews; and
- within a sample of typical urban schools, student samples of 12 students from each school to represent ethnic–race and academic diversity at the 10th grade.

This embedded sampling design enabled us to observe system effects on teaching within comparable school settings and, conversely, to analyze differences in school or subject department settings within a particular school system. In this way, we were able to tease out conditions in particular contexts that influenced teaching practices. For example, in our research on mathematics education, we saw that California's state mathematics framework provided content and strategies for math departments to promote all students' success; in contrast, math departments in Michigan were conducting "business as usual." We saw this difference in our interviews with math teachers across schools in these states and in the results of statistical analyses showing different effects of professional community on teachers' readiness to adapt instruction for all students. (See the Illustration: A Bottom-Up Line of Analysis section.)

An embedded sampling design makes it possible to examine diversity in students' school environments and to assess how layers and conditions of school context combine to affect educational processes and outcomes. In research centrally focused at the student and classroom level, denser samples of students than in the Center for Research on the Context of Teaching (CRC) design are desirable.

Clearly, an embedded sampling design can never represent all important context variables, nor can it adequately represent all combinations of conditions represented at each level. Rather, it ensures variation on context conditions likely to be important for educational outcomes of interest, and it captures the embeddedness of students' school environments. It combines strengths of both large-sample surveys and in-depth case studies and aims to overcome weaknesses of each.

Measurement Strategies

We recommend measurement strategies that integrate large-scale survey research and in-depth case studies of school environments and comparative analyses of quantitative and qualitative field data. General strategies that guide our research in embedded-school samples are summarized in Figure 2 and include the following:

- longitudinal data collection in the embedded-context sample to ensure sufficient depth of analysis in a large field sample;
- iterative development of quantitative and qualitative data for students, teachers, and contexts to refine conceptions of relevant environments and estimates of their effects on teaching and learning;
- emphasis on subjective measures of processes and contexts within school settings to capture differential experiences and constructions of embedded contexts; and

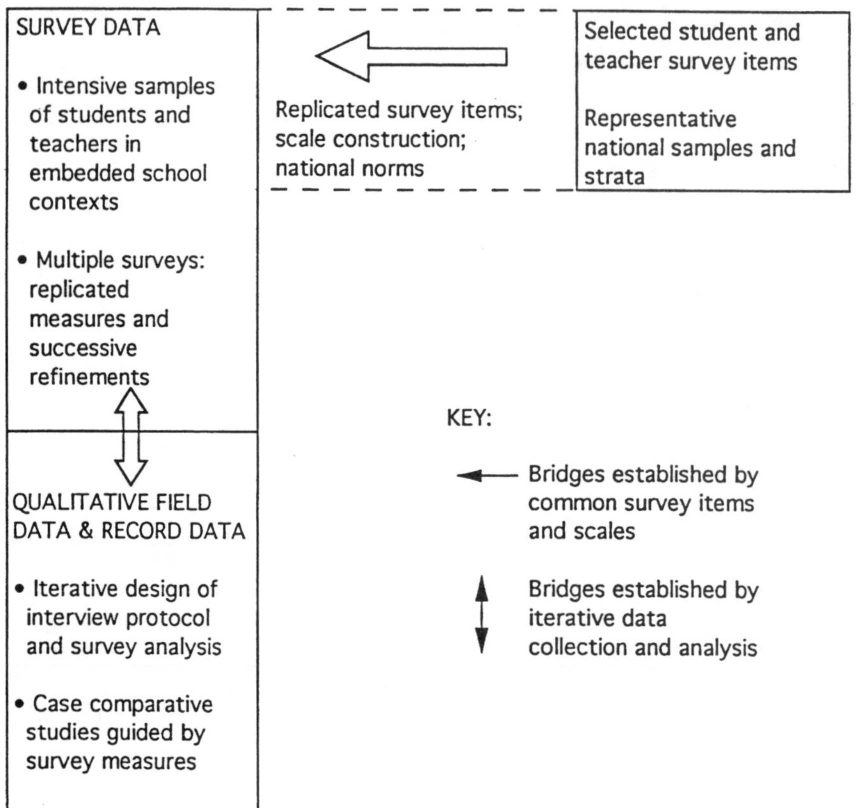

Figure 2. Strategies for bridging quantitative and qualitative measures of school context. NELS:88 = National Educational Longitudinal Survey of 1988.

- establishment of "bridges" between field and national survey measures and samples to obtain norms for assessing sampling biases and for calibration of quantitative scores within the field sample.

An iterative approach to generating survey and interview data turns up common and unique themes across sites. The qualitative data describe meanings of particular context conditions to individuals, groups, and school cultures. Successive development of survey instruments refines measures of variability in the sample. In our study of teachers, for example, we refined measures of collegiality in school and department settings to record overall contrasts among our sites and to capture conditions in the rare teacher learning communities found in our sample (McLaughlin, 1993; McLaughlin & Talbert, 1993a, 1993b; Talbert & McLaughlin, 1994).

Our approach to measuring the school environment emphasizes students' and teachers' subjective realities. It differs from that of researchers and policymakers, who look at practice and school outcomes from the outside in, from the frame of social science theory, without first assessing the relevance of contexts or variables to proximal processes of schooling. Teachers' and students' perspectives on schools and classrooms often yield a strategically different view of what matters most in a particular educational setting.

We establish a crosswalk between field data and large representative samples of students, teachers, and schools by replicating questionnaire items included in national and state teacher surveys in our field instruments. For example, by replicating HS&B national survey measures of "collegiality" and "principal leadership" in our field instruments, we could locate our sites in national school distributions on these variables. This measurement strategy provides a basis for judging sampling and effect–estimate biases, thus overcoming some limitations of a purposive field sample. It considerably extends the analytic capacity of field research and small-scale studies of students' responses to school environments.

Analysis Strategies

A bottom-up strategy for assessing the school environment aims to identify, first, which settings and contexts account for particular student experiences or outcomes and, second, what conditions in the relevant environments affect the criterion. Rather than deciding a priori which level of analysis to adopt for a given study, one should use analysis of variance (ANOVA) techniques, as well as interview data, to address the empirical question of which context levels or units of analysis are significant for a particular criterion. For example, across what level of analysis, or kind of schooling context, do researchers observe systematic variation in students' academic effort or perceptions of adult support? Can patterns shown by the survey data be validated and interpreted by interview data?

Results of bottom-up analyses also point to cases that deviate from a general pattern. For example, ANOVAS in teachers' collegiality scores for our 16-high-school study showed that independent schools and one public school in the sample had strong schoolwide community, whereas most schools had substantial variation within schools and across subject departments (McLaughlin, 1993; McLaughlin & Talbert, 1993a, 1993b; Talbert & McLaughlin, 1994). This pattern directed us to pursue case studies of the strong school communities while pursuing analysis of internal school communities for the other schools. The bottom-up strategy enables one to detect when and where multiple units and lines of inquiry should be pursued.

Of course, this inquiry is guided by prior research and theory. Our emphasis on teachers' social norms as mediating context effects on learning is grounded in considerable research, for example. Also, once contexts that affect particular outcomes are identified, prior research helps to specify variables for measurement and analysis. The bottom-up analysis strategy is both a dialogue of quantitative and qualitative data and a dialogue of data and theory.

ILLUSTRATION: A BOTTOM-UP LINE OF ANALYSIS

Our research on the school environment documents considerable diversity in teachers' work lives and professional behavior across secondary schools (McLaughlin, 1993; McLaughlin & Talbert, 1993a, 1993b; Talbert & McLaughlin, 1994). Here, we illustrate how a bottom-up analysis of students' engagement in academic classes identified multiple, interactive context effects.

As part of our research in the 16-school sample, we conducted a longitudinal study of 54 students in four inner-city high schools (12–14 students in each school; McLaughlin, 1993; McLaughlin & Talbert, 1993a, 1993b; Talbert & McLaughlin, 1994). The students were purposively sampled to represent a range of academic achievement in the 10th grade. (See Phelan, Davidson, & Cao, 1991, for further description of the sample and sites.) These students were interviewed at least three times a year, and a subsample of students in each school were "shadowed" (or accompanied by a CRC researcher) for several days each year during a 2-year period. In addition, the students completed the full NELS:88 10th-grade student questionnaire, and we obtained their high school transcripts. Our bottom-up analysis proceeds through dialogue between the ethnographic and the quantitative data.

Student Engagement

Through interviews with students in our sample, we heard about ways in which individual teachers had helped them to connect with a subject or had supported them to stay in school. The students also told us how some teachers put them down and how they dreaded those class periods. By talking with these students, attending their classes, and listening to their conversations with peers, we learned that their experiences of school varied considerably from class to class, or from teacher to teacher, throughout the day. In particular, the levels of trust among students in the classroom and support for academic learning established by teachers varied substantially across classes for most of these students.

Through interviews with teachers, we learned that different teachers also viewed the same student differently. The profile of a student varied across classes, just as the portrait of "school" varied for students across classes. For example, in one high school, a student we shadowed found himself criticized as "probably overachieving" and "unlikely to succeed" in his very traditional social studies class, where the teacher took center stage, and in the next hour was praised as a "promising writer" and as having "academic potential" by his English teacher, whose classroom cast students in active roles as learners. His different experiences of school, and of himself as student, stemmed from his teachers' different ideas about the ways in which students should involve themselves in subject area content and concepts. These data raised important questions about units of school environments that are meaningful for students.

We pursued the issue with statistical ANOVAs for a variety of academic and affective outcomes, using survey and transcript data for the students in the longitudinal field sample. Included was the subset of students for whom we had NELS:88 survey data, student ratings of classes and teachers, and teacher survey data. Availability of teacher data was essential so that we would be able to relate class-level variance in student outcomes to teacher and teaching variables being addressed in our broader research project. The sample for this analysis included 80 academic classes of 20 students in four subjects in four schools. We considered course grades for 2 years and student survey measures of their levels of understanding and effort in each of their classes (NELS:88, Likert-like scales) and their ratings of how much they liked the class and the teacher (5-point scales).

ANOVAs for these measures of student performance, self-reports on class behavior, and affective ratings addressed the issue of which unit of analysis accounts for a particular kind of student behavior. Is variation mainly between students, or between schools, or between particular academic subjects, or between departments in a high school, or between classes for a student? As shown in Table 1, we found considerable variance at the class level that was not a function of student differences or higher level school differences. Although academic grades varied mainly between students, we also observed considerable between-classes variation for individual students. Students' reports of the level of effort they invested in a class were almost entirely (94%) a matter of variation between classes.[4]

The bottom-up analysis focused on between-classes variance in students' efforts: What class variables and context conditions account for differences in student effort? We focused on mathematics classes to simplify the analysis, to control for institutional culture differences across subjects

[4]Note that the R^2 for Model 4 in Table 1 is not the sum of variance explained by Models 1–4. This is because the sets of dummy variables included in each model are not mutually exclusive. For example, the set of student dummy variables in Model 1 spans the four schools represented in Model 2; the department dummy variables in Model 4 encompass the four schools of Model 2 and the 4 participants of Model 3. If between-students variance were entirely independent of variance related to subjects and school boundaries, then the R^2 for Model 5 would equal the sum of Model 1 (student-level variance) and Model 4 (the Subject × School [Department] variance).

TABLE 1
Isolating Variance in Student Outcomes Unique to Class: Regression Analyses of Outcome Variables on Dummy-Variable Sets

	Model					
Outcome variable	1 Student (ST)	2 School (SC)	3 Subject (SUB)	4 Department (SUB × SC)	5 ST + SC + SUB	6 Estimated class variance[a]
Grades (transcript)						
Class grade						
Year 1 (n = 77)	0.78	0.00	0.06	0.00	0.80	0.20
Year 2 (n = 81)	0.73	0.07	0.00	0.00	0.73	0.27
NELS measure						
Understanding (n = 68)	0.46	0.15	0.00	0.05	0.46	0.54
Effort (n = 68)	0.06	0.00	0.01	0.00	0.06	0.94
CRC measure						
Class rating (n = 79)	0.23	0.07	0.07	0.17	0.37	0.63
Teacher rating (n = 79)	0.00	0.00	0.12	0.15	0.16	0.84

Note. Data indicate adjusted R^2 variance for each dummy variable. NELS = National Educational Longitudinal Survey; CRC = Center for Research on the Context of Teaching.
[a]$1 - R^2$ for Model 5.

and differences in educational policies applied to subjects within a given administrative system. The general bottom-up strategy we used to conduct the analysis is represented in Figure 3.

Teacher Professionalism and Students' Effort

Through longitudinal research on teachers and teaching, we developed a global survey measure of teacher professional commitment. This scale correlates highly with a number of indexes of teacher professionalism, such as a strong service ethic toward students (Talbert & McLaughlin, 1994), and it predicts a range of student experiences and outcomes. Figure 4 shows the strong correlation between students' efforts in mathematics classes as predicted by their math teachers' scores on the Professional Commitment Scale (7-item scale; $\alpha = .71$).

Survey items that make up the Professional Commitment Scale correspond to students' comments about conditions that make them want to do well in a class. Teachers who scored high on the scale put in extra effort, felt that they were improving as a teacher, loved the subject they teach, were eager to learn about ways to improve teaching, and were loyal to the teaching profession. Conversely, students tend to tune out of a class in which the teacher lacks engagement with his or her subject matter and students; when knowledge is transmitted in routine and impersonal ways, students are neither motivated nor able to make the subject matter personally meaningful.

What school environments support or undermine teachers' professional commitments? In our bottom-up analysis strategy, we looked to other proximate settings and external contexts of schooling to address this question.

Settings for Teachers' Professionalism

The next stage of analysis began with the question of which levels of the school context account for variation in teachers' professional commitment. Again we used a dialogue between qualitative and quantitative data to pursue the issue. Our investigation included the ANOVA strategy illustrated for measures of student engagement. We examined variance in teachers' scores on the Professional Commitment Scale and on other related indicators of teacher professionalism. We found that sector, district, school, and department contexts represented in our sample each accounted for some variance in teacher commitment (Talbert & McLaughlin, 1994). We then turned to the issue of what variables at each system level predicted the differences in teacher professionalism.

The strength of teacher community was a strong correlate of teachers' professional commitment and varied systematically at multiple levels of the

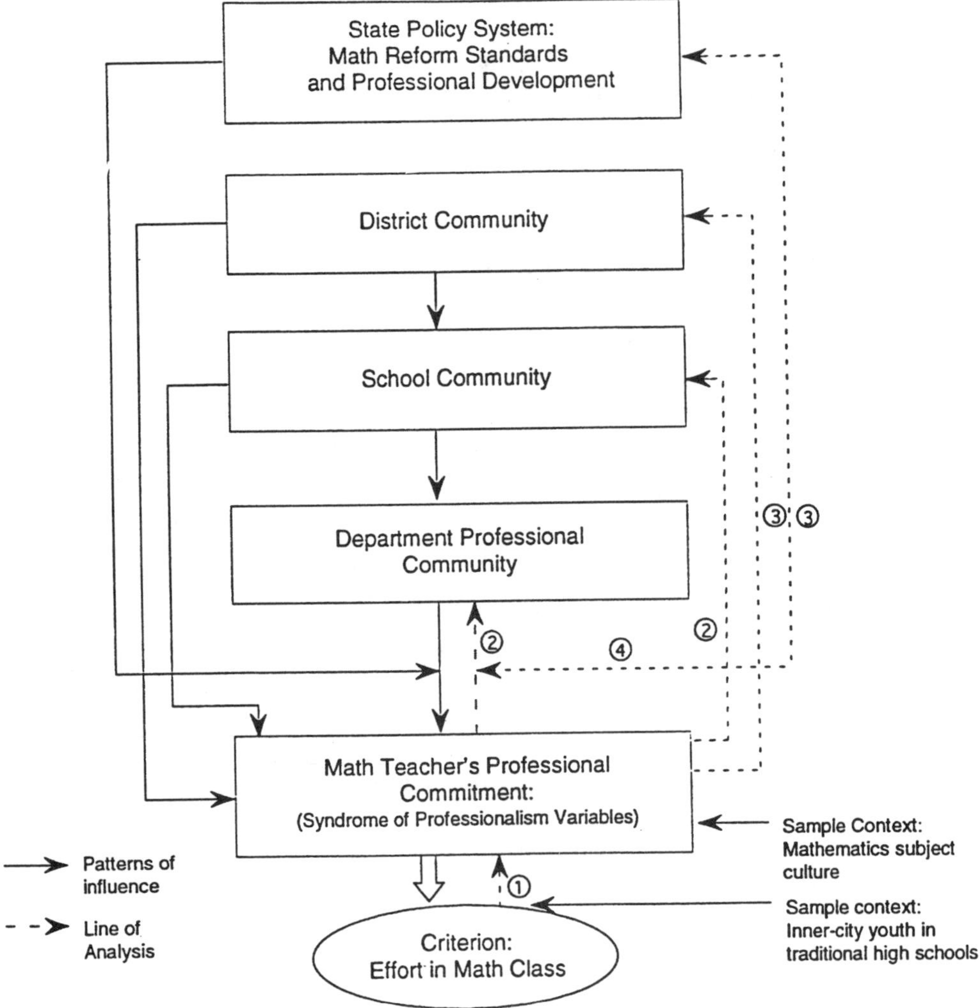

Figure 3. A bottom-up analysis of embedded school contexts that influence student effort in mathematics.

school system. Figure 4 shows the embedded-context boundaries of our 16-school sample and mean school scores on the Professional Commitment Scale and on a Collegiality Scale, a global measure of the strength of teacher community.[5] (These scores are reported in standard deviation units,

[5]This scale, and others reported here, were developed by CRC. See Talbert and McLaughlin (1994) for items making up the collegiality scale and other CRC measures.

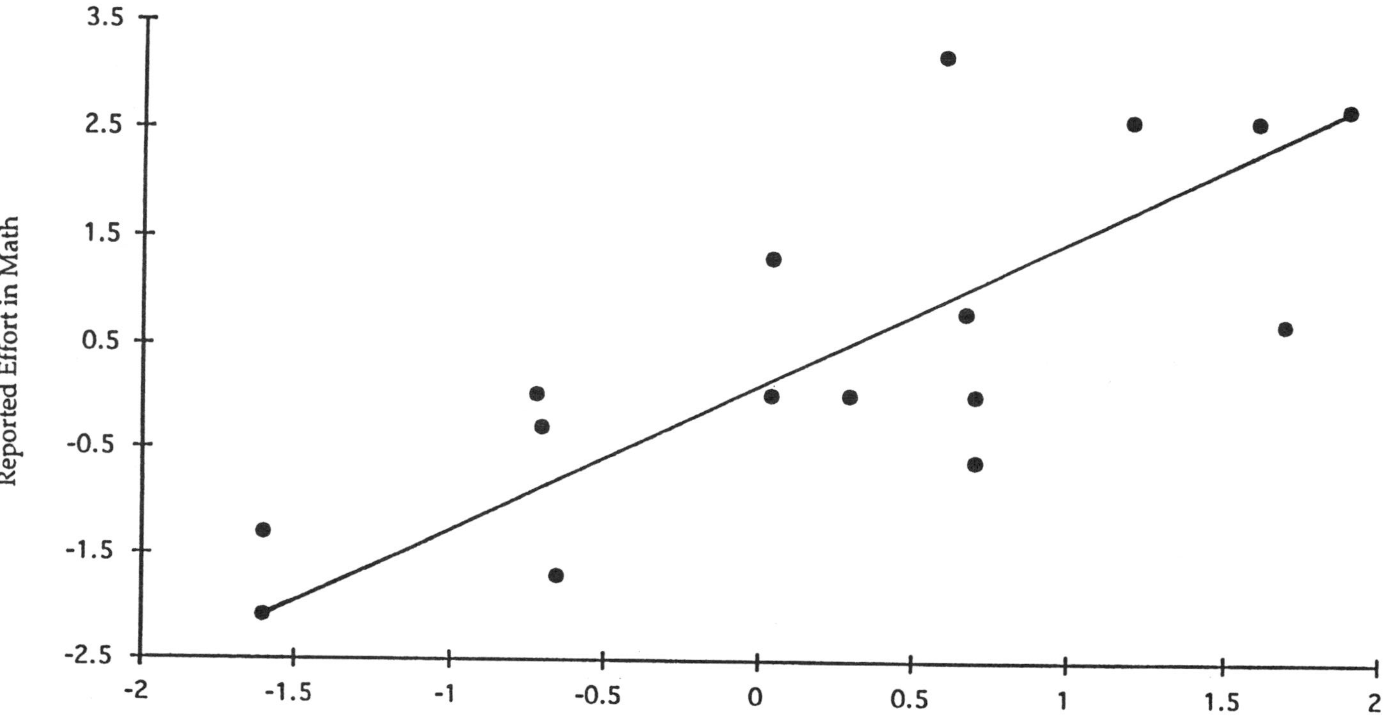

Figure 4. Regression of student-reported effort in mathematics on teacher commitment. Effort scores are standardized according to each student's reported efforts in all of his or her core academic subjects.

with the standard scores computed at the individual level for the full teacher sample.) The graph of school means on teachers' commitment and collegiality shows that schools in our sample differed substantially in providing students access to professionally engaged teachers.

Qualitative case studies of the strong teacher communities in the independent schools (Schools 5, 9, and 4 in Figure 4) and in three California schools (Schools 1, 7, and 8) documented the kinds of interactions among teachers that supported their professionalism. We observed in each case that schoolwide norms encouraged teachers to solve problems collectively, to share teaching resources, and to share information about particular students' needs. Also common across these schools was a norm of "personalization" for teacher–student relations—the expectation that teachers and students come to know one another as whole people and that individual interests, prior knowledge, and needs are central to the teaching and learning process (McLaughlin & Talbert, 1993b; McLaughlin, Talbert, Kahne, & Powell, 1990).

ANOVA results also directed us to look at subject departments within the typical comprehensive high schools as sources of variable teacher community and professionalism. We found substantial differences in the strength and character of subject departments in many of these schools; indeed, in four of the comprehensive high schools, we found subject departments in which their means on our survey scale of collegiality differed by more than one standard deviation. National norms for this score provided a metric for judging the significance of between-departments and between-schools differences observed in our sample.

Case studies of the contrasting department communities revealed ways in which teachers' work and relations with students differed in the strong and weak departments. These comparisons included contrasting department communities within the same school and contrasting departments across schools in the same subject (math and science). Our interviews with teachers in urban high schools indicated how department communities moderated teachers' responses to changing student populations and shaped their sense of professional career and commitment. For example, teachers in weak departments tended to see the students as less capable of academic success than did their school colleagues in strong departments in the same school. They saw the same students differently and brought different expectations and levels of commitment into their classes.

We observed that differences in teachers' attitudes toward students were related to their opportunities to learn from colleagues and, in fact, to improve their chances for success with students. In strong department communities, when a teacher was struggling, he or she turned to colleagues instead of giving up on the students. Quantitative analyses conducted at the department level for 36 departments in eight typical public schools corroborated these findings from interviews and observations: The Teacher

Commitment Scale correlated .52 with department community and .29 with a measure of teachers' sense of responsibility for students (Talbert & McLaughlin, 1994).

Policy Contexts of Student–Teacher Relations

The strong schoolwide communities in our sample were, with one exception (School 7 in Figure 5), special mission schools. Through specialized charters, programs, and policies, the mission schools forged a sense

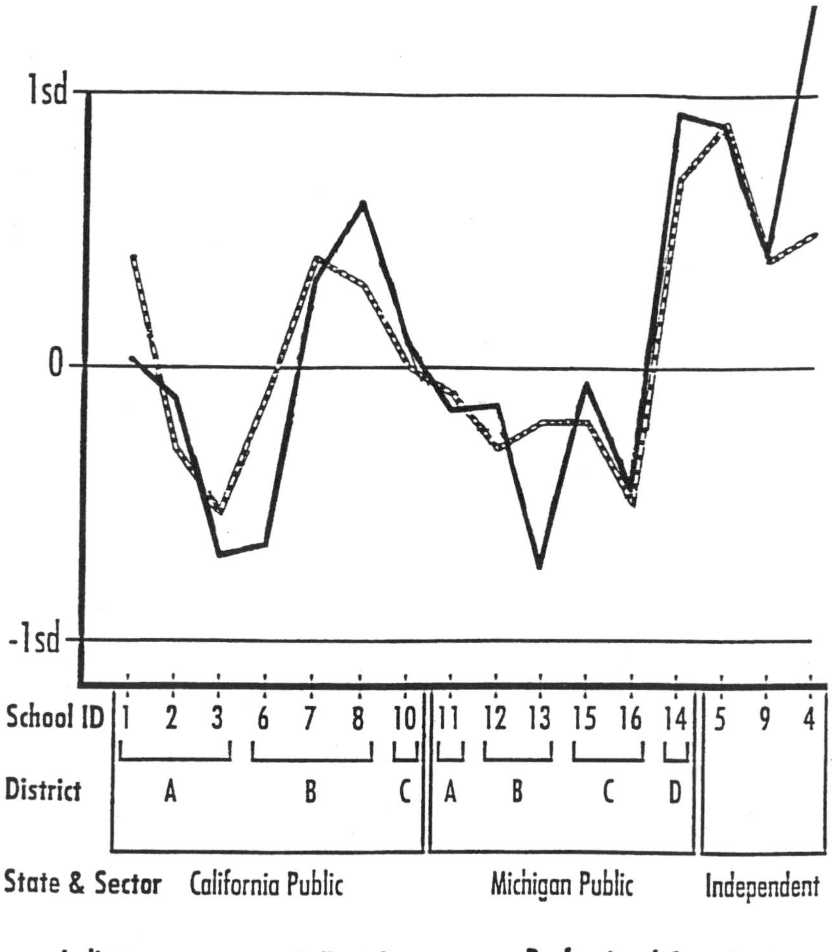

Figure 5. School differences on professional community indicators. The Center for Research on the Context of Teaching (CRC) Collegiality Index is a 5-item scale based on High School and Beyond teacher survey items (α = .84), and Professional Commitment is an 8-item scale (α = .75). Teachers' scores on each scale were standardized to allow for comparability. Averages for each CRC school are plotted in the figure. sd = standard deviation.

of shared goals and interests among teachers and students. These conditions fostered teacher professionalism and supportive personalized relations between teachers and students. Particularly in the performing arts public school in our sample (School 8 in Figure 5), we also saw the key role played by the principal and other school leaders in sustaining the school mission and community.

Apart from communicating school goals and expectations, the mission school leaders challenged institutional norms in the context of schooling that operate against the development of the schoolwide community. For example, subject identities among teachers promoted department versus school loyalties in large high schools, regardless of whether the department community is strong or weak. Furthermore, given a general status order among subjects (with math usually at the top and vocational subjects and the arts at the bottom of the status hierarchy), a sense of social inequalities among teachers can undermine community (Little, 1990). Site-level policies and norms to counter these tendencies are essential to sustaining a schoolwide community. (See Talbert, 1993, for elaboration of this point.)

Another way in which system policies can promote teachers' commitment and responsibility toward students, we saw, is by challenging norms of subject cultures that can inhibit teachers' responsiveness to their students. In particular, we saw the power of a standards-based reform policy for mathematics education challenge taken-for-granted beliefs about math teaching and learning and encourage teachers to rethink ways of connecting students and content. This reconsideration prompted classroom adaptations that enhanced teachers' responsiveness to their students and their capacity to personalize approaches to teaching and learning. We observed this effect as contrasts in findings for the state policy contexts represented in our sample: California, with strong math reform policies and supports, versus Michigan, with no reforms in math underway during the 1980s. Specifically, we observed that math teachers' adaptation to students—a survey scale measuring teachers' belief that they can promote all students' learning—was related to teacher community in California but not in Michigan. This interaction effect is shown in Figure 6.

Quantitative and qualitative analyses of math teachers and departments in the two policy contexts revealed that strong teacher communities tended to either enforce or challenge institutional norms for math instruction that constrained adaptation to students. In strong traditional math departments, teachers generally regarded high rates of student failure as a sign that high teaching standards were being upheld. However, in a policy system aiming to reform mathematics teaching to support all students' success, we found strong departments and teacher networks in and outside of the schools in which teachers were developing new practices and conceptions of effective math education. In these teacher communities, student failure was regarded as the educator's failure to adapt instruction in ways

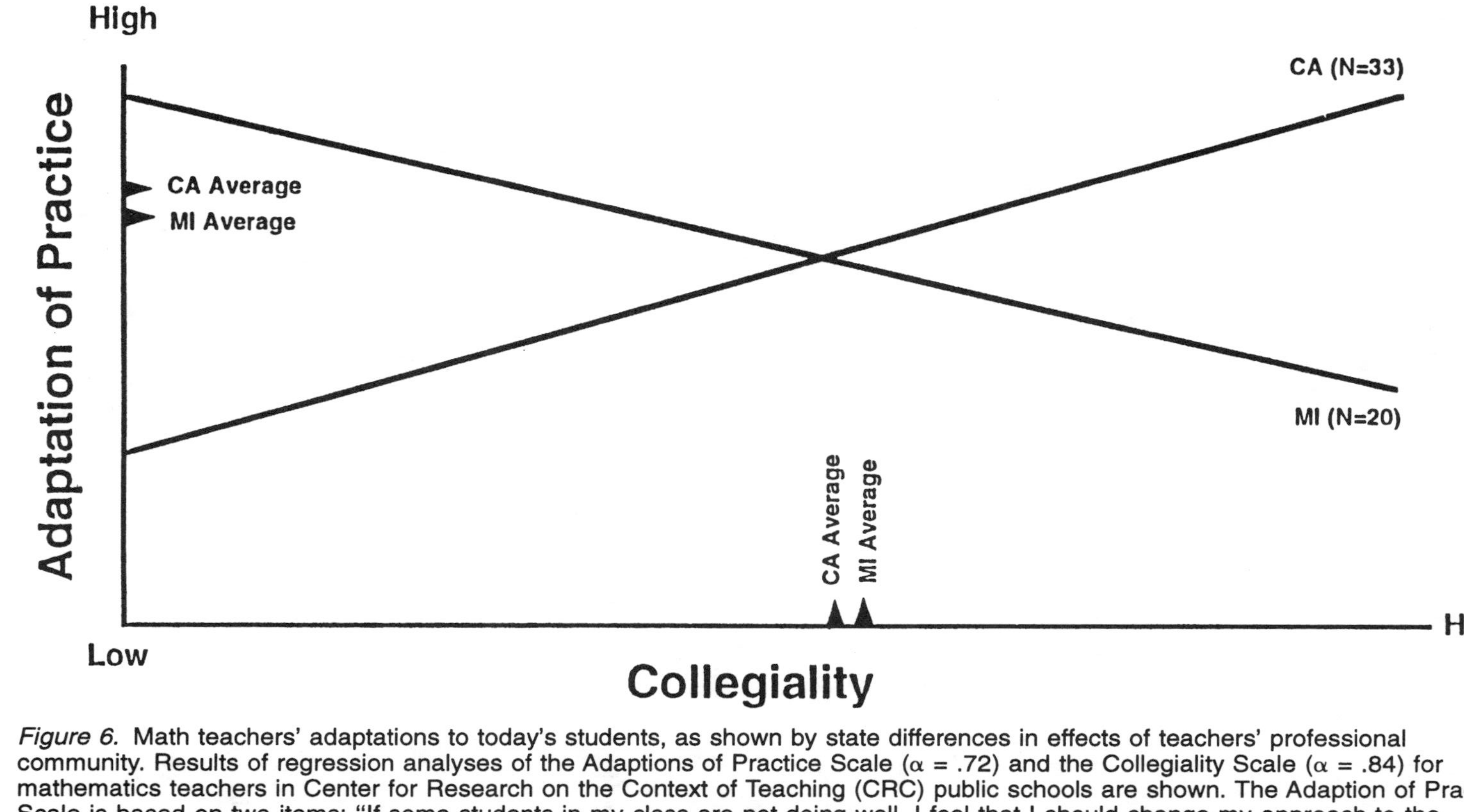

Figure 6. Math teachers' adaptations to today's students, as shown by state differences in effects of teachers' professional community. Results of regression analyses of the Adaptions of Practice Scale (α = .72) and the Collegiality Scale (α = .84) for mathematics teachers in Center for Research on the Context of Teaching (CRC) public schools are shown. The Adaption of Practice Scale is based on two items: "If some students in my class are not doing well, I feel that I should change my approach to the subject" and "By trying a different teaching method, I can significantly affect a student's achievement." The graph shows the regression slope for California (CA) math teachers (β = .23, r = 59) and the slope for Michigan (MI) math teachers (β = −.10, r = −.27, *ns*).

that promote learning for all students. Students in these teachers' classrooms had qualitatively different experiences with mathematics than did their peers in traditional math classes. In each case, students' realities were embedded in a complex and interactive environment of teacher community, institutional norms for mathematics education, and curriculum policies in the school administrative system.

EXTENDING A BOTTOM-UP PERSPECTIVE ON THE SCHOOL ENVIRONMENT

In this chapter we described our conception of the school environment as multiple embedded contexts and illustrated a bottom-up, multimethod approach to assessing context effects on students' educational experiences and outcomes. Compared with the social-address and school community research described in the first section, which frame analyses in terms of particular levels and kinds of variables, our approach analyzes students' realities as embedded in multiple settings and contexts of schooling.

As illustrated by our analysis of students' efforts in high school classes, we analyzed the relevance and interplay of particular contexts and variables from the bottom-up, or from the inside out—from the core classroom setting to broader social, administrative, and institutional contexts. By locating our analysis at the bottom of the school system and in the daily experiences of students and their teachers, we could identify particular units of analysis and cases that shaped differences in students' educational behavior. Multiple theoretical lenses allowed us to see how situated realities of school settings were constructed from institutional, administrative, and social system conditions and processes.

A hierarchical model assuming additive effects across levels would miss the permeability of embedded contexts and the ways in which environments combine to effect proximal processes. Contexts do not simply "add up" for students. A strong district, and a strong principal, for example, do not sum to a positive school experience for a student in a class taught by a professionally disengaged teacher who believes that the students cannot learn the course material. Or, a shift in the broader policy context (e.g., higher standards for high school graduation) may boost student accomplishment in a school setting where faculty ethos and capacity can support more rigorous academic work for all students but can diminish it in the school down the street where faculty are unwilling or unable to enable student success with higher standards. Indeed, our illustration revealed that math teachers in weak communities in the reform state were least likely to adapt instruction to meet all students' needs; this interaction effect spanned multiple levels of school organization.

Our various notions of embeddedness refer to the kinds of interplay we observed between types and levels of school environments. For example, our research on mathematics teaching indicated that subject culture beliefs and standards were enacted in most classrooms and departments and that they differed substantially from the cultures governing science or English teaching. High school teaching, in this view, is embedded in distinct subject cultures that direct professional practice. We observed, however, that teaching is embedded in social networks of teachers who make sense of the multiple contexts in which they teach: the students' capacities and needs, the subject matter and teaching norms, and the policy system and professional environment. We saw that some math departments, for example, rejected norms from their subject culture to construct more successful approaches to teaching their students. Finally, we saw that such community effects were embedded in a broader policy environment, so that the inclination or authority of teacher communities to challenge routines of subject instruction appeared to depend on policies and resources supporting change.

Further research using an embedded-context model of schooling and bottom-up analyses might extend our conceptual model to consider cumulative and longitudinal perspectives on students' school experiences. The model represents a vertical slice of multiple contexts and settings that frame students' school experiences. Our work thus far has not addressed the issue of how multiple settings and experiences—coincident in a day and school year or sequential over years of schooling—combine to affect individuals' educational outcomes.

We learned that high school students experienced substantial diversity across their classes throughout the school day and that students' engagement in a class was strongly related to their teachers' professional attitudes and behavior. However, in measuring the school environment, we have not taken into account thus far the sum of situations experienced by a student. Is the salience and significance of a particular positive or negative classroom experience conditioned by other concurrent school experiences? How do students' out-of-school involvements, with community-based organizations or activities, for example, play out for students in diverse school settings? Given students' comments in our interviews, we can hypothesize that a positive school environment matters more to students whose other life settings are unsupportive or are barren of resources for development; conversely, a school setting experienced as inhospitable or negative will likely mater less to students who find support in their families or community.

A longitudinal perspective on students' school environments would include successive classroom and school settings and contexts, or pathways, across years and developmental stages. How do elementary grade students respond to transitions between qualitatively different classroom settings?

How much weight does a supportive versus nonsupportive setting have over the years, and does this vary with developmental stages? For example, does a child who experienced a strong class learning community one year remain a confident and active learner the next year in a class that promotes deference and routine teacher-directed work? Does the recent setting and experience supplant the former? How lasting or temporal are effects of particular school situations on students' long-term engagement with education or with a particular subject?

Bottom-up measurement strategies are essential to developing longitudinal perspectives on students' school environments and outcomes. Profiles of students' cumulative school environments and patterns of engagement could be constructed, ideally, through longitudinal research or through retrospective interviews and school records. Short of constructing cumulative profiles of students' school environments, research could target transition grades—such as the first grade of middle or junior high school or the first grade of high school—to study students' adaptations to particular kinds of changes in their school environments. Evidence that such school transitions are important periods in individuals' educational biographies, often marking decline or improvements in academic performance, suggests that changes in quality of the school environment may be particularly potent at these school career stages.

Horizontal and longitudinal perspectives on embedded school contexts promise advances in theory on school effects and in educational policies to promote positive educational outcomes for all students. Analyses located in continuities and discontinuities in students' educational experiences and outcomes would afford refinements of notions of embeddedness central to our conceptual model. In this case, the student's educational background would be among the contexts in which school experiences are embedded. Furthermore, analyses focused on students' cumulative experiences in particular school environments would help to identify the higher level contexts and conditions that create continuities, for better or worse, in individuals' educational careers.

REFERENCES

Alexander, K. L., Cook, M. A., & McDill, E. L. (1978). Curriculum tracking and educational stratification: Some further evidence. *American Sociological Review, 43*, 47–66.

Ball, S. J., & Lacey, C. (1984). Subject disciplines as the opportunity for group action: A measured critique of subject sub-cultures. In A. Hargreaves & P. Woods (Eds.), *Classrooms and staffrooms: The sociology of teachers and teaching* (pp. 232–244). Milton Keynes, England: Open University Press.

Becker, W. C., & Gerstein, R. (1982). A follow-up of follow through: The later effects of the direct instruction model on children in fifth and sixth grades. *American Educational Research Journal, 19,* 75–92.

Brown, A. L., & Campione, J. C. (1977). *Memory strategies in learning: Training children to study strategically* (Tech. Rep. No. 22). Urbana: University of Illinois, Center for the Study of Reading.

Brown, A. L., & Campione, J. C. (1980). *Inducing flexible thinking: Problem of access* (Tech. Rep. No. 156). Urbana: University of Illinois, Center for the Study of Reading.

Bryk, A. S., Lee, V. E., & Holland, P. B. (1993). *Catholic schools and the common good.* Cambridge, MA: Harvard University Press.

Chubb, J. E., & Moe, T. E. (1990). *Politics, markets and America's schools.* Washington, DC: The Brookings Institution.

Coleman, J. S., & Hoffer, T. (1987). *Public and private high schools: The impact of communities.* New York: Basic Books.

Coleman, J. S., Hoffer, T., & Kilgore, S. D. (1982). *High school achievement: Public, private, and Catholic schools compared.* New York: Basic Books.

Finley, M. K. (1984). Teachers and tracking in a comprehensive high school. *Sociology of Education, 57,* 233–243.

Gamoran, A. (1986). Instructional and institutional effects of ability grouping. *Sociology of Education, 59,* 185–198.

Gamoran, A. (1987). The stratification of high school learning opportunities. *Sociology of Education, 60,* 135–155.

Greeno, J. G. (1991). Number sense as situated knowing in a conceptual domain. *Journal for Research in Mathematics, 22,* 170–218.

Greeno, J. G., Smith, D. R., & Moore, J. L. (1991). Transfer of situated learning. In D. Detterman & R. Sternberg (Eds.), *Transfer on trial.* Hillsdale, NJ: Erlbaum.

Grossman, P. L., & Stodolsky, S. S. (1994). Considerations of content and the circumstances of secondary school teaching. In L. Darling-Hammond (Ed.), *Review of research in education* (Vol. 20, pp. 179–221). Washington, DC: American Educational Research Association.

Hallinan, M. T. (1990). The effects of ability grouping in secondary schools: A response to Slavin's best-evidence synthesis. *Review of Educational Research, 60,* 501–504.

Hargreaves, D. H. (1967). *Social relations in a secondary school.* London: C. Tinling.

Jencks, C. S., Smith, M., Acland, H., Bane, M. J., Cohen, D., Gintis, H., Heyns, B., & Michelson, S. (1972). *Inequality: A reassessment of the effect of family and schooling in America.* New York: Basic Books.

Lacey, C. (1970). *Hightown grammar.* Manchester, England: Manchester University Press.

Little, J. W. (1990). Conditions of professional development in secondary schools. In M. W. McLaughlin, J. E. Talbert, & N. Bascia (Eds.), *The contexts of teach-*

ing in secondary schools: Teachers' realities (pp. 187–223). New York: Teachers College Press, Columbia University.

Mayer, R. E., & Greeno, J. G. (1972). Structural differences between learning outcomes produced by different instructional methods. *Journal of Educational Psychology, 63*, 165–173.

McLaughlin, M. W. (1993). What matters most in teachers' workplace context? In J. W. Little & M. W. McLaughlin (Eds.), *Teachers' work: Individuals, colleagues and contexts* (pp. 79–103). New York: Teachers College Press, Columbia University.

McLaughlin, M. W., & Talbert, J. E. (1993a). *Contexts that matter for teaching and learning*. Stanford, CA: Center for Research on the Context of Secondary School Teaching.

McLaughlin, M. W., & Talbert, J. E. (1993b). How the world of students and teachers challenges policy coherence. In S. Fuhrman (Ed.), *Designing coherent educational policy: Improving the system* (pp. 220–249). San Francisco: Jossey-Bass.

McLaughlin, M. W., Talbert, J. E., Kahne, J., & Powell, J. (1990). Constructing a personalized school environment. *Phi Delta Kappan, 72*, 230–235.

Metz, M. H. (1978). *Classrooms and corridors: The crisis of authority in desegregated secondary schools*. Berkeley: University of California Press.

Meyer, J. W., & Rowan, B. (1977). Institutionalized organizations: Formal structure as myth and ceremony. *American Journal of Sociology, 83*, 340–363.

National Council of Teachers of Mathematics. (1989). *Curriculum and evaluation standards for school mathematics*. Reston, VA: Author.

National Council of Teachers of Mathematics. (1991). *Professional standards for teaching mathematics*. Reston, VA: Author.

National Council of Teachers of Mathematics. (1995). *Assessment standards for school mathematics*. Reston, VA: Author.

Oakes, J. (1985). *Keeping track: How schools structure inequality*. New Haven, CT: Yale University Press.

Phelan, P. K., Davidson, A. L., & Cao, H. T. (1991). Students' multiple worlds: Negotiating the boundaries of family, peer, and school cultures. *Anthropology and Education Quarterly, 22*, 224–250.

Purkey, S. C., & Smith, M. S. (1983). Effective schools: A review. *Elementary School Journal, 83*, 427–452.

Rosenbaum, J. E. (1976). *Making inequality: The hidden curriculum of high school teaching*. New York: Wiley.

Rutter, M., Maughan, B., Mortimore, P., Outson, J., & Smith, A. (1979). *Fifteen thousand hours: Secondary schools and their effects on children*. Cambridge, MA: Harvard University Press.

Talbert, J. E. (1990). *Teacher tracking: Exacerbating inequalities in the high school*. Stanford, CA: Stanford University, Center for Research on the Context of Secondary School Teaching.

Talbert, J. E. (1993). Constructing a schoolwide professional community: The negotiated order of a performing arts school. In J. W. Little & M. W. McLaughlin (Eds.), *Teachers' work: Individuals, colleagues, and contexts* (pp. 164–184). New York: Teachers College Press, Columbia University.

Talbert, J. E., & McLaughlin, M. W. (1994). Teacher professionalism in local school context. *American Journal of Education, 102,* 123–153.

Talbert, J. E., McLaughlin, M. W., & Rowan, B. (1993). Understanding context effects on secondary school teaching. *Teachers College Record, 95,* 45–65.

Wilson, B., & Schmits, D. W. (1978). What's new in ability grouping? *Phi Delta Kappan, 59,* 535–536.

8

THE WORKPLACE ENVIRONMENT: MEASUREMENT, PSYCHOLOGICAL EFFECTS, AND BASIC ISSUES

CARMI SCHOOLER

In its long-standing survey research program on the psychological effects of occupational and other social-structurally determined environmental conditions, the Laboratory of Socio-Environmental Studies (LSES, now the Section of Socio-Environmental Studies) has developed a distinctive approach to conceptualizing and measuring environmental conditions, particularly occupational ones, and to analyzing their psychological effects. The reports of this research, obviously relevant to many issues in psychology, have appeared almost exclusively in sociological publications and rarely in psychological ones. The core of the present chapter is a description of the development of the LSES's approach to conceptualizing the work environment and a summary of the findings of the empirical longitudinal research program based on this approach. Through this program, the LSES examined a series of theoretically derived hypotheses about causal connections between social-structurally determined aspects of the environment such as occupation and the individual's psychological functioning.

Although the approach developed by the LSES has been highly productive, it has not been without its critics. All too often, these criticisms have been based on questionable and unsupported reductionist beliefs. One of these unfounded beliefs is that the environment, particularly the social and cultural environment, has a negligible impact on development and behavior. A second such belief is that socioenvironmental factors and their effects cannot be studied in a scientifically rigorous way.

Besides affecting the generalizability of many neuroscience and cognitive science findings, the disinterest in studying the environment and its effects can lead to underestimates of the effects of the environment. It is a mathematical fact that error in the measurement of an independent variable tends to result in the underestimation of its effects (Bohrnstedt, 1969). Consequently, if one is comparing the effects of generally well-measured classes of variables, such as biological and genetic variables, with those of classes of variables with generally high degrees of measurement error, such as environmental variables, the relative power of the well-measured class will be overestimated. This is true not only for psychological but also for biological dependent variables.

An example of how better measurement of environmental factors can affect the estimate of the proportion of biological variability explained by the environment can be found in Pérusse, Rice, Bouchard, Vogler, and Rao (1989). These authors used a more carefully developed and extensive set of environmental measures than commonly used in the predictions of blood pressure. Their environmental measures proved to be substantially more powerful than those commonly encountered in other studies. When they limited their analyses to four commonly used environmental predictors of blood pressure, their results were two to three times less powerful than when they used their fully developed set of environmental measures.

The importance of developing better measures and ways of conceptualizing the environment goes beyond assessing the power of environmental effects. Such development is indispensable if researchers are to elucidate the mechanisms through which the environment has its effects. Knowledge of such mechanisms is necessary if researchers are to comprehend how the environment interacts with the biological predispositions of the individual. Only after such interactions are understood can the nature of many of the processes that are of central interest to neuroscientific or cognitive researchers be fully fathomed. Studying the environment with the same levels of both resources and scientific rigor that are brought to bear on neuroscientific and cognitive research is thus not only a meaningful goal in itself but also a necessary prerequisite for realizing the full potential of neuroscientific and cognitive research efforts. This is particularly true given serious questions that have been raised about the generalizability of findings in cognitive studies that rely almost exclusively on college student populations as participants (Schooler, 1989; Sears, 1987).

Given the general purpose of this volume, before the approach and results of the LSES program on the psychological effects of the occupational environment are described, the basic theoretical and philosophical concepts underlying studies such as the LSES's examination of the interrelationship of the individual and the environment are briefly and critically examined.

THE INTERRELATIONSHIP OF INDIVIDUALS AND THEIR ENVIRONMENTS

As Whitehead (1954) noted, "The very essence of real actuality—that is of the completely real—is process" (p. 354). Individual inanimate things or biological beings can be thought of as processes in which the interconnections among the components are patterned in a way that promotes a boundedness and a historical continuity over some period of time. This boundedness and historical continuity can lead to a subjective sense of distinctness from other processes and in some circumstances to a sense of self.

Different types of relatively self-contained processes (i.e., types of individual things or beings) are differentially affected by different external processes (i.e., phenomena). Phenomena that are more or less spatially contiguous and temporally contemporary with the individual are its environment. The more contiguous and contemporary with the individual the phenomena are, the more immediate the environment (e.g., Bronfenbrenner's [chapter 1, this volume] distinction between distal and proximal environmental measures). Depending on the nature of the individual in question, environments can involve different ontological levels of processes (e.g., molecular, chemical, biological and psychological, social, and cultural). Environmental phenomena that may causally affect the individual (i.e., that can change the relatively self-contained ongoing process that the individual is) are distinguishable, not only by the actual nature and magnitude of their causal effects but also by a variety of other characteristics. In terms of their potential effect on the individual, the most salient characteristic of environmental phenomena is their likelihood of occurring in the individual's immediate environment. Another relevant characteristic is the times in the history of the individual during which they may have their effects.

Individual processes differ in the degree to which they appear stable (i.e., do not change). The level of stability of individual processes is a function of the interrelationship of three characteristics: (a) the extent to which its internal dynamics are static (i.e., the degree to which its internal rules of development limit change), (b) the ease with which it can be affected by other processes in its environment, and (c) the likelihood that its immediate environment will contain phenomena likely to change it.

Individuals also differ in the extent to which they change other processes in their environments (e.g., how strong and how wide a ripple a wave makes).

Every known individual process has conditions under which it will change. Some changes are such that the identity of the individual process continues, other changes are "great" enough so that the process loses its identity (e.g., death, destruction, or mitosis, in which the original individual cell splits into two).

Biological reproduction is the emergence of a new individual as a function of the processes of the parent(s). The development of the individual after the initial instant of conception is a joint function of the characteristics of the individual and the environment and thus involves continuous interaction between the individual and the environment (Chein, 1936; Gottlieb, 1992). As I have indicated, and as is also evident from the LSES findings presented in this chapter, what might seem to be biologically determined stability (i.e., relative imperviousness to external processes) may actually be a function of environmental stability—the low likelihood that the individual will encounter novel environmental factors that might affect the particular characteristics under consideration.

Individuals do, of course, attempt to select or alter their environments to meet their biologically and environmentally determined needs. Thus, hungry individuals seek food, many schizophrenic individuals avoid social situations (Schooler & Spohn, 1982). The LSES's own research program on the relationship between occupational conditions and psychological functioning shows a variety of lagged effects from intellectual flexibility and self-directed values and orientations at one point in time to job conditions 10 years later. Although at least part of these results may be a function of selective recruitment and retention on the employers' part, these findings suggest that over time people's psychological characteristics affect the kinds of work they choose to do, the ways that they do their jobs, or both. On the other hand, as discussed later, the same analyses strongly indicate that much of the apparent stability in cognitive and other aspects of psychological functioning is the result of the relative lack of change in the socioenvironmental conditions to which individuals are exposed.

LSES RESEARCH ON THE PSYCHOLOGICAL EFFECTS OF ENVIRONMENTAL CONDITIONS

The study of the psychological effects of occupational conditions has been the central focus of the LSES sociological and social psychological research program for more than three decades. The study was originally conceived in the early 1960s by Melvin Kohn and me as a way of explaining social class differences that he had found in parental values:

> Middle-class mothers give high priority to values that reflect *internal dynamics*—the child's own and his empathic concern for other people's . . . [e.g.,] consideration, self-control and curiosity. Working class mothers, by contrast, give higher priority to values that reflect *behavioral conformity*—obedience and neatness. (Kohn, 1969, p. 21)

Kohn had first observed these differences in the parents of the normal controls whom he interviewed in a study of social class and schizophrenia (Kohn & Clausen, 1959). He then confirmed the differences in a survey of a representative sample of Washington, DC, area parents (Kohn, 1959).

In discussing his findings, Kohn (1963; as stated in Kohn & Schooler, 1983) proposed that "the key to understanding why middle class and working class parents differ in their values lies primarily in their different educational and occupational experiences, particularly the differential opportunity to exercise self-direction in work" (Kohn & Schooler, 1983, p. viii). He interpreted these differences as suggesting that the comparatively greater value that lower socioeconomic status parents place on conformity in their children and the comparatively greater value that higher status parents place on self-directedness are at least in part a function of the different requirements necessary to succeed in the jobs that those parents are likely to hold. In short, self-direction is consonant with an orientation to self and society premised on the possibility, learned from one's job experience, of accomplishing what one sets out to do and of being rewarded for succeeding; conformity is consonant with an on-the-job learned orientation concerned with the dangers of stepping out of line.

After reading an early draft of Kohn's article (1963); I proposed that his "interpretation was certainly subject to empirical test and that we should get to work immediately on that test" (Kohn & Schooler, 1983, p. viii). Kohn and I agreed that our research instrument should be a face-to-face structured interview conducted on a representative sample of employed men. We considered including employed women as part of our sample, but we were concerned that doing so would require almost doubling our sample size. We tried to make as many of our questions as possible closed ended. Pretesting, however, quickly revealed that some of our potentially most important measures (such as complexity of work with things, data, and people) required structured but open-ended questions, adroit on-the-spot probing by experienced interviewers, and in-office coding by trained coders.

While planning the study, we enlarged the scope of our inquiry in several important ways. We expanded our hypothesis to the more general one that social status differences in people's orientations toward themselves and their environments and even in the ways they think are to a notable extent a function of the nature and conditions of their work. To test this more general hypothesis, we expanded the psychological variables we examined beyond the realm of parental values to include values for oneself as well as psychological measures such as self-esteem, anxiety, authoritarianism, and, perhaps most unusually for a survey of that time, intellectual flexibility. (For a complete version of this interview, see Kohn, 1969, Appendix C.)

MEASURING THE WORK ENVIRONMENT

Dimensionalizing Conditions of Work

Fundamental to our approach, and most directly relevant to the topic of this book, was our decision to study dimensions of work rather than particular occupations. Thus, instead of comparing specific jobs (e.g., plumbers vs. surgeons), we conceived of a job in terms of a series of dimensions (e.g., closeness of supervision, routinization, substantive complexity [seen as indicative of occupational self-direction], ownership, bureaucratization, position in the hierarchy, and time pressure).

The dimensionalization of occupations had several advantages. By avoiding the necessity of selecting participants from a relatively limited number of categorical occupations, the dimensionalization of occupational conditions permitted us to use a nonweighted representative sample of employed men rather than limiting us to having to sample relatively large numbers of workers from relatively few occupations. As a result, our findings were readily generalizable to a defined and meaningful population of workers.

Dimensionalization of occupational conditions also made it possible for us to determine exactly which aspects of a job were related to a given type of psychological functioning. It did so not only by permitting us to examine the correlations between different dimensions of work and psychological functioning but also by allowing us to carry out analyses examining how strongly a particular occupational condition is related to a particular aspect of psychological functioning when the effects of other occupational conditions are controlled.

This ability to identify the specific effects of particular occupational conditions was made possible because dimensionalization of occupational conditions permitted us to use regression and other types of analyses in which the independent variables were linear rather than categorical. We had some idea at the time we made our decision to dimensionalize occupational conditions of the advantages that such analyses would have over the more categorically oriented analyses then prevalent in sociology. It was, however, not until the subsequent adaptation of regression-based path analyses to sociology that we began to realize how fortunate we were with our decision. As it turned out, it was only the development of regression-based structural equal modeling (SEM; Joreskog, 1973) in the late 1960s, which opened the possibility of estimating reciprocal effects, that provided us with an analytical tool that would permit us to deal with a focal issue in our research. Only by estimating the reciprocal effects between our dimensions of occupational conditions and our dimensions of psychological functioning could we come to grips with the problem of "whether the relationships between job conditions and personality solely reflect processes of occupational selection and job molding or whether, in addition, the job actually does affect personality" (Kohn & Schooler, 1983, pp. x–xi). In fact, the much earlier acceptance of SEM by sociologists rather than by psychologists is at least part of the reason why our research findings have appeared primarily in sociological journals. (For a further discussion of methodological differences between the two disciplines, see Schooler, 1991.)

The use of SEM also permitted us to develop confirmatory factor analysis (CFA)-based measurement models of our key environmental variables that make it possible to eliminate the effects of measurement error. Problems of measurement error are of particular concern in longitudinal studies such as ours because measurement error of independent variables (e.g., an initial value of a variable modeled to affect its later value) is particularly troublesome. This is so because the regression coefficient of the path of the dependent variable on the independent variable (e.g., the path from the initial to the later measure) will be underestimated in direct proportion to the amount of error in the measurement of the independent variable.

This concern over measurement error may seem finicky, but the problem of measurement error can be made tangible by citing the following two numbers: .59 and .93. Both numbers are estimates of the over-time correlation of ideational flexibility, one of the key psychological variables in our study; both are based on exactly the same measures of the same individuals over the same 10-year time span. However, .59 is the over-time correlation of ideational flexibility factor scores based on principal component factor analyses from the first and second stages of our longitudinal study, whereas .93 is the over-time correlation shorn of measurement error by the use of CFA. Clearly, any conclusions about how earlier levels of ideational flexibility interrelate with other psychological or environmental variables to predict later levels of ideational flexibility would be different, depending on whether or not measurement error is taken into account.

Similarly, measurement error in our environmental measures has to be taken into account if the psychological effects of environmental variables are to be estimated. A central example of the type of environmental variable we developed using CFA is our measure of the substantive complexity of work.

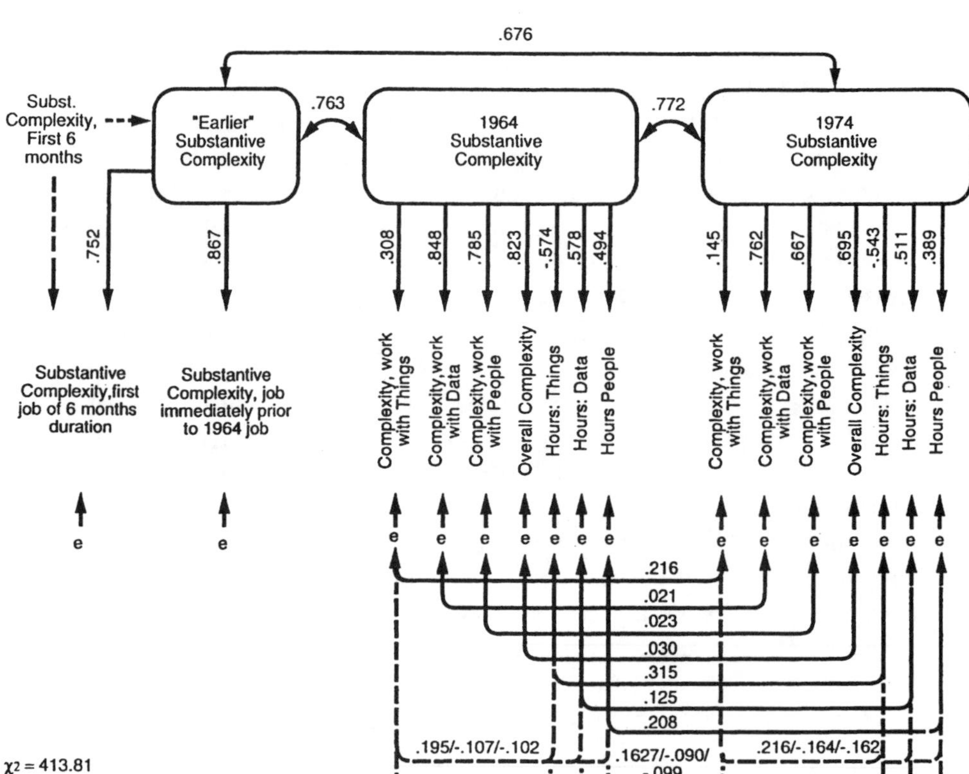

Figure 1. Measurement model for substantive complexity. e = error.

A Measurement Model for Substantive Complexity

Our measurement model for substantive complexity (Kohn & Schooler, 1978, 1983) is presented in Figure 1. By the substantive complexity of work, we mean the degree to which the work requires thought and independent judgment. Substantively complex work, by its very nature, requires making many decisions that must take into account ill-defined or apparently conflicting contingencies. Although in general, work with data or with people is likely to be more complex than work with things, this is not always the case, and an index of the overall complexity of the work should reflect the degree of complexity in each of these three types of activity. Work with things can vary in complexity from ditch digging to sculpturing; similarly, work with people can vary in complexity from receiving simple directions or orders to giving legal advice; and work with data can vary from reading instructions to synthesizing abstract conceptual systems.

Our information about the substantive complexity of men's work is derived from detailed questioning of each respondent about his work with things, data or ideas, and people. The men's answers to these detailed questions provided the basis for seven ratings: an appraisal of the complexity of each man's work with things, data, and people; an appraisal of the overall complexity of this work, regardless of its content; and an estimate of the amount of time spent by each man working at each type of activity. The ratings of complexity of dealing with things, data, and people were made by using the codes developed for the *Dictionary of Occupational Titles* (DOT; U.S. Department of Labor, 1965); the measure of overall complexity was a similar rating developed by us (Kohn & Schooler, 1969).

We treat all seven ratings of the 1964 job as indicators of the underlying but not directly measured construct—the substantive complexity of that job. Each indicator is conceived to reflect the underlying construct, which it measures only imperfectly, together with some degree of error in measurement.

The 1964 survey (Kohn & Schooler, 1969, 1982) also provided us with the titles of the first job the respondent held for 6 months or more and of the job he held immediately before the one he held at the time of the interview. Taking advantage of the fact that our codes for the complexity of work done with things, data, and people were the same as those used for three of the digits in the DOT numerical code of occupations, we were able to use the job titles of these earlier jobs to develop an approximate index of substantive complexity for each of these earlier jobs. We used these two measures as indicators of a latent variable we called *earlier (pre-1964) substantive complexity*. (For a discussion of the procedures, developed from the LSES research, for the use of DOT job titles to estimate the substantive complexity of occupations, see Cain and Treiman [1981]. In this article, the authors also discuss a variety of other work conditions and demands that can be derived from knowledge of the DOT title of a job.)

Our follow-up survey conducted in 1974 (Kohn & Schooler, 1978, 1982) asked the same questions and made the same seven ratings. Again, we treated these ratings as indicators of the underlying construct, in this instance, the substantive complexity of the job held at the time of the 1974 interview. As before, we conceived of each indicator as reflecting the underlying construct, together with some degree of measurement error. We also allowed for the possibility that errors of measurement are correlated over time—that whatever errors there may have been in the measurement of complexity of work with things in the 1964 job, for example, may correlate with errors in the measurement of complexity of work with things in the 1974 job. The fit of the model to data was also improved by taking into account other theoretically plausible correlated errors to measurement—notably, between the complexity of each man's work with things and the amount of time he spends working with things, data, and people.

Besides providing us with a way to control for measurement error, the most interesting information provided by this measurement model is that the overall stability in job complexity, from 1964 to 1974, was rather high: The correlation between the two measures of complexity, stripped of measurement error, was .77. (For a relatively simple general discussion of SEM and for a more detailed discussion of its application to the LSES occupational study data, see Schooler [1983]. For an early application of SEM to the measurement of children's home environments, see Williams [1976]. For the use of SEM to model the substantive complexity of the school environment, see Miller, Kohn, and Schooler [1985, 1986]. For more recent developments in SEM, see Joreskog and Sorbom [1993a, 1993b], Bollen [1989], and Bollen and Long [1993]).

Other Aspects of the LSES Measures of Work

Besides the issue of dimensionalization, another decision we made in developing our measures of the work environment was to focus on "objective conditions of work—what a worker does, who determines how he does it, in what physical and social circumstances he works, to what risks and rewards he is subject—rather than subjective appraisals of those job conditions" (Kohn & Schooler, 1983, p. 298).

An alternative commonly used approach is based on the belief that job conditions become important for psychological functioning only as they are perceived by the workers. This approach deliberately begins with indexes based on respondents' subjective reactions to their job conditions, rather than on job conditions as an outside observer might report them. Those using this approach would measure boredom rather than routinization or alienation rather than lack of control. Such an approach overlooks possible gaps between the conditions to which workers are exposed and their awareness of the effects of those conditions. The presence or absence of such gaps may be social-structurally determined. Moreover, conditions felt to be benign may be deleterious, whereas conditions felt to be onerous or unpleasant may be beneficial.

We did try to get measures not only of objective working conditions but also of the workers' subjective appraisals of those conditions. We did so in order to try to assess empirically how objective conditions become transformed into subjective experience and how both objective conditions and subjective perceptions affect off-the-job psychological functioning and behavior. In order, however, to keep our respondents' reports of their actual job conditions as nonsubjective as possible, our questionnaire began by concentrating on what the respondents did at work and what conditions they worked under. It was only at the end of the occupational section that we asked about how they felt about their work and occupation. Having both the respondents' relatively objective descriptions of their work conditions and their subjective feelings about their work and occupation, we were in a position to use SEM to examine the causal relationship between their work conditions and how they felt about their work.

RESULTS OF THE LSES OCCUPATION STUDY

The original 1964 sample of 3,101 men was representative of all men in the United States, 16 years of age or older, who were employed in civilian occupations at least 25 hours a week (Kohn & Schooler, 1969, 1982). The survey that we designed was conducted by the National Opinion Research Center. Seventy-six percent of the men selected for the sample gave reasonably complete interviews.

Analysis of our respondents' responses supported our hypotheses in several ways (Kohn, 1969; Kohn & Schooler, 1969, 1983). First, we replicated the earlier findings that the higher their social-stratification positions, the more value men place on self-direction and the more confident they are that self-direction is both possible and useful. The lower their social-stratification positions, the more men value conformity to external authority and the more they are convinced that conformity is all that their abilities and the nature of their circumstances allow.

Other findings within the study clearly demonstrated the positive relationship between social-stratification position and the degree to which job conditions allow and require self-direction. Our results also showed that such job conditions are, as we had hypothesized, predictive of self-directed, nonconformist values and orientations and an intellectually flexible cognitive style. Other results indicated that oppressive working conditions produce an overall sense of distress.

Our respondents thus seemed to have generalized from their job experiences to their ways of viewing and dealing with their off-of-the-job circumstances. All in all, our findings provided strong support for our hypothesis that occupational status matters for values and orientations because it helps determine the opportunity and the need for exercising self-direction that jobs provide or preclude. These opportunities, in turn, affect what individuals value and their orientations to and modes of functioning in their environments.

We realized, however, that with the data at hand we could not deal with such issues as the relationship of occupational selection and of "job-molding" to values, orientations, and cognitive function. We clearly recognized the great difference between demonstrating that the relationships of social stratification to our various psychological measures are at least, in part, statistically attributable to occupational conditions and establishing that these occupational conditions actually enter into the processes through which social stratification has its psychological effects. Only with longitudinal data could we attempt to straightforwardly face the issue of causal directionality—of how much the psychological characteristics of the individual affect the conditions of the job and of how much the conditions of the job affect the characteristics of the individual.

In the 1974 follow-up, a representative subsample of 687 of the original respondents, who were less than 55 years old when originally interviewed, were reinterviewed. Their wives and children were interviewed for the first time. Our first longitudinal analysis (Kohn & Schooler, 1978, 1982) focused on what we felt to be the most pivotal job condition, the substantive complexity of work, and one crucial facet of psychological functioning, ideational flexibility. As noted earlier, using the then newly developed technique of SEM (Joreskog, 1973), we developed measurement models of both concepts that showed that, shorn of measurement error, the over-time correlations of both phenomena over the 10-year period were high: .93 for ideational flexibility and .77 for substantive complexity. Nevertheless, our SEM-based causal analyses demonstrated that the effect of ideational flexibility on the substantive complexity of work was, as many would expect, quite pronounced ($\beta = .45$). This effect was lagged, occuring gradually over time. As we had predicted, the reciprocal effect of substantive complexity of work on ideational flexibility was also significant and relatively strong (the standardized path; $\beta = .17$). This effect was about one fourth as great as the effect of the men's 1964 ideational flexibility on their 1974 ideational flexibility (i.e., stability; $\beta = .71$).

Thus, although the correlation of ideational flexibility over the 10-year interval was over .90, our analyses indicated that a notable part of this correlation was due to the actual stability of the environment. After taking into consideration environmental changes coming about because of their initial levels of ideational flexibility, if during the 10-year period between the two surveys, the level of changes in the substantive complexity of the individuals' work environments had been greater, the changes in their ideational flexibility would have been greater and the over-time correlation of that variable lower. The apparent stability of ideational flexibility is thus, in notable and significant part, a function of the stability of the environment.

Further longitudinal analyses (Kohn & Schooler, 1982, 1983) repeatedly demonstrated the psychological importance of occupational self-direction. Job conditions that facilitate occupational self-direction increase men's ideational flexibility and promote a self-directed orientation to self and society as well as child rearing and personal values that reflect such an orientation. Job conditions that limit occupational self-direction decrease men's ideational flexibility and promote a conformist authoritarian orientation to self and society and congruent child rearing and personal values. The longitudinal findings also provided evidence of other ways that job conditions affect personality, the most important being the confirmation that oppressive occupational conditions (e.g., closeness of supervision, dirtiness, and absence of job protection) produce distress.

Other findings demonstrated that the level of a job's occupational self-direction is substantially determined by that job's location in the organizational structure. Ownership, bureaucratization, and high position in the supervisory hierarchy all facilitate the exercise of occupational self-direction. These findings provide strong empirical support for the hypothesis that stratification-related conditions of work actually affect psychological functioning and play an important part in explaining social status differences in personality and cognitive functioning.

The longitudinal analyses also demonstrated that over time, the individual's psychological functioning has important consequences for his or her place in the social structure (Kohn & Schooler, 1982, 1983). Both ideational flexibility and a self-directed orientation lead, in time, to higher status, more self-directed jobs. The fact that most of the personality-to-job effects are lagged rather than contemporaneous suggests that job conditions are not readily modified to suit the individual worker. Nevertheless, over time, many workers either modify their jobs or move to jobs more consonant with their psychological functioning. Thus, the long-term effects of psychological functioning on job conditions are substantial. The process of job affecting worker and worker affecting job is truly reciprocal throughout adult life. (For an extended discussion of the theoretical implications of the apparent difference between the speed with which job conditions affect workers' psychological functioning and the speed with which workers' psychological functioning affects the nature of their jobs, see Schooler [1994]).

These findings about the effects of occupational conditions on men were replicated cross-culturally in studies carried out in collaboration with Japanese (A. Naoi & Schooler, 1985; Schooler & Naoi, 1988) and Polish (J. Miller, Slomczynski, & Kohn, 1985; Kohn & Slomczynski, 1990; Kohn, Slomczynski, & Schoenbach, 1990) investigators. These cross-cultural replications prove the generalizability of our findings to a noncapitalist society (1978 Poland) and to a non-Western society in which individualistic, self-directed autonomy is not particularly stressed (1979 Japan).

The findings about the psychological effects of the conditions of paid work were also extended to women in the United States (J. Miller, Schooler, Kohn, & Hiller, 1979) and in Japan (M. Naoi & Schooler, 1990). In addition, analyses of the psychological consequences of the household work of American wives (Schooler, Miller, Miller, & Richtand, 1984) indicated that the conditions of such work have generally the same psychological effects as those of work done for pay. Preliminary analyses suggest that the same is true for Japanese wives. Other findings strongly suggest that in both sexes, complex self-directed work leads to intellectually demanding leisure-time activities (K. Miller & Kohn, 1983).

Exploring whether a similar pattern of environmental effects occurs at earlier stages of life, LSES researchers examined the data from the interviews of the respondents' children. Our analyses show that self-directed, complex schoolwork increases children's intellectual flexibility and self-directed orientations just as self-directed, complex occupational and housework affect their parents (K. A. Miller, Kohn, & Schooler, 1985, 1986). Other analyses also provided evidence that exposure to a complex environment during childhood has effects on adult psychological functioning similar to the effects on adult functioning of exposure to environmentally complex occupational conditions during the middle of the life span (Schooler, 1972, 1976).

LSES researchers also tested whether a similar pattern of results holds true at the other end of the life span by comparing the effect of substantively complex work on intellectual flexibility in different age cohorts in both the United States and Poland (J. Miller et al., 1985). We found that in both countries, the degree to which substantively complex work increases intellectual flexibility remains constant across the life span. What differs with age is the substantive complexity of the work people do. In both countries, the work of older workers is less substantively complex. Thus, leaving aside the possible effects of retirement, part of the intellectual decrement reported in older adults may result from the reduced complexity of their work environments. In a much more intense and extensive attempt to examine how social-structurally determined environmental conditions affect older adults, we are currently carrying out a follow-up survey of the adult respondents we last interviewed in 1974.

CONCLUSION

The LSES approach to measuring occupational conditions and the findings resulting from it have a number of important methodological, empirical, and theoretical implications. At the methodological level, we have demonstrated the advantages that can be gained by applying, where possible, a dimensional as opposed to a categorical approach to measuring the environment.[1] Thus, we have seen how the dimensionalization of occupational conditions provided us with the conceptual and statistical tools

[1]An argument can be made that measurements should generally be dimensional except when the characteristic in question has only two states (e.g., the switch is on or off or an object is or is not a table) or when a significant interaction exists such that when a particular set of characteristics or dimensional positions occur together, the result is different than when they occur separately. (For a discussion of this approach, as it applies to the issue of diagnosis, see Schooler, 1992.) It should also be noted that although the problem does not seem to be ultimately intractable, the use of categorical variables (or even of dimensional variables that have fewer than six or so values) as dependent variables in many of the techniques used for causal modeling of nonexperimental data is presently problematic. (For a fuller discussion of these issues, see Bollen [1989], Joreskog and Sorbom [1993c], and Muthen [1984].)

to determine how particular aspects of work affect particular aspects of psychological functioning. We have also shown that it is possible to question individuals in such a way as to separate their relatively objective descriptions of their environmental conditions from their subjective affective reactions to those conditions. In addition, this approach freed us from the sampling constraints that would have been imposed if we had been limited to directly comparing the psychological effects of particular occupations.

Our central empirical finding is that all through the life span, for both sexes and for a wide variety of different types of work, environmental conditions that facilitate self-direction increase ideational flexibility and promote a self-directed orientation to self and society and lead to holding values congruent with such an orientation.

In one theoretical extension, our findings have been integrated with other research findings into a rough-hewn theory about the effects of environmental complexity on psychological functioning (Schooler, 1984, 1987). The theory hypothesizes that the more diverse the stimuli, the greater the number of decisions required, the greater the number of considerations to be taken into account in making these decisions, and the more ill defined and apparently contradictory the contingencies, the more complex the environment. To the degree that the pattern of reinforcement within such environments "rewards" cognitive effort, individuals should be motivated to develop their intellectual capacities and to generalize the resulting cognitive processes to other situations. Nonintellective aspects of psychological functioning may also be affected. To the extent that complex environments reward initiative and independent judgment, such environments should foster a generalized orientation favoring self-directedness rather than conformity to external authority. (For a discussion of how environmental complexity may even affect cultural values, see Schooler, 1990.)

Perhaps more important than the validity of any particular hypothesis of environmental effects are several more general conclusions that can be reached from our experience in measuring and assessing the effects of occupational conditions. The nature and relative strength of environmental effects can be legitimately assessed only when theoretically relevant environmental characteristics have been measured in ways that permit sophisticated analyses. These conclusions hold true for any organisms, but they are particularly apropos to humans.

High correlations over time in some particular psychological characteristic, which are often seen as evidence for the importance of stable, innate biological processes, may equally well be a function of environmental stability. It will only be after researchers have come to understand environmental processes and how they interact with the biological processes of the individual that they will achieve a basic understanding of human biology or even be able to make usefully generalizable estimates of heritability. For all of the difficulty in doing so in a scientifically rigorous way, studying the human environment in all of its social-structural and cultural complexity is not merely a luxury to be allowed social scientists in times of plenty. An understanding of the environment is a necessity for biological and psychological researchers if they are to understand fully the human biological and psychological processes that concern them or that contribute to the development of mental health or mental illness.

REFERENCES

Bohrnstedt, G. W. (1969). Observations on the measurement of change. In E. F. Borgatta (Ed.), *Sociological methodology, 1969* (pp. 113–133). San Francisco: Jossey-Bass.

Bollen, K. A. (1989). *Structural equations with latent variables*. New York: Wiley.

Bollen, K. A., & Long, J. S. (Eds.). (1993). *Testing structural equation models*. Newbury Park, CA: Sage.

Cain, P. S., & Treiman, D. J. (1981). *The Dictionary of Occupational Titles* as a source of occupational data. *American Sociological Review, 2,* 253–278.

Chein, I. (1936). The problems of heredity and environment. *Journal of Psychology, 2,* 229–244.

Gottleib, G. (1992). *Individual development and evolution*. New York: Oxford University Press.

Joreskog, K. G. (1973). A general method for estimating a linear structural equation system. In A. S. Goldberger & O. D. Duncan (Eds.), *Structural equation models in the social sciences* (pp. 85–112). New York: Seminar Press.

Joreskog, K. G., & Sorbom, D. (1993a). *LISREL 8 user's reference guide*. Chicago: Scientific Software International.

Joreskog, K. G., & Sorbom, D. (1993b). *LISREL 8: Structural equation modeling with SIMPLIS command language*. Chicago: Scientific Software International.

Joreskog, K. G., & Sorbom, D. (1993c). *PRELIS 2 user's reference guide*. Chicago: Scientific Software International.

Kohn, M. L. (1959). Social class and the exercise of parental authority. *American Sociological Review, 24,* 352–366.

Kohn, M. L. (1963). Social class and parent–child relationships: An interpretation. *American Journal of Sociology, 68,* 471–480.

Kohn, M. L. (1969). *Class and conformity: A study in values*. Homewood, IL: Dorsey Press.

Kohn, M. L., & Clausen, J. A. (1959). Relation of schizophrenia to the social structure of a small city. In B. Pasamanick (Ed.), *Epidemiology of mental disorder* (pp. 69–86). Washington, DC: American Association for the Advancement of Science.

Kohn, M. L., Slomczynski, K. M., & Schoenbach, C. (1990). *Social structure and self-direction: A comparative analysis of the United States and Poland*. Oxford: Basil Blackwell.

Kohn, M., & Schooler, C. (1969). Class, occupation, and orientation. *American Sociological Review, 34*, 659–678.

Kohn, M. L., & Schooler, C. (1978). The reciprocal effects of the substantive complexity of work and intellectual flexibility: A longitudinal assessment. *American Journal of Sociology, 84*, 24–52.

Kohn, M. L., & Schooler, C. (1982). Job conditions and personality: A longitudinal assessment of their reciprocal effects. *American Journal of Sociology, 87*, 1257–1286.

Kohn, M. L., & Schooler, C. (1983). *Work and personality: An inquiry into the impact of social stratification*. Norwood, NJ: Ablex.

Kohn, M. L., Slomczynski, K. M., & Schoenbach, C. (1990). *Social structure and self-direction: A comparative analysis of the United States and Poland*. Oxford, England: Basil Blackwell.

Miller, J., Schooler, C., Kohn, M. L., & Miller, K. A. (1979). Women and work: The psychological effects of occupational conditions. *American Journal of Sociology, 85*, 66–94.

Miller, J., Slomczynski, K. M., & Kohn, M. L. (1985). Continuity of learning-generalization: The effect of job on men's intellective process in the United States and Poland. *American Journal of Sociology, 91*, 593–615.

Miller, K. A., & Kohn, M. L. (1983). "The reciprocal effects of job conditions and the intellectuality of leisure-time activities." In M. L. Kohn & C. Schooler (Eds.), *Work and personality: An inquiry into the impact of social stratification* (pp. 217–241). Norwood, NJ: Ablex.

Miller, K. A., Kohn, M. L., & Schooler, C. (1985). Educational self-direction and cognitive functioning of students. *Social Forces, 63*, 923–944.

Miller, K. A., Kohn, M. L., & Schooler, C. (1986). Educational self-direction and personality. *American Sociological Review, 51*, 372–390.

Muthen, B. (1984). A general structural equation model with dichotomous, ordered categorical, and continuous latent variable indicators. *Psychometrica, 49*, 115–132.

Naoi, A., & Schooler, C. (1985). Occupational conditions and psychological functioning in Japan. *American Journal of Sociology, 90*, 729–752.

Naoi, M., & Schooler, C. (1990). Psychological consequences of occupational conditions among Japanese wives. *Social Psychology Quarterly, 58*, 100–116.

Pérusse, L., Rice, T., Bouchard, C., Vogler, G. P., & Rao, D. C. (1989). Cardiovascular risk factors in a French-Canadian population: Resolution of genetic and familial environmental effects on blood pressure by using extensive information on environment correlates. *American Journal of Human Genetics, 45*, 240–251.

Schooler, C. (1972). Social antecedents of adult psychological functioning. *American Journal of Sociology, 78*, 299–322.

Schooler, C. (1976). Serfdom's legacy: An ethnic continuum. *American Journal of Sociology, 81*, 1265–1286.

Schooler, C. (1983). The application of confirmatory factor analysis to longitudinal data. In D. Ricks & B. Dohrenwend (Eds.), *Origins of psychopathology: Research and public policy* (pp. 155–171). Cambridge, England: Cambridge University Press.

Schooler, C. (1984). Psychological effects of complex environments during the life span: A review and theory. *Intelligence, 8,* 259–281.

Schooler, C. (1987). Cognitive effects of complex environments during the life span: A review and theory. In C. Schooler & K. W. Schaie (Eds.), *Cognitive functioning and social structure over the life course* (pp. 24–29). Norwood, NJ: Ablex.

Schooler, C. (1989). Social structural effects and experimental situations: Mutual lessons of cognitive and social science. In K. W. Schaie & C. Schooler (Eds.), *Social structure and aging: Psychological processes* (pp. 129–147). Hillsdale, NJ: Erlbaum.

Schooler, C. (1990). Individualism and the historical and social-structural determinants of people's concern over self-directedness and efficacy. In J. Rodin, C. Schooler, & K. W. Schaie (Eds.), *Self directedness and efficacy: Causes and effects throughout the life course* (pp. 19–44). Hillsdale, NJ: Erlbaum.

Schooler, C. (1991). Interdisciplinary lessons: The two social psychologies from the perspective of a psychologist practicing sociology. In C. W. Stephan, W. G. Stephan, & T. F. Pettigrew (Eds.), *The future of social psychology: Defining the relationships between sociology and psychology* (pp. 71–81). New York: Springer-Verlag.

Schooler, C. (1992). Statistical and causal interaction in the diagnosis and outcome of depression. In J. House, D. Blazer, & K. W. Schaie (Eds.), *Health behavior and health outcomes*. Hillsdale, NJ: Erlbaum.

Schooler, C. (1994). A working conceptualization of social structure: Mertonian roots and psychological and sociocultural relationships. *Social Psychology Quarterly, 57,* 262–273.

Schooler, C., Miller, J., Miller, K. A., & Richtand, C. N. (1984). Work for the household: Its nature and consequences for husbands and wives. *American Journal of Sociology, 90,* 97–124.

Schooler, C., & Naoi, A. (1988). The psychological effects of traditional and of economically peripheral job settings in Japan. *American Journal of Sociology, 94,* 335–355.

Schooler, C., & Spohn, H. E. (1982). Social dysfunction and treatment failure in schizophrenia. *Schizophrenia Bulletin, 8,* 85–98.

Sears, D. O. (1987). Implications of the life-span approach for research on attitudes of social cognition. In R. P. Abeles (Ed.), *Life-span perspectives and social psychology* (pp. 17–60). Hillsdale, NJ: Erlbaum.

U.S. Department of Labor. (1965). *Dictionary of occupational titles* (3rd ed.). Washington, DC: U.S. Government Printing Office.

Whitehead, A. N. (1954). *Adventures of ideas*. New York: Macmillan.

Williams, T. (1976). Abilities and environments. In W. H. Sewell, R. M. Hauser, & D. L. Featherman (Eds.), *Schooling and achievement in American society* (pp. 61–101). New York: Academic Press.

IV

THE LARGER ENVIRONMENT

9

MEASUREMENT OF THE PHYSICAL ENVIRONMENT AS STRESSOR

GARY W. EVANS

Research on stress has emphasized person-based coping processes (e.g., coping and social support) or psychosocial stressors (e.g., life events and occupational stressors) and has paid scant attention to the role of physical environmental characteristics. The purpose of this chapter is to examine methodological issues in the measurement of environmental stressors that typically confront individuals over the life course. The effects of physical stressors on human health and welfare are not discussed because this topic has been covered elsewhere. (See Evans [1982]; Cohen, Evans, Stokols, & Krantz [1986]; and Evans & Cohen [1987] for general reviews; see Evans, Kliewer, & Martin [1991] and Wohlwill & van Vliet [1985] for physical stressors and child development.) Aspects of the psychosocial environment can also function as stressors (e.g., interpersonal conflicts, work load demands, control, and social support), but these are not discussed in this chapter. My focus is on the measurement of physical stressors across the

I thank Robert Bechtel, Michael Frese, Rachel Kaplan, and Stephen Lepore for critical comments on drafts of this chapter. Preparation of this chapter was partially supported by grants from the National Science Foundation (INT-9013122), the National Institute of Health (R01 HL47325-01), and the U.S. Department of Agriculture Hatch (NY327407).

life span. Two excellent sources on measurement issues with psychosocial stressors are Kasl and Cooper (1987) and S. Cohen, Kessler, and Gordon (1995).

Environmental stressors are potentially relevant to health and behavior throughout the life course for several reasons. First, they are ubiquitous throughout one's life. People spend enormous amounts of time within built structures that contain elements that may create dysfunction. Moreover, people frequently find themselves in situations that are noisy or polluted, and they are often surrounded by too many people.

Second, given the pivotal role of the physical environment in human evolution, it seems reasonable to suspect that the human organism is sensitive to and partially dependent on certain dimensions of the physical environs for its well-being and healthy development. Both the early-experience literature and the psychobiological work with animals, in particular, indicate critical periods of exposure to some modicum level of sensory stimulation for healthy cognitive development (Bornstein, 1989; Denenberg, 1972). The burgeoning field of behavioral toxicology also reveals that exposure to a wide range of chemicals during in utero and neonatal development may portend serious neurobehavioral abnormalities (Weiss, 1983). Behavioral toxicology also exemplifies the critical role of age in transactions between the physical environment and human health.

Third, much of cognitive and social development directly involves interactions with the physical environment. The development of attentional processes is likely influenced by distraction. Motivation is related to learning about the predictability and responsiveness of one's surroundings. Social skills involve the regulation of social interactions that are strongly influenced by physical space and architecture.

More indirectly, parental involvement and responsiveness may be influenced by the physical environment (Bronfenbrenner, 1979). Adults when crowded socially withdraw from those around them (Evans, Palsane, Lepore, & Martin, 1989; Lepore, Evans, & Schneider, 1991). Noise produces lower frustration tolerance, greater irritability, and more potential for negative social interactions among adults (Cohen & Spacapan, 1984). Lower parental responsiveness to young children is associated with ambient noise levels in the home (Wachs & Camli, 1991). Certain architectural elements influence social interaction, may affect competence or self-efficacy, and can foster restoration and recovery from stress.

Moreover, the saliency of physical settings to influence well-being shifts over the life course. The prenatal and neonatal environment is strongly shaped by the mother's options and choices; early childhood is likely to be affected primarily by residential or day-care facilities; middle childhood is affected by home and school settings and, with the onset of adolescence, the addition of the neighborhood setting. With adulthood, the orbit of physical settings is often significantly altered by work or higher educational environments, and for some in old age, greater contact with institutional settings is likely. Thus, one's age is significantly associated with both the type and the range of physical settings typically experienced. With varying setting exposures, the probability of experiencing different kinds of physical and psychosocial stressors shifts accordingly. To begin with, this chapter defines various aspects of the environment and then moves on to measurement issues, focusing on problems inherent in using subjective measurements in assessment of the physical environment.

DEFINITION AND MEASUREMENT

Noise is defined as unwanted sound. It is typically referenced in terms of sound intensity, which is measured in decibels. The decibel scale is logarithmic with a 10-dBA increment perceived as twice as loud. Average exposure to noise is measured over some period of time (e.g., 24 hours), and peak exposures are measured. The dBA scale is usually used, although other weighting scales are available. Another important parameter of noise measurement is exposure duration. Some evidence suggests, for example, that duration rather than peak level (unless extreme) is a better predictor of hearing damage (Kryter, 1985). Another approach to the measurement of noise is to weight nighttime exposure more heavily than other times, as used in measures such as Leq with a nighttime penalty (Ldn) or community noise equivalent level (CNEL). These measures correlate better with community annoyance than a simple average (Leq) or peak exposure. Annoyance with noise is another common index of noise in the environment (Evans & Tafalla, 1987). Some studies with children have also used observer ratings of noise in the home (Wachs & Gruen, 1982). See Kryter for more details on noise measurement.

Crowding occurs when the need for space exceeds the supply and is typically measured by people per room or per square meters in the interior environment and people per acre or per square mile at the external level. Considerable evidence indicates that interior density measures are more meaningful for human health than external density measures (Baum & Paulus, 1987). Variable number of occupants (social density) has also been distinguished from variable space (spatial density), with some suggestion that social density has more potent adverse effects (Baum & Paulus, 1987). There is also evidence that prolonged exposure to residential crowding is necessary before negative effects are apparent (Lepore, Evans, & Schneider, 1991). Rather than relying on density, some research has focused on perceived crowding as the index of environmental condition (Baum & Paulus, 1987). Another aspect of the physical environment that may be similar to crowding is traffic congestion. Research on traffic congestion and health indicates that exposure to peak levels rather than average levels is critical

(Evans & Carrere, 1991). Peak levels are defined as ≥90% of road capacity. Subjective measures of traffic congestion, termed *impedance*, have also been developed (Stokols, Novaco, Stokols, & Campbell, 1978). For further details on the measurement of crowding, see Baum and Paulus.

Air pollution is a collection of toxic agents that includes photochemical oxidants (smog), sulfur oxides, nitrogen oxides, carbon monoxide, particulates, and heavy metals (e.g., lead) in the ambient environment. Indoor pollutants include all of these except photochemical oxidants, plus various gases emitted by products such as glue in building materials. Ironically, although exposure to indoor pollutants is much more common and occurs at significantly higher levels, research and regulation have largely focused on ambient pollutants (Miller, 1992). Interest in indoor air pollution has been spurred significantly by the occurrence of allergylike cold and flu symptoms (sick building syndrome) among a small subset of building occupants. Efforts to pinpoint environmental causes of this syndrome have proven quite difficult, however (Hedge, Erickson, & Rubin, 1992). Typically, either average or peak concentrations are assessed by various sensing instrumentation. Some work on community annoyance with air pollution has relied on subjective estimates of perceived air quality as well, assessing an overall index of air quality (Evans & Jacobs, 1981).

Assessment of *architectural elements* as potential sources of stress has occurred largely within occupational settings. The design of technology, instrumentation, and immediate work implements (e.g., chair and desk) is highly developed in terms of parameters such as biomechanical support (e.g., chair) and range of motion (e.g., shelf height; see Hedge, 1989). This approach has also been applied to interior settings, with a focus on design for the disabled (Mace, Hardie, & Place, 1991) and older adults (Grayson, 1991).

There have been some preliminary attempts to assess the *residential environment* in terms relevant to health outcomes over the life span. Bradley and Caldwell (1987) have examined relationships between social and physical environmental factors and early development. Separate HOME scales have been developed for infant/toddlers, preschoolers, and elementary-aged children. Trained observers rate aspects of the residential setting on a plus-and-minus basis. The infant/toddler and preschool versions of the HOME scales have just a few items on the home physical environment. The elementary-aged HOME scale, however, has an entire subscale devoted to the physical environment. This subscale consists of items of varying relevance to indexes of housing quality. Complexity and variety of the home setting are assessed along with crowding, noise, accessibility to safe play areas, and structural defects. The latter (one item) rates the presence of clear structural defects, such as hazards, peeling paint/plaster, rodent infestation, and so forth.

The Purdue Home Stimulation Inventory (PHSI) (Wachs, 1986) consists of multiple subscales coded by trained observers. One section of the PHSI is devoted to the physical environment and includes items measuring the availability and variety of stimulus materials (play objects and toys), responsivity of the environment (extent to which differential actions of the child produce variable responses from his or her surroundings), noise and crowding, organization and structure of surroundings, and physical exploration allowed (e.g., extent of floor freedom for infants).

The Annual Housing Survey, which draws national as well as regional samples of housing conditions, contains a series of dichotomous questions that have been used to designate housing as adequate or inadequate. Criteria stem from two subsets of items. Items measuring structural adequacy include plumbing, kitchen facilities, heating, and electrical safety. Maintenance quality items include roof upkeep, wall or floor conditions, plaster conditions, paint conditions, and presence of rodents inside. (See Christensen, Carp, Cranz, & Wiley, 1992, for an application to older adults.)

Kasl, Will, White, and Marcuse (1982) have derived a 29-item index of housing quality from the American Public Health Association's Housing Survey. Kasl et al.'s measure includes items rated one through five by the respondent on adequacy of basic facilities—for example, central heating and unit maintenance (e.g., leaky pipes) plus items rated by observers on structural deficiencies (e.g., areas in need of repair).

Some efforts have also been directed toward the measurement of physical properties of *institutional settings*, particularly day-care and senior citizens' facilities. Moore (1987, 1994, in press) found that an important physical feature of day-care settings for social and cognitive development is spatial organization. It is assessed by a 10-item, 5-point rating scale that evaluates various design elements that contribute to a continuum of closed-plan to open-plan designs. The degree of specificity, enclosure, visual exposure, and physical separation from other activity areas as well as traffic corridors constitutes the basic elements of the scale. A second scale assesses the organization and character of activity pockets or learning centers in day-care facilities. Some design variables assessed include spatial definition and enclosure, adequacy of storage, work surfaces and display areas, degree of softness and flexibility, resource availability, and separation from other activity areas.

A somewhat more qualitative approach to environmental assessment of day-care settings is contained within the Pacific Oaks Scales (Prescott, 1987; Prescott, Kritchevsky, & Jones, 1975). Aspects of the physical setting assessed include clarity and appropriateness of traffic corridors, over- and underutilization of physical space, variety of activities supported, complexity of props, softness and hardness of materials, spaces for seclusion, play activity areas, and degree of definition and separation of activity areas.

Moos and Lemke (1992, 1994) have recently supplemented their extensive evaluations of the social climates of different settings (work, home, school, health care, and older adult group homes) with some in-depth evaluation of the designed environment of group homes for older adults. Eight subscales based on 153 dichotomous items assess community accessibility, physical conditions, social–recreational facilitation, prosthetic aids, spatial orientation support, safety hazards, staff support facilities, and spatial adequacy. More specialized scales for the evaluation of facilities for patients with dementia are currently under development (Weisman, Lawton, Norris-Baker, Sloane, & Kaup, 1994). See also Lawton (chapter 4, this volume).

MEASUREMENT ISSUES

Several conceptual and methodological problems are apparent in the measurement of the physical environment as a factor influencing human development over the life course. These problems can be subdivided into difficulties with objective measures and with subjective measures of the physical environment.

Objective Measures

At least three major difficulties stand out in measuring the objective physical environment: environmental sampling, exposure estimation, and construct validity. See Exhibit 1 for a description of the difficulties of measuring the objective physical environment.

Environmental Sampling

Most studies of the environment as stressor have insufficient range in the sampling of environmental conditions. The vast majority of noise and crowding studies, for example, contain two levels, high and low, of the respective environmental conditions (Evans & Cohen, 1987). This precludes examination of essential questions such as what is the nature of the objective–perceptual function. This state of affairs leaves researchers with-

EXHIBIT 1
Methodological Issues in Objective Assessments of Environmental Stressors

Environmental sampling
- Range, kurtosis, linearity, and representative data

Exposure estimation
- Accuracy, individual mobility, and structures

Construct validity
- Appropriateness of descriptive metrics and inadequate taxonomy of salient physical dimensions

out a psychophysics of real-world stimuli (Berglund, 1987; Daniel & Vining, 1983). Estimates of health impacts from environmental conditions may also be insensitive when a limited range of environmental conditions is examined (truncated variance). It is also important to recognize that the distribution of environmental conditions in the ambient environment is frequently badly skewed. Extreme kurtosis significantly reduces the power of statistical tests based on the general linear model (J. Cohen, 1988).

Lack of adequate environmental sampling is also problematic, given the realistic possibility of both nonlinear functions as well as threshold effects between adverse conditions and health or well-being. Researchers know much more about individual variability in responses to a specific level of environmental stressors than they do about how much exposure to a specific stressor, such as noise, air pollution, or crowding, is harmful on average for the general population. Analysis of vulnerable subgroups is important but should not occur to the exclusion of knowledge about the relationship between environmental conditions and the health of the population at large.

Perhaps more important is the lack of information on just what is the typical range of environmental exposures of people to different physical stressors (Brunswik, 1956; Canter, 1991; Petrinovich, 1979). Without such knowledge, researchers are unable to represent ecologically valid stimuli in experimentation or to set appropriate guidelines for public health protection adequately. The latter goal is complicated by data showing that the age of the organism can be a critical factor in estimating both environmental exposure and sensitivity of response (Evans & Cohen, 1987; Wachs & Gruen, 1982).

Ideally, a wider range of environmental exposure should be assessed in research on physical environmental stressors. More basic work is sorely needed to simply determine what is the normal range of physical conditions that people are exposed to across the life span. It is also important to keep in mind that people are typically not randomly assigned vis-à-vis physical stressors. People who are poor are more likely to experience inadequate housing. Women are more likely to suffer from repetitive strain injury from continued keypunching. Thus, careful sampling is required to ensure sufficient exposure to environmental stressors.

Exposure Estimation

Estimates of both level and duration in field studies are extremely crude. People move in space and time and are thus differentially exposed to physical stressors in ways that are not captured by static assessments of residential or work conditions. For example, exposure to residential density is typically assessed by people per room. Yet, for many residences, the number of people at home at different times of the day fluctuates markedly.

The need for multiple observations over time in one setting would address this problem, although exposure to particular environmental conditions across settings would remain unspecified. Noise and pollution estimates are typically dependent on fixed-site monitors, which are costly. Air pollution exposure throughout the entire Los Angeles air basin is based on a set of less than 25 monitors. Furthermore, various structural characteristics that can attenuate or exacerbate exposure are not included in estimates of exposure. Seasonal variation in use of windows, ventilation systems, and building materials themselves can alter individual exposure to physical conditions.

Furthermore, because individuals typically move through space and time, they are often confronted with various combinations of environmental stressors either simultaneously or lagged over time. Although little is known about this issue, there is some reason to believe that exposure to multiple stressors has symbiotic effects that alter the nature of our reactions (Evans, Johansson, & Carrere, 1994; Lepore & Evans, 1996).

The potent role of individual mobility has not been sufficiently appreciated in environmental stress research. Age, particularly at the two ends of the life span, dramatically affects mobility. Mobility affects both the range of exposure and the capacity to regulate exposure to environmental stressors. The friction of physical distance operates differently for people of varying mobility. An interesting example of this is research showing the strong dependence of groups of people with low physical mobility (e.g., poor people) on physical proximity for the development and maintenance of social networks (Fried, 1972). People restricted by physical or economic constraints are highly dependent on physically proximate, accessible social networks.

The problem of exposure estimation is best solved with ambulatory environmental monitoring devices coupled with time budget techniques. Sound levels and many pollutants can be estimated with personal dosimeters. Density levels can be assessed by careful observation. Some architectural elements can easily be measured by floor plans, drawings, or photographs. Time budgets, logs and other diary sources, and random beeper probes can all be applied to track more adequately personal exposure to variation in physical environmental conditions over space and time.

Construct Validity

Researchers do not as yet have well-developed models of human reactions to physical stressors and thus are unclear about what critical properties of the environment they should assess. For example, is duration or intensity of exposure more important? If duration is the most relevant parameter, over what time period should it be considered? Ascertaining onset and offset of exposure to environmental conditions can be difficult. Alternatively, should one use average or peak measures of exposure or perhaps some combination of duration and level exposure? See Lepore (1995) for additional discussion on the importance of accurate duration estimation in the study of chronic environmental conditions and human health.

In the case of the designed environment, investigators have little direction about what the relevant properties of settings are that might relate to human health and well-being. Most design and behavior research focuses on preference or satisfaction and has typically ignored specific design elements, thus responding to the overall setting. When specific aspects of design have been assessed in terms of human satisfaction, they tend to be defined by traditional design theory, based on aesthetics, thus focusing on elements such as color, furnishings, and symbolism and meaning of facades, balance, and order.

Working backward from research on behaviors with potential implications for health, a few preliminary suggestions about potentially stress-inducing properties of the designed environment are possible. Design elements in addition to noise and crowding that create especially high levels of stimulation are candidates for stress-inducing properties of interior design. Novelty and complexity, bright lights and colors, and high levels of movement or change might contribute to information overload. Conversely, extremes of monotony and homogeneity might be taxing because of understimulation. The coherence or underlying structure and organization of spaces may affect legibility and affordances. Users' ability to comprehend the structure or underlying pattern of spaces may strongly influence comprehension of the meaning and logical requirements and uses of space (Kaplan & Kaplan, 1982).

Design can inhibit or facilitate control and a sense of environmental mastery. Spaces or objects that are inaccessible to people because of size, strength, or mobility may affect perceived control and eventually one's motivation to persist in the face of challenges. The flexibility and responsiveness of the designed environment may also play a role in individual sense of competence and mastery. Privacy, for example, is centrally dependent on one's ability to regulate social interaction, which is heavily dependent on variability in the size of the physical spaces one has access to (Sherrod & Cohen, 1979).

Flexibility can also be related to life span. One way to reduce environmental stressors is to change physical surroundings. People with greater cognitive or physical capacities are more apt to change the environment to fit their needs rather than to readjust their expectations or attitudes, thus accommodating themselves to their surroundings. Both the range of options available and personal capabilities to utilize effectively options afforded by the physical environment are partially related to life-span status.

Finally, social interaction and communication can be profoundly altered by the physical environment. Physical proximity, the layout and adjacencies of spaces, the provision of group regulated spaces, the design and placement of meeting spaces, and the permeability of boundaries between spaces can all influence communication and social interaction (Becker, 1990).

Subjective Measures

Many studies of environmental stressors and behavior rely on subjective estimates of the physical environment to gauge environmental exposure. This is especially true for studies of architectural design elements and human well-being. Although the focus herein is on problems with this approach, it is important to briefly acknowledge some of the reasons for utilization of subjective measures in assessments of the physical environment. First, subjective environmental assessments help deal with some of the problems noted for objective sampling. Reliance on individual reports assumes some correspondence with the actual range and extent of individual exposure (Craik & Zube, 1976). Personal appraisals of environmental conditions may better reflect more integrated cumulative exposures over time and place. In this sense, then, objective assessments may be more readily threatened by poor exposure estimation. Second, there are important differences in individual experiences of the same environmental condition (Lazarus, 1966; Lazarus & Folkman, 1984).

Two general classes of problems are endemic with self-report measures of the objective environment. The first class of problems relates to construct validity: What exactly does a perception of the objective environment indicate? The second class of problems focuses on internal validity: What can be concluded when a subjective assessment of the physical environment is related to some index of human functioning?

Construct Validity

There are several theoretical and applied implications of ignoring the stimulus input, the objective physical environment, in human–environment studies: environmental definition, cognitive appraisal, threats to construct validity, and design application. See Exhibit 2 for a description of the validity of subjective assessments of the physical environment.

Environmental definition. Foremost, it becomes impossible to locate the stimulus and to specify the role of the physical environment in human–environment relationships. When the physical environment is operationalized by subjective ratings from the individual, one cannot decipher what aspects of a subjective description or evaluation of the physical environment stem from idiosyncratic emotional processes rather than from actual variation in the physical environment. When a subjective report of the physical environment is used as the independent variable, one cannot

EXHIBIT 2
Construct Validity of Subjective Assessments of Environmental Stressors

Environmental definition
  Location and description of the environment
Cognitive appraisal
  Environment-appraisal function, generic organismic requirements, and imperceptible environmental characteristics
Threats to construct validity
  Minimal objective–subjective convergence, temporal error, and adaptation level
Application
  Designers' requirements for physical parameters

locate the stimulus squarely in the environment or in the person (Archea, 1977; Bechtel, 1987).

There is empirical support for this concern. Reports of psychosocial environmental conditions are strongly correlated to personality characteristics such as Type A behavior (Kirmeyer, 1988; Spector & O'Connell, 1994) or negative affect and locus of control (Spector & O'Connell, 1994). Moreover, the accuracy of reports vis-à-vis independent judges is also affected by personality (Kirmeyer, 1988). Similarly, assessments of the physical environment are also significantly colored by personality (Gifford, 1980; Mehrabian & Russell, 1974). Evaluation of the physical environment can also be influenced by affective states. Fisher (1974) varied feedback regarding attitudinal similarity to a confederate in an experiment. More negative environmental perception occurred with feedback indicating attitudinal dissimilarity.

Cognitive appraisal. By leaving out the objective physical environment, scholars also lack understanding of how cognitive appraisals are influenced by the external environment. It seems reasonable to suspect that one's appraisal of a situation is a joint function of personal and situational variables, yet psychological theory and research have focused nearly exclusively on the former (Lazarus & Folkman, 1984).

An overly strict focus on individual variations in response to environmental quality also overlooks that human beings, as all other organisms, have general functional requirements. By carefully studying changes in health or well-being across a wide range of environmental variation, scientists can better understand the optimum range of environmental stimuli for all or major segments of the population plus gain a better sense of what the basic environment–behavior function looks like (Kaplan, 1983). Identification of vulnerable or sensitive subgroups as a function of developmental status or other individual factors is important but may best be understood in reference to general environment–health relationships in the larger population.

Attention only to perceptible phenomena also ignores the indisputable fact that many physical stimuli that people do not perceive have profound effects on their health and well-being (Wohlwill, 1973). For example, many pollutants with documented health and behavioral consequences cannot be perceived by human beings (Evans & Jacobs, 1981).

Threats to construct validity. There are several threats to construct validity from sole reliance on subjective appraisals of the physical environment as a stressor. Absence of well-documented physical referents for behavior renders it difficult to examine certain measurement properties, particularly validity, in subjective indexes of the physical environment. Jenkins, Nadler, Lawler, and Cammann (1975) and Spector and colleagues (Spector, 1987, 1992; Spector & Jex, 1991; Spector, Dwyer, & Jex, 1988) have examined in some detail the validity of subjective reports of job environment characteristics. Although their focus has primarily been on psychosocial characteristics of the job, the data are relevant for what they suggest about subjective assessments of physical environment conditions. Both research groups found stable but rather small correlations between worker's perceptions and other observer's subjective ratings of various work environment characteristics and found no convergence with some work characteristic ratings. Parallel trends have been noted in life events research (Wethington, Brown, & Kessler, 1995).

Steinberg, Greenberger, and Ruggiero (1982) have extended these analyses of occupant versus observer environmental evaluations, noting that although trained observers' subjective ratings of job conditions correlated somewhat with workers' subjective ratings, objective behavioral measurements did not. For example, worker and observer subjective ratings of time pressure were modestly associated, whereas objective assessments of time pressure (e.g., actual time measures) were not correlated to workers' ratings. These results are consistent with Jenkins et al.'s (1975) data indicating substantial methods variance in their multitrait–multimethod matrix, particularly for the self-report methods. Kirmeyer (1988), on the other hand, found significant but modest correlations between workers' perceived work load ratings and objective observations of work flow (e.g., number of calls for police dispatchers). Wachs (1988) found more substantial associations between decibel readings and trained observers' aggregate evaluations of noise levels in the home. Thus, it is possible that certain types of physical environmental conditions can accurately be assessed vis-à-vis subjective criterion. Both situational characteristics (e.g., complexity) and observability undoubtedly play a role in affecting cross-method validation.

Both laboratory and field investigations suggest that changes in work conditions are reflected in changes in workers' or participants' judgments, but, again, the magnitude of such changes whether in the laboratory (Taber & Taylor, 1990) or in the field (Eden, 1990; Parkes, 1982) was modest at best. Both measurement error and person-based sources are likely contributing variance to individual judgments of environmental characteristics.

Data on citizens' perceptions of community noise or air quality, while reliable, are not highly correlated to physical parameters (Evans & Tafalla, 1987). It is also known that objective ergonomic assessments of machine–operator interfaces do not correlate with worker evaluations (Carayon-Sainfort, Smith, & Lim, 1991). Reactions to various designed or landscape settings that are dependent on verbal scales are markedly stable, regardless of the physical features being assessed. This may suggest that verbal scales seem to be as much about language as they are measures of environmental characteristics (Daniel & Ittelson, 1981).

The passage of time itself can distort environmental assessments. For example, reports of stressful event frequencies decline as one looks back in time (Funch & Marshall, 1984). Raphael, Cloitre, and Dohrenwend (1991) compared events recalled on a monthly basis with those retrospectively recalled over the prior year. They uncovered a marked lack of concordance that worsened over time (e.g., 11-month-old events overlapped only 10% with 1-month reports at the time). Of even greater concern, the rate of decline is associated with certain event characteristics such as controllability (Thoits, 1983) or chronicity (Neilson, Brown, & Marmot, 1989). McQuaid and colleagues also noted that as many as one third of recent acute life events noted are actually chronic in nature (McQuaid et al., 1992). Similar distortions might readily occur in retrospective evaluations of physical environmental conditions. One's mood at the time of recall can also seriously distort retrospective recall of environmental conditions (Broadbent, 1985; Evans & Cohen, 1987).

The range of physical properties one is exposed to either at the time of measurement (Poulton, 1977) or experientially in daily life (Berglund, Berglund, & Lindvall, 1987) can strongly influence subjective assessments of the physical environment. Berglund et al. have shown, for example, that individual judgments of ambient noise levels or ambient air quality are not accurate in comparison to objective indicators. However, when these same data are calibrated to take into account individual range effects, substantial improvements in accuracy occur. In the laboratory, vastly different physical stimuli (e.g., sounds differing by more than 10 dBA) can receive similar loudness judgments if embedded in acoustic stimuli of dramatically different ranges (Poulton, 1977).

Design application. Insufficient attention to the role of the physical environment in human health and well-being leaves researchers with inadequate information to assist professionals interested in reshaping the physical environment to improve human functioning. Study of the subjective meaning of environments indicates little about the stimulus properties, the physical attributes, that make one setting more satisfying or healthier than another (Bechtel, 1987; Wohlwill, 1973). This also makes it impossible to monitor changes in environmental quality over time as they affect human welfare (Zube, 1980).

The preoccupation of environmental psychologists with interindividual differences in responses to the physical environment has also focused attention away from generic environment behavior relationships that underlie most built environments. Recognition of vulnerable subgroups and their special needs is valuable to designers, but the neglect of more general design and behavior requirements has severely handicapped designers' abilities to utilize research linking behavior to the environment because it leads to overly complex design guidelines or general calls for flexibility to accommodate individual needs. Few, if any, meaningful design principles emerge as a result, because instead of the focus being on the physical environment and how it can affect people generally, the focus has been on individual variation in reaction to the same or a very restricted range of setting characteristics.

Scientists need to supplement environmental measures whenever possible with multiple methodological assessments. In this way, researchers can disentangle the method from the construct (Cook & Campbell, 1979; McGrath, 1982; Petrinovich, 1979). To put it differently, multiple-method approaches enable researchers to determine to what degree environment and behavior relations exist independent of the methods used to measure them. Triangulation among different methodological assessments of the same concept not only allows one to assess the psychometric properties of the self-report instrument but also reveals important areas of environmental effects that self-report may be under- or overly sensitive to (Brinberg & McGrath, 1982; Denzin, 1989; Jick, 1979). Methodological triangulation in concert with a life-span perspective may also enable researchers to better understand how age or other personal characteristics contribute to under- or overestimation biases.

Internal Validity

Another set of methodological and conceptual concerns arises when investigators rely on subjective estimates of the physical environment in studies of how environmental stressors affect human health and well-being. Internal validity is sorely tested because of overreliance on subjective indexes of both the environmental condition and the human response. Among the most salient problems are monomethod bias, tautological reasoning, spuriousness, and selection bias. See Exhibit 3 for a description of the problems of internal validity with subjective assessments of environmental stressors.

EXHIBIT 3
Internal Validity of Subjective Assessments of Environmental Stressors

Monomethod bias
  Inflated correlation between environmental stressors and outcome measures because of shared methods variance
Tautological reasoning
  Overlap in content between environmental stressor index and outcome index
Spuriousness
  Misattributions of environmental causes, personality and affect as third variables, and personality
Selection bias
  Personality, ecological covariation, and differential tolerance

Monomethod Bias

Bias can occur when assessments of the physical environmental stressor and the outcome are both subjectively based. Two constructs measured with the same method will tend to share some variance because of the method used in common (Campbell & Fiske, 1959; Cook & Campbell, 1979). Unfortunately, this is particularly true for self-report measures because of their common subjectivity. Subjective measures of both the environment and the presumed outcome emanate from the same human observer. Evidence of monomethod bias occurs in two sources. First, objective indicators of physical work characteristics correlate less with subjective health or job satisfaction measures than do subjective indicators of physical work characteristics (Frese & Zapf, 1988; Kasl, 1986, 1987). Parallel trends have been noted in social environmental factors and subjective indicators of well-being (Thoits, 1983). Second, multimethod–multijob characteristic matrices indicate considerable shared methods variance among self-report indexes of job factors and affect (Jenkins et al., 1975; Williams, Buckley, & Cote, 1989). On the other hand, confirmatory factor analyses indicate that some of the covariation between perceived job characteristics and perceived stress outcomes are substantive (Semmer & Zapf, 1989).

The problem of methodological overlap between environmental and outcome measures is most obviously dealt with by relying on objective environmental measures rather than on subjective estimates of environmental conditions. Use of standardized, well-validated self-report outcome measures should also help minimize the problem of shared methods variance, particularly when both convergent and divergent validity data are satisfactory.

Comparison of conclusions that rely on different types of measures can also prove useful. Differences in correlations between objectively versus subjectively assessed environmental conditions and outcomes may suggest self-report bias. Frese (1985a), for example, showed that self-ratings, other workers' ratings, and trained observers' scaling of work load differed as they correlated with workers' self-reports of psychosomatic symptoms. Structural equation modeling can allow investigators to estimate the extent of over- versus underestimation bias caused by self-report methods when both independent and dependent variables include multiple methodological assessments (Judd & Kenny, 1981; Kessler, 1983). Examination of residual plots may also suggest systematic error in assessments of relationships between environmental conditions and outcomes related to monomethod bias.

Interaction findings predicted a priori can help counter monomethod bias under some situations. Methodological contamination ought to occur among all subgroups and thus is less likely to be present when a significant interaction is found. One important exception to this, however, is when one of the factors is partitioned according to a personal characteristic that might correspond to systematic self-report biases such as negative affectivity. Here, the interaction itself could actually be produced by response bias.

Tautological reasoning

In its worst form, the association between subjective evaluations of the environment and self-report outcome measures simply reflects a tautology because the same thing is being measured. For example, careful analysis of scales measuring stressful events reveals that many of the "events" are in fact symptoms of either physical or psychological health (Dohrenwend, Dohrenwend, Dodson, & Shrout, 1984; Dohrenwend, Link, Kern, Shrout, & Markowitz, 1990). Perhaps the most blatant example is that major illness is one of the items on many standard stressful life events scales. Of particular concern, when such scales are decontaminated by removing items of this nature, substantially smaller correlations are found between stressors and outcome measures (Dohrenwend & Shrout, 1985; Schroeder & Costa, 1984). In the occupational literature (Kasl, 1986, 1987; Spector, 1992), scales that measure satisfaction with job environment conditions, which are then used to predict job satisfaction, mood, or stress, are subject to the same tautological problem. One of the clear advantages of using objective indexes of environmental stressors is that this type of tautological reasoning does not happen.

Spuriousness

Spuriousness threatens internal validity when both the environment and the outcomes are assessed with self-report. Various person-based processes may simultaneously lead to a distortion of reported environmental conditions and self-reported responses thereto. At times, this may be conscious on the part of the respondent. For example, individuals in a high-stress job may desire to change the situation and thus exaggerate for political gains how poor current working conditions are (Frese, 1985a; Frese

& Zapf, 1988). Unintentional misattributions can also occur, particularly when retrospective reports of prior environmental conditions are requested. For example, someone currently sick or experiencing negative psychological symptoms or moods may inadvertently alter his or her assessment of the environment in a negative direction. When something is wrong, people look for causes (Contrada & Krantz, 1987; Parkes, 1982).

Concurrent assessment of environmental conditions is also influenced by levels of health, psychological distress, or mood (Frese, 1985a; Kasl, 1986; Parkes, 1982). Researchers do not know if this occurs because of selective perception (e.g., those in a bad mood pay attention to problems) or if a response bias is created (e.g., Persons see everything the same but report things more negatively). When the outcome measure is a subjective measure such as reported symptoms (e.g., angina pain) rather than an objective health index (e.g., heart attack), not only is the direction of the association cast into doubt but the association itself may be chimerical. For example, retrospective studies have shown associations between stress and angina pain, whereas prospective studies have found no such associations (Contrada & Krantz, 1987).

Two other types of data also raise concerns about spuriousness between self-reports of environmental conditions and human responses. First, workers *within* the same job category or given the same experimental task in a job characteristic simulation (e.g., work load) show consistently modest but significant correlations between self-reported work conditions and job satisfaction or job stress. The problem is that these correlations are at least as large as those found when comparing self-reports between heterogeneous jobs (Spector, 1992). In other words, given a situation in which there is significantly less objective variation in work environment conditions (same job or task), in comparison to considerable objective variation (different job or task), the correlation between perceived job characteristics and perceived outcomes is similar in both cases.

Second, several studies have found that the manipulation of affect significantly alters workers' reports of job conditions (Spector, 1992). People who are instructed to think positively about their jobs, who are told that others like their job, or who experience positive mood, all produce more positive ratings of job characteristics in comparison to controls.

Personality can produce spurious associations between subjective environmental appraisals and self-report outcome measures. Negative affectivity and anxiety have both been shown to influence the positive correlation found between reported job characteristics and self-reports of stress and psychological symptoms (Brief, Burke, George, Robinson, & Webster, 1988; Parkes, 1990; Payne, 1988). Neuroticism and negative affectivity color individual's reports of stressful life events as well as measures of affect and psychological health (Schroeder & Costa, 1984; Watson & Pennebaker, 1989). Recently, Schaubroeck, Ganster, and Fox (1992) have shown that the spuriousness caused by negative affectivity appears to be most salient when utilizing measures requiring evaluations of internal subjective states. Self-reported outcomes that were more descriptive and less evaluative and descriptions of health symptoms were unrelated to negative affectivity.

Personality-based spuriousness can occur in several ways. A personal trait may cause selective perception of environmental conditions (Gifford, 1980; Mehrabian & Russell, 1974). Traits may also bias reporting of certain psychological or physical states or the trait may heighten sensitivity to stressors (Mechanic, 1980; Parkes, 1990).

Spurious associations between environmental variables and human responses can be investigated in several ways. One can measure the variable of concern (e.g., negative affectivity, education, and political views) and then control for it. This approach assumes that one knows what the third variable is. Note also that use of covariance models for statistical controls is fraught with difficulties. These statistical techniques are less robust with respect to assumptions (e.g., homogeneity of variance and normality) and, perhaps more seriously, they assume no interaction. Conceptually, assumptions about controlling out variance can direct attention away from important contextual variables that help define the operation of the physical environment as it impacts human well-being (Bronfenbrenner, chapter 1, this volume).

When complete specification is unlikely, several other approaches can be helpful. If the contamination is due to retrospective bias in recall or description, prospective longitudinal analysis can help. Spuriousness caused by personal characteristics that jointly affect reporting of environmental conditions and outcomes (e.g., negative affect and repressive coping style) cannot definitively be ruled out by prospective longitudinal designs, but their plausibility is lessened.

Self-reports of other variables, and not just of the environment and the outcome, should also be highly correlated if certain individual biases are driving the association of interest. Are people with high levels of symptoms also more likely to be higher on other measures such as dissatisfaction? Person-based bias may also be evident in high intercorrelations among multiple indexes of the environment or may reflect real shared environmental variation. Consistent positive or negative evaluations of physical conditions are an important warning sign. One can also examine whether relations between the independent and dependent variable are consistent for those subgroups of people consistently over- versus underrating environmental conditions (Frese & Zapf, 1988).

An alternative strategy is to use other individuals' judgments about environmental conditions. When trained observer panels are used to assess subjectively the physical environment instead of setting occupants, more stable and sensitive responses can be elicited in response to varying environmental conditions (Craik & Feimer, 1987; Daniel & Vining, 1983). Furthermore, aggregation of observer evaluations across the panel improves the reliability of observer subjective evaluations (Ghisseli, Campbell, & Zedeck, 1981) and heightens the correlation between these subjective evaluations and objective assessments (cf. Wachs, 1988). The role of observer training has been examined in some detail by Stewart (1987), who has shown large improvements in observer accuracy and sensitivity in air pollution judgments through training procedures.

Relying on more consensual indicators may also help to deal with spuriousness. For example, instead of using the individual's ratings of the environment, one could rely on the group mean or median (Moos, 1986). Frese and Zapf (1988) have found that group indexes provide significant estimates of environmental effects on individually measured outcomes in work settings. This approach may be more desirable than using independent observers or supervisors because certain aspects of environments may not be discernible to an independent observer. Furthermore, the representativeness of the sample of observations is of possible concern. In the case of supervisors, their judgments may differ markedly from workers because of personal, political, or other subjective reasons (Spector et al., 1988). Independent observers from the outside might alter behaviors because of reactivity or not see a representative sample because of time or access restrictions. Moreover, as discussed earlier, subjective ratings by trained observers, at least of work environment characteristics, appear to reflect shared method variance (Jenkins et al., 1975; Steinberg et al., 1982).

The wording of self-report instruments can minimize subjectivity by reducing evaluative queries and by emphasizing descriptive scales that minimize inference. Respondents' descriptions of the environment (e.g., lighting levels), not their evaluative judgment feelings about its qualities (e.g., poor lighting)—or worse, its effects (e.g., lighting interferes with work)—may approximate less contaminated objective indicators of environmental conditions (Craik & Zube, 1976). Frese and Zapf (1988) have found that individual descriptive statements correlate substantially higher with independent observers' ratings than do evaluative judgments.

Selection Biases

Although personality may contribute to spuriousness because of bias, personal traits can actually change environmental conditions. Direct effects might occur, for example, if a high-sensation-seeking individual altered his or her surroundings to produce greater variety or intensity of stimulation. Selection might occur as well when either the person or the supervisor assigned an individual to certain types of environments. Certain body types might select into particular types of ergonomically constrained work situations. More hardy, resilient workers might be assigned into more noxious environmental conditions at work. Spector, Jex, and Chen (1993) found that negative affectivity was correlated with objective measures of work-setting characteristics. Thus, some of the reported shared variance between negative affectivity and self-reports of work conditions (e.g., Brief et al., 1988) may reflect not so much spuriousness but instead may indicate naturally occurring covariation between negative affectivity and working conditions.

At a more general level, the concept of niche picking indicates that many organisms select settings that match or optimize individual preferences or tolerances. This becomes a methodological problem if one ascribes variance in some outcome variable to the physical setting, or to niche characteristics, ignoring the possibility that some self-selection factor determined niche selection in the first place, altered aspects of the niche to meet personal needs, or both.

Selection bias can contribute to problems with internal validity in other ways. Exposure to suboptimal environmental conditions is rarely random. People with less economic and political resources tend to reside or work in settings of poor environmental quality (McHarg, 1969; Saegert & Winkel, 1990). Some of these background characteristics could covary with systematic response patterns. In addition, these individuals might also experience greater stressors apart from the target environmental variable. Frese (1985b) noted, for example, that workers in lower level jobs on average live in poorer housing, are exposed to more ambient environmental stressors, and often face a host of other adverse circumstances. These other factors might be the real source of negative health reported. Apart from the methodological difficulties inherent in ecological covariation among multiple risk factors, there is increasing evidence that the more environmental (social or physical) risk factors encountered, the greater normal development is compromised (Lepore & Evans, 1996; Rutter, 1981).

Conversely, if only insensitive or tolerant individuals choose to live or work or remain living or working under crowded, noisy, polluted, or otherwise negative environmental circumstances, their self-reports of distress or malaise may be distorted, but in the opposite direction, suppressing apparent environment–health covariation. Note that self-selection into as well as out of negative environmental conditions needs to be considered as a potential source of bias in measurement (Cohen et al., 1986).

Selection in and of itself does not necessarily mean that no environmental effects occur. An alternative view akin to the evolutionary perspective on genetic expression (Dobzhansky, 1962) is that certain environmental conditions may be necessary for self-selection factors to play out their effects. Thus, it is an individual's predisposition, sometimes genetic, and certain critical environmental factors combined together that lead to negative health or behavioral outcomes.

Another more subtle form of selection bias can occur because of characteristics of the dependent variable. Many subjective factors in addition to level of dysfunction influence use of health-care facilities. Levels of stress, willingness to complain, sensitivity to symptoms, and cultural beliefs are but a few of these variables (Mechanic, 1980). To the extent that variables like these also affect subjective descriptions of environmental conditions, which seems highly likely (Fisher, 1974; Saegert & Winkel, 1990), then any estimate of shared variance between a health symptom and a subjective estimate of environmental conditions is likely to be skewed if one uses samples of the population identified through the health-care system.

CONCLUSION

Measurement of physical environmental stressors relevant to human behavior is still in its infancy. The area is underdeveloped conceptually and suffers from overreliance on subjective estimates of environmental conditions. Multimethodological assessment of conceptually relevant physical parameters is necessary. Additional emphasis also needs to be placed on more thorough, systematic environmental sampling of the physical environment, as experienced through everyday activity. Note that this puts a premium on instrument development to assess interior environments because human beings spend greater than 90% of their lives inside of buildings. Research is needed to systematically examine variation in subjective reports of environmental conditions over time as a function of both environmental variance and person variance. Measures of multiple places by the same set of raters need to be systematically analyzed. Throughout this chapter, I have also noted the potential importance of a life-span perspective in studying environmental conditions and human well-being. Both the type and the duration of environmental stressor exposure and organism sensitivity to some physical conditions of the environment may vary with developmental status.

REFERENCES

Archea, J. (1977). The place of architectural factors in behavioral theories of privacy. *Journal of Social Issues*, *33*, 116–137.

Baum, A., & Paulus, P. B. (1987). Crowding. In D. Stokols & I. Altman (Eds.), *Handbook of environmental psychology* (pp. 533–570). New York: Wiley.

Bechtel, R. B. (1987). The ubiquitous world of paper and pencil tests. In R. B. Bechtel, R. Marans, & W. Michelson (Eds.), *Methods in environmental and behavioral research* (pp. 82–119). New York: van Nostrand Reinhold.

Becker, F. (1990). *The total workplace*. New York: van Nostrand Reinhold.

Berglund, B. (1987). Environmental psychophysics is inter-disciplinary psychology. In R. Ulrich & S. Hygge (Eds.), *Research on environment and people* (pp. 32–41). Stockholm: Swedish Council for Building Research.

Berglund, B., Berglund, U., & Lindvall, T. (1987). Measurement and control of annoyance. In H. Koelega (Ed.), *Environmental annoyance: Characteristics, measurement and control* (pp. 29–44). Amsterdam: Elsevier.

Bornstein, R. (1989). Exposure and affect: Overview and meta-analysis of research, 1968–1987. *Psychological Bulletin, 106,* 265–289.

Bradley, R., & Caldwell, E. (1987). Early environment and cognitive competence: The Little Rock study. *Early Child Development and Care, 27,* 307–341.

Brief, A., Burke, M., George, J., Robinson, B., & Webster, J. (1988). Should negative affectivity remain a measured variable in the study of job stress? *Journal of Applied Psychology, 73,* 193–198.

Brinberg, D., & McGrath, J. E. (1982). A network of validity concepts within the research process. In D. Brinberg & L. Kidder (Eds.), *Forms of validity in research* (pp. 5–22). San Francisco: Jossey-Bass.

Broadbent, D. E. (1985). The clinical impact of job design. *British Journal of Clinical Psychology, 24,* 33–44.

Bronfenbrenner, U. (1979). *Ecology of human development.* Cambridge, MA: University Press.

Brunswik, E. (1956). *Perception and the representative design of experiments.* Berkeley: University of California.

Campbell, D. T., & Fiske, D. W. (1959). Convergent and discriminant validation by the multitrait–multimethod matrix. *Psychological Bulletin, 56,* 81–105.

Canter, D. (1991). Understanding, assessing and acting in places: Is an integrative framework possible? In T. Garling & G. W. Evans (Eds.), *Environment cognition and action* (pp. 191–209). New York: Oxford University Press.

Carayon-Sainfort, P., Smith, M. J., & Lim, S. Y. (1991). Comparisons of objective and subjective ergonomic evaluations of office environments and workstations. In Y. Queinnec & F. Daniellou (Eds.), *Designing for everyone: Proceedings of the Eleventh Congress of the International Ergonomics Association* (pp. 768–770). London: Taylor & Francis.

Christensen, D., Carp, F., Cranz, G., & Wiley, J. (1992). Objective housing indicators as predictors of the subjective evaluations of elderly residents. *Journal of Environmental Psychology, 12,* 225–236.

Cohen, J. (1988). *Statistical power analysis for the behavioral sciences (2nd ed.).* Hillsdale, NJ: Erlbaum.

Cohen, S., Evans, G. W., Stokols, D., & Krantz, D. S. (1986). *Behavior, health, and environmental stress.* New York: Plenum.

Cohen, S., Kessler, R., & Gordon, L. (Eds.). (1995). *Measuring stress.* New York: Oxford University Press.

Cohen, S., & Spacapan, S. A. (1984). The social psychology of noise. In D. M. Jones & A. J. Chapman (Eds.), *Noise and society* (pp. 221–245). New York: Wiley.

Contrada, R., & Krantz, D. S. (1987). Measurement bias in health psychology research designs. In S. V. Kasl & C. L. Cooper (Eds.), *Stress and health: Issues in research methodology* (pp. 57–78). New York: Wiley.

Cook, T. D., & Campbell, D. T. (1979). *Quasi-experimentation: Design and analysis for field settings*. Chicago: Rand McNally.

Craik, K., & Feimer, N. (1987). Environmental assessment. In D. Stokols & I. Altman (Eds.), *Handbook of environmental psychology* (pp. 891–918). New York: Wiley.

Craik, K., & Zube, E. (Eds.). (1976). *Perceiving environmental quality*. New York: Plenum.

Daniel, T., & Ittelson, W. (1981). Conditions for environmental research: Reaction to Ward and Russell. *Journal of Experimental Psychology: General, 110*, 153–157.

Daniel, T., & Vining, J. (1983). Methodological issues in the assessment of landscape quality. In I. Altman & J. Wohlwill (Eds.), *Behavior and the natural environment* (pp. 39–84). New York: Plenum.

Denenberg, V. (1972). *The development of behavior*. Stamford, CT: Sinauer.

Denzin, N. (1989). *The research act*. Chicago: Aldine.

Dobzhansky, T. (1962). *Mankind evolving*. New York: Bantam.

Dohrenwend, B. S., Dohrenwend, B. P., Dodson, M., & Shrout, P. (1984). Symptoms, hassles, social supports, and life events: Problem of confounded measures. *Journal of Abnormal Psychology, 93*, 222–230.

Dohrenwend, B. P., Link, B., Kern, R., Shrout, P., & Markowitz, J. (1990). Measuring life events: The problem of variability within event category. *Stress Medicine, 6*, 179–187.

Dohrenwend, B. P., & Shrout, P. (1985). "Hassles" in the conceptualization and measurement of life stress variables. *American Psychologist, 40*, 780–785.

Eden, D. (1990). Acute and chronic job stress, strain, and vacation relief. *Organizational Behavior and Human Decision Processes, 45*, 175–193.

Evans, G. W. (Ed.). (1982). *Environmental stress*. New York: Cambridge University Press.

Evans, G. W., & Carrere, S. (1991). Traffic congestion, perceived control, and psychophysiological stress among urban bus drivers. *Journal of Applied Psychology, 76*, 658–663.

Evans, G. W., & Cohen, S. (1987). Environmental stress. In D. Stokols & I. Altman (Eds.), *Handbook of environmental psychology* (pp. 571–610). New York: Wiley.

Evans, G. W., & Jacobs, S. V. (1981). Air pollution and human behavior. *Journal of Social Issues, 37*, 95–125.

Evans, G. W., Johansson, G., & Carrere, S. (1994). Psychosocial factors and the physical environment: Inter-relations in the workplace. In C. L. Cooper & I. T. Robertson (Eds.), *International review of industrial and organizational psychology* (Vol. 9, pp. 1–29). Chichester, England: Wiley.

Evans, G. W., Kliewer, W., & Martin, J. (1991). The role of the physical environment in the health and well being of children. In H. Schroeder (Ed.), *New directions in health psychology assessment* (pp. 127–157). Washington, DC: Hemisphere.

Evans, G. W., Palsane, M. N., Lepore, S. J., & Martin, J. (1989). Residential density and psychological health: The mediating effects of social support. *Journal of Personality and Social Psychology, 57*, 994–999.

Evans, G. W., & Tafalla, R. (1987). Measurement of environmental annoyance. In H. Koelega (Ed.), *Environmental annoyance: Characterization, measurement, and control* (pp. 11–28). Amsterdam: Elsevier.

Fisher, J. (1974). Situation-specific variables as determinants of perceived environmental aesthetic quality and perceived crowdedness. *Journal of Research in Personality, 8*, 177–188.

Frese, M. (1985a). Stress at work and psychosomatic complaints: A causal interpretation. *Journal of Applied Psychology, 70*, 314–328.

Frese, M. (1985b). Theoretical models of control and health. In S. Sauter, J. Hurrell, & C. L. Cooper (Eds.), *Job control and worker health* (pp. 107–128). New York: Wiley.

Frese, M., & Zapf, D. (1988). Methodological issues in the study of work stress: Objective versus subjective measurement of work stress and the question of longitudinal studies. In C. L. Cooper & R. Payne (Eds.), *Causes, coping, and consequences of stress at work* (pp. 375–411). New York: Wiley.

Fried, M. (1972). Grieving for a lost home. In R. Gutman (Ed.), *People and buildings* (pp. 229–244). New York: Basic Books.

Funch, D., & Marshall, J. (1984). Measuring life events: Factors affecting fall-off in the reporting of life events. *Journal of Health and Social Behavior, 25*, 453–464.

Ghiselli, E., Campbell, J., & Zedeck, S. (1981). *Measurement theory for the behavioral sciences*. New York: Freeman.

Gifford, R. (1980). Environmental dispositions and the evaluation of architectural interiors. *Journal of Research in Personality, 14*, 386–399.

Grayson, P. (1991). The best of design for the elderly. In W. Preiser, J. Vischer, & E. White (Eds.), *Design intervention* (pp. 121–152). New York: van Nostrand Reinhold.

Hedge, A. (1989). Environmental conditions and health in offices. *International Review of Ergonomics, 3*, 87–110.

Hedge, A., Erickson, W., & Rubin, G. (1992). Effects of personal and occupational factors on sick building syndrome reports in air conditioned offices. In J. Quick, L. Murphy, & J. Hurrell (Eds.), *Stress and well-being at work* (pp. 286–298). Washington, DC: American Psychological Association.

Jenkins, G., Nadler, D., Lawler, E., & Cammann, C. (1975). Standardized observations: An approach to measure the nature of jobs. *Journal of Applied Psychology, 60*, 171–181.

Jick, T. (1979). Mixing qualitative and quantitative methods: Triangulation in action. *Administrative Science Quarterly, 24,* 602–611.

Judd, C., & Kenny, D. (1981). *Estimating the effects of social interventions.* New York: Cambridge University Press.

Kaplan, S. (1983). A model of person–environment compatibility. *Environment and Behavior, 15,* 311–332.

Kaplan, S., & Kaplan, R. (1982). *Cognition and the environment.* New York: Praeger.

Kasl, S. V. (1986). Stress and disease in the workplace: A methodological commentary on the accumulated evidence. In M. Cataldo & T. Coates (Eds.), *Health and industry* (pp. 52–85). New York: Wiley.

Kasl, S. V. (1987). Methodologies in stress and health: Past difficulties, present dilemmas, future directions. In S. V. Kasl & C. L. Cooper (Eds.), *Stress and health: Issues in research methodology* (pp. 307–318). New York: Wiley.

Kasl, S. V., & Cooper, C. L. (Eds.). (1987). *Stress and health: Issues in research methodology.* New York: Wiley.

Kasl, S. V., Will, J., White, M., & Marcuse, P. (1982). Quality of the residential environment and mental health. In A. Baum & J. E. Singer (Eds.), *Advances in environmental psychology* (Vol. 4, pp. 1–30). Hillsdale, NJ: Erlbaum.

Kessler, R. C. (1983). Methodological issues in the study of psychosocial stress. In H. Kaplan (Ed.), *Psychosocial stress* (pp. 267–341). New York: Academic Press.

Kirmeyer, S. (1988). Coping with competing demands: Interruption and the Type A pattern. *Journal of Applied Psychology, 73,* 69–74.

Kryter, K. (1985). *The effects of noise on man* (2nd ed.). New York: Academic Press.

Lazarus, R. D., & Folkman, S. (1984). *Stress, appraisal, and coping.* New York: Springer.

Lazarus, R. S. (1966). *Psychological stress.* New York: McGraw-Hill.

Lepore, S. J. (1995). Measurement of chronic stressors. In S. Cohen, R. C. Kessler, & L. Gordon (Eds.), *Measuring stress* (pp. 102–121). New York: Oxford University Press.

Lepore, S. J., & Evans, G. W. (1996). Coping with multiple stressors in the environment. In M. Zeidner & N. Endler (Eds.), *Handbook of coping* (pp. 350–377). New York: Wiley.

Lepore, S. J., Evans, G. W., & Schneider, M. (1991). The dynamic role of social support in the link between chronic stress and psychological distress. *Journal of Personality and Social Psychology, 61,* 899–909.

Mace, R., Hardie, G., & Place, J. (1991). Accessible environments. In W. Preiser, J. Vischer, & E. White (Eds.), *Design intervention* (pp. 155–176). New York: van Nostrand Reinhold.

McGrath, J. (1982). Methodological problems in research on stress. In H. Krohne & L. Laux (Eds.), *Achievement, stress, and anxiety* (pp. 19–48). Washington, DC: Hemisphere.

McHarg, I. (1969). *Design with nature.* New York: Museum of Natural History.

McQuaid, J., Monroe, S., Roberts, J., Johnson, S., Garamoni, G., Kupfer, D., & Frank, E. (1992). Toward the standardization of life stress assessment: Definitional discrepancies and inconsistencies in methods. *Stress Medicine*, *8*, 47–56.

Mechanic, D. (1980). The experience and reporting of common physical complaints. *Journal of Health and Social Behavior*, *21*, 146–155.

Mehrabian, A., & Russell, J. (1974). *An approach to environmental psychology*. Cambridge, MA: MIT Press.

Miller, G. (1992). *Living in the environment*. Belmont, CA: Wadsworth.

Moore, G. T. (1987). The physical environment and cognitive development in child care centers. In C. Weinstein & T. David (Eds.), *Spaces for children* (pp. 41–72). New York: Plenum.

Moore, G. T. (1994). *Early childhood physical environment observation schedules and rating scales*. Milwaukee: University of Wisconsin, School of Architecture and Planning.

Moore, G. T. (in press). Early childhood physical environment rating scales, dimensions of education rating scales, observation schedules, and behavior maps for the description and measurement of child care centers. *Environment and Behavior*.

Moos, R. H. (1986). Work as human context. In M. Pallak & R. Perloff (Eds.), *Psychology and work: Productivity, change, and employment* (pp. 9–52). Washington, DC: American Psychological Association.

Moos, R. H., & Lemke, S. (1992). *Physical and architectural features checklist manual*. Palo Alto, CA: Stanford University Medical Center.

Moos, R. H., & Lemke, S. (1994). Group residences for older adults. New York: Oxford University Press.

Neilson, E., Brown, G., & Marmot, M. (1989). Myocardial infarction. In G. Brown & T. Harris (Eds.), *Life events and illness* (pp. 310–342). New York: Guilford Press.

Parkes, K. R. (1982). Occupational stress among student nurses: A natural experiment. *Journal of Applied Psychology*, *67*, 784–796.

Parkes, K. R. (1990). Coping, negative affectivity, and the work environment: Additive and interactive predictors of mental health. *Journal of Applied Psychology*, *75*, 399–409.

Payne, R. (1988). A longitudinal study of the psychological well being of unemployed men and the mediating effects of neuroticism. *Human Relations*, *41*, 119–138.

Petrinovich, L. (1979). Probabilistic functionalism: A conception of research method. *American Psychologist*, *34*, 373–390.

Poulton, E. C. (1977). Quantitative subjective assessments are almost always biased, sometimes completely misleading. *British Journal of Psychology*, *68*, 409–425.

Prescott, E. (1987). The environment as organizer of intent in child-care settings.

In C. Weinstein & T. David (Eds.), *Places for children* (pp. 73–88). New York: Plenum.

Prescott, E., Kritchevsky, S., & Jones, E. (1975). *Environmental inventory of children rearing environments*. Pasadena, CA: Pacific Oaks College.

Raphael, K., Cloitre, M., & Dohrenwend, B. P. (1991). Problems of recall and misclassification with checklist methods of measuring stressful life events. *Health Psychology, 10*, 62–74.

Rutter, M. (1981). Protective factors in children's responses to stress and disadvantage. In M. Kent & J. Rolf (Eds.), *Primary prevention of psychopathology* (Vol. 3, pp. 49–74). Hanover, NH: University Press of New England.

Saegert, S., & Winkel, G. H. (1990). Environmental psychology. *Annual Review of Psychology, 41*, 441–477.

Schaubroeck, J., Ganster, D., & Fox, M. (1992). Dispositional affect and work-related stress. *Journal of Applied Psychology, 77*, 322–335.

Schroeder, D., & Costa, P. (1984). Influence of life event stress on physical illness: Substantive effects or methodological flaws. *Journal of Personality and Social Psychology, 46*, 853–863.

Semmer, N., & Zapf, D. (1989). Validity of various methods of measurement in job analysis. In K. Landau & W. Rohert (Eds.), *Recent developments in job analysis* (pp. 67–78). London: Taylor & Francis.

Sherrod, D., & Cohen, S. (1979). Density, personal control, and design, In J. R. Aiello & A. Baum (Eds.), *Residential crowding and design* (pp. 217–228). New York: Plenum.

Spector, P. (1987). Method variance as an artifact in self-report affect and perceptions at work: Myth or significant problem? *Journal of Applied Psychology, 72*, 438–443.

Spector, P. (1992). A consideration of the validity and meaning of self-report measures of job conditions. In C. L. Cooper & I. T. Robertson (Eds.), *International review of industrial and organizational psychology* (Vol. 7, pp. 123–151). Chichester, England: Wiley.

Spector, P., Dwyer, D., & Jex, S. (1988). The relationships of job stressors to affective, health and performance outcomes: A comparison of multiple data sources. *Journal of Applied Psychology, 73*, 11–19.

Spector, P., & Jex, S. (1991). Relations of job characteristics from multiple data sources with employee affect, absence, and turnover intentions, and health. *Journal of Applied Psychology, 76*, 46–58.

Spector, P., Jex, S., & Chen, P. (1993, August). *Personality traits as predictors of employee job characteristics*. Paper presented at the annual American Psychological Association convention, Chicago.

Spector, P., & O'Connell, B. (1994). The contribution of personality traits, negative affectivity, locus of control, and Type A to the subsequent reports of job stressors and job strains. *Journal of Occupational and Organizational Psychology, 67*, 1–11.

Steinberg, L., Greenberger, E., & Ruggiero, M. (1982). Assessing job characeristics:

When "perceived" and "objective" measures don't converge. *Psychological Reports*, 50, 771–780.

Stewart, T. (1987). Developing an observer based measure of environmental annoyance. In H. Koelega (Ed.), *Environmental annoyance* (pp. 213–224). Amsterdam: Elsevier.

Stokols, D., Novaco, R., Stokols, J., & Campbell, J. (1978). Traffic, congestion, Type A behavior, and stress. *Journal of Applied Psychology*, 63, 467–480.

Taber, T., & Taylor, E. (1990). A review and evaluation of the psychometric properties of the Job Diagnostics Survey. *Personnel Psychology*, 43, 467–500.

Thoits, P. (1983). Dimensions of life events that influence psychological distress: An evaluation and synthesis of the literature. In H. Freeman (Ed.), *Psychological stress* (pp. 33–104). New York: Academic Press.

Wachs, T. D. (1986). Models of physical environmental action. In A. Gottfried & C. Brown (Eds.), *Play interactions: The contribution of play materials and parent involvement to child development* (pp. 253–277). New York: Lexington.

Wachs, T. D. (1988). Validity of observer ratings of ambient, background noise in the home. In B. Berglund, U. Berglund, J. Karlsson, & T. Lindvall (Eds.), *Noise as a public health problem: Proceedings of the Fifth International Congress on Noise as a Public Health Problem* (Vol. 3, pp. 301–306). Stockholm: Swedish Council for Building Research.

Wachs, T. D., & Camli, O. (1991). Do ecological or individual characteristics mediate the influence of the physical environment upon mother–infant transactions? *Journal of Environmental Psychology*, 11, 249–264.

Wachs, T. D., & Gruen, G. (1982). *Early experience and human development*. New York: Plenum.

Watson, D., & Pennebaker, J. W. (1989). Health complaints, stress, and distress: Exploring the central role of negative affectivity. *Psychological Review*, 96, 234–254.

Weiss, B. (1983). Behavioral toxicology and environmental health science. *American Psychologist*, 38, 1174–1187.

Weisman, J., Lawton, M. P., Norris-Baker, C., Sloane, P., & Kaup, M. (1994). *Professional environmental assessment protocol: A standardized method of expert evaluation of dementia special care units*. Milwaukee: University of Wisconsin, Department of Architecture and Planning.

Wethington, E., Brown, G., & Kessler, R. (1995). Interview measurement of stressful life events. In S. Cohen, R. C. Kessler, & L. Gordon (Eds.), *Measuring stress* (pp. 59–79). New York: Oxford University Press.

Williams, L., Buckley, M., & Cote, J. (1989). Lack of method variance in self-reported affect and perceptions at work: Reality or artifact? *Journal of Applied Psychology*, 74, 462–468.

Wohlwill, J. F. (1973). The environment is not in the head! In W. F. E. Preiser (Ed.), *Environmental design research association* (pp. 166–181). Stroudsburg, PA: Dowden, Hutchinson & Ross.

Wohlwill, J. F., & van Vliet, W. (Eds.). (1985). *Habitats for children*. Hillsdale, NJ: Erlbaum.

Zube, E. H. (1980). *Environmental evaluation*. Monterey, CA: Brooks/Cole.

10

THE ENVIRONMENT AS CULTURE IN DEVELOPMENTAL RESEARCH

CHARLES M. SUPER AND SARA HARKNESS

Measure all that can be measured, and render measurable all that defies measurement.—Galileo Galilei

To see the environment of human development as a cultural construct offers insights not easily derived from within traditional psychology. It should not be surprising that to achieve this perspective requires methods of investigation that are not well known in the mainstream of psychology—by tradition, a science of the individual. Cultural methods (if they may be called that) are not, however, simply modular attachments to a standard took kit of assessment. To be sure, cultural methods do include some specific techniques of data collection, but, more important, they involve a different, more integrative strategy of investigation.

Central to a cultural understanding is the observation that the humanly constructed environment is not a random mass of unrelated customs, behaviors, situations, beliefs, and values. Rather, this ever-present, sometimes invisible reality has a systematic structure. The structure can be seen in both its stasis and its dynamics. At the static level, it is easy to locate typical features of the environment in a particular culture or subculture that, one by one, are familiar proximal variables for the de-

Preparation of this chapter was supported in part by a grant from the Spencer Foundation. All statements made and views expressed here are the sole responsibility of the authors.

velopmentalist: the nature of verbal interaction between mother and infant, the responsibility training in home activities, the hours per week in day care, or the parental monitoring of children's outside activities. The cultural view augments this list by identifying regularities of such features across cultural domains, across scale, and across time. Such regularities, synergistic and occasionally contradictory, reflect the "organized whole" of a culture, its organic nature. Such regularities present a "message" or create a continuing experience for the developing child far more potent than one would imagine from examining only a single element in this pattern.

A further characteristic of environmental structures is evident in their dynamic response to differences among individuals. Human environments respond differentially to people of divergent age, temperament, gender, social origin, or other inherent or ascribed properties. Psychologists have long recognized this as one aspect of "the active individual" producing "reactive covariance" between the person and the environment (Bell, 1968; Plomin, DeFries, & Loehlin, 1977). The pattern of such differential reaction reflects specific connections among different aspects of the environment, however, and may not be predictable from its more general, static properties. Thus, the pattern of environmental differences associated with individual characteristics may differ from group to group and will itself be a cultural product.

With regard to both these properties of cultural environments, the key methodological issue is in fact a conceptual one. It is not so much a question of how to measure the environment (although that remains an important issue) as of what in the environment to measure; the answer then is not so much a particular element as it is the relationship among elements. Assessment of the environment in its cultural aspects, therefore, requires some kind of model of what human culture is and how it works with regard to guiding and shaping, and ultimately being recreated by, human development.

In this chapter, we discuss two anthropological concepts of culture that can be helpful to environmental psychologists: the immediacy of culture and its integrating nature. We then summarize a theoretical framework—the "developmental niche"—that can guide researchers in applying these ideas. This is followed by several examples of how the connectedness of culture provides an integrating force in development. Next, we present an outline of research methods and strategies that have proven helpful in documenting and evaluating the cultural perspective. We close with a consideration of why this perspective has been difficult to achieve within modern developmental studies and why at the present moment in the discipline's evolution, a cultural perspective on the environment seems increasingly necessary and natural.

THE CONCEPT OF CULTURE

As the central concept in the discipline of anthropology, "culture" has been the topic of definitional discussion throughout this century. This discussion has emphasized a range of sometimes conflicting ideas, including culture as a system external to the person, a cognitive map for everyday action, an adaptation to the local environment, the object of childhood adaptations, all of the humanmade parts of the environment, systems of meaning or symbol shared by community members, or simply a construct in the observer's mind. (See, for example, D'Andrade, 1992; Geertz, 1973; Harkness, 1992; Herskovits, 1955; Kluckhohn, 1945/1962; LeVine, 1973; Murdock, 1945; Romney, Weller, & Batchelder, 1986; Shweder & LeVine, 1984; Spiro, 1951; Steward, 1955; Triandis, 1994a; Whiting & Whiting, 1960.) Whatever disagreements can be noted, however, more relevant to the present topic is the continuing assumption that culture is an immediate, ever-present reality, one that is shared by members of a community and that structures and colors all experience and behavior. "The abstract definition of culture," wrote D'Andrade (1990),

> fails to indicate the pervasiveness and importance of culture in normal human life. If we try to enumerate the actions that a normal person carries out in an average day, we quickly discover that a great deal of what people do is culturally shaped . . . in the sense that both the goal and the means to the goal are part of a learned and shared system of understandings about the appropriate thing to do. For example, an average American adult, on waking, does things like shaving, showering, dressing, eating breakfast, and reading the morning newspaper. These conventional actions, evaluated by conventional standards, are replicated daily by millions of other Americans, but not performed at all by millions of nonAmericans. (pp. 65–66)

In contrast, psychologists, on those occasions when culture is included in their theories, tend to keep it at great distance from the individual. In Bronfenbrenner's (1979) innovative and widely influential ecological model, for example, culture is represented as the macrosystem, "the consistency observed within a given culture or subculture in the form and content of its constituent micro-, meso-, and exo-systems, as well as any belief systems or ideology underlying such consistencies" (Bronfenbrenner, 1979, p. 158). Although this definition is not incompatible with many anthropological approaches, the macrosystem's placement at the top of a nested hierarchy leaves it with no direct connection to the individual. Indeed, as Bronfenbrenner's model is often presented graphically, culture exists as the outermost of several circles, while the developing child stands at the center, insulated from the cultural macrosystem by family, neighborhood, school, and other settings and institutions in the microsystem, mesosystem, and exosystem (e.g., Cole & Cole, 1993, p. 24). Other contextually oriented discussions generally follow this model, showing culture as an outer wrapping to the more immediate influences on development and behavior (e.g., Lerner, 1984).

One consequence of this distancing of culture, as Meyers (1992) pointed out, is the inability of such a model to address the experience of children in the developing world who must move between settings that are organized by different cultural traditions. "Entrance into school [for them]," Meyers wrote, "represents more than a transition from one institution to another within one overarching blueprint; [this] creates a need for articulation between two different blueprints" (p. 68) at the meso-, exo-, and macrosystems level. At the close of the twentieth century, it can be noted, all societies are undergoing rapid change, in part because of external influences from the global integration of commerce and information. Children in all societies, from America to Zimbabwe, are likely to experience multiple cultural "blueprints" and the need for articulation, which Meyers pointed out is increasingly common to development in all cultures.

It is not surprising, given their assumption of a single cultural umbrella, that even ecologically oriented models in psychology give scant attention to cultural aspects of the environment. Rather, the impetus for much of environmentally oriented psychology, at least as it was initially defined in the field of child development (e.g., Bronfenbrenner, 1979; McCall, 1977), was more simply to move developmental psychology from the laboratory into "the real world" outside. That world was, of course, the local, primarily North American environment. The cross-cultural literature was set aside as unhelpful, on the grounds of scientific weakness and "being limited to variations that presently exist or have occurred in the past" (Bronfenbrenner, 1979, p. 40). Subsequent uses of the ecological model generally follow suit, bypassing the macrosystem entirely as a source of influence on developmental processes (e.g., Bronfenbrenner & Crouter, 1983).

In short, a hierarchical model in which culture is an outer layer beyond the experience of daily life actually removes culture from consideration as a part of the growing child's environment. The anthropological insistence on the immediacy of culture not only better reflects the phenomenological experience of daily life but also brings the cultural environment into reach for the empirical scientist.

A second essential characteristic of anthropological concepts of culture is their focus on the integration of cultural elements. This is most evident in the long tradition of research in social and psychological anthropology that includes the work of Margaret Mead, Ruth Benedict, and John and Beatrice Whiting. The Whitings, particularly in their earlier work, emphasized that the cultural systems of beliefs, values, and behaviors are "not only . . . internally integrated, but each type of custom is systematically related to the others. [They] form in combination a blueprint for action that has been called the custom complex" (Whiting & Whiting, 1960, p. 51). In this view, it is the combination of elements that marks the human reality. The Whitings continued as follows:

> Anthropologists in isolating the concept of culture and by studying its manifestations in societies the world over, have [contributed to] a more precise understanding of that which is transmitted to a child in any society. . . . The concept of culture focuses attention not only on the overt behavior of parents in training their children but [also] on the cognitive map that influences the content of what is transmitted, the techniques the parents employ, and their behavior as role models. (pp. 53–54)

Once a cultural complex is identified, there is an analytic urge to tease it apart, to identify the elements, and to specify their unique functions. This is probably essential for understanding how the cultural environment works. There is a danger, however, that in trying to find a specific element as causal for a development outcome, the larger integrative effects will be overlooked. LeVine (1970) summarized the problem for the classical studies of culture and personality this way:

> Customs like child-rearing practices and the variety of cultural behavior patterns with which they have been hypothetically linked tend to be associated with many other customs, and these multiple associations lend themselves to a variety of interpretations, some of them sociological or ecological rather than psychological. In the welter of multiple connections . . . it is all too easy to find support of simple causal hypotheses by limiting one's investigation to a few variables rather than looking at the larger structure of relations in which they are embedded. (1970, pp. 596–597)

In other words, measurement of isolated aspects of the environment, no matter how precise, will necessarily overlook the role of culture. It is the cultural complexes and multiple connections that create culture's effects. Although this makes it more difficult to disentangle societies' "natural experiments" than early comparative researchers imagined (see LeVine et al., 1994), it also suggests a relatively new and promising agenda for interdisciplinary psychologists as they seek a more sophisticated understanding of the environment of behavior and development: Look for structures that integrate experience, and look for their immediacy in everyday life.

THEORETICAL FRAMEWORKS FOR UNDERSTANDING THE CULTURAL ORGANIZATION OF DEVELOPMENT

Several conceptual frameworks have been offered in recent years that draw on the research literature in culture and human development and that emphasize dynamic integration of environmental features and environment–individual interaction. Despite their somewhat different purposes, these models share a number of common features, in part no doubt because their proponents share an interdisciplinary background that includes training in both individual development and psychological anthropology, the latter under John and Beatrice Whiting. The "ecocultural niche" proposed by Weisner, Gallimore, and colleagues pays special attention to the process of family adaptations in constructing daily life, as this process is influenced, for example, by the culturally constituted goals, beliefs, and scripts for conduct (Bernheimer, Gallimore, & Weisner, 1990; Gallimore & Goldenberg, 1993; Gallimore, Goldenberg, & Weisner, 1993; Weisner & Garnier, 1992; Weisner, Matheson, & Bernheimer, 1996). Worthman (1994, 1995; Worthman, Stallings, & Jenkins, 1993) has proposed the "developmental microniche" as a device to model relationships of biology, behavior, and culture in shaping human development, particularly qualitative shifts in growth and health status as a function of developmental transitions and culture change. Finally, we have suggested the "developmental niche" as a way to conceptualize the immediacy of cultural forces in the environment of an individual (Super & Harkness, 1986b).

The concept of the developmental niche draws on three distinctive but complementary conceptualizations of the child's cultural environment that can be found in the research literature. In the first, culture is seen to provide an array of settings for daily life, each characterized by particular kinds of actors and tasks. In the second, culture is seen as a collection of customary practices that convey messages to the child. The third focuses on the psychological reality of culture, as constructed by the caretakers' shared beliefs about children and child care. Each of these research traditions, we argued in a recent review (Super & Harkness, 1997), provides a critical perspective on culture as a developmental environment. However, not one of them successfully accommodates two essential ideas, namely the integration of various elements in the child's cultural environment (which is highlighted in the present chapter) and the endogenous forces in individual development (which are more familiar in the psychological literature). The developmental niche is a theoretical framework that attempts to acknowledge and integrate this set of considerations.

At the center of the model is the individual child (see Figure 1), and the initial view in this scheme is to take the place of the child and look outward to the everyday world. Although this approach can be used to analyze the niche for a specific individual (Super & Harkness, 1993), the usual application has been to derive a generalized description of recurring patterns for children in a cultural community. In most cases, this involves contrasting two or more communities widely separated in geographic place and historical background. However, flexibility in the degree of generalization is a useful feature of the framework, as it has proven helpful in

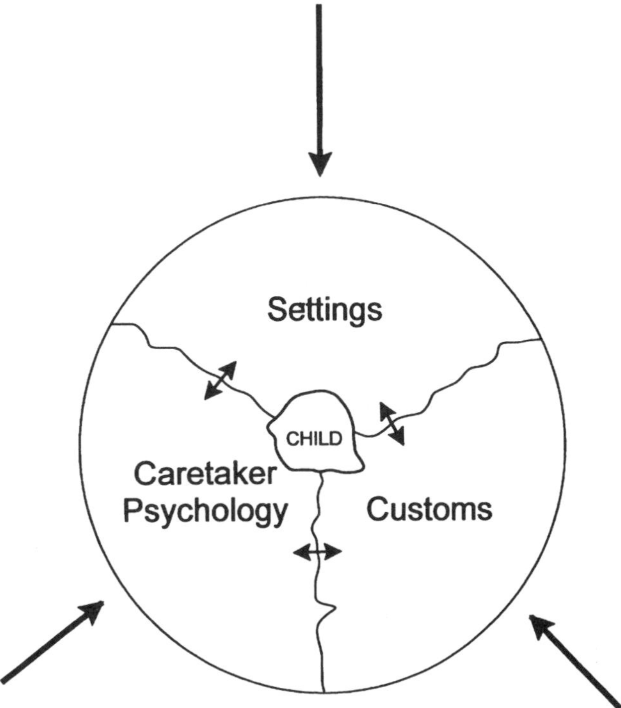

Figure 1. The developmental niche.

examining variation within a single physical community and in documenting changes in child care that are due to migration or seasonal change, as indicated in a number of studies cited in the upcoming discussion.

Surrounding the child are three subsystems of the niche:

1. *The physical and social settings of the child's daily life.* The objects and people around the child determine to a significant degree the risks and supports for growth, as well as the kinds of interactions that are likely to take place.
2. *The culturally regulated customs of child care and child rearing.* These are the meaningful and useful daily practices that are often carried out with little conscious effort and usually seem to the caretaker to be the obvious and natural thing to do. Also included in this subsystem are less frequent institutionalized behaviors that mark developmental transitions, such as initiation rites.
3. *The psychology of the caretakers.* This includes specific beliefs and emotional orientations of caretakers. Parents' culturally organized belief systems, or "parental ethnotheories," concerning child behavior and development are a key part of this subsystem because they can be seen to direct and organize seemingly disparate features of the environment in ac-

cordance with larger cultural meanings (see Harkness & Super, 1996).

In this scheme, the three subsystems constitute elements of the environment as they are culturally structured in the child's experience. Essentially, the same scheme can be applied to the niches for adult development as well, by generalizing the third subsystem to include the psychology of the other relevant actors as they impinge on the target adult.

Three corollaries describe key aspects of the niche's dynamic structure:

1. The three subsystems operate together with powerful though incomplete coordination as a system. Homeostatic mechanisms promote consonance among elements of the niche (such as settings that are consistent with parental beliefs), but there are also inconsistencies that result from historical change, outside influences, limits on resources, and the vagaries of life. Thus, internal dynamics of the niche (represented in Figure 1 as the double-headed arrows connecting the three subsystems) can be a source of change.
2. Each of the subsystems of the niche is functionally embedded in other aspects of the larger ecology in specific and unique ways. This is represented by the separate arrow for each subsystem pointing inward from the outside ecology. Thus, the three subsystems act as the primary channels through which the niche, as an open system, is influenced by outside forces.
3. Each of the subsystems is in a continual process of mutual adaptation with the individual child, including such characteristics as gender, temperament, and developmental level (represented by the irregular shape of the child–niche interface).

The developmental niche framework has been used as an analytic scheme and to direct research efforts in a number of domains: motor skills (Super, 1976, 1981), emotional expression (Harkness & Super, 1983, 1985; Super & Harkness, 1982a), sleep and arousal (Super & Harkness, 1982b; Super et al., 1996), cognitive development (Super, 1991), language development (Blount, 1990; Harkness, 1988, 1990), literacy (Harkness & Super, 1993), mathematical skills (Pellegrini & Stanic, 1993), goodness of fit between child temperament and environmental demands (Super & Harkness, 1986b, 1993, 1994), patterns of developmental dysfunction (Super, 1987), household production of health (Harkness & Super, 1992b; Super, Keefer, & Harkness, 1994), children's transition from home to school (Harkness & Super, 1993, 1995), and the study of immigrant children and families (Eldering, in press). The method of analysis in many of these studies consists of measurement of selected aspects of more than one component of the niche, along with some assessment of developmental status in individual children, followed by the examination of the relationships among all of these. In other reports, the empirical analysis is less complete, but the niche framework is used to suggest promising avenues of future research. In both cases, however, the effort is usually to highlight ways in which different parts of the cultural environment shape development by repeating and elaborating messages to the growing individual.

THE ORGANIZATIONAL POWER OF CULTURE

The metaphor of environmental "messages" containing important cultural information about appropriate belief, emotion, and action is a common one, going back at least to Margaret Mead. As LeVine (1973) explained,

> The transmission of culture from generation to generation is, in Mead's view, a process of communication in which many aspects of the growing individual's cultural environment relay the same messages to him, messages reflecting the dominant configurations of his culture. He acquires his "cultural character" by internalizing the substance of these messages. (p. 54)

The nature of the messages may range from the concrete to the thematically abstract and from explicitly focused to preconscious and even subconscious. At whatever level, however, messages that are more frequent or more intimately linked with a broader message (i.e., those that are part of a cultural complex) are assumed to be more potent (see, for example, Mead, 1930/1966, and Benedict, 1934/1959). Repetition and a multiplicity of channels function, as in any well-engineered system of control and communication, to ensure that the message is adequately delivered, given a variety of situations and possible disturbances. These messages produce the simple, first-order effects of a culture's organizational structure. In addition, there are dynamic, second-order effects that can be seen in how cultures differ in adjusting the pattern of messages to particularities of the individual.

First-Order Effects

There are at least three ways in which the organizational aspects of the developmental niche create powerful effects on, or messages for, the developing individual. They can be labeled as *contemporary redundancy*, *thematic elaboration*, and *chaining*.

Contemporary Redundancy

Contemporary redundancy is the simplest and most direct form of environmental organization to produce significant developmental results. It involves the mutually reinforcing repetition of similar influences from several parts of the environment during the same period of development. A concrete example of this phenomenon can be found in the patterning of early and late attainment of various motor milestones (e.g., sitting and walking) in rural Kenyan (Kipsigis) and urban American (White middle class) infants (Super, 1976, 1981).

Among the Kipsigis, many superficially unrelated caretaker behaviors have been observed, which all have the effect of strengthening an infant's large musculature in the legs and trunk and of providing high levels of vestibular stimulation and experience in maintaining balance. Daily, new mothers carried out a traditional practice called *keguldo* in which the mother, sitting with her legs stretched out in front, held her very young infant under the arms and dangled the baby's feet so they just touched her own legs; this stimulated the stepping reflex, and the ensuing activity was enjoyed by all. A few months later, mothers and siblings would dig a small, shallow hole in the ground, pad it with cloth or animal skins, and place the young baby inside in a sitting position; left this way for several minutes, the infant would gain an assisted experience in maintaining the upright posture. Still later, the baby would be taken daily in the early morning to a grassy spot and given practice in walking, with exactly the same graded series of adult supports used in the standardized tests of motor development.

What ties these and other activities together is an elaborated set of beliefs concerning the primacy of motor responsivity and integrity in early life. Traditional Kipsigis mothers were found to orient their perception and understanding of neonatal behavior around such concepts (Super & Harkness, 1996). As in many other cultural groups in East Africa (Kilbride & Kilbride, 1975), these mothers also held explicit beliefs about the necessity of teaching children to sit and walk, saying that in the absence of such effort—an almost unimaginable abdication of parental responsibility—a child would be very slow in becoming competent, possibly even failing ultimately in acquiring the necessary skills. In addition, it can be noted that the physical setting of life in and around a cluster of mud houses—where the ground might be cold, wet, or dirty; where cooking fires were present; and where insects and other harmful creatures might be found—promoted customary methods of holding and carrying infants on the caretaker's hip or strapped on her back, an experience that is especially stimulating of postural adjustment and large muscle development.

In short, a complex interweaving of beliefs, customs, and settings provided overlapping support and stimulation for the development of specific motor competences. Identical and closely related behaviors were repeated time and again for a variety of different reasons, all within the period of infancy characterized by very rapid growth of the gross motor and locomotion system. The complex was flexible in its overdetermination so that individual differences in infants and families could, and did, exist, but always within the culturally organized pattern that emphasized repeatedly the importance and the exercise of early motor skills. Some families felt more strongly about the importance of teaching than did others; some had more family members to carry out teaching and playful activities; some infants objected to the constraint and irregular movement of being carried on the caretaker's back, whereas others appeared to be soothed—all of these and other variations existed within a larger, shared experience that supported motor development.

In contrast, mothers in a Euro-American sample were found to organize their perception of infant behaviors around cognitive competence, not motoric integrity. They did not, in general, hold strong beliefs about the necessity of teaching their infants to sit and walk. Consequently, the mothers did not regularly carry out exercises to promote physical competence but focused instead on providing an emotional security and a physical environment that promoted learning and the exploration of novelty. Customary methods of infant care during the preambulatory period—in a semireclined infant seat or in a playpen—did not particularly strengthen back and leg musculature.

The joint result of these two divergent patterns was that infants in the urban American group typically mastered the milestones of independent sitting and walking later than infants in the rural Kenyan sample. The developmental advantages were specific to the skills emphasized by the environment, however: The Euro-American babies, who had greater experience lying down, tended to master crawling sooner than their Kenyan peers (Super, 1976).

Two aspects of this example are central to understanding how contemporary redundancy supports development. First is the value of having many factors leading toward the same end, some of them deliberate and some unintended. It is unlikely that any one of the factors summarized earlier could have a profound influence acting alone; rather, the repetitions are diverse and mutually supportive. Second is the set of connections among beliefs, customary practices, and settings of daily life that produces the contemporary redundancy. It would be difficult to see this organizational aspect of culture if the environment were conceptualized more narrowly, or if only one aspect were the focus of inquiry.

Thematic Elaboration

Thematic elaboration, a second pattern of systematic influence, refers to the repetition and cultivation over time of symbols and systems of meaning. This process depends on the remarkable facility of human young to detect, abstract, and internalize patterns of meaning in the environment, even implicit messages that are unstated but embedded in otherwise unrelated phenomena. The acquisition of language and discourse style is perhaps a prototype for this phenomenon, but the learning qualities are not restricted to this domain. In their social and emotional development, and in the regulation of affective expression, children also appear effortlessly to abstract rules of performance and to generate systems of meaning that are specific to their cultural surroundings (Harkness & Super, 1985; Lutz, 1983).

Shweder, Mahapatra, and Miller (1990, p. 195) provided a salient example in their work on moral development in the town of Bhubaneswar, India. In their social communication approach to this topic, they see the child making "unconscious inferences" based on interpretations of events presented by "local guardians of the moral order (e.g., parents)" through the daily routines of family life. The implicit and affect-laden messages are contained in verbal exchanges, visible emotional reactions, and institutionalized behaviors. In their example, Brahmin (upper-caste) children learn about the danger of touching polluted objects and people from many sources. Their mother pulls away and cries, "Don't touch me, I am polluted," to the approaching toddler during her period of menstruation, and the child notices that she eats and sleeps alone and is prohibited from entering the kitchen or indeed from approaching anything of value. The father avoids being touched by anyone between the purifying rite of bathing and worship; the grandmother will not touch the clothes a child wears in the company of "Untouchables" at school. Children play "pollution tag," in which "it" is said to have eaten at the house of the lowest caste Untouchable. "The culture," Shweder et al., write

> is providing the child with a practical moral commentary in which one of the many messages is ultimately that menstrual blood, feces, and lower status go together. For the sake of physical and spiritual well-being, they must be kept at a distance from what is clean, pure, and of higher status. (p. 197)

Repetition over several stages of life enhances the opportunities for thematic elaboration. As in Shweder et al.'s (1990) Indian example, it may be that the most powerful elaborations begin early in life with emotional experiences, which are subsequently developed as symbolic material, and are ultimately realized as culturally explicit systems of morality, religion, or profoundly personal meaning. Pollution, guilt, shame, courage—these grand cultural themes are prototypical of those elaborated across the life span. It is characteristic of thematic elaboration over time, however, that as cultural models are reiterated at subsequent stages of development, there is often further elaboration or an indication of a change in the child's relationship to the thematic material. As we have noted elsewhere (Harkness, Super, & Keefer, 1992), cultural continuities in thematic development contrast with developmental tasks that are posited to differ from age to age (e.g., Erikson's eight stages). "Independence" is such an organizing theme for many U.S. parents, recurring in their discussions about children at every stage, from sleeping through the night in early infancy, through the "terrible two's" and starting school, to romantic relations in adolescence, going off to college, and beyond. Such continuity of thematic material provides both children and caretakers with the opportunity to reinforce emerging concepts of the individual but also to reexamine existing understandings in light of developmental change.

The most profound examples of thematic elaboration also involve repetition of the pattern across several domains of behavior. In the Indian example provided earlier, the emotional is woven together with the intellectual, and the same message is given with regard to food, menstruation, defecation, bathing, physical closeness, worship, caste status, and gender differences. Another, more extended example of cross-domain thematic elaboration is provided by the rich literature on Japanese child rearing (see Shwalb & Shwalb, 1996, for a historical overview). One can trace in this body of work many factors that contribute to the Japanese child's emerging sense of dependence on and closeness with others, compared with the U.S. child's growing separateness and independence. U.S. mothers, for example, have been found to respond more quickly to their infants' vocalization, to promote their infants' physical activity, and to emphasize verbal communication across a distance. In contrast, the Japanese mothers have been found to be more soothing and quieting and to maintain a physical closeness of communication (Bornstein et al., 1992; Caudill & Weinstein, 1969). Similarly, U.S. mothers have been described as more explicitly controlling their young children's behavior through rewards and punishments, whereas Japanese mothers often avoided overt control in preference for a process of "osmosis" through modeling and patience (Hess & Azuma, 1990). Taken together, this body of work describes a complex but coherent divergence in the beliefs and practices from which Japanese and U.S. children read the messages of their respective cultures across infancy and childhood and also across many domains of public and private behavior.

A final feature of thematic elaboration is replication at different scales of magnitude. Recent work in Holland, for example, stresses Dutch parents' use of rest and regularity as organizing ideas for daily life, compared with a U.S. sample (Super et al., 1996). When interviewed, the Dutch parents were explicit about the value of a restful and reliable schedule for children. (Indeed, the ideas had been formalized in the national health service's curriculum for child care for nearly half a century.) They also managed their daily routines to ensure a restful and regular environment for their children: Infants in the Dutch sample were found to sleep significantly more than those in the United States, and their bedtimes were more regular. In addition, within this circadian structure, Dutch mothers were also less stimulating during periods of interaction with their infants, touching and talking to them less than did the U.S. mothers, and apparently using a slower response time for social interchanges. As a result, the Dutch babies tended to remain in a calm, quiet state of arousal, compared with the more stimulated and stimulating state of activity more frequently observed in the United States. Thus, both the low-periodicity circadian pattern and the high-periodicity interactive routines of daily life provided the same differential messages: the value of stimulation and activity in the U.S. sample and of calm predictability among the Dutch.

Replication of patterns across scale is not a well-researched topic in the developmental literature. However, replication across scale joins with repetition over time and domain to produce the multiple redundancy that is characteristic of thematic elaboration.

Chaining

The completion of a causal chain from separable elements in the environment is a third means through which culture can profoundly affect the course and content of development. A concrete example is provided by the work of Zeitlin, Ahmed, and their colleagues among very poor families in a rural area of Bangladesh (Ahmed et al., 1991–1992; Ahmed, Zeitlin, Beiser, Super, & Gershoff, 1993): Through ethnographic methods, including interviews and behavior observations, they identified an interplay of child-care customs, unsanitary settings, and caretaker beliefs concerning the meaning and causes of infantile diarrhea that together resulted in very high rates of infant malnutrition, morbidity, and mortality. Several different routes of infection were delineated, and it was evident that changing any one of several organizing links had the potential to break the causal chains of exposure and infection. Field trials led to interventions aimed at altering three major features of the environment: the caretakers' understanding of germ theory, the child's exposure to unsanitary settings, and the customary methods for washing. Later comparison with a control sample indicated a significant reduction in morbidity and growth retardation. A number of public health issues in children's development are open to this kind of analysis (Harkness & Super, 1992b).

The defining feature of chaining is that no single element of the environment is sufficient *in kind* to produce a particular outcome. There is, rather, a holistic creation that requires a significant contribution from different aspects of the environment to be realized. In the Bangladesh example, were the young child's physical settings not so contaminated with animal manure and other disease-bearing agents, or were it not customary for mothers to dry their damp and contaminated hands on their clothing and (subsequently) carry the infant on the adjacent hip, or were year-old infants not internally motivated to explore the nature of objects by mouthing them, then the parents' lack of knowledge concerning germ theory alone would not have resulted in such high rates of infection. One complete chain of events must be present for the problem to occur.

In contrast to contemporary redundancy and thematic elaboration, which depend on multiple instances of similar environmental events, chaining may be achieved with single instances, if they are organized to achieve some other process. Similarly, in contemporary redundancy and thematic elaboration, no single element is critical, whereas chaining requires a specific kind of event, often at a particular time. Chaining stresses the way certain combinations of elements in the environment coalesce to enable some external process to be completed; a particular combination of elements is necessary to complete the whole.

In summary, there are at least three ways in which the integrative properties of culture coordinate environmental influences: (a) by overdetermining an outcome through repeated instances of specific training, support, or induction of emerging capacities; (b) by thematic elaboration across stages of development of core ideas concerning, for example, the relationship of self and others; and (c) by arranging environmental components so as to permit (or prevent) the completion of some causal chain. These aspects of development in context cannot be accounted for by models of the environment that overlook its systematic structure, nor by individualistic models of the child. It is the mediating and coordinating systems of culture that enable the developmental effects.

Second-Order Effects

The discussion so far has focused on cultural structure in the developmental environment that produces a strong main effect on all individuals. There are, in addition, second-order interactive effects, in which individual variation within the culture can also be recognized as a culturally created pattern. Wallace (1961), a psychological anthropologist, pointed out a generation ago that one feature of cultures is that they organize internal diversity. This is true both in terms of subgroups (i.e., social classes or occupational groups) and at the level of individuals.

There are a variety of personal characteristics that lead to differential consequences in various cultural contexts—gender and temperament being among the most obvious. It is now a widely shared observation that such individual characteristics call forth from the environment disparate responses. The point here is that the way an environment responds to differences among individuals is a product of its cultural organization and that the reasons for the differential reactions may not be evident until broader aspects of life in that setting are specified.

The majority of studies that demonstrate different patterns of response to a particular feature of individuals focus on temperament during infancy or childhood (e.g., Korn & Gannon, 1983). DeVries (1984), in a particularly dramatic example, found that infant characteristics such as a calm, adaptable, and happy temperament, which are generally related to positive outcomes in U.S. samples, were strongly predictive of failure to survive a period of drought in an East African sample of seminomadic pastoralists. One critical factor, he found, was the mother's assumption that an infant will cry if hungry. The more fussy and vociferous infants were therefore nursed more frequently, and during a period of extreme nutritional stress, this increase made the difference between life and death.

A related but less dramatic result in a Kenyan farming community is reported by Super and Harkness (1994). They found that Kipsigis infants who naturally displayed a more regular pattern of hunger and sleep during the day spent more time with their mothers (and less in care of the traditional sibling caretaker), whereas in a metropolitan U.S. sample, the opposite relationship occurred, with the more regular infants spending less time with their mothers and more time in the care of a babysitter or the father. Detailed analysis indicated that in the Kipsigis case, a mother who could predict the timing of her infant's needs might easily arrange garden work and other household chores in order to be available for feeding, followed by a period of socializing, when the infant was awake and ready. The less predictable baby would typically be entertained by the sibling caretaker as long as possible while the mother was busy; when distraction was no longer sufficient, the mother would interrupt her work and nurse the baby, who, by then exhausted from crying, would fall asleep as the mother returned to her chores. In the United States, by contrast, the mother who could predict her baby's schedule apparently felt safer in arranging alternative care while she was out of the house, but the mother with a less predictable infant more typically felt obliged to be personally available whenever her child might need attention.

The power of culture to organize correlations at the individual level is not limited to constitutional variation. Hess and Azuma (Azuma, 1996; Hess & Azuma, 1990) found quite different developmental outcomes associated with parents' style of discipline in their Japanese and U.S. samples. In accord with Bernstein's (1971) hypothesis about the effects of "restricted" versus "elaborated" codes between parent and child, which was the starting point of Hess and Azuma's project, Hess and Azuma found in the United States that mother's preference for discipline that was based on an appeal to authority was negatively correlated with her child's school achievement, as measured 7 years later. In contrast, there was a positive correlation in Japan: Children whose mothers based their discipline on simple authority performed better in school than those whose mothers chose more reasoned approaches. The authors offered as one possible factor that in their Japanese sample, the mother–child relationship was typically based on symbiotic interdependence; hence, the only mothers who dared to attempt direct authority were those who felt very secure about their bond (and through that relationship fostered achievement). One can also speculate about group differences in the kind of authority relations used in the classroom and in other environmental factors as well.

Whatever the mediating factors, examples like this warn researchers that all developmental correlations found in a single cultural setting may be the result of a much larger matrix of practices and meanings that is characteristic only of that society. The same holds true for subgroups within complex societies. It has recently been demonstrated, for example, that the degree of physical punishment (short of abuse) has opposite effects on young children in Euro-American and African American groups. In the former, increased punishment is associated with greater aggressive and other externalizing behaviors, whereas in the latter, it is slightly associated with lower aggression (Deater-Deckard, Dodge, Bates, & Pettit, 1996). As we have commented elsewhere (Super & Harkness, 1986a), monocultural studies risk mistaking the structure of the environment for the structure of development.

METHODS FOR STUDYING THE CULTURAL ORGANIZATION OF DEVELOPMENT

Assessment of the developmental niche generally requires a combination of techniques drawn from anthropological and psychological traditions. Ethnographic field methods for the identification of cultural patterns have been developed in anthropology for over a century, and many of them are directly relevant to the present topic. Systematic quantitative methods have been an important aspect of this tradition, but they have been more broadly developed in the field of psychology. A salient aspect of the best work on culture and development in recent decades is the interweaving of qualitative and quantitative methods. This is necessarily the case as research on culture and human development depends as much on the identification of important qualities for study as it does on the measurement of their presence, frequency, magnitude, and duration.

Table 1 lists several methods of data collection that have proven valuable in research on children's cultural environments, including key ethnographic techniques, observations of naturally occurring behavior, and formal methods for the elicitation of standardized information. For each method, we have listed (in the second column) components of the developmental niche to which it can contribute at least some qualitative understanding, as well as (in the last column) those components for which

TABLE 1
Methods for Studying the Developmental Niche

Method	Components	
	Identified	Measured
Participant observation and ethnographic interviewing	Settings, customs, and caretaker psychology	
Spot observations and diaries	Settings, customs, and caretaker psychology	Settings (and customs)
Behavior observations	Customs and caretaker psychology	Customs
Semistructured interviews and focus groups	Customs and caretaker psychology	Customs and caretaker psychology
Structured questioning		Caretaker psychology and customs
Passive enumeration	Caretaker psychology and customs	Caretaker psychology and customs
Formal methods: free listings, clustering, multidimensional scaling, and consensus analysis	Customs and caretaker psychology	Caretaker psychology and customs

the method can yield quantitative measures. We discuss each of the methods with a particular emphasis on aspects likely to be less familiar to psychologists. Throughout this discussion, however, it should be kept in mind that to understand the environment as culture, the value of any particular measure rests not only on its own centrality to the investigator's hypothesis but also on its contribution to identifying internal structures that form the niche and that in turn produce the kinds of first- and second-order effects discussed earlier.

Ethnographic Methods

It is often the case in psychological research that researchers are familiar in advance with the qualities of behavior or of the environment that they wish to study, and the technical challenges of measurement are addressed through standard concepts of validity and reliability. This is less likely to be true in studies that focus on cultural aspects for two reasons. First, most such research involves a comparative strategy, implying that at least one of the cultural settings is foreign to the investigator and the relevant qualities may be unfamiliar to him or her. Second, even working in one's own culture often involves exploring new territory, because of the relative novelty of a cultural perspective.

Ethnographic methods refers to a loose collection of techniques, developed mostly by anthropologists, to describe the culture or the shared way of life of a group of people. Historically, the typical target of such research has been a preindustrial, non-Western community of farmers, pastoralists, or hunter–gatherers, but more recently, there are also examples of similar approaches to understanding the culture of modern urban groups, including corporations and schoolrooms as well as residential communities. Excellent discussions of the role of ethnographic methods in modern interdisciplinary research are presented by Greenfield (1996), Weisner (1996), and Munroe and Munroe (1986). Goodenough's (1980) broad methodological review is a helpful guide on specific techniques, and Miles and Huberman's (1994) thorough treatment of qualitative methodology is relevant to a number of issues in ethnography.

For the present discussion, ethnographic techniques can be seen to serve three closely related purposes. First, they are necessary to provide a rich description of the context of behavior and development, to give the "feeling" of a cultural setting, or, more strongly, to provide the outsider with an understanding of the local meaning systems that organize and sustain human behavior in that context. Second, it is in developing this description that the researcher may come to identify previously unanticipated features of the environment that warrant more precise investigation and measurement. Third, close insights into the ethnography of development contribute substantially to the identification of the niche's internal structure, which is the origin of contemporary redundancy, thematic elaboration, and chaining.

For all of these purposes, a key strategy in the ethnographic method is to think divergently in the search for patterns. The patterns of interest are to be found within and between the niche's subsystems and also across the individual–niche boundary. Rarely are the patterns evident in concrete behavior, however; rather, they exist in relations among parts and in the meaning systems used by the niche's occupants. They are among the "invisible realities" that Malinowski (1935) pointed to in his description of the ethnographic method:

> The observer should not function as a mere automaton; a sort of combined camera and phonographic or shorthand recorder of native statements. While making his observations the field worker must constantly construct: he must place isolated data in relation to one another and study the manner in which they integrate. To put it paradoxically one could say that "facts" do not exist in sociological any more than in physical reality; that is, they do not dwell in the spatial and temporal continuum open to the untutored eye. The principles of social organization, of legal constitution, of economics and religion have to be constructed by the observer out of a multitude of manifestations of varying significance and relevance. It is these invisible realities, only to be discovered by inductive computation, by selection and construction, which are scientifically important in the study of culture. (p. 317)

Often the identification of invisible realities and the realization of connections among disparate behavior patterns require the perspective of an outside scholar who is looking for cultural themes as well as the understanding of an insider. In traditional anthropological field work, this need for both an insider and an outsider view was met by the visiting ethnographer and a few key informants. As the political, economic, and educational arrangements for comparative research have changed over the past decades, other models have proven useful. The Whitings established a model of "cross-training" in which students from two universities worked with colleagues or faculty from the partner institution, giving advanced academic training as well as bicultural research team experience to all parties. A significant number of U.S. and Kenyan scholars shared this productive experience and now play influential roles in their intellectual and professional fields (Whiting, 1994). Hess and Azuma (see Azuma, 1996) pioneered a very effective collaborative arrangement among senior researchers on the basis of a long-term, bilaterally funded program of research. Short-term collaboration on specific projects is now increasingly evident in the literature. The problem of combining insider knowledge with outsider insights, however, is less easily solved in monocultural projects in which all participants come from the same background; this is the case, of course, for the vast majority of published research on child rearing and child development. Although the formal specification of strategies for qualitative research has made a significant contribution to the reliable identification of themes and meaning systems (e.g., Miles & Huberman, 1994), both the outsider's capacity for surprise and the insider's familiarity with local meaning remain essential assets in finding and understanding cultural practices.

Participant Observation

The process of induction referred to by Malinowski (1935) is especially critical during the early phases of investigation, as the researcher begins to identify events, behaviors, and beliefs that are significant (see Goodenough, 1980). The researcher's observation is facilitated by living in close proximity with the people whose culture one is studying, witnessing the everyday and unexpected as well as the ceremonial. A feeling for the process of discovery of "invisible realities" through participant observation, as this technique is called, can be gleaned from Vogel's (1996) account of her initial realization of dependence as a theme in Japanese child rearing, shortly after she and her husband took up residence in their research community called Mamachi, a suburb of Tokyo, in the late 1950s:

> One evening the usual quiet of our neighborhood was broken by the sound of a child's crying and pounding on the entrance gate next door. Ezra and I quizzically turned to our Japanese maid. She readily ex-

> plained that the grade school child, crying for forgiveness, had obviously been shut out of the house for punishment. My immediate mischievous thought was that any American child so punished would probably run off down the street gleefully. The more usual method of punishment in the USA would be to send a child to his room, or "ground" him for the weekend. Next, we began to notice that mothers walking down the street with unruly toddlers did not hold their hands tightly and command them to stay close and not run off, as we had often seen American mothers do. Rather, the Mamachi mother would run a bit ahead of the straying child, who would then become anxious, run after his mother, and thereafter stay close to her. I mused that our American assumption was that a child wanted to be free and independent, and hence we punished him with confinement or enforced dependence. In contrast, the Japanese assumed a child most wanted dependence and punished him by evoking fear of abandonment. (p. 7)

The products of participant observation potentially contribute to the identification of elements in each of the three subsystems of the developmental niche. The settings of daily life are experientially evident, a variety of customs can be observed, and the accumulation of experiences yields insights into how people in the community organize their thinking about children, family life, group process, and other relevant domains. For many purposes, this level of experiential understanding is sufficient for describing and contextualizing the focal topic of investigation; more important, it also begins the creative process of identifying relevant parts of the environment and their relationship to one another.

There is a general consensus among anthropologists that the most valuable participant observation lasts at least 1 year. This gives the investigator sufficient time to become a familiar figure within the community and to gain access to more informal information, to acquire some of the local common sense that makes meaningful otherwise odd contradictions, to notice and explore patterns that are relevant to one's work, and to see a full cycle of yearly activities. Such extended involvement in field work is not easily available to many researchers, and for multisite comparisons it becomes impossible. As collaborative teams of investigators become more common in cultural research, each working with common methods in their own culture, extended participant observation becomes less important for simply gaining local information and understanding. It remains a primary ethnographic method, however, even for briefer periods of time for the personal insights it offers, and it has proven quite adaptable to short-term variations (e.g., in educational settings).

Ethnographic Interviewing

Vogel's (1996) inquiry to her Japanese maid for help in understanding the evening event illustrates the second unique method of fieldwork, namely, the ethnographic interview. In their extended discussion of this method, Whiting and Whiting (1960) list several ways in which this technique differs from the more psychologically, individually oriented interview. First, the role inequality is reversed: It is the "subject," not the researcher, who is the expert. Second, the "interview" often takes place over an extended period of time, prompted by current events and returning sporadically to important themes. Third, the real target of the discussion is often not the individual but the individual as a representative of socially shared understandings.

One learns many facts through ethnographic interviewing, especially about events that one is unable to see firsthand. The interview can serve as an extension of participant observation (Whiting & Whiting, 1960); its more important purpose, however, is to break the hermeneutic seal surrounding the objective behaviors so as to understand their meaning from within the culture. The includes an evaluative, emotional component, but its core is the web of associations with other actions and motives. In the Japanese example, what is the parents' goal in shutting out the child? What kinds of transgressions would prompt this action? What is the child frightened of? Is this whole event related to the goals and feelings involved when the mother walks away from the straying young child on the sidewalk? Accurate answers to this kind of question constitute what Maxwell (1992) has labeled *interpretive validity*.

It is important to cross-check interpretations and reports from several informants, of course, because from any single person one may get an idiosyncratic notion of a larger shared idea. Wassman and Dasen (1994), an anthropologist–psychologist team, emphasized the importance of interviewing a variety of people—not just "key informants"—to assess the diversity of opinion or knowledge within even a relatively homogeneous group. In its most organized form, this cross-checking takes place as semistructured interviews so that central ideas can be explored with each person.

It is equally important to compare even consensual reports with actual behavior, as it is not unusual to hear of customs that may be universally recognized but that are less frequently carried out. For example, Tharp, Gallimore, and their colleagues (Tharp et al., 1984; Weisner, Gallimore, & Jordan, 1988) found the idea of sibling caretaking to be widely known and approved of among Hawaiian families, but not all families actually used this customary method of child care because the need did not arise. Nevertheless, the kinds of child–child relations instantiated in this practice proved to be important for understanding educational difficulties in the classroom and in designing innovative structures that utilized the widely acknowledged model of child–child relations for the benefit of all children, even those who had not actually participated in this custom at home. The identification of shared customs can index an aspect of caretaker psychology, and of the child's model of the world, that may be important, even if it has never been personally experienced.

Interviewing persons from a different cultural background necessarily introduces special difficulties, because the structure and norms of interpersonal communication are culturally defined. Triandis (1994b) provided a particularly dramatic example, regarding failed negotiations on the brink of the Gulf War between the U.S. Secretary of State and the Foreign Minister of Iraq. More generally, and more prosaically, there is a considerable literature on how the customs of communication are transmitted to children and how they affect the process of conversation and interview (Harkness & Super, 1977; Ochs & Schieffelin, 1984b; Wolfgang, 1979); this is, of course, a continuing area of active research. The relevance here is that ethnographic interviewing is itself a culturally situated activity, and the outcome needs to be subjected to cross-checking not only with other informants but also through other methods, such as participant observation and structured assessments of meaning.

Summary

The methods of participant observation and ethnographic interview are essential methods for identifying and understanding the meaningful elements and organizational structure of the developmental environment. Through observation and inquiry, usually an ongoing process, one learns about the salient customs, the settings, and the psychology that helps organize them. In expert hands, these methods alone can provide a rich and theoretically provocative account of the cultural environment (e.g., see Levy, 1996). In addition, they lay the base for knowing what in the environment is worth measuring and for generating hypotheses about how components of the niche relate to one another.

Systematic Quantitative Techniques

The array of specific measures used in studying the cultural environment is a vast one, and the statistical techniques that have been applied to these measures are equally wide ranging. It is nevertheless possible to outline several kinds of methods that have proven useful in recent research and to indicate which parts of the niche they illuminate. As is shown, most of the techniques can be used to address all three subsystems; once again, the strategy of integrating multiple methods is highlighted as a critical strategy.

Measuring Settings

Participant observation can yield useful impressions of where, with whom, and in what activities children or adults spend their time. More precise measurement, however, offers not only important documentation but also the quantification necessary for testing hypotheses about group differences and individual variations in experience. In general, the measurement of settings in the present sense refers to the recording and description of the kinds of settings that contribute to the developmental niche and also to a tabulation of their relative frequency. Recent comparative research has made effective use of two quite different methods for these purposes: spot observations and diaries.

Spot Observations. Spot observations, which amount to a verbal snapshot of locale, personnel, and activities, were developed in East Africa by Munroe and Munroe (1971), but they have also been used in other locations, especially where most daily life takes place outside and is visible to the researchers as they approach the homestead or household. The method rests on a predetermined random or pseudorandom (balanced) schedule for unannounced observations and on the collection of a sufficient number of observations to permit statistical analysis (Rogoff, 1978). In the original technique, the approaching observer first notices the location, activity, and social context of the target individual (usually a child), then approaches to give the appropriate greetings. The observer may then also ask about factors that are not visually evident, such as the location of the mother and any assigned tasks the child is carrying out, or possibly recent events. If the observer remains in the household for another purpose, the spot observation may be repeated sometime later (Ahmed et al., 1993; Rogoff, Mistry, Göncü, & Mosier, 1993). Because the segment of time recorded is nearly instantaneous and the frequency of observation is rarely more than a few times per day, this method is not adequate for the study of discrete, short-lived behaviors (e.g., specific speech acts or parental response to rule violation). Rather, spot observations are typically used to describe the distribution of recurring combinations of elements in the physical and social settings. The number of observations required depends, of course, on several factors, which can be estimated with the tools of power analysis (Cohen, 1977); for some purposes, several dozen will suffice, but a full data set yielding individual estimates may number well over a thousand.

Common items used in spot observations include the presence or absence of specific individuals (mother and father), the number of other persons present, the identity of the target child's caretaker, the child's activity, the distance from home, and the physical position. Weisner, Gallimore, and their colleagues have especially emphasized patterns of behavior that covary with place, leading to the concept of "activity settings" (Gallimore et al., 1993). The quantitative measures derived from these measures have proven helpful in understanding, for example, between-group variation in methods of infant care, such as infant upright posture, physical contact with caretakers, and use of sibling caretakers (Chisholm, 1983; Konner, 1977; Super, 1981); patterns of caretaking by fathers and other family and group members (e.g., Harkness & Super, 1992a; Munroe & Munroe, 1992); and young children's opportunities for gender identification and activities (Bloch, 1987; Whiting & Edwards, 1988). Repeated at two different times, such descriptions can provide a valuable indication of shifts over time or in response to external factors such as seasonality in maternal work (Gill & Super, 1994). In an urban setting, a telephone-based version of the spot observation may be more efficient and equally effective, at least when mothers can report adequately on the location and activity of their infants and young children (Bloch, 1987; Edwards, Logue, Loehr, & Roth, 1986; Munroe et al., 1983; Super & Harkness, 1994). More generally, spot observations have contributed to the larger study of time allocation in various cultural contexts (Munroe et al., 1983).

Spot observations can also be used to derive stable estimates of individual differences in experience among children in the same population. Munroe and Munroe (1971), for example, demonstrated the relationship between household density and features of infant care of Logoli families, and Ember (1973) assessed the (non-normative) assignment of Luo boys to sibling care as a predictor of learned social behavior. Nerlove, Roberts, Klein, Yarbrough, and Habicht, 1974) used spot observations to investigate individual differences in the activities of Guatemalan children and their level of cognitive development. Edwards et al. (1986) studied young U.S. children's exposure to adult men and women as a function of day-care experience. Sex differences in infant care among various East African groups were documented through spot observations by Super (1984).

Diaries. Diaries are a less frequently used but powerful technique for learning about the settings of development and the activities that take place in them. In one manifestation, these diaries account for the full 24-hour day, divided into segments by the recorder to correspond to major changes in activity or setting. For each segment, the entry may include (in addition to time, place, and activity) all other people present and the identity of specific individuals interacting with the target child. In the comparative literature, diaries have been used primarily to learn about the daily life of younger children (e.g., sleep patterns; Super et al., 1996), when one can rely on the mother or other caretaker to be knowledgeable of the child's changing activities and to be reliable as a recorder. The method is also adaptable to older ages, when participants can keep their own records. Relying on the target child or a caretaker to provide the raw data naturally introduces an opportunity for distortion. Maintaining validity thus rests on the quality of the research relationship (always vital in any field project) and the face value and innocuous nature of the material asked for. The measures derived from diaries are usually time based, and, as in the case of spot observations, they are most practical when concerned with the large-scale flow of daily life and the distribution of settings, persons, and activities therein.

The most obvious measures to be derived from spot observations and diaries address the daily settings of development (see Table 1): Where is the child, with whom, and what is the child doing? In addition, it is sometimes only a small leap also to derive measures of customary practices. For example, in our study of parental behavior in Holland, mentioned earlier, our attention was initially drawn to the importance of regularity in children's sleep patterns through interviews with parents; this identified regular bedtimes as a custom in the sense of having recognized legitimacy. The actual occurrence of the custom, however, was assessed through analysis of diaries kept by the parents, which confirmed that regular bedtimes were more characteristic in the Dutch sample than a comparison group in the United States. Similarly, spot observations have been used to confirm the customary assignment of particular household tasks to boys and girls of particular ages (Ember, 1973). Finally, the specific description of daily settings and the activities that take place in them often suggest to the investigator unexpected features to be explored through ethnographic or semistructured interviews.

In summary, spot observations and diaries are useful methods for describing the physical and social settings of daily life not only in terms of their particular qualities but also in terms of their empirical distributions. There is nothing inherently "cultural" about these techniques—indeed, they have been used to study individual differences—but when examined for patterns, they may focus attention on the cultural regulation of daily life, in comparison with other samples or more simply as quantitative ethnography. The results provide a basis for identifying regularities in settings and activities that may differ between groups, or that one wants to relate thematically to other elements in the niche, or to developmental trends.

Measuring Customs

Customs are a particular combination of the behavioral routines and the psychology that marks them as normative, meaningful, and useful. They correspond, by and large, to the notion of "practices" as that term is now used in cultural psychology (Miller & Goodnow, 1995). As such, their measurement can take place at the level of either psychology or behavior, or preferably both. An example cited by Whiting and Whiting (1960) captured this dual quality:

> To say that an Ojibwa child is brought up by his grandmother from the time he is weaned and may live in a different village from his own parents' from that time forth is of interest, even though, and this is reported to be the fact, this custom is not practiced by all or even a majority of Ojibwa families (Barnow, 1950). That it is a custom, and that any Ojibwa family who practiced it would not be looked upon as

deviant, is the sort of statement that is generally made by anthropologists and can be said to be descriptive of Ojibwa culture. (p. 56)

Two very different techniques are described here as particularly helpful in measuring the existence and prevalence of customs in the developmental niche (beyond those derived from setting measures, as indicated earlier). The first includes three variations of behavior observation, called here *time sampling*, *interpretive observations*, and *behavior sampling*. (For a fuller discussion of types of behavior observations, see Altmann, 1974, or Bakeman & Gottman, 1987.) Second, semistructured interviewing, which is related to but more rigorous than ethnographic interviewing, is a particularly useful technique to identify, document, and understand customs.

Intensive behavior observations that capture aspects of the behavior stream across an extended time provide an important account of customary behaviors. One tradition well represented in the comparative literature is the sampling of time units (e.g., 10-second intervals) with a list of behaviors to be checked for their occurrence. Such *time sampling*, as it is often called, was used in the well-known studies of Caudill and Weinstein (1969), which concerned infant care in Japan and in the United States. In this work, discrete behaviors (e.g., mother touches baby and baby vocalizes) were recorded, and multivariate analysis of variance was used to examine group differences. A number of other cross-cultural studies have used similar methods of behavior observation; earlier ones are reviewed in Super (1981), and there is a continuing literature based on this method (e.g., Bornstein et al., 1992). Advances in understanding the significant limitations of this kind of time sampling (Mann, Ten Have, Plunkett, & Meisels, 1991) suggest caution in its further use, however, particularly for the brief behaviors, such as looking or smiling, which are often the focus of these studies. In addition, there is a striking difference between those studies that, like Caudill's, use behavior observations as one of several methods, including ethnographic ones focused specifically on infant caretaking, and those studies that have behavior observations as the only empirical base, relying on casual or more general notions about the surrounding culture to provide an understanding of observed behavioral similarities and differences compared with other samples. The evident difference in scientific knowledge contributed by these two types of studies reinforces the present emphasis on understanding the connections among components of the niche as essential to understanding whether any single environmental difference might have developmental consequences.

The time-sampling method has been almost exclusively used in the study of behavior by and directed toward infants and toddlers. In these cases, it has been more or less implicitly assumed that the discrete behaviors observed are primarily important in their own right, and whatever symbolic value they might carry is secondary. In studies of older children, this assumption is increasingly untenable, and an appropriate method of observation must capture the subjective, culturally defined meanings of customary behavior as well. Thus, other methods of intensive observation attempt to capture meaning and sequence in the flow of the behavior stream.

Interpretive Observations. Interpretive observations of early social interaction, and particularly studies of early language development, focus specifically on the meaning of customary interactions and the child's acquisition of culture through participation in the daily communicative environment. (See, for example, Miller & Hoogstra, 1992; Ochs & Schieffelin, 1984a.) In the most detailed version, the natural language of young children is recorded in their home environment while the investigator takes notes on the surrounding behavior and settings (e.g., see Ochs, 1988). As a method of measuring the customs or practices of child rearing, this and related techniques have been particularly successful in identifying organized dyadic and triadic speech routines that teach social interaction (Watson-Gegeo & Gegeo, 1977), affective response (Schieffelin, 1979), and social role (Harkness & Super, 1977; Rabain-Jamin, 1994), as well as language.

Whiting and Edwards (1988) and Whiting and Whiting (1975) developed a different method of observing the meaning of customary ways of interacting with young children. The initial recording of naturally occurring behavior is undertaken by observers from the local culture, who have been trained in the system of breaking the behavior stream into units of a goal-oriented "mand" (request or command) and response, in which the mand may be for a physical resource, assistance, obedience, or simply social companionships. Recording is done by hand, as text in consecutive narrative sentences. The observer "follow(s) the eyes of the focal child, identifying, whenever possible, the instigations to the focal child's social behavior and the responses of the partner to the child's social acts" (Whiting & Edwards, 1988, p. 14). Thus, a record might read, "Mother gently asks child to help brother carry the child—child complies but sulkingly." The record is coded by the local, trained observers for content (intention and response) and style. Although a general indication of time is included in the protocol, the analysis of these observations is based on the behavioral unit (mand and response), not on elapsed time. Aggregated over many observation periods, this method allows a detailed analysis of the customary social interactions between people with various combinations of age, gender, and family status. The method has been particularly fruitful in revealing both universals and cultural differences in the social interactions that contribute to the developmental niche. Analyses combining data from multiple research sites have illuminated the pattern of larger cultural features associated, for example, with a relative emphasis on prosocial compared with egoistic behaviors (Whiting & Whiting, 1975) and have also suggested situational universals in the origin of sex differences in behavior (Whiting & Edwards, 1988).

Behavior sampling. Behavior sampling is a variation in the strategy of behavior observation that is particularly useful when a specific focal situation or behavior has already been identified through ethnographic study or on the basis of theoretical prediction. Often the specified behaviors constitute a customary set of practices. For example, Zeitlin, Ahmed, and their colleagues (Ahmed et al., 1991–1992; Ahmed et al., 1993) identified personal hygiene behavior as a culturally regulated domain of theoretical importance to understanding the pattern of diarrheal disease in Bangladeshi infants and constructed observational schedules to document hand-washing and related routines. Munroe and Munroe (1971), in their study of household density and infant care, sampled specific behaviors (e.g., infant cry) to record caretaker responses. In these and other cases, the environment is characterized on the basis of how it responds to particular child behaviors, and this is relevant to the understanding of both settings and customs.

Behavior observation techniques are familiar to psychologists, of course, and the ones outlined here share a history with research that is not culturally oriented. However, as the concept of custom implies a pattern of behavior linked to historical and contemporary systems of meaning, the measurement of custom must involve access to local understandings and motives, as well as to the actual behaviors. One technique that facilitates this connection is the semistructured interview.

Semistructured interviews. Semistructured interviews contain a core of key questions that are asked of each respondent in such a way that the answers can be tallied to evaluate hypotheses about beliefs and values in the sampled population. At the same time, they are more flexible than an oral questionnaire, thus providing the skilled interviewer with an opportunity to probe beyond key questions and learn about how the respondent reasons, with what shared and idiosyncratic concepts and themes. In this manner, semistructured interviews contribute quantitatively and qualitatively to identifying and understanding customary practices. (Consequently, they also bridge the connection between customs and the psychological component of the developmental niche.) On occasion, it is efficient to carry out these interviews in small groups, in which case they may resemble focus groups.

This dual function of semistructured interviews can be illustrated with our recent work on parents' ethnotheories in the town of Bloemenheim, Holland and in the environs of Cambridge, Massachusetts (Super et al., 1996). In our initial interviews, we asked respondents what they thought was important for them to do, as parents, for their child at his or her particular developmental stage. In Bloemenheim, we immediately learned of a cultural formulation for infant care called the "three *Rs*": *Rust*, *Regel-*

mat, and *Reinheid* (rest, regularity, and cleanliness). We also learned that the three *R*s were until recently part of the official guide to infant care in Holland promulgated by the national health service and that they were still widely known and, in general, taken as sensible ideas. In virtually every interview, parents described their customary approach to sleep training during infancy, naps in early childhood, or bedtime for school-aged children as one that valued physical rest and a comfortable, reliable routine of activity. Often these descriptions came naturally in the flow of talking about children's needs; on occasion, we asked specifically about particular routines. As we learned more, we were able to ask more detailed questions about customary decision making. If the parent needs to run a quick errand, but the baby is still asleep, for example, would it be better to leave the infant alone for a short period than wake him or her, or would that be unusual (and considered deviant)? Through repeated discussions of this sort (and taking them, in this case, at face value), we were able to establish that leaving a sleeping baby alone briefly was considered customary, even though not all parents personally agreed with this practice, and approximately one third said they would not do it. We were not able to derive this information from behavior observations or even diaries because the occasion for the practice was infrequent. In this case, then, semistructured interviews played a key role in establishing the existence of the customary practice and in providing a rough indication of its frequency.

In summary, measuring customs adequately usually requires two interactive steps. One is qualitative, in which regularities in practice are identified through either basic ethnography or direct observation. The second step consists of obtaining quantitative measures of individuals' views on the nature and importance of the custom or measures of the frequency of occurrence of the identified practice, or both. Ideally, an inclusive strategy for assessing customs demonstrates their existence, documents their occurrence, and explains their relationship to the settings of daily life and to the psychological theories that guide them.

Measuring Caretaker Psychology

The final component of the developmental niche, the psychology of caretakers, is thought to be of special significance because of its directive properties (Harkness & Super, 1996). That is, within the confines of a given time and place, the beliefs and values held by parents play a major role in deciding among the many choices they face regarding their children. Particularly in modern societies, a variety of settings can be arranged and some resolution must be achieved among overlapping and sometimes conflicting customs. How to discourage night waking, whether to use day care, when to become more firm in handling minor disobedience, or how to build appropriate self-confidence at school—these and a myriad of other decisions are shaped by the ideas and feelings parents bring to the process. The cognitive–affective structures shared with other members of the community (i.e., the parental ethnotheories) are major guides in such decisions.

Measuring parental ethnotheories presents the same two challenges outlined for settings and customs—namely, to identify qualitatively the locally relevant structures and then to derive quantitative measures. All of the methods discussed earlier—ethnographic interviewing, participant observation, spot observations, diaries, behavior observations, and semistructured interviews—are likely to provide the investigator with hypotheses about the way parents think about children and their needs. One can often proceed directly from this generative phase to the development of a questionnaire or structured interview, which might involve several rounds of focused ethnographic interviewing and attention to standard psychometric issues of validity and reliability. The final act of measurement might look very similar to individual measurement techniques familiar to psychologists; the results, however, summarized to describe group parameters such as mean and variance, would be taken to describe ideas within the community sampled, and from there a panorama of inferential statistics enable careful comparison with other groups. Three such sources of data have been used to good effect in comparative studies: structured questioning (oral or written) for the compilation of psychometric scales, more passive enumeration of statements and ideas, and formal methods derived from cognitive science.

Minturn and Lambert's *Mothers of Six Cultures* (1964) is a classic example of *structured questioning*, in which mothers in contrasting groups were interviewed with a standard, fixed protocol of questions. The answers to related questions were combined to create summary scales, as is commonly done in attitude surveys. Although relatively straightforward as a strategy, the comparison of diverse groups on common scales engages a tangle of issues about how—and even whether—one can achieve results that satisfy construct, ecological, and interpretive validity for underlying latent constructs rather than demonstrate only surface differences in scores. Properly done, this psychometric approach is uniquely powerful, but the difficulties in cross-cultural application are considerable and continue to provoke heated discussion (Irvine & Carroll, 1980).

The *passive enumeration* of ideas more spontaneously offered can be illustrated by the Dutch–American project discussed earlier. Alerted by ethnographic procedures and the initial semistructured interviews to Dutch notions of children's need for rest and regularity, we often took the opportunity to ask further about parents' ideas on the nature of infant sleep and how it changes over time. Fortunately, this was also a topic of discussion in our earlier data collection in the United States, and we were able to extract from transcriptions in both samples a large number of statements by parents that included some kind of proposition about the nature of infant sleep (Super et al., 1996).

One view, for example, was that some babies naturally sleep through the night from an early age, whereas others are temperamentally more likely to have difficulty with sleeping through. Another was that sleeping through is essentially a maturational phenomena and cannot be taught or trained. A simple count of the propositions offered by parents in our discussions demonstrated that these two ideas were much more commonly held by the U.S. parents, along with the notion that one could, nevertheless, look for specific strategies, or "little tricks," to get the baby (and oneself) through the night. The Dutch parents, in contrast, much more frequently insisted that a regular sleeping schedule was important and that failure to arrange such a routine would have serious consequences for later development. Again, the counts were amenable to statistical treatment, confirming group differences in the frequency of emphasizing the importance of a regular sleep schedule during infancy. This approach is, of course, strongest when testing is carried out on a different sample from the one generating the hypothesis, a common issue in thematic analysis.

Counting the frequency of naturally occurring statements is probably less likely to risk imposing a concept that does not apply in one context or another, compared with applying a multicomponent scale, as long as the method of elicitation and related social rules are similar. The assumption that differences in the frequency of concept usage reflect differences in internal beliefs or values nevertheless corresponds to the question of construct validity. In both cases, an examination of how the results fit (or fail to fit) with other measures is essential. In the earlier example, the coherence is noteworthy among the face content of parents' statements about rest and regularity, the frequency of mentioning specific concepts, the routines documented in the diaries, and the interactive behaviors observed during home visits. This coherence provided credibility to each of the measures and at the same time revealed redundancy and elaboration in the niche.

Finally, there are a number of intensive *formal methods* derived from cognitive science that can be used to measure psychological structures in the developmental niche. Cognitive anthropologists have adopted and developed such procedures to identify and model cultural domains of knowledge. Within anthropology, these techniques were used initially for studying domains such as ethnobotany and terms of kinship, but they can be applied equally well to developmental issues. There are several good introductory references available (e.g., Borgatti, 1992b; Weller & Romney, 1988), as well as a software package designed to facilitate the collection and analysis of such data (Borgatti, 1992a).

The fundamental strategy for learning about cognition as applied to a cultural domain is first to obtain examples of a given class (e.g., child characteristics that contribute to school success or behaviors that represent "independence") through free listing from participants or selection from an appropriate, previously constructed compilation (such as behavioral descriptions from a standardized questionnaire). Subsequently, selected items from the list are grouped by participants, rated along a relevant scale, compared with one another, or submitted to some other method that yields a measure of their proximity, similarity, or covariation. There are several methods for then analyzing the internal structure of the results, which presumably reflect salient aspects of the cognitive structures that generated them. Most useful and appropriate are clustering techniques and multidimensional scaling. A recent example of how cluster analysis can facilitate elucidation of cultural meanings used by adults (and by extension, adult caretakers) is Menon and Shweder's (1994) presentation on facial expression and shame in the Hindu narrative of the goddess Kali. The meanings that they derive and demonstrate include those spoken of more descriptively in accounts of thematic elaboration in the developmental niche for Oriya childhood (e.g., see Shweder et al., 1990). White (1994) used multidimensional scaling to explore the structure of emotion terms in their studies in South Pacific groups and, from that, to theorize about fundamental issues in the study of culture and emotion. The cultural meanings empirically demonstrated, again, are ones that figure strongly in ethnographic accounts of local child rearing and socialization (e.g., see Lutz, 1988).

When shared cultural meanings and concepts in children's environments are the focus of research, consensus analysis is often an appropriate empirical method of analysis (Romney et al., 1986). A relatively new tool, consensus analysis offers several unique contributions. Most relevant to the present discussion, it allows the investigator to deduce the "culturally correct" answer to questions of knowledge from informants who may vary in their level of expertise. In addition, it provides a test of whether a group of participants (presumably sampled from the same cultural community) do in fact share a common understanding, a common cognitive model for specific domains. Applications of this new technique to the measurement of the psychological component of the developmental niche are few, but promising. In our analysis, mentioned earlier, of U.S. and Kipsigis mothers' conceptual schemes for neonatal behavior, consensus analysis was helpful in demonstrating that two separate, shared cognitive models were involved, not just an arbitrary difference in results. Similarly, Raghavan, Harkness, and Super (1993) used the procedure to show consensus within, but not between, the way South-Asian and native-born U.S. parents conceptualized the nature of adolescent daughters, even though they all lived in the same neighborhoods and in the same general surroundings of a university town in Pennsylvania.

Thus, identification and measurement of the psychological components of the developmental niche—particularly parental ethnotheories—play an important role in understanding regularities observed in the settings and customary practices of everyday life. A broad range of techniques is available to do this, ranging from simple compilation of material in ethnographic interviews to more formal methods of eliciting and rating the content of cultural knowledge domains. As with each of the other components of the niche, examining the relationship among findings from different methods is an important aspect of validation as well as theoretical reward.

Summary

We have outlined several methods of data collection that permit measurement of elements in the three subsystems of the developmental niche. Spot observations and diaries provide prevalence estimates for the settings (and often the routines) of daily life, behavior observations and semistructured interviews establish the existence and estimate the use of customary practices, and cognitive methods ranging from the unobtrusive to the highly formal provide empirical evidence about the psychological structures that guide caretaker behavior. It should be evident, however, that a key feature for understanding culture is the interplay of qualitative and quantitative information garnered from these various methods. Findings in one domain suggest further exploration or reexamination in another, and replication of patterns suggests salient cultural themes.

Integrating Concepts and Measures

Culturally oriented researchers have added significantly to techniques for measuring the specifics of behavioral settings, customary practices, and shared psychology. Their unique contribution, however, has been to provide theoretical structures to guide the integration of singular measures of the environment into a description of its organization. It is from the interrelation and integration of measures and concepts across the niche's subsystems that the developmental power of culture emerges. The final step in cultural research, therefore, is to review the information obtained and assemble from it a rendering of the contemporary redundancy, thematic integration, and chaining that shape development in that context. This step is an iterative one, involving review and reconsideration as a creative process, testing emerging hypotheses against the data.

To achieve this level of description, the most successful research has necessarily specified at least some of the elements in each subsystem of the developmental niche, or, for example, all five core elements of the activity settings in Weisner's eco-cultural model (Weisner & Garnier, 1992). More traditional group-difference reports are less successful by these criteria.

They may demonstrate a divergence in developmental behaviors, but lacking measures of the niche, the interpretation relies on general notions about the cultures involved and thus on speculation about how those general notions translate into the environment for the observed children. A stronger but still insufficient case may be made with evidence of contrasts in one component of the niche, but this remains a limited and possibly distorted view of the constellation of forces involved; in the end, these studies can only speculate on why that one aspect of the environment carries such power.

The more systematic and integrative model endorsed here suggests a strategy for measuring the environment of development on the basis of our current understanding of how culture weaves its influence. Earlier advances in contextualizing development, such as the ecological approach, were developed in response to other needs at the time, and without benefit of the comparative research literature now available. It may be helpful, in closing, to sketch how the present proposal for measuring the environment as culture rests in its historical moment.

SEEING THE ENVIRONMENT AS CULTURE

At the beginning of the twentieth century, the emerging social sciences coalesced into three groups: psychology, to study the human mind (as manifest in local Western cultures); sociology, to study the origin and nature of social institutions (again, as they had recently evolved in Western Europe); and anthropology, to study other, foreign, people and societies. For most of this century, the three disciplines have tended to recruit intellectual and financial resources to develop their own special strengths and to differentiate themselves from one another. The exchange of ideas across their common intellectual borders nevertheless led to constant interdisciplinary mix at the interstices, which on occasion made important contributions back to the mother disciplines, but rarely could they compete with the centralizing forces.

In the past two decades, several shifts have begun to alter this pattern, at least in the field of human development. A critical transition occurred at the end of the 1970s when the discrepancy between laboratory studies (which had seemed to mark developmental psychology's coming of age as a science) and important issues in society became too great to ignore. Within the span of a few years, there were several articulate calls for a larger vision, what Cahan and White (1992) have referred to since as a "second science." McCall (1977) charged the dominant paradigm with ignoring essential questions only because they cannot be modeled in the laboratory, and he attributed the triviality of results to excessive devotion to an experimental model that came "to dictate rather than serve research questions" (p. 333). Bronfenbrenner's (1979) landmark work on "the ecology of child development" appeared in full form 2 years later, opening with the famous statement that "much of developmental psychology, as it now exists, is the science of the strange behavior of children in strange situations with strange adults for the briefest possible periods of time" (p. 19). In the same year, Kessen (1979) declared that after reviewing the major works of several centuries on "the child," he was convinced there was no such thing; he called for a new paradigm with "the-child-in-context" as the primary unit of analysis. Simultaneously, life-span developmental psychology was emerging with a distinctive view of cohort differences that brought historical changes to the fore (Baltes, 1979), and life-course studies, coming in part from sociology, reinforced this broader time perspective (Elder & Rockwell, 1979).

Curiously, as we noted in the opening of this chapter, cultural variation was not included in the broad reexamination undertaken in the late 1970s. The forces that currently bring culture to the theoretical attention of psychologists, particularly developmentalists, are diverse but seem to have followed quickly in the subsequent decade. They include the changing demography of the U.S. population, the globalization of transportation and communication, the emergence of strong developmental science in Europe and Asia, the increasingly robust literature in cross-cultural psychology, and the postmodern relativism that has swept through the social sciences.

All of that leaves the study of human development with a great deal more to explain than it has had to in the past. It is no longer reasonable to think that "child development" can be understood by studying children in only one cultural setting; what was the paradigm of development is now only a single cultural instance. Understanding the variable construction of child development is now part of the mission for developmental science, and new methods are needed. We have suggested in this chapter that the first challenge in pursuing this mission is to conceptualize the kinds of organization that culture imposes on the developmental niche, in order to move beyond an implicitly haphazard model of the environment; the second is to include systems of meaning as critical aspects of the environment, in order to view the environment from the inside; and the third is to collect systematic measures from the major subsystems of this structure, in order to discern their organizing relationships with developmental processes and outcomes. These are the challenges and the rewards of seeing the environment as culture.

REFERENCES

Ahmed, N. U., Zeitlin, M. F., Beiser, A. S., Super, C. M., & Gershoff, S. N. (1993). A longitudinal study of the impact of behavioral change intervention on cleanliness, diarrhoeal morbidity, and growth of children in rural Bangladesh. *Social Science and Medicine, 37*, 159–171.

Ahmed, N. U., Zeitlin, M. F., Beiser, A. S., Super, C. M., Gershoff, S. N., & Ahmed, M. A. (1991–1992). Community-based trial and intervention techniques for the development of hygiene intervention in rural Bangladesh. *International Quarterly of Community Health Education, 12*, 183–202.

Altmann, J. (1974). Observational study of behavior: Sampling methods. *Behavior, 49*, 227–267.

Azuma, H. (1996). Cross-national research on child development: The Hess/Azuma collaboration in retrospect. In D. W. Shwalb & B. J. Shwalb (Eds.), *Japanese child rearing: Two generations of scholarship* (pp. 220–240). New York: Guilford Press.

Bakeman, R., & Gottman, J. M. (1987). Applying observational methods: A systematic view. In J. D. Osofsky (Ed.), *Handbook of infant development* (pp. 818–854). New York: Wiley.

Baltes, P. B. (1979). Life-span developmental psychology: Some converging observations on history and theory. In P. B. Baltes & O. G. Brim (Eds.), *Life-span development and behavior* (Vol. 2, pp. 5–43). New York: Academic Press.

Barnow, C. (1950). *Acculturation and personality among the Wisconsin Ojibwa* (Memoir, Vol. 72). Washington, DC: American Anthropological Association.

Bell, R. Q. (1968). A reinterpretation of the direction of effects in studies of socialization. *Psychological Review, 75*, 81–95.

Benedict, R. (1959). *Patterns of culture*. Boston: Houghton Mifflin. (Original work published 1934)

Bernheimer, L. P., Gallimore, R., & Weisner, T. S. (1990). Ecocultural theory as a context for the Individual Family Service Plan. *Journal of Early Intervention, 14*, 219–233.

Bernstein, B. (1971). *Class, codes, and control. Vol. 1: Theoretical studies towards a sociology of language*. New York: Routledge & Kegan Paul.

Bloch, M. N. (1987). The development of sex differences in young children's activities at home: The effect of social context. *Sex Roles, 16*, 279–301.

Blount, B. (1990). Parental speech and language acquisition: An anthropological perspective. *Pre- and Peri-natal Psychology, 4*, 319–337.

Borgatti, S. P. (1992a). *ANTHROPAC 4.0*. Columbia, SC: Analytic Technologies.

Borgatti, S. P. (1992b). *ANTHROPAC 4.0: Methods guide*. Columbia, SC: Analytic Technologies.

Bornstein, M. H., Tamis-LeMonda, C. S., Tal, J., Ludemann, P., Toda, S., Rahn, C. W., Pecheux, M., Azuma, H., & Vardi, D. (1992). Maternal responsiveness to infants in three societies: The United States, France, and Japan. *Child Development, 63*, 808–821.

Bronfenbrenner, U. (1979). *The ecology of human development*. Cambridge, MA: Harvard University Press.

Bronfenbrenner, U., & Crouter, A. C. (1983). The evolution of environmental models in developmental research. In P. H. Mussen (Series Ed.) & W. Kessen (Vol. Ed.), *Handbook of child psychology. Vol. I: History, theory, and methods* (4th ed., pp. 357–414). New York: Wiley.

Cahan, E. D., & White, S. H. (1992). Proposals for a second psychology. *American Psychologist, 47,* 224–235.

Caudill, W., & Weinstein, H. (1969). Maternal care and infant behavior in Japan and America. *Psychiatry, 32,* 12–43.

Chisholm, J. S. (1983). *Navajo infancy: An ethnological study of child development.* Albuquerque: University of New Mexico Press.

Cohen, J. (1977). *Statistical power analysis for the behavioral sciences.* New York: Academic Press.

Cole, M., & Cole, S. R. (1993). *The development of children* (2nd ed.). San Francisco: Scientific American Books.

D'Andrade, R. (1990). Some propositions about the relations between culture and human cognition. In J. W. Stigler, R. A. Shweder, & G. Herdt (Eds.), *Cultural psychology: Essays on comparative human development* (pp. 66–129). Cambridge, England: Cambridge University Press.

D'Andrade, R. G. (1992). Schemas and motivation. In R. G. D'Andrade & C. Strauss (Eds.), *Human motives and cultural models* (pp. 23–44). Cambridge, England: Cambridge University Press.

Deater-Deckard, K., Dodge, K. A., Bates, J. E., & Pettit, G. S. (1996). Physical discipline among African American and European American mothers: Links to children's externalizing behaviors. *Developmental Psychology, 32,* 1965–1972.

deVries, M. W. (1984). Temperament and infant mortality among the Masai of east Africa. *American Journal of Psychiatry, 141,* 1189–1194.

Edwards, C. P., Logue, M. E., Loehr, S., & Roth, S. (1986). The influence of model infant group care on parent/child interaction at home. *Early Childhood Research Quarterly, 1,* 317–332.

Elder, G. H., Jr., & Rockwell, R. C. (1979). The life course approach and human development: An ecological perspective. *International Journal of Behavioral Development, 2,* 1–21.

Eldering, L. (in press). Child rearing in bicultural settings: A cultural ecological approach. *Psychology and developing societies: A journal.* New York: Garland.

Ember, C. R. (1973). Feminine task assignment and the social behavior of boys. *Ethos, 9,* 135–149.

Gallimore, R., & Goldenberg, C. (1993). Activity settings of early literacy: Home and school factors in children's emergent literacy. In E. Forman, N. Minick, & C. A. Stone (Eds.), *Contexts for learning: Sociocultural dynamics in children's development* (pp. 315–335). Oxford, England: Oxford University Press.

Gallimore, R., Goldenberg, C. N., & Weisner, T. S. (1993). The social construction and subjective reality of activity settings: Implications for community psychology. *American Journal of Community Psychology, 21,* 537–559.

Geertz, C. (1973). *The interpretation of cultures.* New York: Basic Books.

Gill, S., & Super, C. M. (1994, June). *Adaptations in the developmental niche to seasonal variation in agricultural work in a rural Indian setting.* Poster presented at the biannual meeting of the International Society for the Study of Behavioral Development, Amsterdam, The Netherlands.

Goodenough, W. H. (1980). Ethnographic field techniques. In J. C. Triandis & J. W. Berry (Eds.), *Handbook of cross-cultural psychology. Vol 2: Methodology* (pp. 29–55). Boston: Allyn & Bacon.

Greenfield, P. M. (1996). Culture as process: Empirical methodology for cultural psychology. In J. W. Berry, Y. H. Poortinga, & J. Pandey (Eds.), *Handbook of cross-cultural psychology. Vol. 1: Theory and method* (2nd ed., pp. 301–346). Needham Heights, MA: Allyn & Bacon.

Harkness, S. (1988). The cultural construction of semantic contingency in mother–child speech. *Language Sciences*, *10*, 53–67.

Harkness, S. (1990). A cultural model for the acquisition of language: Implications for the innateness debate. *Developmental Psychobiology*, *27*, 727–740.

Harkness, S. (1992). Human development in psychological anthropology. In T. Schwartz, G. M. White, & C. A. Lutz (Eds.), *New directions in psychological anthropology* (pp. 102–121). New York: Cambridge University Press.

Harkness, S., & Super, C. M. (1977). Why African children are so hard to test. In L. L. Adler (Ed.), *Cross-cultural research at issue* (pp. 145–152). New York: Academic Press.

Harkness, S., & Super, C. (1983). The cultural construction of child development: A framework for the socialization of affect. *Ethos*, *11*, 221–231.

Harkness, S., & Super, C. M. (1985). Child–environment transactions in the socialization of affect. In M. Lewis & C. Saarni (Eds.), *The socialization of emotions* (pp. 21–36). New York: Plenum.

Harkness, S., & Super, C. M. (1992a). The cultural foundations of fathers' roles: Evidence from Kenya and the United States. In B. S. Hewlett (Ed.), *The father's role: Cultural and evolutionary perspectives* (pp. 191–211). New York: Aldine de Gruyter.

Harkness, S., & Super, C. M. (1992b). The developmental niche: A theoretical framework for analyzing the household production of health. *Social Science and Medicine*, *38*, 217–226.

Harkness, S., & Super, C. M. (1993). The developmental niche: Implications for children's literacy development. In L. Eldering & P. Lesemen (Eds.), *Early intervention and culture: Preparation for literacy* (pp. 115–132). Paris: UNESCO.

Harkness, S., & Super, C. M. (1995). *Parental ethnotheories, cultural practices, and the transition to school: Progress report to the Spencer Foundation.* Unpublished manuscript.

Harkness, S., & Super, C. M. (1996). Introduction. In S. Harkness & C. Super (Eds.), *Parents' cultural belief systems: Their origins, expressions, and consequences* (pp. 1–23). New York: Guilford Press.

Harkness, S., Super, C. M., & Keefer, C. H. (1992). Learning to be an American parent: How cultural models gain directive force. In R. G. D'Andrade & C. Strauss (Eds.), *Human motives and cultural models* (pp. 163–178). New York: Cambridge University Press.

Herskovits, M. J. (1955). *Cultural anthropology*. New York: Knopf.

Hess, R. D., & Azuma, H. (1990). Cultural support for schooling: Contrasts between Japan and the United States. *Educational Researcher, 20*, 265–288.

Irvine, S. H., & Carroll, W. K. (1980). Testing and assessment across cultures: Issues in methodology and theory. In H. C. Triandis & J. W. Berry (Eds.), *Handbook of cross-cultural psychology: Methodology* (Vol. 2, pp. 181–244). Boston: Allyn & Bacon.

Kessen, W. (1979). The American child and other cultural inventions. *American Psychologist, 34*, 815–820.

Kilbride, J. E., & Kilbride, P. L. (1975). Sitting and smiling behavior of Baganda infants: The influence of culturally constituted experience. *Journal of Cross-Cultural Psychology*, 6, 88–107.

Kluckhohn, C. (1962). The concept of culture. In C. Kluckhohn (Ed.), *Culture and behavior* (pp. 19–73). New York: Free Press. (Original work published 1945)

Konner, M. J. (1977). Infancy among the Kalahari Desert San. In P. H. Liederman, S. R. Tulkin, & A. Rosenfeld (Eds.), *Culture and infancy: Variations in the human experience* (pp. 69–109). New York: Academic Press.

Korn, S. J., & Gannon, S. (1983). Temperament, cultural variation and behavior disorder in preschool children. *Child Psychiatry and Human Development, 13*, 203–212.

Lerner, R. M. (1984). *On the nature of human plasticity*. New York: Cambridge University Press.

LeVine, R. A. (1970). Cross-cultural study in child psychology. In P. Mussen (Ed.), *Carmichael's manual of child psychology* (3rd ed., Vol 2, pp. 559–612). New York: Wiley.

LeVine, R. A. (1973). *Culture, behavior, and personality*. Chicago: Aldine.

LeVine, R. A., Dixon, S. L., Richman, A., Leiderman, P. H., Keefer, C. H., & Brazelton, T. B. (1994). *Child care and culture: Lessons from Africa*. New York: Cambridge University Press.

Levy, R. (1996). Essential contrasts: Differences in parental ideas about learners and teaching in Tahiti and Nepal. In S. Harkness & C. M. Super (Eds.), *Parents' cultural belief systems: Their origins, expressions, and consequences* (pp. 123–142). New York: Guilford Press.

Lutz, C. (1983). Parental goals, ethnopsychology, and the development of emotional meaning. *Ethos, 11*, 246–263.

Lutz, C. A. (1988). *Unnatural emotions: Everyday sentiments on a Micronesian atoll and their challenge to Western theory*. Chicago: University of Chicago Press.

Malinowski, B. (1935). *Coral gardens and their magic* (Vol. 1). New York: American Book.

Mann, J., Ten Have, T., Plunkett, J. W., & Meisels, S. J. (1991). Time sampling: A methodological critique. *Child Development, 62,* 227–241.

Maxwell, J. A. (1992). Undertanding and validity in qualitative research. *Harvard Educational Review, 62,* 279–300.

McCall, R. B. (1977). Challenges to a science of developmental psychology. *Child Development, 48,* 333–344.

Mead, M. (1966). *Growing up in New Guinea: A comparative study of primitive education.* New York: William Morrow. (Original work published 1930)

Menon, U., & Shweder, R. A. (1994). Kali's tongue: Cultural psychology and the power of shame in Orissa, India. In S. Kitayama & H. R. Markus (Eds.), *Emotion and culture: Empirical studies of mutual influence* (pp. 241–283). Washington, DC: American Psychological Association.

Meyers, R. (1992). *The twelve who survive: Strengthening programmes of early childhood development in the Third World.* New York: Routledge.

Miles, M., & Huberman, A. M. (1994). *Qualitative data analysis: An expanded sourcebook* (4th ed.). Thousand Oaks, CA: Sage.

Miller, P. J., & Goodnow, J. J. (1995). Cultural practices: Toward an integration of culture and development. In J. J. Goodnow, P. J. Miller, & F. Kessel (Eds.), *Cultural practices as contexts for development: New directions for child development* (Vol. 67, pp. 5–16) San Francisco: Jossey-Bass.

Miller, P. J., & Hoogstra, L. (1992). Language as tool in the socialization and apprehension of cultural meanings. In T. Schwartz, G. M. White, & C. A. Lutz (Eds.), *New directions in psychological anthropology* (pp. 83–101). Cambridge, England; Cambridge University Press.

Minturn, L., & Lambert, W. W. (1964). *Mothers of six cultures: Antecedents of child rearing.* New York: Wiley.

Munroe, R. H., & Munroe, R. L. (1971). Household density and infant care in an East African society. *Journal of Social Psychology, 83,* 3–13.

Munroe, R. H., Munroe, R. L., Michelson, C., Koel, A., Bolton, R., & Bolton, C. (1983). Time allocation in four societies. *Ethnology, 22,* 355–370.

Munroe, R. L., & Munroe, R. H. (1986). Field work in cross-cultural psychology. In W. J. Lonner & J. W. Berry (Eds.), *Field methods in cross-cultural research* (pp. 111–136). London: Sage.

Munroe, R. L., & Munroe, R. H. (1992). Fathers in children's environments: A four culture study. In B. S. Hewlett (Ed.), *Father–child relations: Cultural and biosocial contexts* (pp. 213–229). New York: Aldine de Gruyter.

Murdock, G. P. (1945). The common denominator of culture. In R. Linton (Ed.), *The science of man in the world crisis* (pp. 51–69). New York: Columbia University Press.

Nerlove, S., Roberts, J. M., Klein, R. E., Yarbrough, C., & Habicht, J. P. (1974). Natural indicators of cognitive ability. *Ethos, 2,* 265–295.

Ochs, E. (1988). *Culture and language development.* Cambridge, England: Cambridge University Press.

Ochs, E., & Schieffelin, B. B. (1984a). *Acquiring conversational competence*. Boston: Routledge & Kegan Paul.

Ochs, E., & Schieffelin, B. (1984b). Language acquisition and socialization: Three developmental stories and their implications. In R. A. Shweder & R. A. LeVine (Eds.), *Culture theory: Essays on mind, self, and emotion* (pp. 276–322). Cambridge, England: Cambridge University Press.

Pellegrini, A. D., & Stanic, G. M. A. (1993). Locating children's mathematical competence: Application of the developmental niche. *Journal of Applied Developmental Psychology, 14,* 501–520.

Plomin, R., DeFries, J. C., & Loehlin, J. C. (1977). Genotype–environment interaction and correlation in the analysis of human behavior. *Psychological Bulletin, 84,* 309–322.

Rabain-Jamin, J. (1994). Language and socialization of the child in African families living in France. In P. M. Greenfield & R. R. Cocking (Eds.), *Cross-cultural roots of minority child development* (pp. 147–166). Hillsdale, NJ: Erlbaum.

Raghavan, C., Harkness, S., & Super, C. M. (1993, March). *Indian and American parents' ethnotheories of female gender role identity*. Paper presented at the annual meeting of the Society for Research in Child Development, New Orleans, LA.

Rogoff, B. (1978). Spot observations: An introduction and examination. *Newsletter of the Institute for Comparative Human Development, 2,* 21–26.

Rogoff, B., Mistry, J., Göncü, A., & Mosier, C. (1993). Guided participation in cultural activity by toddlers and caregivers. *Monographs of the Society for Research in Child Development, 58*(8, Serial No. 236).

Romney, A. K., Weller, S. C., & Batchelder, W. H. (1986). Culture as consensus: A theory of culture and informant activity. *American Anthropologist, 88,* 313–338.

Schieffelin, B. B. (1979). Getting it together: An ethnographic approach to the study of the development of communicative competence. In E. Ochs & B. B. Schieffelin (Eds.), *Developmental pragmatics* (pp. 103–137). New York: Academic Press.

Shwalb, D. W., & Shwalb, B. (1996). *Japanese child rearing: Two generations of scholarship*. New York: Guilford Press.

Shweder, R., & LeVine, R. A. (1984). *Culture theory: Essays on mind, self, and emotion*. Cambridge, England: Cambridge University Press.

Shweder, R. A., Mahapatra, M., & Miller, J. G. (1990). Culture and moral development. In J. W. Stigler, R. A. Shweder, & G. Herdt (Eds.), *Cultural psychology: Essays on comparative human development* (pp. 130–204). Cambridge, England: Cambridge University Press.

Spiro, M. E. (1951). Culture and personality: The natural history of a false dichotomy. *Psychiatry, 14,* 19–46.

Steward, J. H. (1955). *Theory of culture change: The methodology of multilinear evolution*. Urbana: University of Illinois Press.

Super, C. M. (1976). Environmental effects on motor development: The case of

African infant precocity. *Developmental Medicine and Child Neurology, 18,* 561–567.

Super, C. M. (1981). Behavioral development in infancy. In R. H. Munroe, R. L. Munroe, & B. B. Whiting (Eds.), *Handbook of cross-cultural human development* (pp. 181–270). New York: Garland Press.

Super, C. M. (1984). Sex differences in infant care and vulnerability. *Journal of Medical Anthropology, 8,* 84–90.

Super, C. M. (1987). The role of culture in developmental disorder: Introduction. In C. M. Super (Ed.), *The role of culture in developmental disorder* (pp. 1–8). New York: Academic Press.

Super, C. M. (1991). Developmental transitions of cognitive functioning in rural Kenya and metropolitan America. In K. Gibson, M. Konner, & J. Lancaster (Eds.), *The brain and behavioral development: Biosocial dimensions* (pp. 225–257). Chicago: Aldine.

Super, C. M., & Harkness, S. (1982a). The development of affect in infancy and early childhood. In D. A. Wagner & H. W. Stevenson (Eds.), *Cultural perspectives on child development* (pp. 1–19). New York: Freeman.

Super, C. M., & Harkness, S. (1982b). The infant's niche in rural Kenya and metropolitan America. In L. L. Adler (Ed.), *Cross-cultural research at issue* (pp. 47–56). New York: Academic Press.

Super, C. M., & Harkness, S. (1986a). The developmental niche: A conceptualization at the interface of child and culture. *International Journal of Behavioral Development, 9,* 545–569.

Super, C. M., & Harkness, S. (1986b). Temperament, culture, and development. In R. Plomin & J. Dunn (Eds.), *The study of temperament: Changes, continuities, and challenges* (pp. 131–150). Hillsdale, NJ: Erlbaum.

Super, C. M., & Harkness, S. (1993). Temperament and the developmental niche. In W. B. Carey & S. A. McDevitt (Eds.), *Prevention and early intervention: Individual differences as risk factors for the mental health of children—a Festschrift for Stella Chess and Alexander Thomas* (pp. 115–125). New York: Brunner/Mazel.

Super, C. M., & Harkness, S. (1994). The cultural regulation of temperament–environment interactions. *Researching Early Childhood, 2,* 59–84.

Super, C. M., & Harkness, S. (1996). *Differences in the perception of newborn behavior.* Manuscript submitted for publication.

Super, C. M., & Harkness, S. (1997). The cultural structuring of child development. In J. W. Berry, P. Dasen, & T. S. Saraswathi (Eds.), *Handbook of cross-cultural psychology: Vol. 2: Basic processes and human development* (pp. 1–39). Needham Heights, MA: Allyn & Bacon.

Super, C. M., Harkness, S., van Tijen, N., van der Vlugt, E., Dykstra, J., & Fintelman, M. (1996). The three R's of Dutch child rearing and the socialization of infant arousal. In S. Harkness & C. M. Super (Eds.), *Parents' cultural belief systems: Their origins, expressions, and consequences* (pp. 447–466). New York: Guilford Press.

Super, C. M., Keefer, C. H., & Harkness, S. (1994). Child care and infectious respiratory disease during the first two years of life in a rural Kenyan community. *Social Science and Medicine, 38,* 227–229.

Tharp, R. G., Jordan, C., Speidel, G. E., Au, K. H., Klein, T. W., Calkins, R. P., Sloat, K. C., & Gallimore, R. (1984). Product and process in applied developmental research: Education and the children of a minority. In M. E. Lamb, A. L. Brown, & B. Rogoff (Eds.), *Advances in developmental psychology* (Vol. 3, pp. 91–141). Hillsdale, NJ: Erlbaum.

Triandis, H. C. (1994a). *Culture and social behavior.* New York: McGraw-Hill.

Triandis, H. C. (1994b). Culture and social behavior. In W. J. Lonner & R. Malpass (Eds.), *Psychology and culture* (pp. 169–173). Needham Heights, MA: Allyn & Bacon.

Vogel, S. H. (1996). Urban middle-class Japanese family life, 1958–93: A personal and evolving perspective. In D. Shwalb & B. Shwalb (Eds.), *Japanese child rearing: Two generations of scholarship* (pp. 177–200). New York: Guilford Press.

Wallace, A. F. (1961). *Culture and personality.* New York: Random House.

Wassman, J., & Dasen, P. R. (1994). "Hot" and "cold": Classification and sorting among Yupno of Papua New Guinea. *International Journal of Psychology, 29,* 19–38.

Watson-Gegeo, K., & Gegeo, D. (1977). From verbal play to talk story: The role of routines in speech events among Hawaiian children. In Ervin-Tripp & C. Mitchell-Kernan (Eds.), *Child discourse* (pp. 67–90). New York: Academic Press.

Weisner, T. (1996). Why ethnography should be the most important method in the study of human development. In A. Colby, R. Jessor, & R. Shweder (Eds.), *Ethnography and human development: Context and meaning in social inquiry* (pp. 305–324). Chicago: University of Chicago Press.

Weisner, T. S., Gallimore, R., & Jordan, C. (1988). Unpackaging cultural effects on classroom learning: Native Hawaiian peer assistance and child-generated activity. *Anthropology and Education Quarterly, 19,* 327–351.

Weisner, T. S., & Garnier, H. (1992). Nonconventional family life-styles and school achievement: A 12-year longitudinal study. *American Educational Research Journal, 29,* 605–632.

Weisner, T. S., Matheson, C. C., & Bernheimer, L. P. (1996). American cultural models of early influence and parent recognition of developmental delays: Is earlier always better than later? In S. Harkness & C. M. Super (Eds.), *Parents' cultural belief systems: Their origins, expressions, and consequences* (pp. 496–532). New York: Guilford Press.

Weller, S. C., & Romney, A. K. (1988). *Systematic data collection.* Newbury Park, CA: Sage.

White, G. M. (1994). Affecting culture: Emotion and morality in everyday life. In S. Kitayama & H. R. Markus (Eds.), *Emotion and culture: Empirical studies of mutual influence* (pp. 219–239). Washington, DC: American Psychological Association.

Whiting, B. B., & Edwards, C. P. (1988). *Children of different worlds: The formation of social behavior.* Cambridge, MA: Harvard University Press.

Whiting, B. B., & Whiting, J. W. (1960). Contributions of anthropology to the methods of studying child rearing. In P. H. Mussen (Ed.), *Handbook of research methods in child development* (pp. 918–944). New York: Wiley.

Whiting, B. B., & Whiting, J. W. (1975). *The children of six cultures: A psychocultural analysis.* Cambridge, MA: Harvard University Press.

Whiting, J. W. (1994). Fifty years as a behavioral scientist: Autobiographical notes. In E. H. Chasdi (Ed.), *Culture and human development: The selected papers of John Whiting* (pp. 14–41). Cambridge, England: Cambridge University Press.

Wolfgang, A. (1979). *Nonverbal behavior: Applications and cultural implications.* New York: Academic Press.

Worthman, C. M. (1994). Developmental microniche: A concept for modeling relationships of biology, behavior, and culture in development. *American Journal of Physical Anthropology* (Suppl. 18), 210.

Worthman, C. M. (1995). Biocultural bases of human variation. *ISSBD Newsletter, 27*(1), 10–13.

Worthman, C. M., Stallings, J. F., & Jenkins, C. L. (1993). Developmental effects of sex-differentiated parental care among Hagahai foragers. *American Journal of Physical Anthropology* (Suppl. 16), 212.

V

INTEGRATION ACROSS SETTINGS

11

HUMAN DEVELOPMENT IN THE AGE OF THE INTERNET: CONCEPTUAL AND METHODOLOGICAL HORIZONS

DANIEL STOKOLS

The 1970s gave rise to a new and innovative paradigm in human development research—*the ecology of human development* (Bronfenbrenner, 1977, 1979; cf. Wapner, 1987, and Wohlwill & Heft, 1987). This evolving *bioecological* paradigm is broadly concerned with the environmental conditions and transactional processes that occur in multiple settings and that exert a cumulative influence on the course of individuals' development over the life span (Bronfenbrenner, chapter 1 this volume). If developmental psychology prior to the early 1970s focused on "the strange behavior of children in strange situations with strange adults for the briefest periods of time" (Bronfenbrenner, 1977, p. 513), the chapters in this volume demonstrate the profound changes in conceptual and methodological orientation that have occurred over the past two decades in human development research. In contrast to earlier developmental studies, the research programs described in these chapters reveal the broader contextual

I thank Sarah Friedman, Kristen Day, Jeanne Tsai, Ellen Greenberger, and Theodore Wachs for their helpful comments on a version of this chapter.

scope of ecological analyses by encompassing the multiple environmental settings—homes, neighborhoods, child-care settings, schools, workplaces, institutional environments, and whole communities—that make up the ecology of development and the multiple life stages in which developmental processes unfold—infancy, childhood, adolescence, young and middle adulthood, and older adulthood.

The goals of the present chapter are twofold. The first goal is to identify convergent theoretical, methodological, and empirical themes reflected in the preceding chapters. The research programs outlined in these chapters reveal critical environmental conditions and transactional processes that significantly affect developmental outcomes within particular settings and stages of the life course. The concepts and research findings discussed in these chapters have important practical implications for environmental design, community planning, and public policy. The second goal of the chapter is to consider conceptual and methodological issues that have been neglected in prior developmental studies. These research "gaps" pose important questions and directions for future research on the ecology of human development.

The discussion of conceptual and methodological "horizons" in the latter portion of the chapter is organized around a topic that has received scant attention in earlier developmental research, that is, the impact of the Internet on the ecology of human development. This topic raises fundamental questions about the conceptualization and measurement of environment–development transactions and suggests several new directions for future research. The extraordinary growth of the Internet in recent years highlights the accelerating pace of societal change and the developmental significance of macrosystemic shifts that have occurred over the past 20 years. The concluding sections of the chapter explore the ways in which these contextual transformations are likely to alter the developmental processes that take place within the major settings and stages of people's lives.

CORE THEMES IN RESEARCH ON THE ECOLOGY OF HUMAN DEVELOPMENT

The chapters in this volume reflect certain convergent themes and assumptions. These core assumptions include the following: (a) Within each stage of the life course, an individual's routine activity system is made up of multiple, interrelated environmental settings (Bronfenbrenner, 1979; Magnusson, 1981; Stokols, 1982); (b) the different settings and the environmental conditions that exist within them vary in their capacity to affect developmental processes and outcomes for better or for worse; (c) the effects of particular environmental conditions on developmental processes and outcomes may be mediated by personal attributes and dispositions and moderated by contextual circumstances (Bronfenbrenner, 1992, chapter 1, this volume); (d) the environmental conditions that are spatially proximal to the individual may influence not only short-term developmental processes and outcomes but also processes and outcomes that are temporally remote; and (e) the environmental conditions that are geographically removed from an individual's immediate life situation may exert direct or indirect influence on his or her developmental processes and outcomes, both in the short run and over more extended periods.

Taken together, the chapters in this volume reflect the broad *spatial*, *temporal*, and *sociocultural scope* of ecological research on human development. That is, they consider places, processes, and events occurring within an extended rather than a narrow region of an individual's or group's geographical environment and within an expanded rather than an abbreviated period of the life span (Stokols, 1987). Accordingly, these chapters examine not only the environment–development transactions occurring within a specified setting (the microsystem) but also the ways in which functional links between two or more settings (i.e., the mesosystem, exosystem, macrosystem, and chronosystem; cf. Bronfenbrenner, 1986, 1992; Brown, chapter 3, this volume; Friedman & Amadeo, chapter 5, this volume; Talbert & McLaughlin, chapter 7, this volume) influence developmental processes and outcomes. Moreover, a number of the chapters identify developmentally relevant facets of an individual's or group's sociocultural environment and, as such, reflect broader sociocultural scope and explicit concern with macrosystem conditions than has been evident in earlier, more narrowly gauged developmental studies (Brown, chapter 3, this volume; Schooler, chapter 8, this volume; Super & Harkness, chapter 10, this volume).

The broad contextual scope of the bioecological paradigm is rarely encompassed by a single research program, because most empirical studies tend to focus (because of resource and time constraints) on developmental processes occurring within delimited categories of settings (e.g., homes, child-care settings, or workplaces) and phases of the life span (e.g., infancy, adolescence, or adulthood). Faced with practical constraints on gathering developmental data over multiple life stages and across diverse community settings, many if not most ecologically oriented research programs concentrate their attention on more fine-grained analyses of the linkages between environmental conditions, developmental processes, and outcomes as they occur within particular categories of settings. Yet, by comparing the methods and findings presented in each of the preceding chapters, it is possible to gain a broader view of the ecology of development as a whole and to identify conceptual and methodological issues that have been neglected in earlier studies and that warrant greater attention in future research.

The Effective Context of Development Within Particular Settings and Life Stages

Each of the research programs presented in this volume identifies environmental conditions that affect developmental processes and outcomes within specified settings and life stages. By revealing these psychologically significant qualities of settings, each chapter broadens our understanding of the *effective context* of development—those contextual circumstances that exert the most profound influence on developmental processes and that afford the greatest explanatory power in analyses of the relationships between environment and development (Stokols, 1987; Wachs, 1989).

The effective context for a given set of environment–development transactions is never completely specifiable, because the range of situational factors that influence those transactions is potentially infinite and the future environmental conditions that may impinge on individuals and groups can only be estimated rather than predicted unequivocally (Manicas & Secord, 1983). Nonetheless, the hypothetical notion of an effective context is useful in prompting researchers to consider the plausible range of situational factors that are likely to influence development within specified times and places and to distinguish (on the basis of prior theory, research, and intuition) among those factors in terms of their relative affect on developmental processes and outcomes.

The notion that some environmental conditions influence development more profoundly than others is reasonably straightforward. However, the process of identifying the effective context of development is a painstaking and complex endeavor. First, the developmental processes and outcomes that occur within specific settings and life stages must be identified by the researcher. Then, the environmental circumstances associated with these settings and life stages that may influence developmental processes and outcomes must be cataloged. Finally, empirical relationships among the specified environmental factors, developmental processes, and outcomes can systematically be observed.

The research programs presented in the preceding chapters have begun to address these complexities of ecological research on human development in at least three important respects. First, at a conceptual level, the chapters contribute taxonomies of key environmental conditions, developmental processes, and outcomes within particular types of environmental settings and stages of the life course. Second, the chapters reveal the methodological pluralism inherent in ecological studies of human development. That is, they effectively combine multiple methods (e.g., adults' and children's self-reports, behavioral observations, time-use surveys, standardized achievement tests, and analyses of archival or ethnographic data) to yield convergent information about the form and consequences of environment–development transactions. Third, by using these multiple methodologies, the chapters empirically document setting-specific and stage-dependent linkages among environmental conditions, developmental processes, and outcomes.

Taxonomic, Methodological, and Empirical Contributions of Earlier Research

An emphasis on descriptive and taxonomic concerns is characteristic of new scientific paradigms during their early stages of development (Altman, 1968). The definition and classification of potentially important predictor, moderator, mediating, and outcome variables provide the necessary foundation for theory development and inferential research. Over the past two decades, several useful taxonomies of environmental variables, developmental processes, and developmental outcomes have emerged. For example, Wachs (1989) contributed a classification of environmental conditions within infants' residential environments. Wachs's taxonomy incorporates three major dimensions of stimulation (background vs. focal, responsive vs. nonresponsive, and animate vs. inanimate) to identify eight prototypic clusters of physical and social conditions within infants' homes. These eight categories of environmental stimulation are arrayed along a continuum ranging from background/nonresponsive/inanimate stimulation at one extreme to focal/responsive/animate stimulation at the other. The former category characterizes primarily physical environments, whereas the latter category is more descriptive of the social qualities of home environments.

Wachs's chapter (chapter 12, this volume) offers an elaboration of his earlier taxonomy by incorporating the additional dimensions of physical stimulus modalities (visual, auditory, and tactual–kinesthetic), the complexity of the developing person's psychological environment, and the stability or variety of objective features of the individual's physical environment. These additional dimensions, in combination with those included in Wachs's (1989) earlier classification system, provide a framework for studies of environment–development transaction in which individual and environmental characteristics are integrated within the same conceptual units, rather than treated as separate and independent of each other.

The taxonomy developed by Wachs (1989) to classify the environmental conditions of infants' homes provided the conceptual framework for subsequent empirical studies documenting the adverse impact of distracting background stimulation (resulting from higher levels of crowding, traffic, and noise in the home) on parents' involvement with and responsiveness toward their infants (cf. Wachs & Camli, 1991; Wachs & Gruen, 1982). Wachs (1979) also found that the intensity and duration of background noise in the home are negatively correlated with various measures of infants' cognitive development over a 1-year interval. Yet, the availability of a "stimulus shelter" in the home (a room or other area where the child can be alone, out of the range of noise and other people) is positively correlated with infants' cognitive development.

Wachs's (1989; Wachs & Camli, 1991; Wachs & Gruen, 1982) research is valuable in that it classifies developmentally relevant features of home environments into theoretically meaningful categories and demonstrates the ways in which distracting background stimulation can interfere with critical developmental processes (e.g., sustained parent interaction with, and parents' responsiveness toward, their children). These critical environment–development transactions exemplify what Bronfenbrenner (chapter 1, this volume) refers to as "proximal processes" (i.e., sustained patterns of interaction between the developing person and his or her surroundings that occur over extended periods).

Bradley's (chapter 2, this volume) program of research on home environments also contributes a classification of developmentally significant features of residential settings (e.g., parental responsivity and acceptance, diversity of stimulation, and presence of learning materials), in which the relative impact on development varies over the stages of infancy, early childhood, middle childhood, and adolescence. Bradley's research on the developmental effects of these variables as reported in this chapter examines four major categories of proximal processes associated with home environments: (a) *sustenance* of the child, (b) *stimulation* of developmentally enhancing activities, (c) *support* of the child's self-sustaining capacities, and (d) *control* over the amount and pattern of inputs experienced by the child. The effective context of development encompasses environmental conditions that either enhance or impair these processes (e.g., the diversity of play materials available to infants, the predictability of activity schedules in the home, and the levels of social and emotional support provided to children; Bradley & Caldwell, 1976). An especially important feature of home environments, identified by Bradley & Caldwell, is the extent to which an ambience of family cohesion and harmony (vs. conflict) prevails in the home—a contextual circumstance that exerts a highly positive influence on children's social and intellectual development.

The research described by Friedman and Amadeo (chapter 5, this volume) on child-care environments further highlights the central importance of classification systems in ecological studies of development. Even within particular categories of settings and life stages, there are striking variations in the structure and organization of child-care environments. For instance, Friedman and Amadeo define the child-care environment as "a place as well as a social milieu in which children spend time on a regular basis when their mother is unavailable" (p. 127). They also note that to assess the child-care environment, the researcher must first determine who provides the care, who is cared for, where the care is provided, and how the care is provided (e.g., the diverse arrangements reflected in relatives' and family-based care vs. center-based care). Moreover, children's experiences of child care can be measured "in terms of the interactions the child has with the provider, peers, and objects in the child-care environment" (p. 128) as well as the duration and stability of those interactions (cf. Clarke-Stewart, Gruber, & Fitzgerald, 1994; McCartney, 1984). The researcher's decisions about which environmental features and interactional processes to focus on, and at what level of detail, depend largely on the goals of the assessment (e.g., for licensing, accreditation, or research purposes), the conceptual framework underlying the research, and the methods of measurement that are available.

To the extent that child care is provided in places located away from the child's home, the nature of the relationships between these different settings making up the home/child-care environment mesosystem must be considered—especially the ways in which multiple environments jointly influence developmental processes and outcomes. Friedman and Amadeo (chapter 5, this volume) note, for example, that it is important for parents to limit the number of different environments that they place their children in, because transitions in care from one setting to the next are difficult for children. They also suggest that developmental processes and outcomes are enhanced to the extent that functional links between the home and the child-care environment are established (e.g., parents' active involvement in and visitation of the child-care setting or child-care providers' periodical visitation of children in their homes).

The chapters by Talbert and McLaughlin (chapter 7, this volume) on assessing school environments, Vandell and Posner (chapter 6, this volume) on conceptualizing after-school settings, and Brown (chapter 3, this volume) on the measurement of adolescent peer environments also examine the ways in which multiple settings outside the home influence developmental processes and outcomes. For example, Talbert and McLaughlin use a bottom-up approach to analyze the ways in which children's classroom settings and proximal educational processes, in combination with the more distal qualities of school administrative structures and institutional cultures, jointly affect students' academic performance (e.g., their effort and achievement in math classes). They report that schools and school districts in which teachers report a strong sense of community and commitment to professionalism in their work effectively enhance students' educational experiences and academic achievement. This research reveals the strong exosystem influence of teachers' involvement in cohesive professional communities on their students' intellectual development.

Vandell and Posner (chapter 6, this volume) examine the links between children's homes, schools, neighborhoods, and after-school environments and document the ways in which these mesosystem relationships can influence the developmental effects of participation in after-school settings. They distinguish between different after-school arrangements (e.g., self-care, formal after-school programs, and informal after-school settings) and suggest that the developmental outcomes associated with these arrangements depend largely on the contextual circumstances present in children's homes, neighborhoods, and schools. For example, the self-care that occurs when children are left by their parents at home alone, or in the company of unsupervised peers, is less likely to have a positive influence on development than that which occurs when children remain at home under the supervision of a responsible older sibling. Also, the developmental benefits associated with children's participation in self-care or formal after-school programs may depend on the extent to which their neighborhoods have high or low rates of crime. Moreover, highly formalized after-school programs when combined with very structured and demanding curricula at school may exert a negative influence on children's social and emotional development by curtailing their opportunities to engage in self-initiated recreational and exploratory activities.

Brown's (chapter 3, this volume) conceptualization of peer environments reveals the complex ways in which adolescents' homes, neighborhoods, and cultural milieus are intertwined and jointly influence their emotional, social, and intellectual development (cf. Super & Harkness, chapter 10, this volume). Brown distinguishes among the adolescents' friendship groups on the basis of frequent face-to-face contact, the reputational "crowds" that they identify with at school or in their neighborhoods, and the more pervasive aspects of youth culture conveyed through the mass media and societal (generational) norms. The influence of these different facets of peer environments on adolescents' socioemotional and intellectual development can vary widely in relation to other contextual circumstances, such as authoritative versus nonauthoritative parenting styles, family educational values, school policies and curricula, ethnic composition of the childrens' neighborhood, adolescents' involvement in part-time employment settings, and community norms regarding cultural diversity (cf. Greenberger & Steinberg, 1986; Steinberg, Darling, Fletcher, Brown, & Dornbusch, 1995).

As individuals progress from childhood through adolescence and into adulthood, the geographic range of their routine activities widens as their personal autonomy and independence increase. Ecologically oriented studies of adults and older adults, thus, must grapple not only with the joint effects of multiple life settings on contemporaneous developmental processes and outcomes but also with the cumulative influence of environmental conditions experienced in earlier life stages on more recent developmental sequelae (Bronfenbrenner, 1992). In the research summarized by Schooler (chapter 8, this volume; Kohn & Schooler, 1982), he uses time series data to evaluate the links between the substantive complexity of adult workers' jobs (the extent to which a job requires thought and independent judgment), on the one hand, and their ideational flexibility and self-directed (vs. conformist) orientations, on the other. Schooler reports significant lagged correlations between job complexity and measures of intellectual flexibility and personal autonomy gathered 10 years later. Moreover, his analyses reveal that children's exposure to complex school work and family settings that encourage autonomy enhances their intellectual development and increases the likelihood that they will choose careers later in life involving complex work and independent judgment (cf. Schooler, 1984).

A recurring theme in several of the preceding chapters is that certain age groups and socioeconomic strata of the population are more vulnerable than others to the potentially harmful effects of environmental demands and stressors (Bronfenbrenner, chapter 1, this volume; Friedman & Amadeo, chapter 5, this volume; Vandell & Posner, chapter 6, this volume). For example, very young individuals and infirm older individuals may be especially susceptible to developmental disturbances caused by chronic exposure to noise, overcrowding, and inadequate housing (Evans, chapter 9, this volume; Lawton, chapter 4, this volume; Wachs, 1989). Moreover, individuals living in poverty are more likely to experience these stressors on a regular basis than are those who are economically and socially advantaged (Bullock, 1990; Huston, 1993). On the other hand, children raised in affluent households and older individuals who are in good health and psychologically proactive cope more effectively with complex environments and are better able to avoid the adverse health and developmental impacts of exposure to environmental stressors. Thus, the evidence from several research programs suggests that the level of congruence, or "fit," between an individual's environmental arrangements and his or her personal dispositions and resources may be a more crucial determinant of developmental outcomes than either environmental or personal factors considered separately (Caplan & Harrison, 1993; Kahana, 1982; Lawton, chapter 4, this volume; Michelson, 1985).

In summary, the preceding chapters contribute valuable taxonomic schemes for categorizing key environmental conditions, developmental processes, and outcomes associated with particular life settings and stages. Moreover, the chapter authors used in their research a variety of measurement strategies to assess the interrelations among these variables and the ways in which multiple settings influence development over the life course. Finally, the findings reported in these chapters suggest a variety of environmental design strategies to enhance developmental processes and outcomes over the life course. Some of these strategies are outlined in the following paragraphs.

Environmental Design Strategies to Enhance Human Development

Wachs' (1979, 1989) and Bradley's (chapter 2, this volume) studies of residential environments indicate that children's cognitive development is hindered by high levels of noise and other distracting stimuli in the home (cf. Wohlwill & Heft, 1987). Similarly, a field-experimental study conducted by Cohen, Glass, and Singer (1973) demonstrated the negative effects of chronic exposure to traffic noise on the development of children's reading and auditory discrimination skills, especially among those living in apartments closest to the highway. Together, these findings suggest the developmental value of incorporating adequate sound insulation materials in the design of home environments, providing secluded interior spaces (or stimulus shelters) that are separated from noisier family areas, and locating homes and apartments away from airports, freeways, and other sources of noise in the community.

The negative impacts of noise and distraction on developmental processes have also been documented in child-care and school settings. For instance, Moore's (1986; Moore & Lackney, 1993) research suggested that the provision of architecturally well-defined study spaces (or "activity pockets") in preschool and elementary school settings helps reduce children's susceptibility to noise distraction and, thereby, significantly increases their engagement with learning activities, attention span, exploratory behavior, and cooperation with peers in the classroom (Moore & Hart, 1989). Also, field experiments conducted by Cohen, Evans, Stokols, and Krantz (1986) and Evans, Hygge, and Bullinger (1995) reveal the adverse effects of chronic noise exposure (on short-term attentional tasks, reading comprehension, long-term memory, tolerance for frustration, and blood pressure) among third and fourth graders attending schools under the flight paths of major metropolitan airports and underscore the importance of locating schools and child-care environments in areas that are sufficiently distant from community noise sources.

At the neighborhood level, design strategies aimed at reducing traffic volume and noise can reduce or prevent environmental conditions that have the capacity to disrupt developmental processes and outcomes. For instance, Appleyard's (1981) field-experimental study of vehicular traffic in residential neighborhoods demonstrates the profoundly negative impact of exposure to heavy traffic volume and excessive traffic noise on social contacts among neighbors, neighbors' collective sense of community, and parents' concerns about children's exposure to traffic hazards when they venture outside their homes or apartments. Appleyard's findings suggested that urban planning strategies aimed at diverting heavy vehicular traffic away from residential neighborhoods will, in the long run, effectively promote a variety of positive developmental consequences for residents and their children.

The negative effects of ambient noise and distraction on developmental processes and outcomes have been observed across a variety of environmental settings and life stages. Thus, the empirical evidence for designing homes, neighborhoods, child-care environments, and schools in ways that protect children from unwanted noise and distraction is quite strong. There is also considerable evidence that the ability to avoid unwanted distraction and to regulate privacy in social settings is psychologically important to adults working in offices and factories (Sundstrom, 1986), patients in health-care settings (Carpman & Grant, 1993), and older adults residing in urban neighborhoods (Carp & Carp, 1987; Lawton, chapter 4, this volume). However, the empirical links between chronic noise exposure in these settings and impaired developmental outcomes (other than stress and environmental satisfaction indices) are less well established for these populations than among noise-exposed children in home, school, child-care, and neighborhood settings.

The developmental outcomes associated with exposure to alternative design arrangements warrant further study in future research. In addition to documenting the developmental benefits of environmental designs that reduce individuals' exposure to noise and other distracting stimuli, future studies also should evaluate the developmental value of design arrangements that (a) enhance the responsivity and informational quality of children's home, day-care, and school settings (Bradley, chapter 2, this volume; Friedman & Amadeo, chapter 5, this volume; Vandell & Posner, chapter 6, this volume); (b) incorporate flexible design elements (e.g., adjustable interior partitions) to facilitate privacy regulation and environmental controllability in residential and work settings (cf. Altman, 1975; Stokols, 1998; Sundstrom, 1986); (c) enhance residents' sense of security and "defensible space" in their homes and neighborhoods (cf. Newman, 1973; Taylor, 1987; Taylor, Shumaker, & Gottfredson, 1985); (d) increase older residents' opportunities for environmental "proactivity" by providing them ready access to commercial and transit services in their neighborhoods (cf. Carp & Carp, 1987; Lawton, chapter 4, this volume; Parmelee & Lawton, 1990); (e) afford children and adults access to natural elements (e.g., plants, water, views of parks, and wooded areas) and opportunities to participate in "restorative" settings (cf. Hartig, Mang, & Evans, 1991; Kaplan & Kaplan, 1989); and (f) provide symbolic elements in residential and community settings to enhance individuals' sense of personal and collective identity (Carr, Francis, Rivlin, & Stone, 1992; Rochberg-Halton & Csikszentmihalyi, 1981; Rowles, 1981; Stokols, 1990).

CONCEPTUAL AND METHODOLOGICAL HORIZONS OF HUMAN DEVELOPMENT RESEARCH

The articulation (and validation) of environmental design strategies to enhance human development over the life course is but one of several important directions for future research. The remaining sections of the chapter examine additional issues that warrant greater attention in future research on the ecology of human development. The discussion of conceptual and methodological horizons of developmental research is organized around the emergence and rapid growth of the Internet, because the advent of modern telecommunication technologies highlights the growing importance and influence of macrosystem changes on developmental processes and outcomes over the life course.

Implications of the Internet for the Ecology of Human Development

During the past 5 years, the World Wide Web and the Internet have grown exponentially. According to a recent survey of Web usage, the number of recorded sites on the World Wide Web grew from 10,022 to 650,000 between December, 1993, and January, 1997—a 65-fold increase (Gray, 1996). Moreover, between January, 1993, and July, 1997, the number of Internet hosts (i.e., machine addresses on the Internet reported by name servers) expanded from 1.3 million to 19.5 million (Network Wizards, 1997). The number of American households using the Internet grew from 3.1 million in 1994 to an estimated 28 million by 1998 (Emerging Technologies Research Group, 1997). Although it is impossible to measure precisely the number of individual Internet users, a recent survey estimated that in the United States alone, nearly 40 million adults now use the Internet, as compared with 8.4 million adult Internet users in 1995, and more than 9.8 million American children presently use the Internet—a 444% increase since 1995 (Find/SVP, 1997a, 1997b).

The rapid growth of the Internet during the 1990s has dramatically altered the ecology of human development and raises profound questions about the conceptualization and measurement of environment–development transactions in the foreseeable future. On the one hand, the Internet might appear to be an exotic and limited influence on human development, considering that its use is confined to relatively affluent populations and to regions of the world where the requisite equipment and telecommunication infrastructure for Internet access (e.g., phone lines, desktop computers, and high-speed modems) are available (U.S. Department of Commerce, 1995). Moreover, the developmental influence of the Internet would seem to be confined to those age groups most frequently exposed to this new technology—especially older children, adolescents, and working adults (Yankelovich Partners, 1995).

On the other hand, it is conceivable that the Internet will also exert a profound, albeit indirect, influence on those populations and age groups that are least likely to use it. For example, developmental deficits among children living in poverty may become more severe as the Internet widens the rift between information-rich and information-poor segments of the world's population. Also, parents' use of desktop computers in the home may have either positive or negative developmental consequences for their infants and toddlers, depending on whether the time they spend on the Internet enhances the educational quality of the home or, alternatively, diminishes their responsiveness to their children during the hours they are on-line.

The preceding observations suggest that the capacity of the Internet to influence developmental processes and outcomes depends largely on the context surrounding its use and availability. In the context of affluence, access to the Internet can engender positive developmental processes and outcomes by exposing individuals to new information and stimulation, thereby fostering a more active and structuring orientation toward the environment. Under these circumstances, the Internet functions as a "developmentally instigative" feature of the individual's environment (Bronfenbrenner, 1992; cf. Schooler, 1984, chapter 8, this volume). In the context of poverty, however, restricted opportunities to learn about and use the Internet can impede children's developmental progress, in contrast to that of more affluent children who have ready access to this increasingly prevalent and powerful technology.

The bivalent nature of the Internet (i.e., its capacity to either support or constrain developmental processes and outcomes depending on contextual circumstances) is evident even among relatively affluent groups. For instance, the Internet and the World Wide Web afford convenient access to a tremendous amount of information, "distance learning" opportunities, and the capacity to communicate regularly and informally with an ever-widening circle of friends, colleagues, and on-line acquaintances. Yet, daily exposure to a surfeit of information and the demands of on-line communication can lead to stimulation overload, distraction from important tasks, and, ultimately, chronic stress and fatigue among working parents and professionally oriented adults (cf. Davidson, 1996; Glass & Singer, 1972; Hartig et al., 1991; Kaplan & Kaplan, 1989). Moreover, concerns have been raised about the questionable authenticity of information posted on the Web (much of which is designed for quick consumption and marketing purposes) and the potentially negative impacts of excessive Internet use on the depth and quality of individuals' thinking and research skills (cf. Noam, 1995; Postman, 1992; Rothenberg, 1997; Stoll, 1995).

Also, as was noted earlier, parents' frequent use of home-based computers may interfere with developmental processes by constraining opportunities for parent–child interaction, thereby promoting an ambience of nonresponsiveness in family environments (cf. Bradley, chapter 2, this volume; Wachs, 1989). However, when families are geographically dispersed for prolonged periods, the Internet can facilitate information exchange and mutual support by enabling parents, grandparents, children, and siblings to stay in frequent contact with one another through the use of electronic mail. Thus, the developmentally instigative and socially supportive qualities of the Internet are likely moderated by the socioeconomic and situation-specific circumstances surrounding its use.

The burgeoning growth of the Internet and the World Wide Web and their capacity to exert both positive and negative effects on developmental processes and outcomes suggest that these telecommunication technologies be given more thorough consideration in future research. The next sections of the chapter identify important theoretical and methodological questions that remain to be examined in ecologically oriented studies of human development over the life span.

Theoretical Questions Concerning the Impact of the Internet and the World Wide Web on Human Development

The Internet encompasses the vast array of electronic connections that links millions of computers and their users throughout the world. The Internet is a highly diversified technology in that it supports several different forms of computer-mediated communication (CMC), such as electronic mail, electronic mail list serves (groups of electronic mail users organized around certain topics), electronic bulletin boards and newsgroups, and sites on the World Wide Web that range from noninteractive to interactive displays of textual, graphical, and auditory information and media. Among the most interactive of these Web sites are the multiuser domains (MUDs), which offer visitors and members opportunities to enter chat rooms, communicate with each other in real time, and manipulate graphical objects displayed at the site.

Individuals gain access to the Internet through either their desktop computers or their cable television systems. However, in contrast to television programming, which is passively received by viewers once a particular channel is selected, the Internet offers unprecedented opportunities for interactive exploration of electronic Web sites, MUDs, bulletin boards, and data archives (cf. Rheingold, 1993; Schuler, 1996). Under the best of circumstances, an individual's engagement with the Internet can function as a "developmentally instigative" proximal process—a sustained pattern of interaction between the person and his or her surroundings that fosters a more active and structuring orientation toward the environment (cf. Bradley, chapter 2, this volume; Bronfenbrenner, 1992, chapter 1, this volume; Schooler, 1984, chapter 8, this volume).

Yet, the capacity of the Internet to bring geographically distant information sources and electronically simulated, virtual places to one's computer or television screen raises several intriguing questions about the ecology of human development. These questions pertain to (a) the relative influence of proximal versus distal processes on human development, (b) the extent to which one's participation in a virtual environment via the Internet constitutes a mesosystem (spanning two or more settings in which the person is directly involved) or simply a microsystem (a particular place where one's computer is located and to which symbolic information is delivered electronically), (c) the circumstances under which an individual's participation in the Internet is likely to promote either positive or negative developmental processes and outcomes, and (d) the developmental implications of the Internet's exponential growth in light of humans' limited capacities for coping with information overload and accelerating rates of environmental change or "turbulence" (Emery & Trist, 1965).

Proximal and Distal Influences on Human Development

Studies of environment–development transactions typically focus on the conditions in one's immediate environment that influence his or her developmental processes and outcomes. This explicit focus on the developmental impacts of the perceptually salient, proximal environment is rooted in Lewin's (1936) conceptualization of the *psychological life space*—the totality of psychobiological conditions (e.g., perceptions, motivations, and salient features of the environment) that determines one's behavior at a specific moment within a particular place. Lewin referred to the nonsalient (nonperceived) features of the sociophysical environment as the *foreign hull* of the life space—those contextual circumstances located beyond the boundaries of the life space that, according to Lewin, are more amenable to sociological and biophysical studies than to psychological research.

Prior to the Internet's emergence as a powerful and pervasive force in society, the relative salience and developmental impact of environmental conditions were generally correlated with their geographic proximity and immediacy to the individual. With the advent of the Internet and the World Wide Web, however, individuals' opportunities to experience distant places and events are now much less bounded by spatial and temporal constraints (cf. Meyrowitz, 1985; Mitchell, 1995). Although non-Internet forms of communication (e.g., reading a book, watching television, talking with others on the telephone, or corresponding with them by surface or air mail) can bring geographically distant people and places psychologically closer to the individual, the Internet differs from these other media in some important respects.

First, electronic mail and the World Wide Web make it possible for an individual to communicate simultaneously and interactively with scores, and even hundreds, of other people (e.g., by participating in virtual chat rooms or through "instant messaging" among acquaintances who find themselves on-line at the same time). By contrast, television programs are experienced more passively than interactively, and telephone conversations are usually restricted to dyads (or to slightly larger groups participating in conference calls). In addition to affording simultaneous contact with a large number of other people, Internet-based communications often combine textual, graphic, and auditory modalities (e.g., real-time video images of the people one is communicating with as well as dynamic views of their physical surroundings). Printed media are quite capable of depicting faraway people and places through photographs, drawings, and text, but they do not provide real-time, interactive views of distant people and events, nor can they deliver nearly instantaneous, multimodal communications, as exemplified by electronic mailings that contain document, voice, and video attachments. Finally, in addition to the instantaneous, interactive, and multimodal qualities of electronic communications, the Internet and the World Wide Web also afford serendipitous encounters with large numbers of strangers in cyberspace and opportunities to explore hundreds and even thousands of communication channels (or Web sites) within relatively short intervals of time.

The capacity of the Internet to make remote places and events psychologically salient to those who use this new technology has important developmental implications for various age groups. Young children and adults with regular access to the Web, for example, are likely to be exposed to diverse cultural influences and vast stores of information, thereby broadening their understanding of the world and strengthening their sense of connection with remote people and places. Similarly, working adults can use the Internet to expand their personal skills and knowledge so that they are better equipped to perform effectively in their jobs. Also, older adults can now use the Internet to maintain a proactive orientation toward other people and places and their symbolic ties to the outside world and to counter feelings of loneliness and isolation, even as their physical mobility becomes more constrained with the passage of time (cf. Lawton, chapter 4, this volume; Rook, 1984; Rowles, 1981; SeniorNet, 1998; Seniors Computer Information Project, 1998).

In short, the rise of the Internet has altered the relative significance of proximal and distal features of the ecology of human development. A much broader array of remote places and events can now be brought squarely into the individual's consciousness or life space, through multimodal electronic simulations of virtual places and seemingly unlimited opportunities to experience those places and events via the Internet and the World Wide Web (cf. Mitchell, 1995; Rheingold, 1993; Stokols, 1995).

Delimiting the Micro-, Meso-, and Exosystem Contexts of Development

According to the bioecological paradigm, the ecology of development includes the major settings that make up an individual's micro-, meso-, exo-, and macrosystems within each stage of the life course. Before the Internet was established, the number and range of micro-, meso-, and exosystems making up a person's ecological environment at each stage of the life course were, for the most part, limited by the geographic and temporal boundaries of the individual's routine (e.g., daily, weekly, and monthly) activity system. With the rapid growth of the Internet in recent years, however, these earlier assumptions have become outmoded. Today, people with access to the Internet can explore and participate in a vast array of virtual places. Also, as these opportunities for involvement in virtual environments have expanded, the boundaries among one's micro-, meso-, and exosystems have become increasingly blurred.

Children, adolescents, and adults can now go to chat rooms, MUDs, and other electronic environments to interact with other people in real time. Is the contextual unit of these interactive processes the microsystem in which one's computer happens to be located or is it a new category of mesosystems that encompasses a particular sociophysical environment (e.g., a residence, classroom, day-care setting, and work site) and the virtual places that are experienced in that environment through computer-based access to the Internet? Similarly, when a parent or teacher accesses the Internet from a home office or classroom, do the electronic linkages between these real and virtual places constitute a new type of exosystem that has developmental consequences for the children participating in those residential and classroom environments?

Blanchard (1997), drawing on the principles of behavior setting analysis developed by Barker (1968) and Wicker (1987), defined *virtual behavior settings* as electronic sites on the Internet that are created through the shared interactions of members and that develop a symbolic sense of space or place through sustained computer-mediated communications among the participants in those sites (cf. Mitchell, 1995; Rheingold, 1993). The fact that virtual behavior settings are nested within face-to-face behavior settings (i.e., those from which the individual accesses the Internet and the World Wide Web via computer or cable television) raises further questions about the psychological and interpersonal tensions that can arise from a person's concurrent involvement in real and virtual behavior settings and the circumstances under which participation in the Internet either fosters or impedes positive developmental processes and outcomes.

Positive and Negative Effects of the Internet on Development

It might be assumed that the presence of a desktop computer wired to the Internet within a particular home, classroom, or work site is analogous to having a standard television set (one that is not connected to the Internet) available in those same environments. That is, both the computer and the television are inanimate objects that can transmit large amounts of symbolic information to those individuals participating in a particular environment—information that can be either educational and developmentally enhancing, on the one hand, or inane and distracting, on the other. This line of thinking would suggest that it is unnecessary, and even misleading, to invent new units of ecological analysis, such as virtual places and behavior settings, and pseudo meso- and exosystems that are defined in terms of the electronic and ephemeral links between virtual places nested within real ones.

Yet, in contrast to the more passive medium of television, it is the capacity of interactive Web sites to engage the exploratory tendencies of children and adults and to facilitate real-time communication between so many geographically dispersed people that makes the experience of virtual environments so similar to participating in real environments. In these respects, participating in the Internet and the World Wide Web via a desktop computer located in a particular place is tantamount to being in two or more places at the same time. Also, it is these highly engaging qualities of the Web that can lead to either detrimental conflicts or developmentally enhancing complementarities between one's simultaneous experiences of real and virtual environments.

To better understand the ways in which simulated electronic environments on the World Wide Web can influence developmental processes and outcomes, it is useful to differentiate between (a) meso- and exosystems that involve links between two or more real (sociophysical) settings and (b) those that involve a link between an actual environmental setting and at least one virtual setting on the Internet. The former categories of meso- and exosystems can be designated as *(r–r) units* that span two or more real settings and the latter as *(r–v) units* encompassing one or more real settings and at least one virtual environment.

For both (r–r) and (r–v) contextual units, the relationships between the different settings included in the specified meso- or exosystem can be characterized as complementary, neutral, or conflicting. *Complementary settings* are those in which the organizational goals and activities are consistent with each other and are mutually reinforcing. *Neutrally linked settings* are those in which the respective goals and activities neither reinforce nor interfere with each other. *Conflicting settings* are those in which the goals and activities are noncomplementary and are in opposition with each other.

Accordingly, *complementary (r–v) units* are those meso- and exosystems in which the virtual setting supports the goals and activities of the *host setting* (i.e., the sociophysical environment from which the Internet is accessed via computer or cable television). In terms of the bioecological perspective on development, the virtual setting in a complementary (r–v) unit enriches and supports the developmentally instigative qualities of the host setting. *Neutral (r–v) units* are those in which the virtual setting neither supports nor detracts from the activities and developmental resources of the host setting. Finally, *conflicting (r–v) units* are those in which the virtual setting disrupts or interferes with the activities and developmentally instigative qualities of the host setting.

The preceding definitions of complementary, neutral, and conflicting (r–v) units suggest that one's participation in virtual environments is most likely to promote positive developmental processes and outcomes in the context of complementary (r–v) units and is most likely to disrupt those processes and outcomes within a conflicting (r–v) meso- or exosystem. This prediction assumes, of course, that the goals and activities of the host setting are, themselves, developmentally positive rather than negative. To the extent that the goals and activities of the host setting are developmentally negative, conflicting inputs from virtual settings may actually promote rather than impair positive developmental processes and outcomes. For purposes of the present discussion, it is assumed that the goals and activities of the host setting are developmentally positive (or neutral) rather than negative.

An example of a complementary (r–v) mesosystem is an elementary school classroom where the teacher encourages his or her students to access educational Web sites from classroom computers, as an adjunct to the information covered in assigned readings and lectures. An example of a conflicting (r–v) unit, on the other hand, is a college dormitory room where students' excessive participation in computer-based chat rooms or virtual game sites detracts from their (or their roommate's) concentration on reading assigned texts or writing term papers. Similarly, an employee's participation in recreational Web sites while at work can decrease his or her productivity, undermine team performance, and evoke resentment among coworkers and supervisors. A more neutral (r–v) context would be one in which students' or employees' participation in interactive Web sites while at home, school, or work has neither positive nor negative impacts on the functioning of the host environment and neither disrupts nor enhances developmental processes and outcomes within that setting.

Although the inclusion of virtual environments in individuals' meso- and exosystems can sometimes be distracting and developmentally disruptive, the complete lack of opportunities to participate in the Internet is especially problematic for economically disadvantaged groups in society (U.S. Department of Commerce, 1995). The relative deprivation created by restricted access to the Internet among particular segments of society and regions of the world may have important developmental consequences for both individuals and groups. These issues are addressed later.

The Internet as a Source of Macrosystem Change

A unique feature of the Internet is its capacity to initiate and amplify macrosystemic changes in the ecology of human development. For instance, the fact that people separated by thousands of miles and multiple time zones can now communicate with one another in real time via Internet-based video, voice, and textual media suggests that the rate of information exchange across cultural and national boundaries will continue to accelerate in the coming decades. The increasing scope and pace of global communications have important implications for professional collaboration in scientific research, international cooperation in environmental management, and people's conceptions of the interdependent links between their immediate environments and more remote regions of the world.

An essential starting point for considering the Internet's potential to initiate and amplify macrolevel changes in the ecology of development is Bronfenbrenner's (1992) definition of the macrosystem:

> The macrosystem consists of the overarching pattern of micro-, meso-, and exosystems characteristic of a given culture, subculture, or other broader social context, with particular reference to the developmentally-instigative belief systems, resources, hazards, life styles, opportunity structures, life course options, and patterns of social exchange that are embedded in each of these systems. The macrosystem may be thought of as a societal blueprint for a particular culture, subculture, or other broader social context. (p. 228)

Consistent with this definition, the Internet and the World Wide Web are developmentally instigative resources (or opportunity structures) afforded by some macrosystems (e.g., affluent communities or cultural groups that emphasize educational values and achievement), but not others (e.g., economically disadvantaged communities or cultural groups that place less emphasis on educational attainment). Among those populations and world regions that have ready access to the Internet, the exchange of information through electronic mail and interactive Web sites is bringing diverse cultures and belief systems into closer contact with each other on a more frequent basis. This cross-pollination of cultural perspectives and world views has the potential to enhance cognitive and social development by encouraging greater ideational flexibility and a more exploratory, proactive orientation among Internet users (Schooler, chapter 8, this volume).

At the same time, the Internet and the World Wide Web are growing so quickly and are facilitating the exchange of so much information that the users of these new technologies are becoming more vulnerable to chronic distraction, stress, and stimulation overload (cf. Davidson, 1996; Glass & Singer, 1972; Kaplan & Kaplan, 1989). At societal and global levels, the exponential growth of the Internet and the rapid rate at which information is now transmitted and received are prompting unprecedented structural changes in economies, health care systems, educational institutions, informal social networks, leisure activities, and patterns of professional and scientific collaboration. Some of these societal changes are desirable and may promote positive developmental processes and outcomes. The extremely fast pace of these changes, however, poses certain dangers for the overall stability and predictability of the macrosystem. A fundamental proposition of bioecological theory posits that

> the degree of stability, consistency, and predictability over time in any element or level of the systems constituting an ecology of human development is critical for the effective operation of the system in question. Extremes either of disorganization or rigidity in structure or function represent danger signs for potential psychological growth, with some intermediate degree of system flexibility constituting the optimal condition for human development. (Bronfenbrenner, 1992, pp. 240–241)

One way in which the Internet can reduce levels of predictability in macrosystems is by facilitating individuals' spontaneous discovery of new information and their serendipitous encounters with strangers from far-flung regions of the world. As use of the Internet and the World Wide Web becomes more pervasive in society, chance encounters with other people and frequent exposure to new information are likely to have a greater influence on individuals' developmental processes and outcomes than in previous years (Stokols, 1988).

The Internet not only can reduce predictability by enabling chance encounters with other people and new information but can also amplify preexisting macrosystem conditions. This "deviation-amplifying" quality of the Internet is reflected in its capacity to magnify previously existing polarities or contradictory states within a macrosystem (Maruyama, 1963). For example, unequal access to the Internet and the World Wide Web among affluent versus low-income groups is likely to widen the rift between information-rich and information-poor segments of society—unless and until these technologies are made more available to economically deprived and underrepresented groups in future years. Similarly, preexisting tendencies in society toward racism, sexual harassment, strident political discourse, social incivilities, child abuse, and other criminal activities are now being channeled toward an increasingly large audience of Internet users (cf. Holman & Stokols, 1994; "Internet a Molester's Tool," 1997; Miller, 1995).

Finally, it is conceivable that individuals' routine use of the Internet will further restrict their participation in civic activities, thereby accelerating present trends toward the decline of "social capital"—those "features of social organization such as networks, norms, and social trust that facilitate coordination and cooperation for mutual benefit" (Putnam, 1995, p. 67). Alternatively, the emergence of virtual communities (Blumenstyk, 1997; Mitchell, 1995; Rheingold, 1993) may actually counter these trends by reinforcing democratic processes (Sclove, 1995) and by encouraging individuals' civic engagement and participation in communities of interest (Blanchard & Horan, 1997).

The impact of the Internet on macrosystem stability and predictability warrants explicit attention in future developmental research, in view of the potentially crucial consequences of these societal-level changes for individuals' development at each stage of the life course. Along these lines, Bronfenbrenner (1992) stressed "the importance of assessing the degree of stability vs. instability, both with respect to characteristics of the person and of context, at each level of the ecological system" (p. 241) in future research (cf. Wachs, chapter 12, this volume). This call for focused studies of the relationships between macrosystem change, unpredictability, and human development over the life course poses complex methodological questions, as outlined in the following paragraphs.

Methodological Challenges Posed by Studies of the Internet, the World Wide Web, and the Developmental Outcomes Over the Life Course

A major methodological challenge confronted in bioecological research is the difficulty of specifying and measuring the effective context of development—those conditions within multiple settings and life stages that have the greatest cumulative impact on developmental processes and outcomes (cf. Stokols, 1987; Wachs, 1989). Specification and measurement of the effective context are complex endeavors, owing to the broad geographic, temporal, and sociocultural scope of the developing person's ecology. Children and adults are typically engaged in multiple micro- and mesosystems and are influenced by numerous exo- and macrosystem conditions as well. Thus, it is perhaps not surprising that many if not most ecologically oriented studies have focused on developmental processes and outcomes that occur within a particular type of setting (e.g., a home, school, daycare center, and work site) and during delimited phases of the life span (e.g., infancy, childhood, and middle or older adulthood).

The strategy of focusing empirical studies on delimited categories of settings and life stages yields in-depth information about the targeted contexts of development and reduces the complexities associated with ecological research—especially the challenges of documenting (a) the complex array of contextual influences on development found within an individual's micro-, meso-, exo-, and macrosystems and (b) the cumulative developmental impact of these conditions over multiple life stages. Yet, the bioecological paradigm emphasizes the importance of studying the cumulative influence of contextual factors on development across multiple settings and stages of the life course (Schooler, chapter 8, this volume). For example, Bronfenbrenner (1992) stated the following:

> The concept of macrosystem includes not only the subculture in which the person has been raised, but also the subculture in which the person lives. The latter is defined by the personal and background characteristics of those with whom the person associates in the settings of everyday life. Any research design that includes a macrosystem contrast should therefore, to the extent possible, provide for securing identifying criteria from both of these domains. (p. 237)

The challenges of specifying the effective context of development across multiple settings and life stages are compounded by the difficulty of measuring the cumulative influence of virtual (as well as real) environments on developmental processes and outcomes. During a single computer session, individuals are capable of participating in a large number of virtual behavior settings located at several different Web sites (Blanchard, 1997; Mitchell, 1995; Rheingold, 1993; Schuler, 1996). Identification of the developmentally instigative qualities of these virtual environments, let alone their cumulative effects on the individual over extended periods, is a daunting task because of the ephemeral nature of electronically simulated settings and the difficulties of recording the duration, quality, and psychological impact of one's experiences with those settings while participating in the Internet and the World Wide Web.

To address these complex issues in future studies, a variety of methodological strategies will be required. Time budget analyses, such as those developed in the field of behavioral geography, can be used to assess individuals' time allocation to both real and virtual settings (cf. Lenntorp, 1978; Michelson, 1985). Also, physical trace measures (Zeisel, 1981) of individuals' participation in MUDs on the Internet, including printed transcripts of their America Online chat room conversations, have been used to record the duration and content of people's experiences with virtual environments (Wall, 1997). Retrospective, autobiographical interviews probing individuals' experiences with real and virtual environments—especially those that are highly memorable and that are perceived to have had a significant impact on one's life—may prove particularly useful as a method for revealing the cumulative influence of environmental conditions on developmental processes and outcomes over the life course (cf., Rowles, 1981; Stokols, 1982).

Perhaps more important than recording the duration and quality of individuals' encounters with particular environments will be the measurement of complementary versus conflicting relationships between the virtual and real settings included in one's meso-, exo-, and macrosystems. These complementarities and conflicts among closely linked settings may exert a greater impact on developmental processes and outcomes than the environmental circumstances present within each individual setting. Moreover, the creation of new measurement strategies for gauging levels of macrosystem instability and unpredictability, and the developmental consequences of these conditions, remain as a relatively neglected but important direction for future research. Finally, ethical questions raised by the study of people's encounters with the Internet and the World Wide Web (especially those pertaining to potential violations of privacy) will need to be addressed in future research on the developmental consequences of participation in virtual environments (Jones, 1994).

CONCLUSION

The chapters in this volume reflect several contributions of earlier research to the study of contextual influences on development over the life course. In particular, ecologically oriented research programs have (a) established valuable taxonomic schemes for categorizing environmental conditions, developmental processes, and outcomes associated with various life settings and stages; (b) introduced and validated multiple measurement strategies to assess the empirical links among these variables and the ways in which environmental settings influence development over the life course; and (c) suggested a variety of environmental design strategies to enhance developmental processes and outcomes over the life course.

Earlier studies also reveal some neglected areas of research on the ecology of human development. The present chapter suggested certain conceptual and methodological horizons for future ecological research, particularly in light of the rapid growth of the Internet and the World Wide Web in recent years and the developmental significance of these macrosystemic changes. These conceptual horizons present new opportunities for developing theoretical models that facilitate a broader understanding of (a) the relative influence of proximal versus distal processes on human development; (b) the emergence of new meso-, exo-, and macrosystem units that incorporate both real and virtual settings; (c) the circumstances under which individuals' participation in the Internet and the World Wide Web is associated with either positive or negative developmental processes and outcomes; and (d) the developmental ramifications of the Internet's exponential growth in light of humans' limited capacities for coping with information overload and accelerating rates of environmental change.

At a methodological level, several complex issues remain to be addressed in future studies of the ecology of development over the life course. These issues generally pertain to the challenges of specifying the effective context of development across multiple settings and life stages and the difficulty of measuring the cumulative influence of virtual (as well as real) environments on developmental processes and outcomes. Some promising directions for future methodological research were discussed in relation to these concerns, including the following: (a) the combined use of multiple methodologies (e.g., time budget analyses, physical trace measures, and retrospective interviews) to assess individuals' time allocation to both real and virtual settings; (b) the creation of new measures to denote either complementary or conflicting relationships between real and virtual settings making up a person's meso-, exo-, and macrosystems; (c) the establishment of new measurement strategies for gauging macrosystem instability and unpredictability and the developmental consequences of those conditions; and (d) the resolution of ethical questions raised by the study of people's participation in the Internet and the World Wide Web, especially those relating to potential infringements on personal privacy.

REFERENCES

Altman, I. (1968). Choicepoints in the classification of scientific knowledge. In B. P. Indik & F. K. Berrien (Eds.), *People, groups, organizations* (pp. 47–69). New York: Columbia University Press.

Altman, I. (1975). *The environment and social behavior*. Monterey, CA: Brooks/Cole.

Appleyard, D. (1981). *Livable streets*. Berkeley: University of California Press.

Barker, R. G. (1968) *Ecological psychology: Concepts and methods for studying the environment of human behavior*. Stanford, CA: Stanford University Press.

Blanchard, A. (1997). *Virtual behavior settings: An application of behavior setting theories to virtual communities*. Claremont, CA: Claremont Graduate Universtiy, the Center for Organizational and Behavioral Sciences.

Blanchard, A., & Horan, T. (1997, August). *Can we surf together if we're bowling alone? An examination into virtual community's impact on social capital*. Paper presented at the American Sociological Association Symposium on the Internet and Social Change.

Blumenstyk, G. (1997, January 17). An experiment in "virtual community" takes shape in Blacksburg, VA: The "electronic village" shows the promise and some of the limitations of the idea. *Chronicle of Higher Education*, p. A24.

Bradley, R. H., & Caldwell, B. M. (1976). Early home environment and changes in mental test performance in children from 6 to 36 months. *Developmental Psychology, 12*, 93–97.

Bronfenbrenner, U. (1977). Toward an experimental ecology of human development. *American Psychologist*, 513–530.

Bronfenbrenner, U. (1979). *The ecology of human development: Experiments by nature and design*. Cambridge, MA: Harvard University Press.

Bronfenbrenner, U. (1986). Ecology of the family as a context for human development: Research perspectives. *Developmental Psychology, 22*, 723–742.

Bronfenbrenner, U. (1992). Ecological systems theory. In R. Vasta (Ed.), *Six theories of child development: Revised formulations and current issues* (pp. 187–249). London: Jessica Kingsley Publishers.

Bullock, R.D. (1990). *Dumping in Dixie: Race, class, and environmental quality*. Boulder, CO: Westview Press.

Caplan, R. D., & Harrison, R. V. (1993). Person–environment fit theory: Some history, recent developments, and future directions. *Journal of Social Issues, 49*, 253–275.

Carp, F. M., & Carp, A. (1987). Environment and aging. In D. Stokols & I. Altman (Eds.), *Handbook of environmental psychology* (Vols. 1 & 2, pp. 329–360). New York: Wiley.

Carpman, J. R., & Grant, M. A. (1993). *Design that cares: Planning health facilities for patients and visitors* (2nd ed.). Chicago: American Hospital Association.

Carr, S., Francis, M., Rivlin, L., & Stone, A. (1992). *Public space*. New York: Cambridge University Press.

Clarke-Stewart, K. A., Gruber, C. P., & Fitzgerald, M. M. (1994). *Children at home and in day care*. Hillsdale, NJ: Erlbaum.

Cohen, S., Evans, G. W., Stokols, D., & Krantz, D. S. (1986). *Behavior, health, and environmental stress*. New York: Plenum Press.

Cohen, S., Glass, D. C., & Singer, J. E. (1973). Apartment noise, auditory discrimination, and reading ability in children. *Journal of Experimental Social Psychology, 9*, 407–422.

Davidson, J. (1996). *Handling information overload*. Retrieved from the World Wide Web: http://www.brespace.com/artspub-overload.html.

Emerging Technologies Research Group. (1997). *U.S. Internet Household Forecast*. Retrieved from the World Wide Web: http://etrg.findsvp.com/timeline/forecast.html.

Emery, F. E. & Trist, E. L. (1965). The causal texture of organizational environments. *Human Relations, 18*, 21–32.

Evans, G. W., Hygge, S., & Bullinger, M. (1995). Chronic noise and psychological stress. *Psychological Science, 6*, 333–338.

Find/SVP. (1997a). *Children on the internet*. Retrieved from the World Wide Web: http://www.findsvp.com/cgi-bin/RetrieveItem.cgi?pub=ET013.

Find/SVP. (1997b). *The 1997 American Internet User Survey*. Retrieved from the World Wide Web: http://etrg.findsvp.com/internet/overview.html.

Glass, D. C., & Singer, J. E. (1972). *Urban stress*. New York: Academic Press.

Gray, M. (1996). *Internet statistics: Growth and usage of the Web and the internet*. Retrieved from the World Wide Web: http://www.mit.edu/people/mkgray/net/.

Greenberger, E., & Steinberg, L. (1986). *When teenagers work: The psychological and social costs of adolescent employment*. New York: Basic Books.

Hartig, T., Mang, M., & Evans, G. W. (1991). Restorative effects of natural environment experiences. *Environment and Behavior, 23*, 3–26.

Holman, E. A., & Stokols, D. (1994). The environmental psychology of child sexual abuse. *Journal of Environmental Psychology, 14,* 237–252.

Huston, A. (1993, November). *Poverty as environment.* Paper presented at the National Institutes of Child Health and Human Development Workshop on Measurement of the Environment Across the Life Span, Bethesda, MD.

Internet a molester's tool, police warn. (1997, November 11). *Los Angeles Times Orange County Edition,* pp. B1, B4.

Jones, R. A. (1994). The ethics of research in cyberspace. *Internet Research, 4,* 30–35.

Kahana, E. (1982). A congruence model of person environment interaction. In M. P. Lawton, P. G. Windley, & T. O Byerts (Eds.), *Aging and the environment: Theoretical approaches* (pp. 97–121). New York: Springer.

Kaplan, R., & Kaplan, S. (1989). *The experience of nature: A psychological perspective.* New York: Cambridge University Press.

Kohn, M. L., & Schooler, C. (1982). Job conditions and personality: A longitudinal assessment of their reciprocal effects. *American Journal of Sociology, 87,* 1257–1286.

Lenntorp, B. (1978). A time–geographic simulation model of individual activity programmes. In T. Carlstein, D. Parkes, & N. Thrift (Eds.), *Human activity and time geography* (pp. 162–180). New York: Wiley.

Lewin, K. (1936). *Principles of topological psychology.* New York: McGraw-Hill.

Magnusson, D. (1981). A psychology of situations. In D. Magnusson (Ed.), *Toward a psychology of situations: An interactional perspective* (pp. 9–32). Hillsdale, NJ: Erlbaum.

Manicas, P. T., & Secord, P. F. (1983). Implications for psychology of the new philosophy of science. *American Psychologist, 38,* 399–413.

Maruyama, M. (1963). The second cybernetics: Deviation-amplifying mutual causal processes. *American Scientist, 51,* 164–179.

McCartney, K. (1984). Effects of quality of day care environment on children's language development. *Developmental Psychology, 20,* 244–260.

Meyrowitz, J. (1985). *No sense of place: The impact of electronic media on social behavior.* New York: Oxford University Press.

Michelson, W. H. (1985). *From sun to sun: Daily obligations and community structure in the lives of employed women and their families.* Totowa, NJ: Rowman & Allenheld.

Miller, L. (1995). Women and children first: Gender and the settling of the electronic frontier. In J. Brook & I. A. Boal (Eds.), *Resisting the virtual life: The culture and politics of information* (pp. 49–57). San Francisco: City Lights Books.

Mitchell, W. J. (1995). *The city of bits: Space, place, and the infobahn.* Cambridge, MA: MIT Press.

Moore, G. T. (1986). Effects of the spatial definition of behavior settings on children's behavior: A quasi-experimental field study. *Journal of Environmental Psychology*, 6, 205–233.

Moore, G. T., & Hart, R. A. (Eds.). (1989). Child care environments: Policy, research, and design [Special issue]. *Children's Environments Quarterly*, 6(4).

Moore, G. T., & Lackney, J. A. (1993). School design: Crisis, educational performance, and design applications. *Children's Environments, 10*, 99–112.

Network Wizards (1997). *Internet domain survey, July, 1997*. Retrieved from the World Wide Web: http://www.nw.com/zone/WWW/report.html.

Newman, O. (1973). *Defensible space: Crime prevention through urban design*. New York: Collier Books.

Noam, E. (1995). Electronics and the dim future of the university. *Science, 270*, 247–249.

Parmelee, P. A., & Lawton, M. P. (1990). The design of special environments for the aged. In J. E. Birren & K. W. Schaie (Eds.), *Handbook of the psychology of aging* (3rd ed., pp. 464–488). New York: Academic Press.

Postman, N. (1992). *Technolopoly: The surrender of culture to technology*. New York: Vintage Books.

Putnam, P. D. (1995). Bowling alone: America's declining social capital. *Journal of Democracy*, 6, 65–78.

Rheingold, H. (1993). *The virtual community: Homesteading on the electronic frontier*. Reading, MA: Addison-Wesley.

Rochberg-Halton, E., & Csikszentmihalyi, M. (1981). *The meaning of things: Domestic symbols and the self*. New York: Cambridge University Press.

Rook, K. S. (1984). Promoting social bonding: Strategies for helping the lonely and socially isolated. *American Psychologist, 39*, 1389–1407.

Rothenberg, D. (1997, August 15). How the Web destroys the quality of students' research papers. *The Chronicle of Higher Education*, p. A44.

Rowles, G. D. (1981). Geographic perspectives on human development. *Human Development, 24*, 67–76.

Schooler, C. (1984). Psychological effects of complex environments during the life span: A review and theory. *Intelligence*, 8, 259–281.

Schuler, D. (1996). *New community networks: Wired for change*. Reading, MA: Addison-Wesley.

Sclove, R.E. (1995). Making technology democratic. In J. Brook & I. A. Boal (Eds.), *Resisting the virtual life: The culture and politics of information* (pp. 85–101). San Francisco: City Lights Books.

SeniorNet (1998). *Research on SeniorNet by Xerox Palo Alto Research Center and the Institute for Research on Learning*. Retrieved from the World Wide Web: http://www.seniornet.org/nsf/intro.html.

Seniors Computer Information Project. (1998). *Overview of the Seniors Computer Information Project*. Retrieved from the World Wide Web: http://www.crm.mb.ca/scip/scipinfo.html.

Steinberg, L., Darling, N. E., Fletcher, A. C., Brown, B. B., & Dornbusch, S. M.

(1995). Authoritative parenting and adolescent adjustment: An ecological journey. In P. Moen, G. H. Elder, & K. Luscher, (Eds.), *Examining lives in context: Perspectives on the ecology of human development* (pp. 423–466). Washington, DC: American Psychological Association.

Stokols, D. (1982). Environmental psychology: A coming of age. In A. Kraut (Ed.), G. *Stanley Hall Lectures* (Vol. 2, pp. 155–205). Washington, DC: American Psychological Association.

Stokols, D. (1987). Conceptual strategies of environmental psychology. In D. Stokols & I. Altman (Eds.), *Handbook of environmental psychology* (Vol. 1, pp. 41–71). New York: Wiley.

Stokols, D. (1988). Transformational processes in people–environment relations. In J. E. McGrath (Ed.), *The social psychology of time. New perspectives* (pp. 233–252). Beverly Hills, CA: Sage.

Stokols, D. (1990). Instrumental and spiritual views of people–environment relations. *American Psychologist, 45*, 641–646.

Stokols, D. (1995). The paradox of environmental psychology. *American Psychologist, 50*, 821–837.

Stokols, D. (1998). Environmental design and occupational health. In J. Stellman & C. Brabant (Eds.), *International Labor Office (ILO) encyclopedia of occupational health and safety, 4th edition* (pp. 34.19–34.22). Section IV, psychosocial and organizational factors (S. L. Sauter & L. Levi, section co-editors). Geneva, Switzerland: International Labor Office.

Stoll, C. (1995). *Silicon snake oil: Second thoughts on the information highway*. Garden City, NY: Doubleday.

Sundstrom, E. (1986). *Workplaces: The psychology of the physical environment in offices and factories*. New York: Cambridge University Press.

Taylor, R. B. (1987). Toward an environmental psychology of disorder: Delinquency, crime, and fear of crime. In D. Stokols & I. Altman (Eds.), *Handbook of environmental psychology*, (Vol. 2, pp. 1433–1467). New York: Wiley.

Taylor, R. B., Shumaker, S. A., & Gottfredson, S. D. (1985). Neighborhood-level links between physical features and local sentiments: Deterioration, fear of crime, and confidence. *Journal of Architectural and Planning Research, 2*, 261–275.

U.S. Department of Commerce. (1995). *Falling through the net: A survey of the "have nots" in rural and urban America*. Retrieved from the World Wide Web: http://www.ntia.doc.gov/ntiahome/fallingthru.html.

Wachs, T. D. (1979). Proximal experience and early cognitive–intellectual development: The physical environment. *Merrill-Palmer Quarterly, 25*, 3–41.

Wachs, T. D. (1989). The nature of the physical microenvironment: An expanded classification system. *Merrill-Palmer Quarterly, 35*, 399–419.

Wachs, T. D., & Camli, O. (1991). Do ecological or individual characteristics mediate the influence of the physical environment upon maternal behavior. *Journal of Environmental Psychology, 11*, 249–264.

Wachs, T. D., & Gruen, G. (1982). *Early experience and human development*. New York: Plenum Press.

Wall, L. (1997). *Invisible communities: A conceptual framework for understanding how a sense of community develops in cyberspace*. Irvine: University of California, Irvine, Department of Environmental Analysis and Design, School of Social Ecology.

Wapner, S. (1987). A holistic, developmental, systems-oriented environmental psychology: Some beginnings. In D. Stokols & I. Altman (Eds.), *Handbook of environmental psychology* (Vol. 2, pp. 951–987). New York: Wiley.

Wicker, A. W. (1987). Behavior settings reconsidered: Temporal stages, resources, internal dynamics, context. In D. Stokols & I. Altman (Eds.), *Handbook of environmental psychology* (Vol. 1, pp. 613–655). New York: Wiley.

Wohlwill, J. F., & Heft, H. (1987). The physical environment and the development of the child. In D. Stokols & I. Altman (Eds.), *Handbook of environmental psychology* (pp. 281–328). New York: Wiley.

Yankelovich Partners. (1995). *Cybercitizen: A profile of online users*. Retrieved from the World Wide Web: http://www.yankelovich.com/cyber/FINDINGS.HTM.

Zeisel, J. (1981). *Inquiry by design: Tools for environment–behavior research*. New York: Cambridge University Press.

12

CELEBRATING COMPLEXITY: CONCEPTUALIZATION AND ASSESSMENT OF THE ENVIRONMENT

THEODORE D. WACHS

In many disciplines, there exists what researchers may call the "gold standard" of measurement—the state-of-the-art procedure for measuring a specific variable against which all other measurement approaches must be compared. For example, monitoring of the metabolism of specific water isotopes (the double-labeled water method) has become the preferred technique when it it necessary to assess total energy expenditure of adults and children in naturalistic settings (Prentice, Velasquez, Davies, Lucas, & Coward, 1989). As pointed out by a number of authors in this volume, although there are multiple ways of assessing the environment, there is no specific method that can be viewed as the gold standard. In the absence of a gold standard, a variety of criteria are utilized to determine what aspects of the environment should be assessed and how these aspects should be assessed. All too often, the choice of environmental assessments is based

I thank Dan Stokols for his comments and suggestions on the thoughts contained in this chapter.

on what is cheap, available, or easy to use (Bradley, chapter 3, this volume). Such a strategy, while perhaps easy for the researcher, does not necessarily make for good science because the most cheap and available measures may be highly imperfect or even invalid reflections of what it is he or she is trying to measure.

In the best of all possible worlds, the choice of what aspects of the environment researchers measure and how they measure these aspects would be dictated by criteria such as the questions they are asking (e.g., Bradley, chapter 2, and Brown, chapter 3, this volume) or by the theoretical framework within which they are working (e.g., Super & Harkness, chapter 10, this volume). Even more fundamental than questions or theory, it also seems clear that the choice of what to assess or how to assess is dictated by the assumptions that are made about the nature of the environment and about how the environment operates to influence development (e.g., Brown, chapter 3, and Lawton, chapter 4, this volume). Consider, for example, three different views of the nature of the environment and the implications of each of these views for environmental assessment. In Scarr's (1992) gene → environment framework, the environment is assumed to operate in a threshold fashion, with only extreme environmental influences viewed as influencing behavioral or development variability and with individual elements of the environment being viewed as functionally equivalent, except at the extremes. Within this set of assumptions, to assess the environment, researchers will need only to identify which individuals live in extreme environments, with little concern for the specific details of the environments that these individuals live in. Hence, social-address assessments that allow classification of individuals living in poverty or who are subject to child abuse would be viewed as the most appropriate way to assess the environment.

Scarr's (1992) assumptions about the environment can be contrasted with the assumptions contained in my specificity model of environmental action (Wachs, 1992). Within a specificity framework, I assume that a wide range of environmental influences is salient and that different aspects of the environment act to influence different aspects of development. For researchers working within this framework, it is necessary to utilize detailed assessments of specific aspects of the individual's proximal environment to be able to link specific aspects of the environment to specific aspects of development. Finally, if researchers operate under the assumptions found in Bronfenbrenner's (chapter 1, this volume) hierarchical model of the environment, then it becomes essential to measure not only specific aspects of the individual's proximal environment but also aspects of the individual's distal environment that are linked to the proximal environment (e.g., socioeconomic status and culture).

Although the assumptions made about environment and environmental influences are essential for determining the choice of environmental assessment strategies, the major thesis of this chapter is that researchers no longer need to make such assumptions. What has been documented in previous chapters in this volume, as well as what I expand on in the present chapter, is a detailed empirical literature that allows researchers to describe accurately not only the structure of the environment but also many of the processes whereby environmental influences act on individual behavior and development. This literature is sufficient to allow empirically based decisions to be made about what the environment is, how the environment operates, and how to best assess the environment without the need to rely on unverified assumptions about the structure of nature of the environment. The questions then become as follows: (a) What does the empirical literature tell researchers about the nature of the phenomena they are assessing and (b) what is the nature of the environment, both in a structural (taxonomic) and in a dynamic (process) sense? Answers to these questions are given in the following sections of this chapter.

THE STRUCTURE OF THE ENVIRONMENT

The Objective Structure

A generally accepted "working" definition of what is meant by the environment would be as follows: organized conditions or patterns of external stimuli that impinge on and have the probability of influencing the individual (Wachs, 1992, p. 39). Implicit in this definition and implicit in many of the taxonomic environmental structures presented in this volume is the idea of the environment as a multilevel, multidimensional hierarchical system ranging from physical ecological features down to specific proximal transactions between child and caregiver. (In this volume, for example, see Bronfenbrenner, Evans, Lawton, and Stokols.) A schematic illustrating the hierarchical-linked multilevel, multidimensional nature of the environment is shown in Figure 1. The hierarchical dimensions shown in Figure 1 are based on Bronfenbrenner's (chapter 1, this volume) structural model of the environment and range from fundamental lower level microsystem characteristics (e.g., proximal processes in the home environment) up through broad-based macrosystem influences (e.g., cultural). As also shown in Figure 1, the multiple hierarchical levels making up the environment are not independent of each other but rather are linked in various ways. For example, in the chapter by Vandell and Posner, linkages between characteristics of the after-school environment and neighborhood characteristics are discussed. Other chapters describe linkages between the school and the larger community (Talbert & McLaughlin) and between the peer environment and the broader cultural context (Brown). Furthermore, each level of the environment is not homogeneous but rather can be further subdivided into various linked subunits. Thus, at the level of the home environment, there is a highly differentiated structure encompassing both the functions served by various aspects of parent–child transactions, as well as by variability in the sources and modality of stimuli encountered by the child (Bradley). Similar complex differentiations are also discussed at the level of the peer environment (Brown), the school environment (Talbert & McLaughlin), the work place (Schooler), and the culture (Super & Harkness).

Although there is general agreement on the hierarchical multilevel, multidimensional nature of the environment, complete agreement is not found on some of the finer details of the environmental structure. Conceptually, although a number of chapter authors (e.g., Bronfenbrenner, Talbert, and McLaughlin) emphasize bidirectional linkages among different levels of the environment, other chapter authors (e.g., Brown, Vandell, and Posner) focus on the asymmetrical nature of such linkages. For these authors, the directionality of linkages, both in terms of strength or extent, is more likely to go from background context or distal environmental characteristics to more proximal environmental characteristics than from proximal to distal. There are two points I would make in regard to these contrasting viewpoints. First, in terms of the nature of linkages available, evidence clearly shows that the detrimental impact of macrosystem influences such as societal violence or poverty can be attenuated when the child's proximal environment is supportive or when sensitive and responsive caregiving practices are utilized (Bradley et al., 1994; Dawes, 1990; Masten, Best, & Garmezy, 1990). Similarly, Stokols (chapter 11, this volume) details how proximal technological supports like the Internet can have major consequences for various aspects of the macrosystem. Such findings, illustrating how the impact of higher level environmental stressors can be moderated by more proximal conditions, support the hypothesis of bidirectional proximal ↔ distal linkages. What the evidence also shows, however, is that it is far easier to document how the impact of proximal processes can be moderated by higher order contextual factors than the reverse pattern (Wachs, 1992). Taken as a whole, the evidence clearly illustrates that linkages between different levels of the environment, while bidirectional, are also asymmetrical.

Second, in response to the question of the operation of higher order moderators, this issue is one that is still not yet resolved. Many studies, both in this volume (Friedman & Amadeo, and Vandell & Posner) and in the literature, show that the impact of proximal processes on individual behavioral developmental variability varies as a function of background contextual conditions like socioeconomic status, culture, or physical–ecological settings (Stokols, 1988; Wachs, 1996). For example, moderation of relations between adolescent school performance and parental rearing strategies varies as a function of ethnic membership (Steinberg, Dornbush,

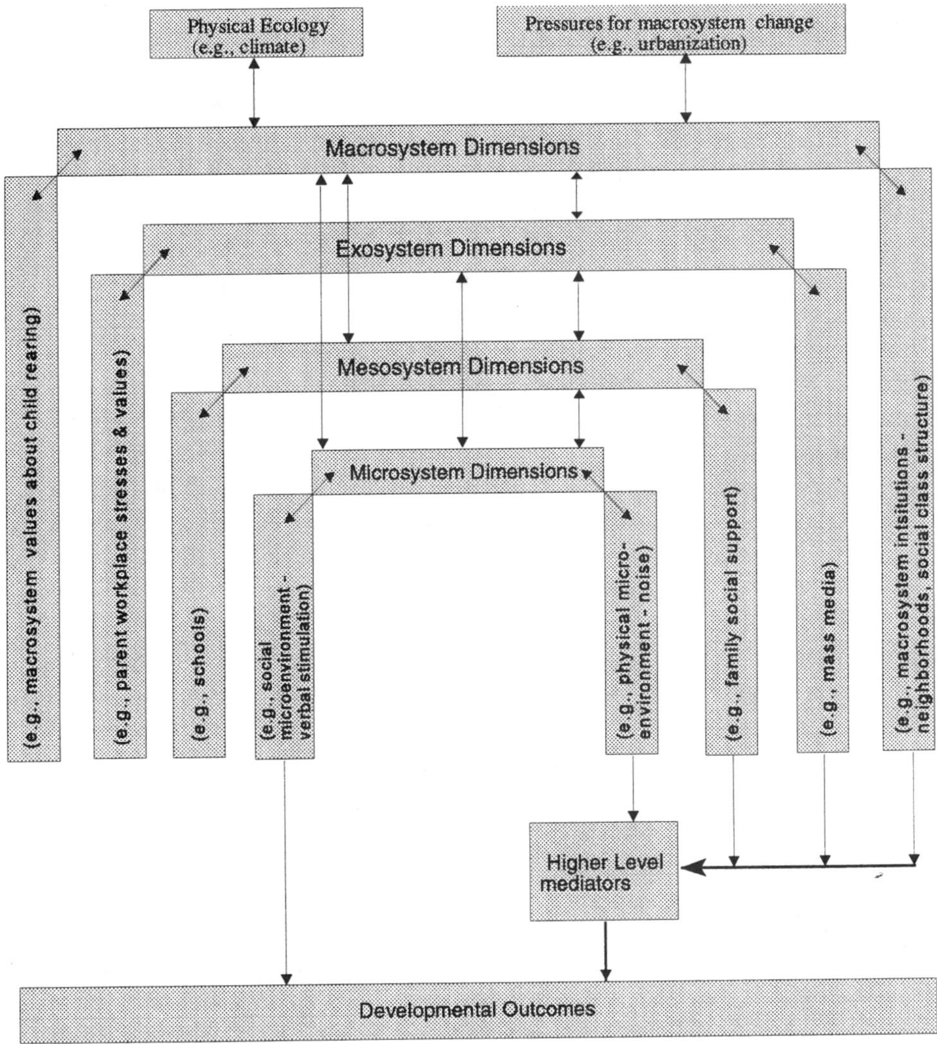

Figure 1. Structural model of the environment. Double-headed arrows refer to bidirectional levels of influence across the environment. Single-headed arrows refer to direct or mediating influences of the environment on development. From T. D. Wachs, *The Nature of Nurture* (p. 41). Newbury Park, CA: Sage. Copyright 1992 by Sage Publications, Inc. Adapted with permission.

& Brown, 1992), whereas relations between parental–occupational level and children's cognitive performance vary as a function of area of residence within a country (Goduka, Poole, & Aotaki-Phenice, 1992). On the other hand, there are all too many examples in which higher order moderation has not been shown to occur, so that similar patterns of relations between patterns of parental stimulation or family structure and children's development are found across widely different cultures (Bornstein, Azuma, Tamis-LeMonda, & Ogino, 1990; Ogilvy, 1990; Wachs et al., 1993). Similarly, there is little evidence for higher level moderation seen in the cross-cultural research described by Schooler (chapter 8, this volume). Although in some cases a lack of higher order contextual moderation of more proximal processes can be attributed to methodological factors, such as low statistical power, methodology per se is not a sufficient explanation in all cases. Rather, there appears to be a genuine discrepancy with some studies showing higher order moderation, whereas other, equally well-done, studies report that even if children in different contexts perform at different levels, the pattern of relations between proximal environmental influences and outcomes is the same across the different contexts. The discrepancy in results noted among different chapters, and in the literature, illustrates one of the fundamental questions that environmental researchers need to deal with, namely, under what conditions is higher order environmental moderation of more fundamental proximal processes most or least likely to occur?

This discrepancy has major implications for strategies used to assess the environment. If higher order moderation of more proximal environmental processes is occurring, then multiple-level assessment is essential. Under conditions of higher level environmental moderation, both the extent and the nature of proximal environment–outcome relations will vary, depending on the nature of the background context within which the individual functions. Indeed, as noted by Super and Harkness (chapter 10, this volume), even the choice of methods used to study more proximal environmental processes may also be influenced by higher order contextual characteristics. On the other hand, if higher level moderation is not occurring, then it becomes unnecessary to assess background context because researchers can safely operate under the assumption that the same pattern of relations found in one context will hold equally well across different contexts.

If higher order environmental moderators are operating, an important question has to do with the appropriate statistical procedures to be utilized. The typical response of all too many researchers has been to use statistical controls, such as analysis of covariance, to reduce the "nuisance" value of higher order moderating influences. Such a strategy has been described by several authors in this volume (e.g., Friedman & Amadeo, and Schooler) as a way of isolating the critical environmental influence. However, other chapter authors (e.g., Bronfenbrenner, Evans, and Vandell & Posner) recommend against the routine application of statistical control, if only because statistical controls may partially mask what the researcher is looking for. I find myself very much in agreement with the latter set of chapter authors in regard to the undesirability of statistical partialling. My position in this matter is based on the conclusion by Rutter and Pickles (1991)—that the choice of statistical techniques should reflect the nature of the phenomena under study. The use of statistical partialling techniques as a way of isolating the critical environmental influence is a procedure that would reflect the environment, if the structure of the environment involved a unidimensional–unilevel set of independent influences. This simply is not the case. Thus, use of statistical partialling techniques to isolate the critical environmental influence, when the very nature of environmental influences is based on a multilevel, multidimensional bidirectional-linked structure, is a strategy that denies rather than reflects existing reality.

Given that researchers do not yet have a set of validated decision rules that would allow them to estimate accurately when higher order moderators may or may not be operating, plus the fact that statistical partialling techniques do not reflect the nature of the environment, what are environmental researchers to do when designing studies to reflect accurately the structure of the environment? I would argue that the most appropriate strategy at present is an inductive one, namely, assuming that higher order environmental moderation may be occurring and building assessment strategies into studies to test the potential operation of higher order moderators. The problem, of course, is that one cannot adequately measure all aspects of the environmental structure. As noted by chapter authors, besides traditional higher order contextual markers such as culture, social class, and ethnic group membership, researchers may also need to consider other less pervasive but nonetheless critical contextual features such as neighborhood, work or school characteristics, nature of peer cultures, or level of physical environmental stressors such as physical barriers or pollution levels. A study that attempted to assess all of these various higher order dimensions, as well as more proximal processes, would either be so low in power that existing relations would be impossible to detect or would require such large sample sizes as to make the study unfeasible. A more viable strategy is seen in the work of Talbert and McLaughlin (chapter 7, this volume), using an embedded model that selectively samples across levels and across dimensions within levels, choosing higher order moderators that are most likely to be operating, given the nature of the outcome phenomena under study.

Within an embedded framework, can researchers specify what specific higher level contextual dimensions need to be integrated within a given study on the role of proximal processes? Unless this can be done, the espousing of the integration of more distal–contextual aspects in studies of the role of proximal environmental influences is an exercise in well-meaning vacuity. Fortunately, the chapter authors have provided good initial starting points in regard to the question of which aspects of context should be integrated into specific studies. Conclusions from the various chapters are summarized in Table 1. For example, when outcomes involve individual competence versus individual dysfunction, Bronfenbrenner (chapter 1, this volume) notes the importance of integrating measures of proximal processes with measures of contextual advantage and disadvantage (e.g., socioeconomic level) and contextual stability. Obviously, the list of higher order contextual dimensions shown in Table 1 is not exhaustive. As D. Stokols (personal communication, June, 1997) has noted, given the increasing interdependence of the various countries that make up the world, researchers may also need to consider linkages between proximal environments and macrodistal conditions such as global economic or climatological change.

By targeting specific contextual measures that can be integrated into studies of proximal processes, and by sampling participants who differ on the specific targeted contextual measures (e.g., living in good vs. poor neighborhoods, urban vs. rural residence, and high vs. low socioeconomic status), it is possible to generate research on environmental influences that accurately reflects the nature of the environment and yet is feasible from both a practical standpoint (e.g., number of participants) and a statistical standpoint (e.g., adequate power). Lest readers think I am still talking hypothetically, I would refer them to Talbert and McLaughlin (chapter 7, this volume), which demonstrates exactly how this can be done in regard to one aspect of the environment (viz., school influences).

TABLE 1
Integration of Distal–Contextual Features Into Studies of Proximal Environmental Processes

Proximal environment	Distal–contextual features to be integrated	Chapter
Child's home environment	Ethnic group membership and day-care quality	Bradley Friedman & Amadeo
Older adult's home environment	Physical distances and physical barriers	Lawton
Adolescent peer environment	Peer crowd characteristics and cultural values about appropriate adolescent behaviors	Brown
Classroom environment	Community characteristics and cultural beliefs about the importance of education	Talbert & McLaughlin
After-school care	Neighborhood characteristics, family socioeconomic status, and ethnic group membership	Vandell & Posner

The Subjective Structure

As discussed by a number of the authors in this volume, the environment involves more than just the objective structure presented earlier. In addition to the objective environmental structure, there also appears to be a "parallel" environmental universe, namely, the individual's subjective perception of his or her objective environment (the subjective environment). Examples of this parallel subjective environment include children's feelings about their after-school environment (Vandell & Posner), what teachers and pupils feel is most important about their school (Talbert & McLaughlin), workers' appraisals of their job characteristics (Schooler), and distinctions between noise and sound (Evans). Although not directly referred to as the subjective environment, the concept of ambience can also be viewed in this way. Ambience can be defined in terms of the pervading style of the home (Bradley), the reputational nature of peer crowds (Brown), or the abstraction of culturally relevant themes by children (Super & Harkness).

In the environmental framework presented by Lawton (chapter 4, this volume), at each level of the environmental structure there is a parallel level of the subjective environment. For example, at the level of the personal environment, objective dimensions would include the individual's marital status or the family's social network, whereas the subjective parallel environment would include how an individual feels about others in his or her social network. At the level of the suprapersonal context, the objective environment might be measures of neighborhood characteristics, whereas the subjective parallel environment could be the individual's feelings about the degree of neighborhood safety or the target group whom the person compares him- or herself to in his or her neighborhood.

Developmental researchers have tended to shy away from assessing the subjective environment, in good part because of the many measurement problems associated with measuring individual perceptions. Many of these problems have been described by Schooler and Evans in their respective chapters (e.g., the continually nagging question of whether subjective perception measures assess the individual's perception of the environment or assess aspects of the individual's personality and temperament, and the increased likelihood of common method variance occurring when self-report perception and outcome measures are used). Alleviation of concerns about the ability to assess the subjective environment has not been helped by reports of the relatively modest correlations between parental attitudes and parental behaviors (Miller, 1995) or of the questionable psychometric characteristics of parent attitude assessment instruments (Holden & Edwards, 1989). Such concerns are not unique to environmental assessment (e.g., see the continuing debate over whether parent report measures of a child's temperament better reflect child temperament or parent personality; (Rothbart & Bates, 1998). However, in spite of these concerns, there are compelling reasons that support the importance of assessing the individual's subjective perceptions of his or her environment.

One major advantage of assessing the subjective environment of the individual is methodological. As discussed by Schooler (chapter 8, this volume), there is a direct relation between the preciseness of the environmental measures and the extent of environmental effects found, with greater error of measurement being associated with less chance of detecting existing environmental influences. As noted by a number of chapter authors (Bradley, Bronfenbrenner, and Super & Harkness), stable and converging aspects of the environment are among the most powerful proximal processes acting on individual developmental behavioral variability. Both in this volume (e.g., Evans and Super & Harkness) and elsewhere (Wachs, 1987), the importance of using aggregated environmental measurement has been stressed. Application of aggregation procedures means that the measurement of the environment is based on multiple measures obtained either across multiple occasions, or on the reports of multiple observers, or on the use of different instruments converging on the same aspect of the environment. Aggregating measurements of the environment across occasions, observers, or measures acts to average out errors of measurement, resulting in more precise and stable assessments (Rushton, Brainerd, & Pressley, 1983). In addition, reducing error of measurement through aggregation can also act to increase statistical power, thus further increasing the chances of detecting existing environmental influences (Wachs, 1991).

Unfortunately, aggregating across multiple observers not only can be costly in terms of time and effort but also can increase the chances of participant reactivity to being observed, particularly in situations such as peer groups in which the presence of observers may disrupt natural behavioral sequences (Brown, chapter 3, this volume). Assessing the environment across multiple observation sequences can also be extremely costly in terms of time and effort, even when relatively brief spot observations are used (Super & Harkness, chapter 10, this volume). Although the use of subjective perceptions of the environment has methodological drawbacks, combining objective and subjective measures of the same environmental dimension offers a relatively low-cost way of obtaining converging environmental data that can be used for purposes of aggregation.

In addition to allowing low-cost aggregation, obtaining subjective perceptions of the individual's environment may allow for more precise predictions. What may be critical in determining individual behavior patterns may be how the individual perceives the nature of his or her environment rather than the actual environment itself. For example, the child's reactions to specific parental disciplinary actions may well be a function of whether the child perceives the parent's overall disciplinary strategy as authoritative or authoritarian in nature (Darling & Steinberg, 1993). Similarly, choice of residential area or acceptance of neighborhood change may be more a function of psychological–perceptual than objective tangible characteristics (Stokols, 1992).

Given the potential benefits found when the subjective environment is assessed, there remains the question of the best way to assess the individual's subjective environment, given the measurement problems noted by chapter authors. A related question is how researchers can measure the individual's subjective environment in populations in which individuals are too young to respond accurately to traditional measures of the subjective environment, such as structured questionnaires and interviews. With regard to the first question, one approach suggested by Evans and by Super and Harkness is that of consensual validation, namely, obtaining multiple reactions of different individuals to a common objective situation, such as the neighborhood, the school, or the workplace. Consensual validation is one way of determining what features of the subjective environment may be more or less accurately assessed, as well as differentiating features of the subjective environment that are common to groups of individuals versus features that are unique to a particular individual in the group. When perceptions are common to multiple individuals in a group, researchers would need to be less concerned about the possible confounding of environment with personality characteristics for these specific dimensions. Differentiating between subjective perceptions of the environment and individual personality characteristics would be an issue primarily when perceptions are unique to the individual within a group.

With regard to the second question of assessing the subjective environment in populations that are too young to respond to traditional measures, one way of dealing with this question is through the concept of internal working models. Internal working models refer to integrated sets of memories, expectancies, and associations between stimuli and affectual responses that act to filter individual perceptions of the environment and that help individuals organize responses to the environment (Calkins, 1994). The operation of internal working models leads children to attend selectively to certain stimuli and to be more likely to react to certain experiences in certain ways. For example, children who have consistently supportive primary caregivers are more likely to act toward the environment as if the environment were likely to be supportive in nature, whereas children who have been repeatedly rejected by their primary caregivers will attend to rejecting cues from their environment (Belsky & Cassidy, 1994). Behavioral markers of such internal working models include attachment relations in infancy (Elicker, Egeland, & Sroufe, 1992) and aggressive behavior patterns in young school-age children (Dodge & Feldman, 1990).

These behavioral markers have the potential to serve as an index of children's subjective environment when more direct subjective measures are either impossible to obtain, as with infants, or more likely to be unreliable, as in the case of young school-age children.

Temporal Structure of the Environment

A point made by a number of chapter authors is that the environment operates not only in space (the objective environment) and within the individual (the subjective environment) but also across time (the temporal environment). The importance of temporal features of the environment has been a central focus in Bronfenbrenner's theoretical framework, both in his previous writings (e.g., Bronfenbrenner, 1989) and in his chapter (chapter 11) in this volume. The importance of viewing the environment within a temporal framework has also been emphasized in the writings of both life-span developmentalists (e.g., Caspi, 1998; Moen, Elder, & Luscher, 1995) and environmental psychologists (e.g., Stokols, 1988). The importance of the temporal environment is also seen in studies on the impact of differences in developmental timing (Spear & Hyatt, 1993) and in predictions derived from chaos theory, which suggest that small initial differences early in development can result in widely divergent developmental outcomes later in life (Gottman, 1991). Obviously, coverage of all aspects of the role of temporal factors in understanding environmental influences would require at least a separate chapter, if not a separate book. However, there are three issues raised by chapter authors that I consider in more detail: (a) the role of age-specific environmental influences, (b) the importance of the individual's personal developmental history, and (c) the question of whether a continuity (cumulative influence) model is the most appropriate one to use when looking at the interaction of temporal and environmental influences.

Age Specificity

As discussed by a number of chapter authors, the nature of the individual's environment changes as a function of age. Age-related environmental changes are seen along such varied dimensions as degree of exposure to environmental toxins (Evans), structure and function of peer groups (Brown), and strategies parents use to transmit culturally relevant messages to their children (Super & Harkness). Also discussed is evidence showing how the impact of specific environmental influences may vary as a function of the age of the individual, even if the nature of underlying environmental dimensions remains constant over time (Lawton and Stokols, this volume)—what I have called *age specificity* (Wachs, 1992). For example, Vandell and Posner (chapter 6, this volume) report that although unsupervised after-school care is related to an increased risk of behavior problems for third graders, increased risk is not seen for fifth graders who are in unsupervised after-school care.

In understanding the nature of differential reactivity to environmental input as a function of age, it is important to keep in mind that age per se usually acts as a demographic marker for more fundamental underlying processes. It is these underlying processes that actually mediate age-related differential reactivity (Wohlwill, 1973). Specific underlying processes include level of maturation of various areas of the *central nervous system* (Wachs & King, 1994), age-associated changes in *hormonal patterns* (Brooks-Gunn & Warren, 1989), or age-related difference in aspects of *executive function* such as selective attention (Enns & Akhter, 1989) or the ability to integrate information from multiple sources (Sophian, 1986). One implication of the operation of age specificity is the importance of including participants from at least two different age levels in environmental research designs. An excellent example of how this might be done in an economical way is seen in a suggestion by Bronfenbrenner (chapter 1, this volume), which is to look at the role of experiences that affect entire families. Such familywide experiences are encountered at the same time by individuals who differ in age. This strategy thus allows comparison of age specificity for adults versus children and, depending on family composition, for children at different ages.

Individual History

Bronfenbrenner (chapter 1, this volume) notes that environmental influences cannot be isolated from the historical period the individual is living in. This concept is mirrored in Brown's (chapter 3, this volume) hypothesis that the nature of peer groups reflect the nature of the historical epoch within which the peer group is nested. These discussions of historical factors apply primarily at a population level, but historical factors can also be relevant at the individual level. Specifically, there is an increasing interest in charting changes in life-course trajectories as a function of prior turning points such as school change or military service (Caspi, 1998; Clausen, 1995; Elder, 1995); there is also an increasing usage of "causal chain" models illustrating how developmental outcomes can be understood as a function of the linkage of individual environmental elements operating at specific time points. For example, Rutter, Quinton, and Hill (1990) have documented how the probability of a woman's having behavior problems as an adult can be traced back to a time-linked series of events in the individual's history, including the level of early adverse rearing experiences, whether subsequent school experiences were positive or negative, and whether marriages were planned or unplanned. Within this framework, development is not viewed as a function of any one experience but rather as the linkage between specific experiences occurring over the individual's history.

Another way of viewing individual historical factors involves the degree to which the individual's previous history can influence reactivity to his or her current environmental context. In their chapter, Talbert and McLaughlin document how a child's previous history in school settings can affect his or her perception of the current school environment. Rutter (1983) has postulated two ways in which an individual's history can affect current reactivity to the environment: *sensitizing* or *steeling*. Sensitizing refers to a situation wherein a history of previous risk decreases the individual's ability to cope with current environmental stressors. Steeling refers to a situation in which a person's previous exposure to risk situations increases the individual's ability to cope with current environmental stress. Steeling is particularly likely to occur if the individual has a history of successfully surmounting past stress or environmental challenges. In addition to sensitizing and steeling, there are two other ways in which past experiences can act to moderate the impact of current environmental influences. One is *buffering*, wherein an individual's ability to meet current environmental challenges is a function of the extent and nature of environmental supports he or she has had in his or her past history. Like steeling, buffering processes act to increase the individual's ability to deal with ongoing stress conditions. An excellent example of buffering is seen in studies of attachment, wherein a child with a secure early attachment is better able to deal with later challenges from the environment than a child who has a history of insecure attachments (Sroufe & Egeland, 1991). A final possibility is *blunting*, wherein past exposure to stressors reduces the individual's ability to make use of current environmental supports. Like sensitizing, blunting acts to decrease an individual's level of competence. For example, children from highly disorganized home environments who coped with environmental chaos by adopting highly rigid coping strategies were unable to adapt these strategies to benefit from later exposure to more structured and supportive environments (Pavenstedt, 1967). A relatively economical way of approaching questions involving how past experiences can moderate reactivity to current environment would be to obtain information on the individual's history of supports and stressors, even if such information were gathered only at a relatively global demographic level.

Temporal Continuity and Discontinuity

The importance of environmental continuity has been a major theme of this volume. Bronfenbrenner argues that unstable environmental contexts can act to undermine the impact of positive proximal processes, whereas both Bradley and Evans emphasize that the strongest environmental impact will come from those aspects of the environment that the individual repeatedly encounters over time. Friedman and Amadeo hypothesize that the greater the continuity between home and child-care environments, the happier the child will be in child care, whereas Super and Harkness postulate that the elaboration over time of culturally relevant themes is a major medium through which cultures get critical messages across to individuals living in these cultures.

However, it also seems clear that the idea of the more environmental stability, the better is an oversimplification. For example, as Schooler (chapter 8, this volume) notes, environmental stability is not an all-or-none phenomena. Different dimensions of the environment may well have different degrees of stability. Furthermore, too much environmental stability may be as problematic as too little stability. When environmental stability is viewed within the framework of variety of experiences a child encounters, a child who is in a highly stable environment (e.g., a highly structured school environment followed by a highly structured after-school environment) may be experiencing relatively low stimulus variety (Vandell & Posner, chapter 7, this volume). Exposure to an adequate amount of environmental change over time has been documented as being a critical proximal environmental influence on development (Wachs, 1992). Furthermore, as suggested by Stokols (chapter 8, this volume), the increase in environmental variability associated with the Internet may become an increasingly salient influence on individual development. The fact that different dimensions of the environment may be salient at different ages (age specificity) is one reason underlying the importance of exposure to a variety of environmental stimuli over time. Over and above the question of variety, it is also important to recognize that the impact of environmental stability cannot be divorced from the quality of the environment the child is in. Being in a stable, developmentally facilitative environment is a very different thing than being in a stable, developmentally inhibiting environment. For example, for infants moving from foster to adoptive homes, degree of similarity between the home settings was a poor predictor of infant adaptation, whereas the quality of the environmental change (moving from a relatively poor to a relatively good environment, or vice versa) was a significantly stronger predictor of infant adaptiveness (Yarrow & Klein, 1980). Similarly, for older children, Finn (1989) has documented how remaining in a stable yet poor school environment decreases the individual's engagement with the educational process while increasing the probability of ultimate school dropout.

Finally, there is a fundamental question as to whether environmental stability resides in the environment, the individual, or both. For the majority of chapter authors, environmental stability is treated essentially as an environmental characteristic. However, initiating a theme that I elaborate on later in this chapter, I would argue that environmental stability cannot be divorced from the individual. The linkage of individual and environmental stability can be looked at on two levels. At a perceptual level, it may well be that the individual's perception of how stable or unstable his or her environment is may be more critical than the actual degree of stability. As discussed by Vandell and Posner (chapter 7, this volume), although a child may seem to be in a bewildering variety of after-school activities, he or she may be able to discern regularity in what looks to outside observers like chaos ("It's Monday, it must be basketball practice after school" and "It's Tuesday, it must be Spanish lessons followed by going to the next-door neighbor's house to wait for my parents"). This suggests the importance of linking both objective and subjective assessment procedures when assessing stability.

At a more active–reactive level, it is important to view stability of the environment not only in terms of the environment per se but also in terms of the individual's own contributions to such stability (Caspi, 1998; Schooler, chapter 8, this volume). For example, in his chapter, Brown describes how some children may be "assigned" by peers to more or less desirable peer groups. Although some children will passively remain in the peer group to which fate or their peers have relegated them (stability of environment), other individuals may behave in ways that allow them to be accepted into more or less desirable peer environments (environmental discontinuity). A critical question deriving from Brown's work is, What individual characteristics result in some children accepting their peer group environments versus the individual characteristics that lead other children to challenge their assignments and by such challenge change the nature of their peer group environment? This question taps a fundamental issue going beyond just the peer environment, an issue that I discuss at greater length later in the chapter.

Structural Aspects of the Environment: Summary

Up to the present, I have shown that the environment operates across objective space, individual perceptions, and time—a complex mix indeed. At the level of space—the objective environment—it is clear that a hierarchical multilevel, multidimensional–linked environmental structure is being dealt with. At the level of the individual—the subjective environment—it is clear that there is a parallel universe consisting of the individual's perceptions of the environment at multiple levels. At the temporal level, it is clear that the objective and subjective environments not only operate across a background of time but also that the nature of temporal processes can influence how the objective and subjective environments affect the individual. Surprisingly, given the major emphasis placed on temporal influences, little is shown in the way of a formal elaboration of how temporal processes fit within existing environmental models, akin to that seen for structural features of the environment. Empirically, there are major gaps between theory and practice with regard to issues involving temporal environmental influences. For example, although repeated measurement is seen as essential for assessing issues such as environmental stability-discontinuity, the overwhelming body of research on environmental influences, is based primarily on single short-term observations. Furthermore, as noted by Evans, rarely do researchers have data on duration of exposure to a particular environmental factor.

Clearly, not all the dimensions of the objective, subjective, and temporal environment can be represented in a single study of environmental influences. However, if studies of environmental influences are to represent accurately the nature of the environment, then such studies must include representative aspects of all three dimensions of the environmental structure. The choice of specific measures from each dimension will depend on both the nature of the research question being asked and the preciseness of available measures (Bradley, Brown, and Friedman & Amadeo). Examples of how relatively low-cost measures of the three major dimensions of the environmental structure could be incorporated into environmental research studies have been noted earlier. However, even studies that encompass representative measures from each of the major dimensions of the environmental structure may not be sufficiently complex to be an accurate representation of the environment. In addition to structure, it is also important to take into account the nature of environmental action processes when studying the environment. Such processes are discussed in the next section.

ENVIRONMENTAL ACTION PROCESS

Specificity

In a global model of environmental action, such as that espoused by Scarr (1992), all aspects of the environment are functionally equivalent, so that any extreme aspect of the environment can predict any aspect of development. In none of the chapters in this volume is support shown for Scarr's hypothesis that the various dimensions of the environment operate only globally or only at the extremes. Lack of support for the idea that only global extreme environments matter is also found in other reviews of this question (Wachs, 1998). In contrast, in a specificity model, the full range of the environment operates in a highly specific framework, with different aspects of the environment being uniquely salient for different aspects of development (Wachs, 1992). The operation of specificity is seen in Vandell and Posner's discussion of how variability in outcomes is a function of specific aspects of the child's after-school, family, and neighborhood characteristics. Similarly, Talbert and McLaughlin note that factors that influence quality of teaching in one subject area may well be different than factors relevant to quality of teaching in a second subject area. Examples of specificity can also be seen in Table 3 in the Friedman and Amadeo chapter (e.g., level of caregiver provider training is positively related to children's cognitive competence but is negatively related to indexes of social competence). Specificity also operates at the temporal level, as shown in evidence indicating that the developmental salience of experiences encountered at different ages will vary as a function of the developmental outcome under consideration (Bradley, Caldwell, & Rock, 1988; Sack, Clarke, & Seeley, 1996). To the extent that siblings living under the same roof encounter different microenvironments, specificity may also explain what behavior genetic researchers have called "nonshared" environmental variance (Wachs, 1996).

In addition to operating at the structural level, specificity can also operate at the process level, with the nature of salient environmental processes varying as a function of the developmental outcomes under consideration (Wachs, 1998). For example, Brown (chapter 3, this volume) illustrates how peer norms are most salient for crowd influences, modeling processes are more critical for interaction group influences, and direct pressures appear to be a more critical process in dyadic relationship influences. Similarly, evidence cited by Bronfenbrenner (chapter 1, this volume) illustrates how differential linkages between the proximal processes and the nature of the background context vary as a function of whether researchers are dealing with outcomes involving developmental competence or developmental disfunction.

One obvious implication of specificity is the importance of not generalizing environment development relations beyond the specific environmental and outcome measures that are being studied. This means that environmental researchers should be wary of grandiose claims made for particular environmental dimensions such as responsivity or scaffolding. At an assessment level, the operation of specificity dramatically reduces the chances of relating specific developmental outcomes to social-address predictors, if only because highly specific predictor–outcome relations may be lost when specific environmental characteristics are collapsed into a global total environmental score (Friedman & Amadeo, chapter 7, this volume). Integration of both specificity and context, as in the research frameworks developed by Bronfenbrenner, Bradley, and Lawton (this volume), illustrates one way in which researchers can measure both the highly specific proximal processes and the background context within which such processes operate.

Covariance

As exemplified in the three-dimensional environmental structure described by Bradley, (chapter 2, this volume) it is possible to set up a taxonomic matrix of the environment on the basis of orthogonal environmental factors. The difficulty with an orthogonal framework is that specific dimensions of the environment rarely appear in isolation. Rather, what is shown are specific environmental combinations appearing together at a rate that is greater than what would be expected by chance alone—that is, *environmental covariance*. As a result, an individual does not just encounter a specific environmental influence but rather encounters both the influence and other aspects of the environment that covary with this influence (Wachs, 1996). For example, a child who lives in a poor-quality neighborhood is also more likely to encounter poor-quality after-school care (Vandell & Posner) while being less likely to have exposure to new information sources like the Internet (Stokols). Similarly, Schooler describes how an individual in a low-status work environment is more likely to encounter psychosocial environmental stressors.

In understanding environmental covariance linkages, it is important to keep in mind that such linkages are probabilistic in nature, Thus, as noted by Talbert and McLaughlin, having a strong school district and a strong principal does not guarantee a child having a committed teacher. Even with this caution, the existence of covariance among different environmental influences means that it is incorrect to assign causality to a specific environmental influence without also taking into account what other environmental domains may covary with this influence.

It is equally important to keep in mind the idea that covariance processes are not restricted just to environmental influences per se. Inherent in the discussion by Evans of how poverty and exposure to physical toxins covary is the fundamental idea that the environment does not operate in isolation from other nonenvironmental developmental influences. Available evidence shows how environmental influences systematically covary with an individual's genetic characteristics, nutritional status, and illness patterns (Wachs, 1996). In addition, as discussed by Vandell and Posner, individual characteristics also covary with specific aspects of the environment. The implications deriving from covariance between environmental and nonenvironmental influences on development are similar to those drawn in regard to environmental covariance. Specifically, researchers must not assign primacy to a specific environmental influence without considering what the linkages are between this environmental influence and covarying nonenvironmental influences; the reverse also holds in that researchers must be careful not to assign primacy to a specific nonenvironmental influence without also looking at its environmental covariates (Wachs, 1992).

When covariance occurs, the traditional response has been to attempt to control statistically (if not ignore) the covariance so the critical environmental influence can be isolated. The various problems associated with statistical control have been described earlier, both in this chapter and in previous chapters in this volume (Bronfenbrenner, Evans, and Vandell & Posner). As I have argued previously, when covariance processes are operating, the unit of analyses should not be the individual variable considered in isolation but rather the covariance among multiple influences (Wachs, 1996). One way of making covariance among influences the unit of analyses is through the use of pattern, or cluster-analytic, techniques. In pattern, or cluster, analysis, individuals are clustered into different groups on the basis of multiple psychosocial and biological characteristics, in such a way as to minimize intergroup resemblance while maximizing intragroup similarity (Magnusson & Bergman, 1990). In this approach, the unit of analyses for predicting developmental outcomes becomes the group; the fundamental question becomes, Does a group of individuals that covaries systematically on a variety of different influences differ in its developmental outcomes from a second group of individuals with different covariance patterns? By using cluster pattern techniques, researchers can build on existing covariances, rather than acting as if they were dealing with isolated environmental and nonenvironmental influences on development. If the fundamental principle is accepted that environmental assessments and analyses must reflect the nature of the environment, then clearly a cluster analysis strategy is one that is a far more accurate representation of how the environment actually functions than is an assessment strategy that ignores existing covariances.

Interaction

Active–reactive covariance refers to a situation in which individuals with different characteristics are more likely to encounter different aspects of the environment. Organism–environment interaction refers to a situation in which the level or nature of reaction to similar environmental input is different for individuals with different characteristics. For example, in his discussion of the impact of proximal experiences on older adults, Lawton (chapter 4, this volume) argues that the less competent the person, the greater the impact of the environment. Individual characteristics that have been shown to interact consistently with environmental influences include difficult temperament, family risk history (e.g., schizophrenic parents), sex, age, and early chronic antisocial behavior patterns (Wachs, 1992).

Both conceptually and empirically, the study of organism–environment interaction processes at the human behavioral level has had a highly controversial history. This history is mirrored in many of the chapters in this volume. For example, interactions are a central feature of some chapters (e.g., Vandell & Posner) and environmental theories presented here (e.g., Bronfenbrenner's Proposition 2) but are barely mentioned in other chapters (e.g., Brown, Friedman & Amadeo, and Talbert & McLaughlin).

Summarizing across a highly complex set of findings, the following conclusions can be made with regard to organism–environment interaction:

1. Although some consistent organism–environment interactions have been documented at the human behavioral level, for the most part, research on the extent and nature of organism–environment interactions tends to be quite inconsistent, with findings rarely being replicated (Cronbach & Snow, 1977; Wachs & Plomin, 1991).
2. A major reason for much of the inconsistent evidence appears to be multiple methodological and statistical problems that reduce the chances of detecting existing organism–environment interactions in human behavioral studies (Evans & Lepore, 1997; McClelland & Judd, 1993; Wachs & Plomin, 1991; Wahlsten, 1990). A brief listing of the many methodological and statistical factors that preclude detecting existing interactions would include the following: (a) lack of power to detect existing interactions, particularly when traditional statistical tests are utilized; (b) use of inappropriate or imprecise measures of both organismic and environmental characteristics; (c) underrepresentation of extreme groups in studies of organism–environment interaction; (d) interactions being masked by either covariance processes or higher order interactions; and (e) atheoretical research leading to broad-based tests of interaction rather than to tests for specific organism–environment combinations.

Environmental Action Processes: Summary

In discussing structural aspects of the environment, I concluded that environmental assessment strategies must reflect the complex structure of the environment as it exists. A similar conclusion also holds with regard to environmental action processes. At the very least, an adequate assessment of the environment must build in tests for the operation of environmental specificity, environment–environment and organism–environment covariance, and for organism–environment interactions. Only when such tests are not confirmed can researchers accept the traditionally preferred environmental action model of a single isolated environmental factor equally influencing multiple aspects of development. The critical point is that researchers cannot design environmental studies under the assumption that specificity, covariance, and interaction processes will not be occurring. On the basis of what is known about the nature of the environment, the likelihood is that these processes will be operating.

Both in earlier writings (Wachs, 1991, 1992, 1996) and in the present section of this chapter, I have discussed assessment and research design features that need to be incorporated into environmental research to reflect the operation of specificity, covariance, or interaction. Rather than repeating myself, I wish to devote the remainder of this chapter to a central question related to process issues, of which there is major disagreement among chapter authors. I refer to the question of whether researchers can or should separate the individual from the environment in research on environmental influences.

Should Researchers Measure the Environment Without Simultaneously Measuring the Individual?

Not surprisingly, there is major variation among chapter authors with regard to the question of whether researchers can and should assess the environment in isolation from the individual. Some chapter authors (Bronfenbrenner and Super & Harkness) argue that the individual and the environment are essentially inseparable and that researchers cannot understand the extent and nature of environmental influences without integrating information on the individual as well, and vice versa. Other chapter authors (e.g., Bradley and Lawton) take what I call a "promissory note" view. This approach is based on the idea that although, ultimately, researchers need to integrate environment and individual, such integration should wait until they have better empirical data and conceptual schemes to guide them toward integrating specific individual and environmental characteristics. Evans, while noting the importance of individual characteristics and individual reactivity to the environment, focuses on the importance of obtaining population-relevant measures of adequate levels of environmental stimulation (equivalent to the dietary construct of required daily allowance), so as to define what is meant by too much or too little stimulation.

The question of whether and how to integrate the individual and environment is one that is not restricted to this volume. Debates between proponents of interactional (two separate units of analysis: individual and environment) and transactional (single unit of analysis: integrated person and environment) world views have been going on for well over a half century (Altman & Rogoff, 1987). My own position on this question is very close to that espoused by Bronfenbrenner and Super and Harkness in this volume; namely, it is essential to begin to integrate individual and environment if researchers are to understand how best to measure the environment and how environmental influences operate. In contrast to Bradley and Lawton, on both conceptual and empirical grounds, I would argue that there is sufficient evidence to begin to postulate specific person–environment linkages that can empirically be tested. My disagreement with the population-level approach of Evans is based on my belief that focusing on population environmental requirements and individual environmental requirements is not a case of either/or. I agree with Evans that it would be quite useful if researchers had the equivalent of an environmental daily allowance (EDA), showing both minimal levels of specific environmental input needed to facilitate development as well as maximal levels beyond which development might be inhibited. However, besides an EDA population mean, of equal importance would be the standard deviation of this EDA population mean. For dimensions of the environment in which the standard deviation is relatively low, researchers could apply population means without being overly concerned about individual differences in reactivity. However, for those dimensions of the environment in which there is wide intrapopulation variability (high standard deviations), general population EDA means would be relatively unhelpful and the focus should be on subpopulation or even on individual environmental requirements. For example, some evidence suggests that Hispanics (Korn & Gannon, 1983) and African Americans (Allen & Boykin, 1991) may have a greater tolerance for higher stimulation levels than do European American populations. For these subgroups, general population requirements on maximal stimulation levels could be highly misleading.

Given the nearly infinite number of possible organism–environment combinations, unless researchers have clear conceptual or empirical guidelines that allow them to focus on specific environment–individual combinations, their research could well turn into a tangle of atheoretical fishing expeditions. In this sense, Bradley and Lawton would be correct in urging the need for caution. However, my reading of the literature convinces me that researchers do have a sufficiently strong empirical and conceptual framework to enable them to begin to propose and test for specific targeted linkages between environmental and individual characteristics. Relevant writings include the work of Strelau (1983), Rutter and Pickles (1991), and Kendler and Eaves (1986) on moderation of environmental stress as a function of individual-difference characteristics such as constitutional differences, stimulus sensitivity, or family history of biological risk; the writings of Dodge (1986) and Rothbart, Derryberry, and Posner (1994), showing how levels of perceived threat in the environment will vary as a function of individual characteristics such as level of anxiety and level of antisocial behavior; the writings of Sroufe and Egeland (1991) and Werner and Smith (1982) on how children differing in attachment patterns or level of sociability also differ in their ability to make use of environmental supports; and the work of Kochanska (1993) and Chess and Thomas (1984) on how different developmental outcomes are associated with specific combinations of caregiver behavior patterns and children's temperament. As an example of how it is possible to formulate predictions linking specific environmental and individual characteristics, I use the objective physical microenvironment as a test case. The three-dimensional matrix shown in Figure 2 is an expansion of a previously presented conceptualization of the objective physical microenvironment (Wachs, 1989). My original conceptualization included the dimensions of animate/inanimate, responsivity, and background/foreground. To these dimensions, I have added modality, complexity, and temporal components, given the utilization of these components in other environmental frameworks presented in this volume.

The bottom dimension of the three-dimensional matrix refers to different physical stimulus modalities, these being (a) *visual* (varying in amount), (b) *auditory* (varying in intensity), and (c) *tactual–kinesthetic* (varying in regularity). The side dimension of the matrix involves what I call physical features of the psychological environment that cut across modalities. These include *complexity* and *responsivity* (varying from low to high), as well as whether stimuli are animate or inanimate and whether stimuli are background or foreground. The third dimension reflects the stability and variety of objective aspects of the physical environment. The numbered lines reflect individual characteristics that previous research or theory has shown as potentially relevant for understanding the impact of a specific dimension of the objective physical environment on individual behavior and development. The arrows associated with these numbers point to those dimensions of the physical environment for which the specific individual characteristics are potentially most relevant. Critical individual characteristics are included in the following paragraphs.

Past Experience

Past experiences can act to set individual adaptation levels for different types or degrees of stimulation (Helson, 1959). For example, one of the consequences of early exposure to high noise levels may be a later screening out of developmentally appropriate auditory stimulation such as language (Finkelstein, Gallagher, & Farran, 1980). Past experience may also operate by intrinsic motivation, as seen in Hunt's (1965) famous formulation with regard to intrinsic motivation: The more a child sees or hears, the more a child wants to see or hear. Past experience may also function by influencing the level of familiarity a child has with different classes of physical objects. Such familiarity may influence the child's reactivity to different classes of objects later in life (Rothbart, 1989).

Organismic Integrity

The individual's ability to attend to or process specific aspects of the physical environment may vary as a function of the degree to which the individual is biologically compromised. Biological factors that have been shown to relate to individual differences in the extent or nature of reaction to physical stimulation include preterm birth (Rose & Feldman, 1990),

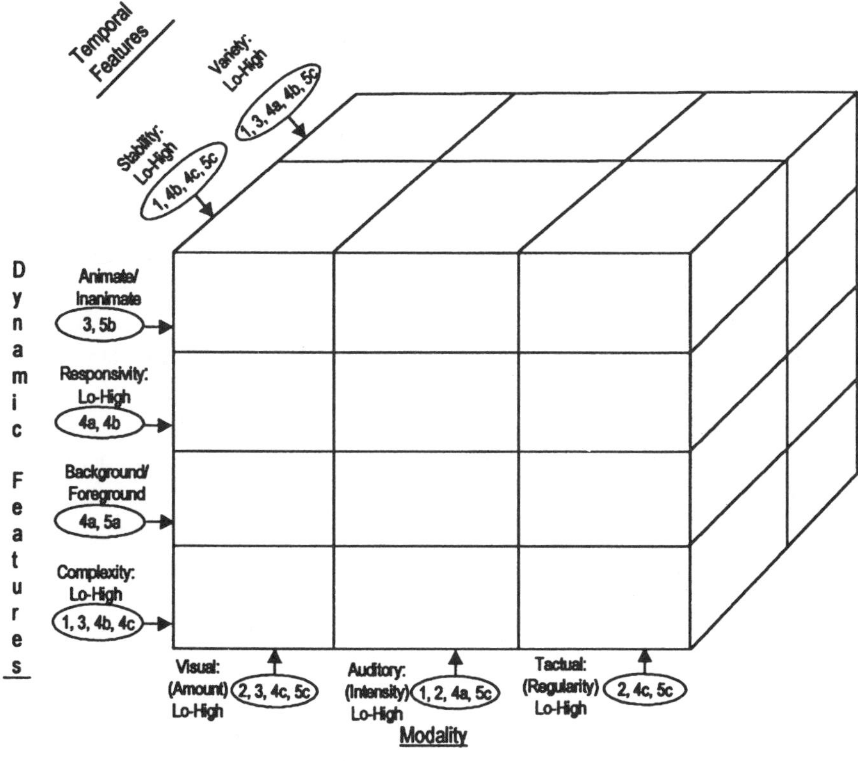

Relevant Individual Characteristics:

1. Past Experience.
2. Organismic Integrity.
3. Cognitive Capacity.
4. Level of Information Processing.
   a. Attentional Processes.
   b. Memory Storage and Retrieval.
   c. Stimulus Processing Strategies.
5. Temperament and Personality.
   a. Field Independence/Dependence.
   b. Motivational Orientation.
   c. Reactivity and Self-Regulation.

(Oval) → Refers to potential interface of individual and environment. The numbers in each oval refer to the individual characteristics that can act to moderate the impact of specific features of the physical environment. For example, individual differences in attention (4a) and field independence (5a) will influence the relative salience of background and foreground stimulation for different people.

Figure 2. Integration of proximal environmental features and individual characteristics in the study of the physical microenvironment.

malnutrition (Grantham-McGregor, 1995), and iron deficiency anemia (Pollitt, 1993).

Cognitive Capacity

Individual differences in level of cognitive capacity can influence the individual's reactivity to, or processing of, stimulation from the physical environment. For example, less cognitive capacity can result in slower information-processing speed, making it difficult for an individual to deal with fast-paced stimulus input or with more complex stimuli that require a response within a given time period (Kail, 1992).

Information Processing

Relevant aspects of individual information-processing abilities are included in the following paragraphs.

Attentional processes. Although biological status can influence how the individual reacts to the physical environment, not all individuals with compromised reactivity patterns have clear-cut biological impairments. Individual differences in attentional processes that are relevant to how a nonbiologically compromised individual reacts to and processes dimensions of the physical environment include selective attention, duration of attention, and ability to shift attention to different stimulus dimensions (Kinchla, 1992; Rothbart & Bates, 1998).

Memory: storage and retrieval. Closely related to the role of past experience is the ability of the child to store and retain these experiences, for later use in comparing level or type of previous stimulation with current stimulation (Nelson, 1994). This retrieval comparison process has been the basis of optimal stimulation models, wherein an individual's preference for different degrees or types of stimulus complexity and variety depend on the degree to which current stimulation matches what has previously been encountered (McCall & McGhee, 1977). In addition, the ability of the child to retain and retrieve past contingency experiences may influence the degree to which the child can respond to current environmental contingencies (Rovee-Collier, 1984).

Processing strategies. Individual differences in cognitive capacity may reflect differences in overall storage space or may reflect the efficiency with which the individual processes incoming information. Use of information-processing strategies, such as efficiently reorganizing input into more accessible units or utilizing automatic processing strategies rather than strategies that require effortful processing, can influence the degree to which the individual can attend to and respond to novel or more complex stimulation (Belmont, 1989).

Stimulus Preference Styles

Individual differences in reactivity to or processing of the physical environment can also vary as a function of individual differences in stimulus preferences. One classic cognitively based individual preference style is the degree of field independence versus field dependence (Witkin & Berry, 1975). Individual differences in this area may influence what aspects of the total physical environmental surround are most likely to be attended to by the individual. From a motivational point of view, individual differences in object versus social orientation may act to influence the degree to which the individual is motivated to engage physical versus social aspects of his or her environment (Wachs & Combs, 1995).

Temperament

Reactivity to the physical environment need not be influenced just by cognitive or cognitively related individual-difference characteristics. There is a rich tradition in the temperament literature illustrating how the individual structures and reacts to his or her physical environment can be moderated by individual differences in approach versus inhibition to novel object situations, level of reactivity to the environment, degree of sensation-seeking behavior shown by the individual, and individual differences in persistence (Kagan, Arcus, & Snidman, 1993; Rothbart & Bates, 1998; Strelau, 1994).

As an example of how these individual characteristics can be integrated with research on the objective physical microenvironment, let us look at the dimension of *environmental complexity*. As discussed by Bradley, environmental complexity influences how motivated a child is to engage his or her environment and how likely a child is to assimilate specific aspects of the environment. As discussed by Schooler, while job complexity can influence the intellectual ability of workers at all ages, older workers are less likely to be involved in more complex job situations. The discussions of complexity by both Bradley and Schooler could easily fit within an optimal stimulation framework, wherein both environment and individual are characterized on their level or range of complexity. Within an optimal stimulation framework, an individual is more likely to be motivated toward and to assimilate environments that are optimally discrepant from his or her own intrinsic complexity range; similarly, an individual's pattern of behavior and development is more likely to be facilitated by levels of environmental complexity that are optimally discrepant from his or her own level (Wachs, 1977).

Environmental complexity would be inherent in specific features of the environment, whereas individual complexity is a function of both the past experience with environments of different complexity and the degree to which the individual can store and process stimuli at different complexity levels. (See Figure 2.) Although it is possible to assess and quantify the degree of environmental complexity in a given physical microenvironment, it cannot necessarily be assumed that all individuals within this environment have the same level of ability to process existing environmental complexity efficiently or have a level of intrinsic complexity that matches well with what is afforded by the environment. Individuals with more efficient memory storage and retrieval systems, who are better able to make accurate judgments about the degree of person–environment match, should be more able to utilize existing environmental complexity than individuals with less efficient storage retrieval mechanisms. Furthermore, individual differences in the degree to which individuals encounter environments of greater or lesser complexity will, in part, be a function of individual differences in temperamental characteristics such as reactivity. As discussed by Strelau (1983), high-reactive individuals will tend to avoid more complex environments, whereas low-reactive individuals will tend to prefer such environments.

All of this illustrates the benefits of integrating individual and environment in studies of environmental complexity, rather than treating environmental complexity in isolation from the individual. Integration leads to a more detailed understanding of how complexity can act to influence individual development and behavior. Integration also increases the chances of researchers finding significant results by developing differential predictions for individuals with different environmental histories or for individuals having different levels of stimulus processing efficiency, memory, or temperament patterns.

CONCLUSION: CELEBRATING THE COMPLEXITY OF THE ENVIRONMENT

A fundamental thesis of the present chapter is that it is essential for the environmental assessment strategies to match the actual nature of the environment as researchers know it. The importance of such a match does not rule out other traditional criteria for gauging the validity of environmental assessments studies, such as accuracy of measurement, but the end result of inaccurate measurement of the right things or accurate measurement of the wrong things will lead researchers to the same dead end. Current environmental research and theory point to certain specific features as being characteristic of the environment. These features are listed in the Appendix.

Although the characteristics of the environment shown in the Appendix may seem unduly complex, this complexity is not due to a plot by environmental researchers to make things more complicated than they actually are. Rather, the previous description is an accurate reflection of what the environment actually is and how the environment actually operates. When faced with descriptions of the environment, as shown in the Appendix, the reaction of many nonenvironmental researchers is to question whether it is possible to study the nature and impact of the environment, given its complexity (Loehlin, 1996; Spitz, 1996; Thompson, 1996). To the extent that studying the environment requires that researchers assess all relevant characteristics of the environment in a single study, the concern of nonenvironmental researchers would be correct. However, environmental studies that accurately reflect the nature of the environment do not need to encompass all of the characteristics shown in the Appendix. At a minimum, such studies must not assess the environment in ways that violate what is known about the environment and how the environment operates. Going beyond the minimum, the structural and process aspects of the environment that need to be represented in researchers' studies will in part be defined by the nature of the questions that are being asked. What has been shown in the various chapters in this volume, and in the present chapter, are ways to assess relevant environmental characteristics that are both economical and feasible and that accurately reflect the nature of the environment and how the environment operates. Examples of how distal environmental assessments can economically be integrated into studies of proximal environmental influences are shown in Table 1. Further examples of how assessment of different environmental characteristics can be built into environmental studies in ways that are both feasible and accurate are shown in Table 2.

TABLE 2
Strategies for Economically Assessing Different Characteristics of the Environment

Assessment procedure	Environment characteristics
Obtain both objective and subjective repeated assessments of specific environmental features and environmental ambience.	Objective and subjective environmental linkages and temporal (cumulative) perceptions of environmental ambience
Obtain low-cost data on individual characteristics by using parent report measures (temperament), existing records (biomedical, school, or family risk history), or direct measures (sex age, and anthropometric measures).	Organism–environment covariance, organism–environment interaction, and age specificity
Obtain data on the impact of major environmental events by using all individuals within a family.	Age specificity
Develop a common core of proximal environmental measures that can be used in different studies encompassing different outcomes and populations with different characteristics. These data can be used systematically to compare results from different studies.	Specificity of environmental action: impact of higher order moderators such as population characteristics
Use clustering procedures in which the unit of analysis is the group and not the individual.	Covariance of different aspects of the environment or covariance between environmental and nonenvironmental influences.

In terms of selection of individual characteristics or nonenvironmental influences that may covary or interact with proximal environmental influences, existing research can be used as a guide for what variables to select when the focus of interest is a specific aspect of the proximal microenvironment (e.g., Wachs, 1992, 1998). Existing reviews of the environmental literature can also serve as a guideline for what specific linkages between higher and lower levels of the environment ought to be integrated in a particular study (e.g., Bronfenbrenner, 1989; Wachs, 1992). An excellent example of how linkages between higher and lower levels of both the objective and the subjective environments can be studied is found in the chapter by Talbert and McLaughlin (chapter 7, this volume). The approach described by these authors not only deals with questions like how many levels of the environment and what levels but also illustrates how the study of multiple levels of the environment is both feasible and reflective of the complex environmental system of the school. Concerns about the drain on statistical power when using multiple levels or multiple dimensions of the environment, or when using measures of individual or nonenvironmental characteristics, are always important to consider. However, such concerns must be viewed with the understanding that statistical power can be increased both by reducing errors of measurement (e.g., the use of more precise participant groups) and by analyzing for specific targeted patterns of relations rather than using global overall tests of significance (Wachs & Plomin, 1991).

The bottom line is that researchers can design research that is feasible and that reflects the nature of the environment through both judicious selection of specific proximal processes, higher order environmental characteristics, and individual and nonenvironmental characteristics and appropriate use of known analytic procedures (e.g., aggregating across time and place). Put another way, researchers can have both complexity and test it too. Celebrating rather than denying the complexity of the environment is a strategy that is long overdue in environmental research. Hopefully, this is a celebration that both current and future generations of environmental (and nonenvironmental) researchers will join.

REFERENCES

Allen, B., & Boykin, W. (1991). The influence of contextual factors on Afro-American and Euro-American children's performance. *International Journal of Psychology, 26*, 373–387.

Altman, I., & Rogoff, B. (1987). World views in psychology. *Handbook of environmental psychology* (Vol. 1, pp. 7–40). New York: Wiley.

Belmont, J. (1989). Cognitive strategies and strategic learning. *American Psychologist, 44*, 142–148.

Belsky, J., & Cassidy, J. (1994). Attachment: Theory and evidence. In M. Rutter & D. Hay (Eds.), *Development through life* (pp. 373–402). London: Oxford University Press.

Bornstein, M., Azuma, H., Tamis-LeMonda, C., & Ogino, M. (1990). Mother and infant activity and interaction in Japan and in the United States. *International Journal of Behavioral Development, 13*, 267–288.

Bradley, R., Caldwell, B., & Rock, S. (1988). Home environment and school performance. *Child Development, 59*, 852–867.

Bradley, R., Whiteside, L. Mundfrom, D., Casey, P., Kelleher, K., Pope, S. (1994). Early indications of resilience and their relation to experiences in the home environments of low birth weight premature children living in poverty. *Child Development, 65*, 346–360.

Bronfenbrenner, U. (1989). Ecological systems theory. *Annals of Child Development, 6*, 187–249.

Brooks-Gunn, J., & Warren, M. (1989). Biological and social contributions to negative affect in young adolescent girls. *Child Development, 60*, 40–55.

Calkins, S. (1994). Origins of individual differences in emotion regulation. *Monographs of the Society for Research in Child Development, 59* (240), 53–72.

Caspi, A. (1998). Personality development across the life course. In N. Eisenberg (Ed.), *Handbook of child psychology: Social emotional and personality development* (Vol. 3, pp. 105–176). New York: Wiley.

Chess, S., & Thomas, A. (1984). *Origins and evolution of behavioral disorders*. New York: Brunner-Mazel.

Clausen, J. (1995). Gender, context and turning points in adult lives. In T. Moen, G. Elder, & K. Luscher (Eds.), *Examining lives in contexts* (pp. 365–392). Washington, DC: American Psychological Association.

Cronbach, L., & Snow, R. (1977). *Aptitudes and instructional methods*. New York: Wiley.

Darling, N., & Steinberg, L. (1993). Parenting style as context. *Psychological Bulletin, 113*, 487–496.

Dawes, A. (1990). The effects of political violence on children. *International Journal of Psychology, 25*, 13–31.

Dodge, K. (1986). Social information processing variables in the development of aggression and altruism in children. In C. Zahn-Waxler, E. Cummings, & R. Ianotti (Eds.), *Altruism and aggression* (pp. 280–302). Cambridge, England: Cambridge University Press.

Dodge, K., & Feldman, E. (1990). Issues in social cognition and sociometric status. In S. Asher & J. Coie (Eds.). *Peer rejection in childhood* (pp. 119–155). Cambridge, England: Cambridge University Press.

Elder, G. (1995). The life course paradigm. In T. Moen, G. Elder, & K. Luscher (Eds.), *Examining lives in context* (pp. 101–140). Washington, DC: American Psychological Association.

Elicker, J., Egeland, M., & Sroufe, A. (1992). Predicting peer competence and peer relationships in childhood from early parent child relationship. In R. Park & G. Ladd (Eds.), *Family peer relationships* (pp. 77–106). Hillsdale, NJ: Erlbaum.

Enns, J., & Akhter, M. (1989). A developmental study of filtering and visual attention. *Child Development, 60,* 1118–1119.

Evans, G., & Lepore, S. (1997). Moderating and mediating processes in environment behavior research. In G. Moore & R. Marans (Eds.), *Advances in environment behavior and design* (Vol. 4, pp. 255–285). New York: Plenum.

Finkelstein, M., Gallagher, J., & Farran, D. (1980). Attentiveness and responsiveness to auditory stimuli of children at risk for mental retardation. *American Journal of Mental Deficiency, 85,* 135–144.

Finn, J. (1989). Withdrawing from school. *Review of Educational Research, 59,* 117–142.

Goduka, I., Poole, D., & Aotaki-Phenice, L. (1992). A comparative study of Black South African children from three different contexts. *Child Development, 63,* 509–525.

Gottman, J. (1991). Chaos and regulated change in families: In P. Cowan & M. Hethrington (Ed.), *Family transitions* (pp. 247–272). Hillsdale, NJ: Erlbaum.

Grantham-McGregor, S. (1995). A review of studies of the effect of severe malnutrition on mental development. *Journal of Nutrition Supplement, 125,* 2233S–2238S.

Helson, H. (1959). Adaptation theory. In S. Koch (Ed.), *Psychology: A study of a science* (Vol. 1, pp. 565–621). New York: McGraw-Hill.

Holden, G., & Edwards, L. (1989). Parent attitudes toward child rearing. *Psychological Bulletin, 106,* 29–58.

Hunt, J. McV. (1965). Intrinsic motivation and its role in psychological development. In M. Levine (Ed.), *Nebraska Symposium on Motivation* (pp. 189–287). Lincoln: University of Nebraska Press.

Kagan, J., Arcus, S., & Snidman, N. (1993). The idea of temperament. In R. Plomin & G. McClearn (Eds.), *Nature, nurture, and psychology* (pp. 197–212). Washington, DC: American Psychological Association.

Kail, R. (1992). General slowing of information processing by persons with mental retardation. *American Journal on Mental Retardation, 97,* 333–341.

Kendler, K., & Eaves, L. (1986). Model from joint affects of genotype on environment on liability to psychiatric illness. *American Journal of Psychiatry, 143,* 279–299.

Kinchla, R. (1992). Attention. *Annual Review of Psychology, 43,* 711–742.

Kochanska, G. (1993). Toward a synthesis of parental socialization and child temperament in early development of conscience. *Child Development, 64,* 325–347.

Korn, S., & Gannon, S. (1983). Temperament, cultural variation and behavior disorders of preschool children. *Child Psychiatry and Human Behavior, 13,* 203–212.

Loehlin, J. (1996). The environment and intelligence. In D. Detterman (Ed.), *Current topics in human intelligence: The environment* (Vol. 5, pp. 151–156). Norwood, NJ: Ablex.

Magnusson, D., & Bergman, L. (1990). A pattern approach to the study of pathways from childhood to adulthood. In L. Robins & M. Rutter (Eds.), *Straight and devious pathways from childhood to adulthood* (pp. 101–115). Cambridge, England: Cambridge University Press.

Masten, A., Best, K., & Garmezy, N. (1990). Resilience in development. *Development and Psychopathology, 2*, 425–444.

McCall, R., & McGhee, P. (1977). The discrepancy hypothesis of attention and affect in infants. In I. Uzgiris & F. Weizmann (Eds.), *The structuring of experience* (pp. 179–210). New York: Plenum.

McClelland, G., & Judd, C. (1993). Statistical difficulties of detecting interactions and moderator effects. *Psychological Bulletin, 114*, 376–390.

Miller, S. (1995). Parents attribution for their children's behavior. *Child Development*, 66, 1557–1584.

Moen, P., Elder, G., & Luscher, K. (1995). *Examining lives in context.* Washington, DC: American Psychological Association.

Nelson, C. (1994). Neural basis of infant temperament. In J. Bates & T. D. Wachs (Eds.), *Temperament: Individual differences at the interface of biology and behavior* (pp. 47–82). Washington, DC: American Psychological Association.

Ogilvy, C. (1990). Family type and children's cognition in two ethnic groups. *Journal of Cross Cultural Psychology, 21*, 319–324.

Pavenstedt, E. (1967). *The drifters: Children of disorganized lower class families.* Boston: Little, Brown.

Pollitt, E. (1993). Iron deficiency and cognitive functioning. *Annual Review of Nutrition, 13*, 521–538.

Prentice, A., Velasquez, L., Davies, P., Lucas, A., & Coward, W. (1989). Total energy expenditure of free living infants and children obtained by the doubly-labeled water method. In B. Schurch & N. Scrimshaw (Eds.), *Activity, energy expenditure and energy requirements of infants and children* (pp. 83–102). Lausanne, Switzerland: International Dietary Energy Consultative Group.

Rose, S., & Feldman, J. (1990). Infant cognition: Individual differences and developmental continuities. In J. Colombo & J. Fagan (Eds.), *Individual differences in infancy* (pp. 229–246). Hillsdale, NJ: Erlbaum.

Rothbart, M. (1989). Temperament in childhood. In G. Kohnstamm, J. Bates, & M. Rothbart (Eds.), *Temperament in childhood* (pp. 59–76). New York: Wiley.

Rothbart, M., & Bates, J. (1998). Temperament. In N. Eisenberg (Ed.), *Handbook of child psychology* (Vol. 3, pp. 105–170). New York: Wiley.

Rothbart, M. Derryberry, D., & Posner, M. (1994). A psychobiological approach to the development of temperament. In J. Bates & T. D. Wachs (Eds.), *Temperament: Individual differences at the interface of biology and behavior* (pp. 82–116). Washington DC: American Psychological Association.

Rovee-Collier, C. (1984). The ontology of learning and memory in human infancy.

In R. Kail & N. Spear (Eds.), *Comparative perspectives on the development of memory* (pp. 103–134). Hillsdale, NJ: Erlbaum.

Rushton, P., Brainerd, C., & Pressley, M. (1983). Behavioral development and construct validity: The principle of aggregation. *Psychological Bulletin, 94,* 18–38.

Rutter, M. (1983). Statistical and personal interactions. In D. Magnusson & V. Allen (Eds.), *Human development: An interactional perspective* (pp. 295–320). New York: Academic Press.

Rutter, M., & Pickles, A. (1991). Person environment interaction. In T. D. Wachs & R. Plomin (Eds.), *Conceptualization and measurement of organism environment interaction* (pp. 105–141). Washington, DC: American Psychological Association.

Rutter, M., Quinton, D., & Hill, J. (1990). Adult outcome of institution reared children. In L. Robins & M. Rutter (Eds.), *Straight and devious pathways from childhood to adulthood* (pp. 135–157). Cambridge, England: Cambridge University Press.

Sack, W., Clarke, G., & Seeley, J. (1996). Multiple forms of stress in Cambodian adolescent refugees. *Child Development, 67,* 107–116.

Scarr, S. (1992). Developmental theories of the 1990's. *Child Development, 63,* 1–19.

Sophian, C. (1986). Early development and children's spatial monitoring. *Cognition, 22,* 61–88.

Spear, N., & Hyatt, L. (1993). How the timing of experience can effect the ontogeny of learning. In G. Turkewitz & D. Devenny (Eds.), *Developmental time and timing* (pp. 167–208). Hillsdale, NJ: Erlbaum.

Spitz, H. (1996). Commentary. In D. Detterman (Ed.), *Current topics in human intelligence: The environment* (Vol. 5, pp. 173–178). Norwood, NJ: Ablex.

Sroufe, A., & Egeland, B. (1991). Illustrations of person–environment interaction from a longitudinal study. In T. D. Wachs & R. Plomin (Eds.), *Conceptualization and measurement of organism environment interaction* (pp. 68–86). Washington, DC: American Psychological Association.

Steinberg, L., Dornbush, S., & Brown, B. (1992). Ethnic differences in adolescent achievement. *American Psychologist, 47,* 723–729.

Stokols, D. (1988). Transformational processes in people–environment relations. In J. McGrath (Ed.), *The social psychology of time* (pp. 223–252). Newbury Park, CA: Sage.

Stokols, D. (1992). Establishing and maintaining healthy environments. *American Psychologist, 47,* 6–22.

Strelau, J. (1983). *Temperament personality and activity*. New York: Academic Press.

Strelau, J. (1994). Concepts of arousal and arousability as used in temperament studies. In J. Bates & T. D. Wachs (Eds.), *Temperament: Individual differences at the interface of biology and behavior* (pp. 117–142). Washington, DC: American Psychological Association.

Thompson, L. (1996). Where are the environmental influences on IQ? In D.

Detterman (Ed.), *Current topics in human intelligence: The environment* (Vol. 5, pp. 179–184). Norwood, NJ: Ablex.

Wachs, T. D. (1977). The optimal stimulation hypothesis and human development. In I. Uzgiris & F. Weizman (Eds.), *The structuring of experience* (pp. 153–178). New York: Plenum.

Wachs, T. D. (1987). Short term stability of aggregated and nonaggregated measures of parent behavior. *Child Development, 58*, 796–797.

Wachs, T. D. (1989). The nature of the physical microenvironment. *Merrill-Palmer Quarterly, 35*, 399–420.

Wachs, T. D. (1991). Environmental considerations in the study of nonextreme groups. In T. D. Wachs & R. Plomin (Eds.), *Conceptualization and measurement of organism environment interaction* (pp. 44–67). Washington, DC: American Psychological Association.

Wachs, T. D. (1992). *The nature of nurture*. Newbury Park, CA: Sage.

Wachs, T. D. (1996). Environment and intelligence: Current status, future directions. In D. Detterman (Ed.), *Current topics in human intelligence* (Vol. 5, pp. 69–86). Norwood, NJ: Ablex.

Wachs, T. D. (1998). Family environmental influences and the development of undernourished children. In N. Lewis & C. Feiring (Eds.), *Family risk and competence* (pp. 245–268). Hillsdale, NJ: Erlbaum.

Wachs, T. D., Bishry, D., Sobhy, A., McCabe, G., Shaheen, F., & Galal, O. (1993). Relation of rearing environment to adaptive behavior of Egyptian toddlers. *Child Development, 67*, 586–604.

Wachs, T. D., & Combs, T. (1995). The domains of infant mastery motivation. In R. MacTurk & G. Morgan (Eds.), *Mastery motivation: Conceptions and applications* (pp. 147–164). Norwood, NJ: Ablex.

Wachs, T. D., & King, B. (1994). Behavior research in the brave new world of neuroscience and temperament. In J. Bates & T. D. Wachs (Eds.), *Temperament: Individual differences at the interface of biology and behavior* (pp. 307–336). Washington, DC: American Psychological Association.

Wachs, T. D., & Plomin, R. (1991). *Conceptualization and measurement of organism–environment interaction*. Washington, DC: American Psychological Association.

Wahlsten, D. (1990). Insensitivity of the analysis of variance to heredity–environment interaction. *Behavior and Brain Sciences, 13*, 109–161.

Werner, E., & Smith, R. (1982). *Vulnerable but invincible*. New York: McGraw-Hill.

Witkin, H., & Berry, J. (1975). Psychological differentiation: A cross cultural perspective. *Journal of Cross Cultural Psychology*, 6, 4–87.

Wohlwill, J. (1973). The study of behavioral development. New York: Academic Press.

Yarrow, L., & Klein, R. (1980). Environmental discontinuity associated with transition from foster to adoptive homes. *International Journal of Behavioral Development, 3*, 311–322.

APPENDIX

Known Structural and Process Features of the Environment

Structural features

The environment is multilevel–multidimensional and hierarchically organized.

There are bidirectional linkages among the various levels of the environment.

Influences from higher levels of the environment (e.g., the macrosystem) both structure and moderate the characteristics and influence of lower levels of the environment (e.g., the microsystem).

Although influences can flow from lower to higher levels of the environmental structure, both the extent and the strength of directionality are more likely to flow from upper to lower levels than the reverse.

The environment exists on both an objective physical level and on a subjective interpersonal level. The structure of the objective environment is paralleled by the structure of the subjective environment.

The environment operates across a background of both historical and individual time.

The impact of historical time influences is seen primarily at a population level.

Individual temporal influences are seen with regard to differential reactivity to current environmental input as a function of both the characteristics of the individual's past history and as a function of individual differences in age (or more precisely, what covaries with age).

Process features

Both extreme and nonextreme environmental influences are relevant for explaining individual developmental–behavioral variability.

Environmental influences tend to be specific rather than general in nature.

Specific environmental influences are more likely to be salient only for a restricted range of developmental outcomes.

Specific dimensions of the environment are not orthogonal but rather covary with other dimensions of the environment.

The environment does not function in isolation.

The environment covaries with both nonenvironmental influences (e.g., genetics, nutrition, and biomedical status) and individual characteristics (e.g., intelligence, attachment, and temperament).

The environment interacts with both nonenvironmental influences and individual characteristics.

AUTHOR INDEX

Numbers in italics refer to listings in the reference sections.

SUBJECT INDEX

ABOUT THE EDITORS

Sarah L. Friedman, PhD, earned her MA in Educational Psychology from Cornell University in 1971 and her PhD in Developmental and Experimental Psychology in 1975 from the George Washington University. She is Fellow of the American Psychological Association, American Psychological Society and American Association of Applied and Preventive Psychology. While employed by the National Institute of Mental Health (NIMH), the National Institute of Education (NIE) and the National Institute of Child Health and Human Development (NICHD), she has published scientific papers and edited books addressing the effects of preterm birth on cognitive, educational and social development of children; the interface of brain, cognition and education; the development of planning skills; and environmental influences on psychological development. Between January, 1987 and July, 1998 she was responsible for the NICHD grant portfolio on cognitive, social and affective development. Since 1989, she has been the NICHD scientific coordinator and one of the investigators of a collaborative longitudinal research project on contexts of development and their effect on the social, emotional, cognitive, linguistic and health development of children from birth through middle childhood.

Theodore D. Wachs, PhD, is a professor of psychological sciences at Purdue University. He received his PhD in child clinical psychology in 1968 from George Peabody College. He is a fellow of the American Psychological Association and was the 1995–1996 Golestan fellow at the Netherlands Institute for Advanced Studies in the Humanities and Social Sciences. His current research concerns the relation between early development, environmental characteristics and nutritional status in young children. He has authored or edited 5 books and has written numerous articles on developmental psychology.